E

GENTLEMEN
&
PLAYERS

GENTLEMEN

&

PLAYERS

Conversations with Cricketers

MICHAEL MARSHALL

GRAFTON BOOKS
A Division of the Collins Publishing Group

LONDON GLASGOW
TORONTO SYDNEY AUCKLAND

Grafton Books
A Division of the Collins Publishing Group
8 Grafton Street, London W1X 3LA

Published by Grafton Books 1987

British Library Cataloguing in Publication Data

Marshall, Michael, *1930–*
Gentlemen and players: conversations with
cricketers.
1. Cricket—Anecdotes, facetiae, satire,
etc.
I. Title
796.35'8   GV919

ISBN 0-246-11874-1

Printed in Great Britain by
Robert Hartnoll (1985) Ltd,
Bodmin, Cornwall

CONTENTS

For Caroline

ACKNOWLEDGEMENTS

My first thanks must go to all those whose contributions are quoted in the book and whose names are listed on the back of the dust jacket. In a few cases they relate to conversations several years ago and, sadly, some have died since they were interviewed. However, recognizing the lasting appeal for cricket-lovers of many of these great names, no attempt has been made to differentiate between those who have gone and those who remain. Indeed, it is the author's fervent wish that all these recollections may serve, in some small way, as tributes to the amateurs and professionals who played in the last four decades of the era of the Gentlemen and Players. To all of them, warmest thanks are due for giving so generously of their time and enthusiasm.

A similar debt is owed to the many others who have assisted in providing facilities for the research which has made this so enjoyable a project. They include the President, Chairman, Secretary and Committee members of all seventeen first-class counties; the curator, librarian and record-keeper of MCC (Stephen Green), Surrey County Cricket Club (Peter Large), Yorkshire County Cricket Club (Tony Woodhouse) and the Scarborough Cricket Club (Les Franklin); and R. L. Arrowsmith, R. J. Atkins, MP, M. R. Barton, P. Baxter, W. E. J. Bishop, H. Blofeld, V. Broderick, W. A. Brown, S. Cama, B. Coleman, G. A. Copinger, A. M. Crawley, G. P. S. Delisle, M. H. Denness, A. H. A. Dibbs, A. Evans-Jones, D. Frith, A. Gibson, R. Harrington, R. Hayter, C. H. Hirst, C. G. Howard, C. Martin-Jenkins, D. Knight, P. J. Loader, G. A. R. Lock, P. J. Lough, D. H. Macindoe, B. Matthews, D. Mosey, A. J. Murtagh, P. J. Noakes, G. Parker, R. Parkin, A. G.

Robinson, A. C. Smith, P. Smith, E. E. Snow, R. W. Taylor, F. E. Templer, J. R. Thompson, M. Tindall, J. F. M. Walker, G. de W. Waller, T. J. Walsh, P. West and G. A. Wheatley.

There are a number of others to whom a special debt of gratitude is due: to Don Rowan for contributing additional interview material; to Philip Defriez and Patrick Allen for their help with the statistical and additional material in the appendices and for work on the draft manuscript; to Geoffrey Copinger for additional pictorial material, and to John Arlott and Jim Swanton for their help and hospitality and for so generously providing written contributions.

Among the cricketers, certain names also require special mention: Ted Dexter and Freddie Trueman for making the preparation of the Foreword so enjoyable and for general assistance during the preparation of the book; Sir Leonard Hutton for allowing the distilled wisdom of his cricketing thoughts to emerge like precious droplets despite his natural tendency to keep the bottle well-corked; Don Kenyon for adding a splendid Black Country dimension; Billy Griffith for constant support and encouragement in my own corner of Sussex; and Colin Cowdrey for giving a special dimension to the study despite his heavy commitments as President in MCC's bicentennial year.

Finally, I cannot end without referring to others without whom this book could not have been completed. Two to whom I returned on many occasions are among our greatest cricketers. Bill Bowes reminded me of my Yorkshire roots and of my BBC broadcasting days on the northern circuit, and gave wise and patient counsel from the standpoint of the model northern professional. Similarly Sir George (Gubby) Allen brought to the study not only the contrasting views of southern amateurs among whom I was educated but also the unique standpoint of one who has been at the heart of the game at Lord's for most of this century.

In the preparation of the book, I am indebted to my secretaries Marybride Watt, who undertook the main burden of the work, and to Polly Andrews, who gave timely help in meeting deadlines. I was fortunate in my editor, Richard Johnson, who conceived the project and showed great patience in awaiting its completion once he was aware of the author's lifelong fascination with its underlying theme. As for my wife, Caroline, the dedication in this book is but small recompense for her forbearance and support.

PLAYING FOREWORD

By E. R. Dexter and Trueman, F. S.
in conversation with Michael Marshall

Shortly before completing work on this book, I was fortunate in persuading Ted Dexter and Fred Trueman to provide material for its Foreword. As the two captains of the last Gentlemen versus Players match at Lord's in 1962, each has a special place in the social history of English cricket and, as old friends, both agreed that their thoughts and reflections on the role of the amateur and professional cricketer might flow freely over dinner.

So, on the Monday evening of a Lord's Test match, the author (M.M.) sat down to dine with his guests: the captain of the Gentlemen (E.R.D.) and the captain of the Players (F.S.T.). The conversation went, in part, as follows:

M.M.   Can you tell me what made each of you decide on playing first-class cricket as an amateur or as a professional? Ted, you won the toss and batted in '62 – perhaps you'll take first knock?

E.R.D.   I suppose that my decision to play as an amateur in county and Test cricket followed a sort of inevitable progression. I loved the game when I was at school at Radley. We had that marvellous combination of a first-class cricket professional and a dedicated cricket master which, historically, has been responsible for bringing so many young amateurs through to the county and Test game. Our pro., Bert Robinson, is still going strong at Radley after nearly forty years. He was not a great one for giving advice but he was a splendid net bowler who would keep encouraging you by saying, 'Come on Sir, get your feet to the ball.' Ivor Gilliat, our cricket master, was a brilliant confidence trickster. He would take each member of the team aside and say, 'In all my years, I've never seen anyone who had your talent.' As a result, we would all walk seven feet tall. On the other hand, he was a stickler for discipline and he ensured that there was a sort of chivalry about the game. For example, when the opposing team arrived, we'd be already changed into whites and flannels and go out to meet the other team and help them carry their cricket gear. I rather doubt that you'd see much of that kind of thing today but I felt that it added to the glamour and sense of occasion in school cricket.

And certainly there was a glamour about the chance to play at Cambridge against the counties and the great professionals like Fred here. When it came to Test cricket it was harder work. There was more at stake. But I suppose, if I'm honest, when I came into the game it was still possible for a Cambridge Blue and an England amateur to mix in a social world where there were real prospects of being offered a good career because you were a well-known cricketer. So, while I was still up at Cambridge, I decided that I would go all out to get Blues and to captain the University at cricket and golf. I reckoned that, if I did, no one would ever ask me what kind of degree I got, and that's exactly how it turned out.

F.S.T. As far as I was concerned, I never gave it a thought. If you have the choice of working underground as a miner or going round the country playing cricket for Yorkshire you don't need to think about it for long. But it wasn't just one long social whirl. I bowled a hell of a lot of overs – many more than they do today – and you had to face a long and tough apprenticeship before you were accepted by Yorkshire. When I started, I shared the junior professional's job and that meant doing all kinds of chores – we didn't exactly have the same kind of arrangements for helping each other with the baggage as they did with Ted at Radley. In our case it was the junior professional's job to get the rest of the team's kit from ground to ground and we were often humping it about in a hurry to catch the last train. There have been occasions when we had so many problems in travelling long distances across country that I've arrived at our hotel at two in the morning when all the bedrooms had been allocated and I've had to share a bed with another junior professional. And the senior pros would expect us to run errands for them – to get their cigarettes and so on. But, make no mistake about it, I was proud to be a professional cricketer playing for Yorkshire and, later, for England. And I was absolutely delighted when they made me captain of the Players. It was a great surprise because Tom Graveney was senior to me in the England side and it really was an honour because that was the ultimate expression of acceptance by our profession.

M.M. Did any of the old cricketers influence you in your early days, and how did you feel about playing both with and against amateurs and professionals? And, again, leaving yourselves out of it, who did you feel was your greatest opponent as a bowler or batsman?

E.R.D. We always called the professionals 'The Professors' and that's what they were – the truly dedicated men of cricket. I learned a lot from them. But it was an old amateur, Gubby Allen, who in so many ways shaped my career. He gave me tremendous encouragement while I was still up at Cambridge and we would spend many hours talking about technique and the technical aspects of the game, and I was fortunate that he had faith in me as chairman of the selectors when I got into the England side. As a batsman – and especially when playing for the Gentlemen – I knew I was up against the best challenge in the country because, throughout my career, there were only a few good amateur bowlers and the Players attack was as good as you'd find in any Test side. If I have to pick one of them out it would be Brian Statham. He was at you all the time and you virtually never got a gift to ease the tension.

F.S.T.   We called the amateurs 'Fancy Caps' or 'Coloured Caps'
         when we came across them in the university and county
         matches and, I must admit, there was something about
         those exotic colours which added a yard or so to my
         pace. Certainly I, and the other professionals, took a lot
         of pleasure in showing them a thing or two. But at
         county and certainly at Test level I never complained
         about the inclusion of an amateur – if he was good
         enough. And when it came to captaincy, there was no
         question in my mind that the independence of the
         amateur who was willing to speak up for his team and if
         necessary take on the County Committee was the best
         combination we ever had. That's not to say that I wasn't
         critical sometimes about the selection of amateurs. For
         example, I protested when David Sheppard was
         brought back into the Test side as a result of his innings
         for the Gentlemen in that last match at Lord's which
         we're celebrating tonight. I made the mistake of setting
         an attacking field for him and giving him the gaps which
         allowed him to get a hundred. He was a magnificent
         batsman – technically one of the best – and a good fielder
         when I first came across him in the early fifties, but you
         can't come back into Test cricket from outside the first-
         class game without something suffering and in his case it
         was his fielding. And that meant that I had to suffer in
         turn. What I preferred to see was an amateur captain
         who was a full-timer like Peter May. P.B.H. was the
         finest batsman in the game after Len retired and there's a
         lot of rubbish talked about him today saying that Surrey
         and England began to decline when he took over the
         captaincy from Len and Stuart Surridge. The fact was
         we were going through a period of change and P.B.H.
         did a fantastic job – not least in bringing me back into
         Test cricket!

E.R.D.   I'm with you in all you say about Peter May but I think
         you're a bit unfair to David Sheppard, Fred. Surely you
         must remember that century he got for us at Melbourne
         in 1963, which was a real match-winner.

F.S.T.   Yes, fair enough. I always admired him as a man and as a
performer but it was the principle I objected to. I still
think it was wrong to bring a man back into the game at
Test level with virtually no recent first-class experience,
knowing that he would only be playing in the one tour
before returning to the Church.

M.M.   Are there any particular matches between the Gentlemen and Players that you recall apart from the 1962
game?

E.R.D.   My first game in 1957 meant a lot to me. I didn't do
much with the bat but I got eight wickets including
Denis Compton, who was captaining the Players in his
last match for them. I'd hardly taken any wickets in
first-class cricket at that stage and I've pulled Denis
Compton's leg ever since about him being my 'bunny'.
But I keep coming back to the 1962 match because that
was the one which really brought me to the fore when I
was chosen to take the side to Australia. They were
tough matches, those games at Lord's, particularly at a
time when the ridge meant that the bounce was unpredictable and chaps like Fred and Brian Statham made life
very uncomfortable. But we did have our lighter
moments. In the 1958 game, there was no play on the
first day because of rain and we thought 'They'll never
bowl a ball tomorrow' and we all went off to a nightclub, The Milroy. Next morning, when we rolled up at
Lord's, the sun was shining and the groundsmen had
done a fantastic job. So we went out into the field and it
was obvious that one of our opening bowlers, J. J. Warr,
was labouring under a severe handicap. He'd been in the
nightclub later than anyone else in the side. He was
never really all that quick and his bowling got progressively slower. After a while, he finally struggled to the
wicket and let the ball go with a groan you could hear all
round the ground. It pitched miles outside the leg-
stump and Roy Marshall, the Players' opening batsman,
winds himself up to hit it out of the ground. But the pace
is so slow that he is half-way through his shot before the

ball arrives and he gets a top edge and the ball goes on to his chin and he has to retire. So that was the origin of what became known as the Milroy ball.

F.S.T. Rain comes into my recollections, too, because it spoilt that last match we had at Lord's with fairly dramatic consequences for me. I was disappointed when the bad weather prevented what I thought was a certain win for the Players. But, like Ted, I made the most of the extra time off. I was due to go with Yorkshire down to Taunton, but I'd been invited to a television show and a party afterwards with a girlfriend who was a leading light in the theatre. Anyway, to cut a long story short, I finished up in our hotel in Taunton at two in the morning and because of the mix-up in the rooms I didn't get my morning call. I woke up at 10.15 and I knew I was due at the ground at 10.30. Vic Wilson was the Yorkshire captain – our first professional leader in modern times – and he was fed up because we'd just lost to Derbyshire in the previous match. Anyway, when I got to the ground ten minutes late he said, 'I'm sending you home.' Well, the effect of that was I missed the game against Somerset and the happiest man on the ground at Taunton was Peter Wight. He was a good West Indian attacking batsman who scored a lot of runs for Somerset, but I regarded him as my rabbit. We'd had a bit of a barney a year or two before when he said I couldn't bowl as fast as his mother and I broke two of his ribs. After that, I think his highest score against me was 13. Anyway, when he heard the news, he had the biggest grin I've ever seen and he got a double-century. So, all in all, I think that drop of rain not only robbed me of leading the Players to a victory in the last match of the series at Lord's but it put a blight on my last years with Yorkshire and was part of the reason why I finished up playing for Derbyshire.

M.M. You've both indicated why the 1962 match was significant for you, but the ending of the amateur and professional distinction really dates from 26 November

1962 when the Advisory Committee for County Cricket resolved that the distinction should be abolished. Now, you were both on tour in Australia at that stage. How did you react to the news that, in future, you would all be cricketers?

E.R.D. It came as a great surprise. We thought the matter had been decided by the MCC only a year or two earlier, when a previous committee under the chairmanship of the Duke of Norfolk had recommended the retention of amateur status. Of course, there was a bit of leg-pulling when we were in Australia that winter, but the Duke of Norfolk was there as our manager and Alec Bedser was his deputy. He was also a strong believer in the old values and they certainly didn't encourage us to regard the recommendation as one by which we all became equal overnight. The old Duke was a marvellous man and you knew exactly where you were with him. His standards were plain for all to see – he was never 'one of the boys'. But he had a style that made the team adore him. I remember early in the tour when he was changing with us in our dressing-room, the question came up as to how we should address him and he said, 'You should call me Duke or Sir in public but you may call me Bernard in the bath.' Oh yes, he certainly set a standard for gentlemanly conduct and he had that marvellous dry sense of humour. If the old distinctions had to go (as was really inevitable by then) they certainly went out in style under his direction.

F.S.T. Style is the word. And it wasn't just confined to the Duke. Ted is right to think of that tour as the last fling of the amateur, and what with the Duke, Ted and our cricketing parson there were times when cricket seemed almost a sideshow. For example, when we had our first press conference, the Duke insisted that the whole team turned up in blazers and flannels. The Australian press really didn't seem interested in the cricket. 'Now Your Grace,' said one of them, 'will you be running any of your horses while you're out here?' The Duke told him all about his plans and who would be his jockey and so on. Then they turned to Ted. 'Skipper, we hear your wife will be modelling at various stages of the tour. Can you give us any details?' And Ted told them all about Susan's appearances in Sydney, Melbourne and so forth. So they went on to David Sheppard. 'Now then Rev.,' they said, 'we hear you'll be preaching in some of our cathedrals. Have you got a fixture-list for us?' And David Sheppard gave them all the details. When we were leaving the room after the press conference, one of the journalists asked me what I thought of the proceedings and I said, 'I'm not sure who I'm working for – the Jockey Club, Dexter Enterprises Limited or the Church Commissioners.' And that's when I lost most of my good-conduct money for the tour! But I'll tell you what. I wouldn't have missed that last outing of the Gentlemen and Players for all the world.

INTRODUCTION

E. R. ('Lord Edward') Dexter of Radley, Cambridge University, Sussex and England and F. S. ('Fiery Fred') Trueman of Maltby Modern School, Maltby Main Colliery, Yorkshire and England each represented the classical upbringing of amateur and professional cricketers and the perpetual battle between North and South. As performers, too, Dexter's attacking batsmanship and Trueman's explosive fast bowling were part of a tradition stretching back a century and a half by which the Gentlemen provided the carefree strokemakers and the Players the hard graft of bowling labour.

They followed in a distinguished line of nineteenth-century Gentlemen and Players captains at Lord's. Records of the early matches from 1806 onwards do not indicate to whom the leadership of the two sides was entrusted, but, for Dexter, the link is clear with the first great Gentlemen's triumvirate of Lord Frederick Beauclerk, Edward Hayward Budd and William Ward, MP, who did much to make the game popular and to provide for the future of both Lord's and the MCC itself; with their successors – another lordly-led trio – Lord Bessborough, his brother the Hon. Spencer Ponsonby and their friend the wealthy C. G. Taylor, who in the 1840s were among the first of the great output of public-school and Oxbridge cricketers that were part of the stream of potential leaders of the nation and the Empire; and with the two distinguished commoners who brought a semi-professional approach to amateur cricket in the form of the schoolmaster Nicholas Wanostrocht, better known as Felix (1804–76), and Alfred Mynn, the 'Lion of Kent' (1807–61).

The Trueman line of early Players can be traced to many of those who stood out from among the professional ranks, including 'Silver Billy' Beldham, who in 1806 came from the first great cradle of cricket in the village of Hambledon to play at the new headquarters of the game at Lord's; William Lambert (1843–1927), who was typical of Surrey's rural strength long before the County Club was established at the Oval; William Lillywhite (1792–1854) and 'Jem' Broadbridge (1796–1843) of Sussex, who were in the forefront of the move to legalize roundarm in place of underarm bowling; Fuller Pilch (1840–70), who would establish himself as the leading professional batsman of the day but who was first employed as one of the 'given men' bowlers for the Gentlemen; and, towering over all the early professionals, the landlord of the Trent Bridge Inn, William Clarke (1798–1856), who would ensure that his professional side and its imitators took cricket at the highest level to the furthest corners of Britain in challenge matches against local sides.

From the 1870s onwards, the formal listing of Gentlemen and Players captains gives an even clearer line of succession. For the Gentlemen, there was a seeming reluctance on the part of MCC to put the Gloucestershire giant, W. G. Grace, in charge of the side at Lord's (possibly because his batting and bowling meant that he frequently won matches almost single-handed). Thus, until the Golden Age – the two decades before the First World War – the side was led by the Lancastrian contemporaries A. N. Hornby and A. G. Steel; I. D. Walker of the many Middlesex cricketing brothers; and Lord Harris, who would go on to dominate MCC as well as Kent for the rest of his life. By the nineties, 'W.G.'s role as the elder statesman of cricket was recognized when, in his fifties, he took charge of the side virtually to the end of the century. Thereafter the captaincy was increasingly seen as a form of recognition which might be liberally shared, so that it included an Australian Test match player in the genial fast-bowling giant S. M. J. Woods, who became for many years the life and soul of Somerset cricket; the Scottish rugger international and wicket-keeper for Middlesex, Gregor MacGregor; the lordly Lancastrian A. C. MacLaren; the perfect gentle knight from Yorkshire, Sir Stanley Jackson; H. K.

Foster, the most successful of the seven brothers who played for Worcestershire; and, in the last years before the First World War, Sir Pelham ('Plum') Warner and C. B. Fry in rotation.

These last appointments foreshadowed the rivalry which would be repeated at later stages in the series, when leadership of the Gentlemen was seen as a stepping-stone to the England Test captaincy. In 1908 when the MCC chose Plum Warner over more senior contenders, including Ranjitsinhji and C. B. Fry, there was discontent among the club's membership. However, Charles Fry had the final pre-war say as captain of the Gentlemen while Plum Warner became the patron saint of the series when he captained the team both before and after the First World War and went on to select the sides for many years thereafter.

The Players' captains were usually rotated on a regular basis as a form of leadership recognition when, for so many years, similar status in Test and county cricket was denied to professional cricketers. During the Golden Age, however, there was a period of relative stability in leadership on both sides which added much to the character and colour of the series when the Gentlemen were led by 'W.G.' and the Players by Arthur Shrewsbury. Shrewsbury (of whom 'W.G.' had simply said when asked for his choice of a Test opening partner, 'Give me Arthur') had raised professional cricket to a new status when, in the 1880s with James Lillywhite and Alfred Shaw, he arranged tours of Australia and led England in seven Test matches.

The restoration of professional standing was badly needed after the proliferation of touring sides such as the All England XI (1846–79) and the United England XI (1852–69) led to internal and external rivalries which, ultimately, became arguments over money. These, in turn, hastened the rise of county cricket and the reassertion of MCC and thus amateur control of the game.

However, the selection of professional captains of the Players at Lord's towards the end of the century recognized a number of those who had taken first-class cricket to every corner of the United Kingdom. They included such independent and relatively affluent figures as Richard Daft, who had first played for Nottinghamshire as an amateur and who would later captain their side as a professional from 1871 to 1880 and whose Nottinghamshire career, together with that of William Gunn (who came into the side in 1880 and who was one of the founders of Gunn & Moore, the Nottingham cricket bat manufacturers), spanned over half a century; William Midwinter (1851–90), who was born in Gloucestershire, played his early cricket in Australia and became the only man to play for England in Australia and for Australia in England; and two great Yorkshiremen, George Ulyett (1851–98), one of the first of the county's internationally recognized opening batsmen, and Tom Emmett (1841–1904), a direct predecessor in the Trueman line of Yorkshire fast bowlers.

Other Players' captains at the turn of the century were, following Arthur Shrewsbury, increasingly drawn from those who had made their names in Test matches as well as county cricket: the tiny Bobby Abel and his opening partner for Surrey, Tom Hayward; the first long-established English Test wicket-keeper A. A. Lilley; and the two Yorkshire giants who linked the Golden Age with the modern game, George Hirst and Wilfred Rhodes. Finally, Jack Hobbs, who would make almost as great an impact on the series for his team as 'W.G.' did for the Gentlemen, was rewarded with the captaincy of the Players in the last match of the series before the First World War, in which the two teams were as follows:

The Gentlemen	*The Players*
C. B. Fry (Capt.)	J. B. Hobbs (Capt.)
A. H. Hornby	F. A. Tarrant
A. P. Day	J. W. Hearne
P. F. Warner	C. P. Mead
S. G. Smith	G. Gunn
J. W. H. T. Douglas	F. E. Woolley
F. R. Foster	E. Humphreys
G. L. Jessop	W. Hitch
P. G. H. Fender	A. S. Kennedy
H. G. Garnett	S. F. Barnes
A. Jaques	H. Strudwick

This match, which the Gentlemen won by 134 runs, may be seen as a watershed at the end of the Golden Age, and it would be twenty years before the amateurs beat the professionals again at Lord's. It also saw the last appearance in these games of such giants as C. B. Fry, G. L. Jessop and S. F. Barnes. Subsequent wartime injuries ended the playing career of F. R. Foster and the lives of H. G. Garnett and A. Jaques. However, happily there were survivors from this game who were willing to share their thoughts when this book was being prepared in the seventies and eighties.

It is written, in short, with the help of many of those who took part in Gentlemen v. Players matches, i.e. those who played first-class cricket for the most part after 1919. While referring to many of the Gentlemen versus Players matches from that date onwards, it is through their participants – the last of the Gentlemen and Players – that we can trace the evolving relationship between amateurs and professionals in county, Test and other cricketing and social situations.

While the book does not seek to present a definitive cricketing social history of the period, it is hoped that, in allowing so many survivors to tell as much of the story in their own words as possible, new light may be thrown on such a longstanding relationship. For I share the views of those who feel that cricket mirrors the social life around it and cannot and should not be regarded as some kind of spearhead for change.

It seemed best, therefore, to let the practitioners describe, in their own way, an age which has gone but whose standards are often seen in sharp contrast with those of the first-class game today. In telling their story, it is, with a few exceptions, from among the great cavalcade who took part in the annual battle for supremacy between the 'Coloured Caps' and 'The Professors' that we shall seek our evidence. No attempt has been made to emulate Sir Pelham Warner's standard text *Gentlemen Versus Players* but, because his book includes matches only up to 1949, the averages and score-cards in the Appendices complete the post-war record and correct some earlier factual errors.

As to the balance of power, it is simply stated in the two-to-one advantage the Players enjoyed over the Gentlemen in the decisive matches at Lord's, the Oval and Scarborough – 117 victories to 61 from 1806 to 1962. But a certain subtlety is needed to understand what was simultaneously a rivalry and a partnership. When matched against each other, it was predictable that the full-time professional would triumph over his amateur counterpart (although, as we shall see, there were some notable exceptions). However, the rivalry was evident in a more complex form when we consider the growth of both county and Test cricket. For here, while there was obvious competition for selection, there was also a community of interest when amateurs and professionals played together as team-mates. In the days before huge prize money and major commercial sponsorship (and their logical extension, limited-overs cricket), English crowds came to see the independent as well as the paid performer.

While hardly any leading amateur cricketer of the twentieth century could deny that his playing success had an actual (or at least a potential) commercial spin-off, his true independence stemmed from the fact that, unlike his professional counterpart, he was not paid by results. At its best, this produced a chemistry involving the carefree amateur and the dedicated professional (with occasional role reversals) that, for so long, English crowds found to their liking. If this book has a theme, therefore, it is in the combination of both partnership and rivalry between Gentlemen and Players which we shall not see again but which is so much a part of our cricket history – a history which was exemplified nowhere more strongly than at Lord's.

It is there that we begin, therefore, in considering the evidence – the evidence of the last of the Gentlemen and Players.

PART ONE

Between the Wars

LORD'S

Lord's in 1919 returned to its traditional role as the home of two major interest groups: the Marylebone Cricket Club – the guardian of the soul as well as the laws of cricket – and Middlesex County Cricket Club, soon to be established as post-war County Champions. The attitude and approach of both clubs made this, still, a truly amateur playground.

The perceptive West Indian cricket historian C. L. R. James has described the twenties as a period of the slow but inevitable decline of the amateur cricketer. In the sense that the war had shaken the old social order, it was true that the pool of amateur talent was severely depleted. No longer could the heirs to the great estates and the private industrial empires count on the freedom to pursue a sporting career as in the Golden Age. Yet these things were relative, and the leadership of both MCC and Middlesex was firmly established in the hands of Lord Harris and Sir Pelham Warner who, together and in succession, ensured that Lord's would continue as the true home of amateur cricket. Another who would maintain the same tradition was Sir George Allen, who was knighted in 1986 but who was then known (and throughout this book is referred to) as Gubby Allen. He was at this time emerging on the Lord's scene by way of Eton and Cambridge, from which vantage-point he had (and still has) a clear view not only of the role of both men but also of their encouragement of amateur talent in the early post-war years.

Citing the two games at Lord's in 1919 (see Appendix I) when the Gentlemen of England defeated the all-conquering Australian Service Team and the traditional fixture between the Gentlemen and the Players was resumed in July, Gubby Allen comments:

I'm not sure that I agree with the view that there was really such a steady decline in amateur cricket between the wars. It was after the Second World War when one really noticed the shortages.

If you look at the Gentlemen's squad of thirteen for those two games in 1919 you can get the flavour of the people who were around. Plum Warner was captain in both games and he had a hell of a job persuading Lord Harris that a Gentlemen's side could cope with the Australian Imperial Forces Team (which would form the nucleus of the great Australian side of the twenties). So the Gentlemen's victory was hailed as a great day for amateur cricket.

Their side included what you might call traditional representatives of the Church and the Services in the Rev. F. H. Gillingham and Col. D. C. Robinson. Then there were the schoolmasters (often referred to as the 'August amateurs') like D. J. Knight of Surrey, famous for his Malvern off-drive, and 'Father' Marriott of Kent, who couldn't field for toffee but who could bowl leg-breaks and googlies on the spot for hours on end because of all his coaching practice at Dulwich. They also included some of the county and Test captains who all had sufficient independent means to play a lot of cricket, like J. W. H. T. Douglas of Essex, who had the family timber business on tap; Arthur Carr of Notts, who came from a wealthy family; and Jack White, the traditional successful west country farmer of whom it was said that if the problem was cows or batsmen he had the remedy. They also had some all-round sportsmen and characters to make up the side, like Michael Falcon, who ran Norfolk cricket for years but who might easily have played for England if he hadn't been in minor county cricket. Then there was A. J. Evans, who escaped from a German prisoner-of-war camp and had written a book about it – he got Blues for golf and rackets as well as cricket at Oxford. So did The Hon. C. N. Bruce, who became Lord Aberdare. He was the finest amateur rackets player of his generation and a damn good middle-order batsman for Middlesex.

For the Lord's match in July, White and Marriott were

replaced by George Louden and Greville Stevens. They became stockbrokers like me, although I only went into the City much later. There were still enough City types around in those days who could get time off for cricket. Greville was an infant protégé. He was in the Middlesex side with me for years. When he first appeared for the Gentlemen he was still at University College School. He was a bit of a glamour boy and had a large female following but he also had a dry sense of humour. He played for the Gentlemen for nine years consecutively and, after the second, at the age of nineteen, he was heard to remark, 'This match isn't what it was and I'm bored with it.'

Gubby Allen's reference to the selection of the Gentlemen's side by Lord Harris and Plum (later Sir Pelham) Warner underlines the dominance which these two men exerted on Lord's for much of the post-war period – a dominance strengthened by the physical alliance of Middlesex and the MCC. As one who would himself bestride the Lord's scene for many years after his own playing career for Middlesex, MCC and England was over, and of whom it might be said the term 'éminence grise' could have been invented, Gubby Allen is widely regarded as encompassing many of the attributes of both men which he sums up as follows: 'Lord Harris was a complete autocrat but a brilliant administrator. Plum Warner on the other hand had no financial brain but was a great picker of men.'

Lord Harris, the treasurer of MCC, served in that post from 1916 to 1932 – a role which he used as the iron man of cricket – while the Middlesex and England captain Plum Warner was now nearing the end of his playing career. He led Middlesex to the County Championship at the age of forty-six in 1920 and went on to a long career as an administrator who would play a major role in the development of Test cricket as a selector. He also achieved a considerable reputation in his writing both as editor of *The Cricketer* and as cricket correspondent for *The Morning Post*. Together, Harris and Warner represented a link with the Golden Age of cricket. Their views tended, therefore, to hark back to the more autocratic and spacious era of independently wealthy amateur cricketers who were in undisputed command of the first-class game.

There were numerous examples of Lord Harris's iron rule. 'Rules are made to be broken,' he once said; 'laws are made to be kept.' In his role as chairman of the MCC Cricket Committee and later as treasurer he provided continuity in the first-class game. He was prominent in shaping and revising the laws of cricket at a time when the interpretation given by Lord's was accepted without question throughout the world. Nearer home, he ensured that the entire Lord's establishment was ruthless in stamping on any sign of dissent which went against the spirit of the game.

Frank Lee, the Middlesex and Somerset professional opening batsman (and later Test umpire), described how, when still on the groundstaff at Lord's, he had hesitated when playing in a minor match before returning to the pavilion after the umpire had given him out leg-before. He was immediately summoned to the office of the secretary, the stern disciplinarian Sir Francis Lacey, who demanded an explanation. Frank Lee produced a piece of his bat and told Sir Francis that the reason why he had paused before leaving the wicket was to retrieve this fragment of wood, which had been dislodged from his bat by the ball from which he had been adjudged lbw. Despite his explanation, he was sternly rebuked and told that if there were a repetition of this kind of behaviour he would be dismissed.

This example of insistence on the gentleman's code of conduct (contrasting so strongly with our own times) was also seen by senior professionals as part of the amateurs' contribution to the game, and they were equally tough in instilling the same kind of discipline into newcomers. There was, however, a generally unspoken complaint on the part of the professionals when it came to relationships between amateur cricketers and the umpires. Such officials depended for their livelihood on the match reports submitted by amateur captains, and it was said that every amateur got the benefit of the doubt from umpires.

J. W. H. T. Douglas was frank in confirming this charge when he continued to play for Essex while no longer county captain:

They said that I seemed to have lost form, to which I replied, 'Loss of form be hanged!' When I was relieved of the captaincy of Essex it cost me thirty wickets and two hundred runs a season.

The bloody umpire couldn't say anything but 'Not out' when I appealed and they only said 'Out' when I was appealed against.

Gubby Allen has described how, when playing his first match for the Gentlemen at Lord's in 1925 (see Appendix I), he was given out leg-before-wicket by the umpire W. A. J. West. Returning to the pavilion without hesitation, he was met by Lord Harris in the amateur dressing-room with the enquiry: 'Well, young feller – satisfied with that decision?' When Allen indicated he was extremely unhappy about it, Lord Harris had umpire West (who was considered good enough to stand in Test matches) struck off the first-class fixture-list.

As Gubby Allen recalls today:

So far as the actual decision was concerned, there was a sequel which taught me a good deal about the game. As we were going out into the field, Bill West came up to me and said, 'Mr Allen, I'm terribly sorry about that decision.' So I just said, 'Don't worry, Bill. Just give them out when I shout.' In my first over, Jack Hobbs got the most tremendous tickle to a ball which the keeper caught. Everyone on the ground appealed and he was given not out.

When Jack got up to my end, I said at the end of the over, 'Jack, you know you hit that, don't you?' 'I did no such thing, G.O.' (he always called me G.O.), he replied. I was really rather shattered. I admired Jack Hobbs, he had helped me a lot and I thought he could do no wrong and certainly would never tell a lie. We were up at Scarborough a short while after and playing on the same side. He was fielding at cover and I was at extra. At the fall of one of the wickets, I went up to him and said, 'Now look, Jack, you know you hit that ball in the Gents v. Players match.' He said, 'Of course I did, G.O. But you mustn't say that in front of the umpire. It's unfair on him and, furthermore, if I had, he would almost certainly have given me out at the next possible opportunity.'

So far as Bill West's sacking was concerned, I'd no idea that Lord Harris would take such a strong line. Bill was a dear old boy and I was terribly upset.

*

The exercise of such autocratic powers was not always welcomed by other MCC members. While there was general agreement that His Lordship played a vital part in eliminating some of the chuckers' in the nineteenth century, his views on matters such as birth qualification could sometimes be carried to excess. Walter Hammond, who had been educated and brought up in Gloucestershire (for whom he was registered), had been born in Kent while his father was stationed there in the Army. When Lord Harris learned of this, he effectively (perhaps with the joint interests of Kent as well as the laws of the game in mind) ensured that he was required to miss the whole of the 1922 season. This led to one of the most famous lordly exchanges in the Long Room at Lord's when Lord Dearhurst, president of Worcestershire, met the treasurer of MCC with the question: 'Good morning my Lord. How many more young cricketers' careers have you buggered up this year?'

A few years later there was a further exchange when Worcestershire played a young professional called Fox who was not properly qualified for the county. Responding to a stiff note from Lord Harris, Lord Dearhurst – perhaps because Worcestershire were in the wrong – used more tactful words in his letter than those which he had previously employed in the verbal exchange at Lord's. In seeking support for his case, however, he wrote a separate note to Lord Hawke of Yorkshire in which he described the difficulties he was having with 'that bloody old fool, Lord Harris'. Unfortunately, the correspondence was despatched in the wrong envelopes and Lords Harris and Dearhurst resumed their strained relationship.

By contrast, Plum Warner had fewer problems regarding Middlesex birth qualifications, since it was often said that the only residential link between Middlesex cricketers was their need to make use of the main London railway stations. He also showed consistent faith in bringing on new players. In the case of his leading professional, the Cockney Irishman Elias Henry (Patsy) Hendren, an examination of that player's early records shows that Warner's faith in him was sustained through the years of limited success before the First World War. His reward came when Patsy blossomed into a brilliant late developer in a career with Middlesex and England which kept him in the first-class game until he was almost fifty.

Gubby Allen also recalled how Plum's encouragement and patronage helped him to sustain a first-class amateur cricketing career despite financial pressures:

I am sure he had a hand in my first appearance for Middlesex. Imagine: Plum had taken the team to the County Championship in 1920 and his successor Frank Mann was well set to repeat this in 1921. Yet at a critical stage in the race, I got this telegram from Frank inviting me to appear in two games for the county in August. I was only just nineteen and hadn't even got a Blue at that stage.

Frank Mann's succession as Middlesex captain had been announced with all the flourish and ceremony of one receiving a sacred trust when his predecessor, Plum Warner, said in a press statement:

My successor in the captaincy will be F. T. Mann – a man in every sense of the word – loyal, straight as a die, gallant soldier and great sportsman. He hits sixes as most men hit fours and there have been few, if any, braver mid-offs. The County Club is lucky indeed in having him as its captain in the coming years and it is certain that he will carry on the great tradition of Middlesex cricket – a tradition of playing the game in the best and truest spirit, never exulting overmuch in times of victory, never being unduly cast down in days of defeat, and always adopting an attitude of generous appreciation towards his opponent – in other words, straight bat and a modest mind.

Frank Mann's dependence on amateur talent in the Middlesex team reflected the situation which was mirrored in many other counties up and down the country. In his scrapbooks, so lovingly compiled by his widow and faithfully maintained by his son George – who would also captain Middlesex and England – some flavour of the glamour and attractions of the life of a first-class amateur cricketer emerges in the enthusiastic tributes of an almost universally 'pro-Gentlemen' press.
Before the start of the 1921 season, the captain Frank Mann was

able to announce that he and Nigel Haig (who would later succeed him as captain) would be available for the entire season while, in May and June, the Hon. C. N. Bruce, E. L. Kidd, G. E. V. Crutchley, L. V. Prentice and A. R. Tanner would join the side and, after the 'varsity match, G. T. S. Stevens. *The Morning Post* cricket correspondent who, in the recently recruited form of Plum Warner, had good reason to know, said that the Champion County should be a merry side under Frank Mann's captaincy, adding, 'He is one of Malvern's most famous cricketing sons, and has imbibed the doctrine which is always taught there of hitting the ball hard and often.' *The Times* saw even greater prospects open for the Middlesex captain, suggesting that he would make an excellent choice for the England captaincy against Warwick Armstrong's 1921 Australian eleven and adding, in period prose, 'He has the wise geniality that makes eleven men into an eleven of brothers.'

After a drawn game in the opening match at Oxford which was affected by rain (when the headlines raved about the Middlesex captain's hitting), the side began a run of six successive victories in the Championship which, together with their nine successive wins at the end of the 1920 season, created a record upon which Plum Warner commented: 'The batting strength of the present side is exceptional and F. T. Mann who is proving himself such an admirable captain must be puzzled in how to write out his order. In these days when some people are apt to decry amateur cricket, it is pleasant indeed to note the success gained by the captain and his amateur colleagues.' The occasion of Plum Warner's report was the Middlesex victory over Nottinghamshire in which Mann had scored 53 runs in nineteen minutes, driving the first ball he received into the pavilion for six so that, added Warner, 'Not even a Thornton, a Bonner, a Jessop or a Lyons can point to a quicker rate of scoring.'

Such attractive batting, particularly when reinforced by Patsy Hendren's consistent high-scoring form, drew enormous crowds. In the Mann scrapbook there are splendid pictures taken on 14 May 1921 during the first day of the match between Middlesex and Sussex. The captions refer to 'Twenty-five thousand people who prefer watching cricket to the more strenuous forms of holiday-making', while the correspondent adds, 'The number of people who can find time to spend the whole day watching cricket astonishes me. Not only was every seat in the cheaper parts occupied but there were rows of people squatting on the roped-off portion of the pitch. They were by no means all the type somewhat loosely spoken of as the "idle rich". Clerks hobnobbed with 'varsity students, labourers with clergymen and mechanics with stock-brokers. The thought struck me that mortality among grand-mothers must have gone up alarmingly over the last weekend.'

The accompanying photographs in the scrapbook are full of social touches. One action shot of the archetypal amateur Major W. G. M. Sarel, the Sussex secretary, shows him wearing a Free Foresters cap and apparently hitting the ball one-handed just out of reach of the Hon. C. N. Bruce while, in the standing-room-only crowd, trilby and homberg hats predominate without a bare head in sight.

Similar large crowds attended the match at Lord's between Middlesex and Warwick Armstrong's all-conquering Australian touring side which ended the Champion County's record run of success. However, the match had its compensations for Frank Mann at a time when the political and social worlds were so closely interconnected. On Monday 6 June, the Middlesex captain attended the dinner in honour of the Australian cricket team at the House of Commons at which the toast of the evening was proposed (in the absence of the Prime Minister) by the Lord Privy Seal, Austen Chamberlain, who, with a candour that could hardly be seen as vote-catching, confessed that he had never played cricket and had only watched the game at school when compelled to do so.

After the loss of the Australian match, Middlesex went on their winning way again before losing to Surrey at the Oval. But the press seemed less concerned with the ending of this run of Cham-pionship victories (which had lasted over twelve months) than with the return to form of the occasional amateur G. T. S. Stevens. One correspondent wrote: 'He was again the schoolboy who went up to Oxford two years ago an England player in embryo. It was not the Stevens that had those failures at Lord's this year; it was the real Stevens at Lord's who can be bracketed with the Ashtons, Chap-man, Jardine, Marriott and Gibson – a famous group of the new school in English cricket.'

Similarly, the Middlesex victory in the return game with Surrey at the end of August 1921, which gave them the Championship, was the occasion for the press to eulogize the part played by R. H. Twining as an opening bat in a crucial match in only his third game for Middlesex that season. Twining, who had been badly wounded in the knee during the Gallipoli campaign, would only play thirty-two matches in fifteen years for Middlesex. Yet, as one correspondent said: 'Mr Twining played as the Badminton Library insists that a batsman should. His left leg was thrown boldly to the pitch of the ball and Mr R. A. H. Mitchell himself would have been proud of some of his strokes on the offside. That is to say they were the perfection of the Eton batting of the old days – and there can hardly ever have been anything better.'

Photographs of the match show Twining batting in his Harlequin cap, and the team picture of the County Champions reflected the amateur flavour of the side with all the professionals wearing their Middlesex blazers and caps while the six amateurs sported a wide range of coloured blazers including the Harlequins, Oxford University, the Free Foresters and the Eton Ramblers. These social distinctions are reflected more subtly in the photograph of the banquet to celebrate Middlesex's second successive Championship victory. At the top table sat the President of MCC, Sir Stanley Jackson, together with Lord Harris, Plum Warner and Frank Mann – all in white tie and tails, as are several of the Middlesex amateurs on the surrounding tables. The senior professionals around them are mostly wearing dinner jackets with wing collars and black bow-ties with a few of their juniors in dark lounge suits.

While Mann's scrapbook gives the flavour of the amateur dominance in the Middlesex side in the early post-war years, at the end of the 1921 Championship season the three highest scorers for the county were all professionals – Patsy Hendren, Jack Hearne and Harry Lee – although there were ten amateurs in the first thirteen places in the county's batting averages. The bowling figures show how heavily Middlesex depended on their unusual amateur and professional combination of Nigel Haig and Jack Durston (both of whom took over a hundred wickets for the county) while further down the list appears, for the first time, the name of G. O. Allen with two wickets in his two matches at 35 runs apiece.

Gubby Allen reflects today on how he was encouraged to build upon this modest start:

Apart from Frank, who gave me my county opportunities in the twenties, I always felt that Lord Harris and Plum Warner were my two great patrons at Lord's – particularly when it came to intermittent appearances at the international level. Because I had to earn my living, I found it difficult to play as regularly as I could wish in the first-class game and as a fast bowler I had fitness problems. Plum in particular was always a great help and encouragement. I got plenty of good club cricket every weekend with teams like the Eton Ramblers or the Free Foresters, and I would go to Lord's almost every evening during the week to bat and bowl in the nets and run endless circuits round the ground.

There's no doubt that Plum took all this in and later, as a Test selector, he gave me opportunities which might never have come my way. I like to think I justified his confidence because, as I said, he was a marvellous picker of men. I only played under him as captain once and I realized then what an inspiring leader he was and how well he read the game. After I'd bowled just a few balls he came across and told me exactly what the two batsmen's strengths and weaknesses were and suggested field changes, all of which proved to be absolutely spot on. What's more, as I went on bowling I experienced the famous Warner treatment in which he would encourage me by suggesting that I was likely to take a wicket at any moment by saying things like 'He can't spot your yorker' or 'Your slower ball has got him foxed'.

After Plum's departure the Middlesex team continued to take much of its character from its amateur leaders. As we have seen, Frank Mann personified the wartime hero. Even his fielding problems, compounded by his wartime injuries, had about them a heroic quality. ('He was like Gibraltar if the ball came straight at him,' recalls his son George, 'but there was no hope if it was either side of him.') He led from the front whether in the field or in persistently hitting enormous sixes. Thanks to what we now know as Watney Mann he was able to devote himself throughout the summer to Middlesex before returning to his work with the brewery in the winter months.

His successor in 1929, Nigel Haig, took over not only with the blessing of his uncle, Lord Harris, but also with his direct financial support. Later he married the glamorous stage actress Unity Moore, who had played Peter Pan in the West End of London. With such financial backing from the family, Nigel Haig could afford to play as an all-rounder for Middlesex for over twenty years while filling in his winters with gentlemanly pursuits that included private cricket tours as well as other games at which he excelled such as real tennis, squash, rackets and golf.

Despite his comfortable circumstances, he showed a keen interest in the matter of cricketing expenses. Greville Stevens would often recall how, on one of the first occasions when he was playing for Middlesex under Haig's captaincy, he was asked what travel expenses he would claim. As he lived in St John's Wood he declined to ask for reimbursement of the tuppenny bus ride, only to be told by his captain: 'I'm not having you rocking the boat. You can put in for expenses in coming up from your parents' place in Hampshire!' On another occasion, when Haig was appearing for MCC, he put in for such heavy expenses that Sir Francis Lacey commanded one of his minions to return the claim to the Middlesex captain with the suggestion that he might like to have another look at it. 'Oh of course,' said Nigel Haig, 'I'm very much obliged,' whereupon he promptly amended the expenses form by doubling the amount claimed.

Haig's successor in 1935, R. W. V. Robins, was another who showed a certain robustness in his attitude to the matter of financial support for amateurs. His son Charles, who would also play for Middlesex, recalls how his father felt that he could easily have played as a professional and claimed two benefits and therefore suggested that there was no reason why he and his son should not gain reasonable reimbursement for loss of earnings while playing the game. All his cricketing life, whether bowling leg-breaks, batting aggressively or offering a challenge as captain, R. W. V. Robins loved to display his daring. However, his son recalls that he did not have the easiest of introductions to the Middlesex side or to the succession as captain:

He really came up the hard way. His father had been a sergeant in the Army and although my father was at Highgate School, I think there was a certain amount of snobbishness directed towards him. He was a marvellous athlete and good enough to play first-division football as well as first-class cricket. But like a lot of small men he hid his insecurity by a manner which many regarded as cocky. He was certainly given a tough time by Nigel Haig when he came into the Middlesex side. If the wicket was doing anything Haig and Durston would bowl all day. If it was a plum wicket then my father would be given an opportunity to bowl. Apart from that, Nigel Haig and Greville Stevens ganged up to put him down, but I think his record as a player and as a captain speaks for itself.

One particular aspect of Walter Robins's attacking cricket was his constant desire to give opposing bowlers the charge. On one occasion this left him open to the antics of so notorious a leg-puller as Patsy Hendren. Hendren, who, with Jack Hearne, continued to provide the main backbone in the professional batting for Middlesex through the whole of the twenties and most of the thirties, could not resist on one occasion when, as was his habit, his captain gave an opposing slow bowler the charge, missed the ball and continued straight on down the wicket towards the pavilion. 'He's missed it,' yelled Patsy, pointing dramatically at the wicket-keeper; 'get back!' Robins dived frantically for the crease, only to arise covered in dust and confusion to find that the wicket-keeper had long since removed the bails.

Robins's successor in 1939 as the last of the inter-war years captains of Middlesex was another leg-break bowler, Ian Peebles. This elegant Scot brought to the game the same kind of style that Jack Buchanan gave to the musical comedy world, and he would give special pleasure with his later work as a cricket writer. A product of the Aubrey Faulkner Coaching School, where he worked for several years, he found his effectiveness was eventually ruined by too much indoor bowling.

Yet for some years he, together with Robins, Haig and Stevens, provided virtually unique bowling strength in speed, swing and varied spin. But in the thirties the irregular availability of amateurs became a growing problem for Middlesex as well as for other counties, and it was only with the emergence of Jim Sims and Jim Smith as professional bowlers and the new generation of Middlesex professional batsmen that the side began to develop the solidity which took it to second place in the Championship for four successive seasons in the last pre-war years.

In three out of these four years, Middlesex had to give pride of place to Yorkshire (who won the Championship seven times in the thirties). The rivalry between the two sides reached a new intensity when Walter Robins was leading Middlesex and Brian Sellers was captain of Yorkshire. A certain ill-will had built up following incidents in games between the two sides, which, as the bespectacled Yorkshire fast bowler Bill Bowes recalls, became personalized in some of the duels between northern professionals and southern amateurs:

Over the years, the Yorkshire and Middlesex encounters really turned into grudge matches. Like all these things it is hard to pin down precisely how this happened, but cricketers have long memories. They claimed Abe Waddington had deliberately tripped and injured Jack Hearne when he was playing a long defensive knock against us in the twenties. We felt that Walter Robins and Gubby Allen had been overdoing short-pitched bowling in the thirties. Anyway, things came to a head when Gubby Allen and I 'had a do' at Lord's. I was pitching them short at him, and he made some threatening noises to which I replied in kind.

Gubby Allen's recollections of the incident are still vivid:

When Bill Bowes started giving me the works I just said, 'Don't forget that I can bounce them too, and I know a Yorkshire tail-ender who will have to bat against me in glasses.' Oh yes, there was some edge in those games with Yorkshire and it affected both amateur and professional alike.

Of the new Middlesex professional batsmen, two names were to stand out almost immediately. In 1936, D. C. S. Compton made his first-team début against Sussex batting at number eleven. This début became the subject of another Gubby Allen umpiring story:

> I had been injured while fielding, so I was batting at number ten when Compton came in to bat. We still needed thirty for a first-innings lead and I went out to meet him to warn him about Maurice Tate, who had been running through our side. I told him that whatever he did he should play forward to Tate, but he persisted in playing back. He was only eighteen at the time and I said, 'You silly little boy – what did I tell you?' But we stayed together and took our side into a first-innings lead when Denis was given out by the umpire, Bill Bestwick, who had been a fast bowler for Derbyshire but who was now in his sixties. When we went out to field I said to him: 'Bill, that wasn't a very good decision, was it?'
>
> 'I'm very sorry, Mr Allen, I had to pump ship. Pity, he may become a good player.'
>
> 'He'll do a bloody sight better than that, Bill.'

This setback did not deter the young Denis Compton who, by the end of the season, had scored over a thousand runs. From the first, his success was based on an unorthodox brilliance which defied analysis although, Gubby Allen has always argued, when the chips were down he could be as orthodox as the best of them, particularly because he played so straight. He himself is proud to recall today that he 'was delighted when they said I played like an amateur'. But, as his team-mates also testify, he could not understand why others did not find it as easy as he did because he had a genius which few could share.

Denis Compton's views on the amateur/professional relationship in the Middlesex side in those pre-war days are interesting:

> I had the greatest admiration for the amateurs in my early days. When I first saw them, the majority were very, very good cricketers and so many of them had played for England. People today would say 'How humiliating, coming out of different entrances' but it wasn't so. Perhaps we didn't have anything on

which to make comparisons but when I started in the game the amateur was certainly not a snob. They were a terrific bunch and they would come down to the professionals' room to pick out somebody's contribution and say 'How marvellous' and 'Jolly well done' or, even better, 'Drinks on me'. I would say my relationship throughout my career with the amateur was rather a special one. I mean, I never looked at him and said, 'Well, why in the hell shouldn't I come through the amateur entrance?'

Denis Compton's partner in many long stands for Middlesex, W. J. Edrich, shared his views on the value of the amateur during his time in first-class cricket. Bill Edrich had no doubt acquired much of the amateur's approach to the game during his five seasons in Minor County cricket as part of the famous Norfolk clan, and he was to turn amateur for Middlesex after the Second World War:

It's often been said that I owed a good deal to Plum Warner for my early start with Middlesex and even more so in Test matches, and this is certainly true. He was typical of the great amateurs of my early days – and every county had a clutch of them – who would go on from a playing career to become administrators. They were certainly dedicated to the game and although I have been criticized for enjoying myself away from the cricket, I always tried to follow the examples which Plum, Gubby Allen and others at Lord's set in encouraging up-and-coming cricketers.

Both Compton and Edrich also had reason to thank Plum Warner for their débuts in the Gentlemen v. Players matches, although both had the unhappy distinction of making a duck on their first appearance. For Denis Compton, selection in the 1937 match (see Appendix I) was equivalent to a Test trial:

Strangely enough, people today and especially the modern player would think 'Oh well, that was just a bun fight' but in fact it was highly competitive. I think it was both amateurs and professionals trying to prove a point. Freddie Brown got me for a duck in my first appearance for the Players and in those days he was a magnificent leg-spinner. The '37 match was a low-scoring game. Although we won by six wickets, we had to fight every step of the way and I think it was because of the runs that I got in the second innings that I was given my chance to appear in a Test match against New Zealand a few weeks later.

For Bill Edrich, the Gentlemen v. Players match at Lord's in 1938 (see Appendix I) was also a Test trial at a time when, having made his début for England against Australia, he was in the middle of a run of low scores in Test matches. To add to his problems, Ken Farnes, the Gentlemen's leading fast bowler, had been dropped from the England team when it was said by some selectors that he was not as quick as in the past. Bill Edrich would later recall:

We had twenty minutes' batting overnight after Hugh Bartlett had made a magnificent hundred for the Gentlemen. Ken Farnes had just been left out of the Test side at Old Trafford. I went out to open with Len Hutton and, as he was the senior partner, I said, 'Which end would you prefer?' and Len said, 'We'll go as we are', which meant that I went to face Ken Farnes. Well, in the event, only one over was bowled in twenty minutes, at the end of which we were no runs for two wickets. For about half that time, I was unconscious. Ken was about six foot four, he was a very powerful chap and normally a very nice gentle person. You had to make him angry to bowl well and he had been made angry by the selectors' decision. I only had two balls. The first was about a foot outside the off-stump but it went through head high from only just short of a length. I thought 'Hello, hello'. The second one was pitched about off-stump so I had to play it and all that I remember was it coming straight at my eyes. It clipped my glove and went on to my head and laid me out. When I recovered, Wally Hammond, who was captaining the Gentlemen for the first time that year (he later told me it was the quickest over he'd ever seen), asked me if I was all right. I said 'Yes' and went back to the crease whereupon Jack Stephenson, who was fielding in the gully and had caught the ball, said 'How was that?' and I was given out.

When I got back into the pavilion, Frank Woolley, who was

the Players' captain (following the usual tradition of honouring an outstanding professional in his last season), was desperately trying to find somebody to go in as night-watchman. Eventually he turned to Bill Price, who was our Middlesex wicket-keeper and was known as 'Gibraltar' Price for his dogged defence when we needed it. 'Would you like to go in for us now?' he asked. 'No, I bloody well wouldn't,' said Bill. Well, he went in and came out again for a quick duck saying, 'I've got a wife and children to think about.' Oh yes, those Gents and Players matches brought out some real competition between professional pride and amateur enthusiasm, and Lord's was the perfect place to bring the best of both together.

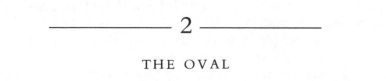

2

THE OVAL

The battles between the Gentlemen and Players at the Oval were never quite as intense as those at Lord's but the rivalry between the two cricket centres was of long standing.

There was something of the 'upstairs–downstairs' relationship between cricket north and south of the Thames, and this was well illustrated in the rivalry between Middlesex and Surrey as personified by Sir Timothy O'Brien. Sir Timothy was an Irish aristocrat – good enough to play for England between 1884 and 1896 – whose middle-order batting was in the grand manner of the Golden Age. Such was his enthusiasm for the game that he was a member of both the MCC and Middlesex as well as Surrey County Cricket Club. However, during one match between Middlesex and Surrey, he caused such deep offence to the Surrey committee that he was expelled from their club. Some years later he was seen in the Long Room at the Oval. When the county secretary reminded him that he was no longer a member, Sir Timothy blithely replied: 'Oh, that's all right. My man has signed me in.'

By the early twenties, the rivalry between Lord's and the Oval was both personal and institutional. As at Lord's, cricket was dominated by the activities of an administrator and a county captain: in this case H. D. G. (later Sir Henry but better known as Shrimp) Leveson Gower, who had captained Surrey from 1908 to 1910, and P. G. H. (Percy) Fender, who was captain from 1920 to 1931. To this pair should be added the name of Jack Hobbs as the senior professional whose standing in the game was such that he would soon bring honour to his profession with a knighthood, as a county committee man and as a Test selector.

On the face of it, Shrimp and his team should have had a good deal in common with Plum Warner and the men at Lord's. Leveson Gower had been Plum Warner's cricket captain at Oxford (which is perhaps a preferable way of describing their relationship – rather than a Shrimp captaining a Plum); both were Test selectors and each enjoyed his outside domain – for Plum within MCC and for Shrimp in choosing sides for the Gentlemen and Players matches at the Oval and as the long-serving organizer of the Scarborough Cricket Festival. Yet there was little love lost between the two. Both were jealous of their preserves and the clash of temperaments was such that the rivalry which we have already noted between the two counties was intensified.

The Surrey captain, Percy Fender, was ever a fighter. Talking, shortly before his death, in the depths of Sussex in his study with its famous black-bound set of *Wisden* and shelves littered with cricket balls which were souvenirs of his bowling or batting performances (as for example that which had been knocked almost out of shape in his record century in thirty-five minutes in the match against Northampton in 1920), he made it plain that he was not averse to tilting at authority, whether at Lord's or the Oval:

> I never really hit it off with Lord Harris. He particularly objected to some of my earlier efforts in bringing the team together. For example, I insisted that the whole team came out on to the field together instead of via the traditional separate amateur and pro-fessional entrances. The first time I took Surrey out on to the field all together against Middlesex at Lord's I was hauled in by His Lordship who said, 'It may be all right at the Oval but we don't do that kind of thing here at Lord's.'

Percy Fender, who had played for Sussex and then Surrey be-tween 1911 and 1914 (and who took over captaincy at the Oval full-time in 1921 after sharing it with C. T. A. Wilkinson), was able to present a unique view of the changes in the game as between the pre- and post-First World War periods:

> There was no disguising that there was a big change. There

wasn't the money about after the war that there'd been before. So far as the amateurs were concerned we'd been able to call on many young men from wealthy families, but with disappearing fortunes and rising income tax they became fewer in number. Those of us who wanted to play as amateurs had to find other opportunities to earn a living. It was partly for this reason that I took up writing first as a journalist – which led to a lot of criticism when I combined this with playing for England on tour – and later in writing books. But I made no bones about it. I used my cricket connections while I was still playing to help my business. For example, as Surrey captain, I could have guests to lunch in the pavilion and many people with whom I did business very much liked to have that kind of opportunity to be on the inside.

Percy Fender's frankness about his use of cricket in combination with his business interests (which as a wine supplier continued despite near-blindness well into his eighties) was matched by his candour over the general difficulties which he had had with his own cricketing establishment:

I had a lot of problems with Shrimp over the question of team selection. So far as amateurs were concerned, my basic rule was that I would always try and include some of the promising youngsters who might go on to become potential captains and leaders in the game, but I regarded it as the normal rule that people of this kind would have obtained a Blue. There were plenty of such people about, but Shrimp, who made his living by acting as a contact man, suggested that I should include two young cricketers who were sons of some of his business friends when they had been barely good enough to get into their college side at university. I said I wasn't willing to accommodate him.

One of the amateurs to whom Surrey gave a trial under Percy Fender's captaincy was T. J. Molony:

It was said that he got his chance because Jack Hobbs deliberately gave away his wicket to him in a trial match early in the season. He was certainly unorthodox and, I believe, the last underarm

bowler to play first-class cricket. When I put him on to bowl
against Nottinghamshire at Trent Bridge in a Bank Holiday
game, a wag in the crowd called out, 'Don't take him off, Fender,
I want to go home and get my old woman. She hasn't had a good
laugh in months.' As it happened, he proceeded to take three
cheap wickets but he bowled so wide of the stumps that one of
them was caught by our wicket-keeper Herbert Strudwick off a
full-blooded hit which he had to catch or be almost decapitated.
Struddy came up to me afterwards and said, 'It's him or me – if
you go on playing him, I'm off.' After that, Molony's days were
numbered.

Whatever their respective views on the opportunities for occasional amateurs, the arguments between Percy Fender and Shrimp
Leveson Gower were not helped by the captain's mordant wit at his
chairman's expense. As Fender recalled, 'I suppose I was a bit
inclined to make the odd joke against Shrimp and these got back to
him.'

These thoughts and confessions of Percy Fender in old age no
doubt explain in part why, as one good enough to play for England
and recognized as the best county captain in the country, he was
never asked to lead the Test side. As one of his Surrey contemporaries remarked, 'He was often his own worst enemy.' It is also
revealing to learn how his attempts to introduce egalitarianism into
the Surrey team were blocked from another and perhaps more
surprising direction. In addition to bringing the team out on to the
field together, Percy Fender sought to change the practice whereby
amateurs and professionals changed in separate dressing-rooms and
experimented with arrangements which would bring the whole
team together. He was approached by his senior professional, Jack
Hobbs, who said, 'We all know what you're trying to do, Skipper,
and we appreciate it. But you know we do like to have a chance to
moan about your efforts at the end of the day's play!'

Jack Hobbs's fellow professional and opening partner Andrew
Sandham had a quiet sense of humour which served him well
during the many years he was obliged to live under the shadow of
'the Master'. Talking shortly before he died in 1982 in his daughter's house at St John's Wood, the old Surrey cricketer – then living

almost a throw-in distance from Lord's – was as philosophical as ever about what he saw as his limited recognition despite his captain's best endeavours:

> I know he put in a word for me at Lord's but I don't think his face fitted and perhaps this didn't always help. After all, I scored over a hundred first-class centuries but, you know, I was never considered good enough to play for the Players at Lord's. But bloody so-and-so was.

'So-and-so' referred to a Surrey player of post-Second World War vintage to whom we will refer later but Sandham's comment underlines the competition and prestige attached to a place in the Players' side at Lord's. By contrast, the Gentlemen and Players match at the Oval drew more extensively on the southern counties. In the 1919 match (see Appendix I) five of the professional side were from Surrey and Middlesex, three from Hampshire and one from Kent, with Lancashire providing the last two places.

Andrew Sandham, who had made his début for Surrey in 1911, had lost some of his best playing years during the war but he might reasonably have hoped for recognition in Shrimp Leveson Gower's selection for the Players side at the Oval. Yet it was hard to gain selection even on his home ground, whether in the 1919 side or its successors:

> Johnny Tyldesley, the 1919 captain, was getting on a bit but he was being honoured as a model professional cricketer and the Players captaincy was one way of doing this near the end of your career. He brought Cecil Parkin down with him from Lancashire. He was a card all right – they called him cricket's comedian but he was a bit too independent for the powers that be and he didn't last with the Players. Of my Surrey team-mates, you couldn't quarrel with Hobbs, Hitch and Strudwick – they were the best batsman, bowler and wicket-keeper in the game just then and Jack took three hundreds off the Gents that year – and no one did that before or since. From Middlesex, Hearne and Hendren were solid choices for the all-rounder and the middle-order slot. And who could quarrel with Phil Mead of Hampshire and Frank

Woolley of Kent as the two best left-hand batsmen around or of Alec Kennedy pegging away at medium pace?

So perhaps it wasn't too surprising that I was over thirty when I got in the side in 1921 [see Appendix I] and, even then, I had to settle for a middle-order place. I remember getting my first hundred for the Players in 1924 [see Appendix I]. I hit Arthur Gilligan for five fours in one over. He kept bowling down the legside and I love to hook. In fact, Jack and I opened together for the Players (at last) in that game and we put on over a hundred as we did on sixty-two other occasions but it seemed as though they wanted us to confine this to county matches.

Of Surrey's playing record during his county career, which lasted until 1937, Andrew Sandham's chief recollection was of the ability of Percy Fender to make do with limited resources:

He would try the most outrageous things. In those days we had tremendous batting strength but our bowling was thin. 'Percy George', as we called him, would suddenly decide to open the bowling with a spinner – often himself. And he had those great personal rivalries with some of the other county captains like Arthur Carr of Notts. When he was batting, Percy George would bring himself on to bowl and when he tugged his collar in a certain way whoever was at short leg would know he had to throw himself to the ground because up would come a legside full toss and Percy George would be shouting out 'Caught Squires bowled Fender' and sure enough out on the long-leg boundary Stan Squires would be pocketing another catch.

Surrey's bowling resources received substantial reinforcement when Alf Gover came into the side in 1928. He would go on to play for his country and continues to support the game through his internationally renowned cricket school in Wandsworth, London. The school, first formed in partnership with his old Surrey colleagues Andrew Sandham and Herbert Strudwick, has been a nursery for cricketers from all over the world, including several of the contemporary West Indian fast bowlers. In 1986, Alf Gover – who at the age of seventy-eight was bowling regularly at his school

– was dining out on the story of the young Indian batsman who, when out of position on a defensive back stroke, tactfully remarked, 'You beat me by sheer pace, Sir.'

When he first joined the Surrey side, Alf Gover recalls that Herbert Strudwick, a great judge of the game, counselled him to bowl at or just outside off-stump, adding, 'That way, you will worry all but the very best.' Percy Fender concurs with the view that Herbert Strudwick was one of the best judges of the game but adds:

> You couldn't wish to have a better man on your side and his suggestions were always immensely valuable. However, there was a problem for someone like Struddy who was not accustomed to authority in practice. I remember, one day, I was called off the field and I asked him if he would look after the side while I was away. He was obviously delighted and I had no qualms about leaving my team under his control. Two of our chaps had been bowling very steadily immediately before I left the field and, when I returned, I saw that they were both still bowling. I went up to Struddy and said, 'I suppose you gave them a breather and brought them back on again?' 'Oh no, Skipper,' he replied; 'they were bowling so well that I never thought to take them off.'

One of the bowlers in question was Alf Gover. Today he retains the looks of an amiable grey fox with the lean figure of his playing days. Despite his consistent success as one of the leading wicket-takers between the wars, he has retained an endearing ability to make fun of himself. In recalling his limited batting pretensions and his enthusiasm to get at the opposition, he has told how, as Surrey's number eleven, he would occasionally waive the umpire's offer to give him guard with the remark: 'Oh, don't worry about that. I played down here last year.'

He has also demonstrated the regard which he felt towards the team's professional, Jack Hobbs:

> When I first came into the side he was a great help and encouragement to me. He was literally worshipped by the whole team. He used to arrange a match to raise funds for a local hospital in

Wimbledon every September. The year I got married, I said to him, 'I do hope you will be a wedding guest.' 'When is it?', Jack replied. 'September 17th,' I said. Well, Jack told me that this was the date of his annual charity match and he wanted me to play for him. So I went to my future in-laws and told them of my difficulty. And my father-in-law to be was a man who loved Surrey cricket and he just said, 'No problem. We'll postpone the wedding until the 18th.' ,

Some of Alf Gover's other anecdotes reveal his respect for his opponents, particularly in his duels with some of the greatest batsmen of the day. He received his first experience of professional gamesmanship early on:

I was in the dressing-room changing for my first game against Middlesex when in came Patsy Hendren. He asked me if I was the new Surrey fast bowler and when I said 'Yes' he said, 'Well, I hope you won't bounce them at me. My eyes aren't as good as they used to be.' Naturally, when he came out to bat, I immediately bounced a couple at him and he hooked the first one for four and the second one for six. Jack Hobbs came across from cover-point and asked me what the devil I was doing. When I told him about my conversation with Patsy he said, 'You idiot. Patsy's the best hooker in the game.'

Later in his career, Alf Gover joined the widespread circle of professional cricketers who regarded Wally Hammond as the greatest English batsman against whom they had bowled. However, on one occasion Alf felt that he had a better than usual opportunity to dismiss the great man:

When we reported for the match against Gloucestershire at Bristol, I went in to see the masseur to get myself toned up a bit before the start of the game. I found Wally Hammond stretched out on one of the side tables fast asleep. 'What's the matter with him?' I asked the masseur. 'Oh, he's been out on the town for the best part of the night' was the reply. As it happened, we were in the field and I got an early wicket and in came Wally. He was shaking himself as he came out towards the wicket and he certainly didn't look at his best. Anyway, I was greatly encouraged, and I delivered one of the best first balls I've ever sent down to anyone. It was the perfect yorker. And you know what happened? Wally gave a sort of half yawn and hit it straight through the covers for four. He then proceeded to lay about him and when he'd got 162 he said to me, 'Alf, you'd better bowl me a straight one. I've had about all the exercise I can take for one day.'

On another occasion, Alf Gover had a typical encounter with one of the amateurs for whom he retains a lasting respect:

Brian Sellers had just been made captain of Yorkshire. He hadn't seen much of my bowling but, from the first, he was quick to try it on. When he came in to bat, he said, 'I'm not in such good nick at the moment. Will you give me one?' So I said, 'Sure, I'll give you one.' I went in fast and bowled him the quickest bouncer I could manage. 'All right,' he said. 'That's the way it is then. Come on. Let's have a bloody do!' I don't think he got a big score that day, but he was certainly a fighter and he knew how to get the best out of his side. In that sense, he and Percy Fender were very much alike.

Alf Gover shares Andrew Sandham's enthusiasm for Percy Fender's wholehearted involvement:

I can see him now persistently beating the bat with his leg-breaks and lifting up his arms to the skies and saying, 'Is there no God in heaven?' And he got very angry when I burst out laughing. He threatened to drop me for some games from the side for failing to take seriously his invocation to the Almighty.

Alf Gover also shared Andrew Sandham's appreciation of Percy Fender's captaincy and relates it to the other amateurs he played with and against:

'Percy George' was so totally dedicated. There have been others – no names, no pack drill – of whom you couldn't quite say the same. I remember one Surrey amateur after Percy George's time who was captaining the side when we had a splendid opportunity to wrap up a match in two days. I went over to him and said, 'Let's claim the extra half-hour, Skipper', because I knew we could get through their tail. He refused for the simple fact – which we all knew – that he was staying with some very smart company and he wanted to stay on for a grand dinner party that night. Mind you, Percy George would not have any amateur passengers in the side. You'd sometimes see some in the opposing teams who were 'Coloured Caps' and the more brilliant the colours some of them wore, the more I fancied my chances as a bowler. We had a range of terms for those boys. Sometimes we would say 'Here comes another BA' and the chap would think we were being respectful about his academic achievements but what we meant was 'bloody amateur'. Mind you, it was all in fun and the amateurs in our pre-war side were top class as many of them showed by playing for England as well as Surrey. You certainly couldn't complain about that sort of amateur.

Several of these leading Surrey amateurs were in the Gentlemen's team which met the Players at the Oval in 1934 when Alf Gover made his highly successful début in the series (see Appendix I). That match was of particular interest; it was not only Alf Gover's first game for the Players but also the last appearance for Percy Fender and, as it proved, the last match ever played between the Gentlemen and the Players at the Oval.

There was another notable farewell appearance later in the same season when Jack Hobbs appeared for the Players for the last time as their captain in the match against the Gentlemen at Folkestone (see Appendix I). One of the Surrey amateurs taking part in that match was M. J. C. (Maurice) Allom. He was one of the rare amateurs who strengthened Surrey's bowling and had a brief but successful career both for the county and for England before business commitments led to his premature retirement from the game. He came from a generation of Cambridge undergraduates who lived life to the full, including, in his case, occasional appearances with his banjo in the dance band at the Savoy.

Still the same immaculate figure who would give long service to

Surrey as their president half a century later, he recalls the background to his brief but enjoyable first-class cricket career:

I had no real help at Wellington College but Len Braund was specially helpful in the brief period which we had for pre-season coaching at Cambridge. We were so lucky in those days, there wasn't the academic pressure they have today and we could put out a side which gave the counties a real run for their money. The 1927 Cambridge side I played in under Eddie Dawson was unbeaten and never bowled out twice.

But I really learned my cricket when I came into the Surrey team, particularly in how to vary my bowling. I had previously been concentrating on bowling reasonably fast but with help from the Surrey pros I learned to develop both the in-swinger and the out-swinger and that gave me my chance to play for England.

I am often asked whether any of the professionals resented it when I came into the Surrey side. The senior pros then were Jack Hobbs, Andrew Sandham, Andy Ducat, Tom Shepherd and Alan Peach and they were wonderful chaps. And the fact that I played as an amateur and replaced one of the pros – there was never resentment of any sort or kind and I was made very welcome. Mind you, as Surrey were short of bowling I was perhaps of some immediate use.

I think there were two factors which prevented any resentment generally about an amateur taking a professional's place. The first was that you had to be pretty good to get into the side, and the second was that the senior pros like Jack Hobbs would come down like a ton of bricks on any signs of 'bolshiness' by the junior professionals.

Maurice Allom was always regarded as a genial giant in his playing days but he recalls how, in reacting to the rivalry between Percy Fender and Arthur Carr, he once showed an excess of zeal:

It was at the height of the bodyline business. I don't remember why but I was very annoyed with Arthur Carr and I bowled him the best bouncer I've ever delivered. He finished up flat on his back with his bat a dozen yards away. There was a stunned silence when the rest of the Surrey team realized the enormity of what I'd done and with the prospect of facing Larwood and Voce later in the game. Then virtually everyone rushed forward – somebody picked up Arthur's bat, people were dusting him off and they all looked at me as if I was the biggest bloody fool in the game.

Andrew Sandham, as a Surrey opening batsman who would have to face the new-ball attack, spells out his concern at the prospect of Arthur Carr's retaliation:

When we played Nottinghamshire, we all knew that Larwood and Voce would have seven or eight pints of beer at lunchtime with a cheese sandwich, and somehow they seemed to bowl faster after lunch than before. I preferred facing Harold Larwood rather than Bill Voce with his left-arm bowling which brought the ball into the body and got you under the ribs. We always used to think that they had a running bet on at lunchtime as to who would hit which of our batsmen the most. So you can understand why we weren't overjoyed by Maurice Allom's youthful enthusiasm.

Another Cambridge blue who followed Maurice Allom into the Surrey side was F. R. (Freddie) Brown in 1931. Ever the bluff red-faced figure, he paints a picture of the school and university influence which took him to a long playing career in county cricket, for the Gentlemen and for England:

I was lucky in getting the best coaching there was in the shape of Aubrey Faulkner. Like many British families between the wars, my father worked overseas and actually played cricket in Peru against Plum Warner's MCC side. I was born in Lima and came as a boarder to my prep school, St Piran's in Maidenhead, in January 1921. At the end of the Easter term, the Major (that was how we referred to Aubrey Faulkner because he was not only a great South African all-rounder but a war hero as well) said, 'Come on, I'll give you a net.' Well, the net was his bowling off rubble into a fives court. It was the best lesson I have ever had in getting into line. If you missed the ball it hit you on the back of the head. Then he got me opening the bowling but he also showed me how to spin the ball. When I went on to the Leys, our cricket master was the old Sussex amateur 'Nipper' Holloway who encouraged me to throw in the odd spinner to vary the medium pace. But when I went on to Cambridge, Aubrey Faulkner, who by then had his own coaching school where I spent as much time as possible, said, 'Don't be a bloody fool. There'll be forty who can bowl the quicker stuff. Concentrate on your spinners.' He was an enormous influence. You look at the 'varsity sides of 1930 and 1931. Virtually every one of them had been to him for coaching. He was the greatest spotter of faults I've ever seen.

Then when I came into the Surrey side, I was lucky in two respects. I had the residential qualification for either Middlesex or Surrey but I chose the Oval because the wickets were so much quicker and you got the bounce. And of course I had Percy Fender as my skipper. He had a reputation for gamesmanship and I saw a bit of that. Before I joined Surrey it was said that, when he was opposed by a new county captain, he'd toss for first innings on the balcony of the pavilion, throw the coin down the stairs and run like hell after it and return with it in his hand saying, 'Bad luck old boy. We'll bat.' Certainly, when we were in the field he was full of tricks. At the end of an over he'd come over to me and say, 'I think this chap has spotted your googly. I'm going to leg slip which will make him think you're going to bowl him the googly. But don't.' That's the kind of thing he did — and he made you think too. He would talk to you all the time.

We had five regular amateurs in the team when I joined it: Fender, Jardine, Allom, Spencer Block and the superbly named Roger de Winton Kelsall Winlaw. Alan Ratcliffe also got a game from time to time. So that meant, excluding the skipper, there were six amateurs — all Oxbridge Blues, at a time when university cricket was at its strongest — who might expect to play for Surrey. They were all selected on merit and they could all get on with the game. If we won the toss, Percy would play hell with us if we didn't get 400 quickly. We could look to our pros for a solid start and then Percy always used to say he could rely on what he called the 'biff bang boys' – the amateurs usually batting at numbers six, seven and eight – to get quick runs and bring in another 10,000 at the Oval after four o'clock. Then we'd expect to bowl at the other side for an hour or so on the first day. The outfield at the Oval was rough in those days and there was no shine after ten overs. So Percy made sure I got a good spell early on and we bowled twenty overs an hour without rushing.

Percy Fender, who, as we have seen, provided a link with cricket prior to the First World War, went on as captain of Surrey with Jack Hobbs as his senior professional until 1931 and played for the county under his two successors D. R. Jardine and E. R. T. Holmes. He recalled:

Of Jack Hobbs, one can only use that overworked cliché about nature's gentlemen because that is what he was. He really did give stature to his profession and no one could have had a better supporter as senior professional than he was to me.

He had his own almost schoolboy sense of humour but there was often a point to it. I remember he once rang Douglas Jardine up on the old-fashioned intercom – you know the kind of thing that you had to blow into and then put to your ear – which was typical of what you'd expect to find in the servants' hall, and I suppose it fitted the image in the Players' pokey little dressing-room in the basement. Anyway, I was with Douglas in the captain's room at the top of the pavilion (he had taken over the side from me by then) and I heard Jack say, 'Skipper, we've got an argument going on down here. It's about the proper extent of the follow-through for an off-drive. Would you come and settle it for us?' Well, Douglas and I went down there and it really was a bit of a rabbit hutch. 'Now then, Skipper,' Jack said, handing him a bat, 'you've got that model off-drive they taught you at Winchester; would you mind showing us your follow-through?' Douglas had originally jibbed a bit at the whole suggestion but I could see he was intrigued and the reference to his Winchester upbringing didn't hurt Jack's case a bit. Anyway he swung the bat through and Jack and the boys all said, 'Oh no, Skipper.

That's nothing like your full follow-through.' So Douglas had another go and – wham – he knocked out the overhead light. We both beat a hasty retreat with various irreverent remarks round our ears about 'Not being room to swing a bat – let alone a cat'.

Douglas did have his own pawky Scottish sense of humour. I remember one day when we had come in from another long day in the field because our limited attack had been hammered and the dressing-room attendant asked if he could get anything for us. 'Just slip out and get me twenty Players,' I said. 'Make mine twenty bowlers,' said Douglas.

Douglas Jardine's successor in 1934, Errol Holmes, had little in common with his Scottish predecessor (apart from the same commitment to wearing the Harlequin cap). He brought a zest for the game and a determination to ensure that everyone enjoyed their cricket. He was a classic example of the Malvernian whose off-driving was typical of his enthusiasm in leading from the front and, in later years, he would regale undergraduate audiences with his approach to the bowling giants of his day. Referring to Harold Larwood, he would describe his fearsome pace, unparalleled accuracy and remarkable stamina. When asked how he dealt with so difficult and dangerous an opponent he simply replied, 'I just hit him through the covers, my boy. I just hit him through the covers.'

It fell to Errol Holmes to end Percy Fender's long association with Surrey, and the occasion was vividly recalled almost half a century later by 'Percy George':

He asked me if I'd like to play a couple of games for Surrey under his captaincy. I wasn't very impressed by that offer and I thought I might still be of some use to my county in rather more games. In any case, I just said, 'All right. Put me down for the Yorkshire match – home and away.'

3

THE NORTHERN
COUNTIES

Percy Fender's enthusiasm for playing against Yorkshire was one shared by all the best amateurs, although it was said that an interesting list could be compiled of those Gentlemen who were never available for games on the northern tour. Alf Gover, for example, always said that there was no shortage of Surrey amateurs keen to play against Yorkshire and contrasted this with the apparent reluctance of some Middlesex amateurs to travel north.

For the northern counties, professionalism was the dominant feature in what became a private Championship battle. Apart from the Middlesex victories in 1920 and 1921, the title between the wars went to Yorkshire twelve times and Lancashire five, with Nottinghamshire and Derbyshire winning once each. In almost all these years, Yorkshire and Nottinghamshire relied on an amateur captain and ten professionals while Lancashire and Derbyshire, after experimenting with a few amateurs in the twenties, generally adopted the successful 'one Gentleman and ten Players' principle.

For Yorkshire, amateur leadership was not confined to the field of play. Lord Hawke, who, like Lord Harris of Kent, combined both a county and national role in cricket administration, had been captain for an unprecedented twenty-eight seasons. For part of this time he was also the club's President, a position he held for over forty years. He also took his turn as President of the MCC and succeeded Lord Harris as the club's treasurer.

But it is for his work on behalf of professionals that he is best remembered. He introduced winter pay, a fairly based talent money system and, above all, arrangements for investing benefit money to look after players in their retirement. When he first took over the Yorkshire side in 1883 it had been described as a drunken rabble, and he had shown his authority by dismissing as great a left-arm slow bowler as Bobby Peel for eccentric behaviour while under the influence of drink. (It was typical of Yorkshire playing strength at that time and of Hawke's perspicacity that Peel's replacement, Wilfred Rhodes, would achieve even greater success for Yorkshire and England.) Gradually, the Hawke style of auto-cratic and firm leadership, together with his interest in his players' welfare, gave the Yorkshire side a stability and pride which was a key element in its Championship successes, and other counties sought to emulate the Yorkshire approach.

Yet Hawke was not without his critics. He retained the cap-taincy for too long (until 1910), and Sir Leonard Hutton today recalls some of the irreverent thoughts which were expressed about 'Lordy' in the Yorkshire dressing-room:

> Wilfred Rhodes said he was a very good captain because he always did what he was told. For example, Wilfred would say, 'Now my Lord, you go into the outfield. I'll go in close and have a natter with the boys.' David Denton, who was one of the greatest fieldsmen of his day, used to say that His Lordship often scored more runs with his fingers than off the bat. Then there was the matter of expenses. Lord Hawke took expenses; Sir Stanley Jackson did not.

This definition of the true amateur as one who could afford to play first-class cricket without financial support of any kind was one which applied to only a handful of those representing the Gentlemen. In Sir Stanley Jackson's case, however, this true amateurism was also emphasized by the fact that his appearances had been limited and, although an outstandingly successful captain of England, he never captained Yorkshire. He continued to be a power behind the scenes in Yorkshire cricket and eventually suc-ceeded Lord Hawke as the county's president. His opportunities for close involvement in the game were limited as his career developed as a Member of Parliament, a Government Minister and later

Governor of Bengal, but he set a standard for the 'true amateur'.

After Lord Hawke's long reign as captain of Yorkshire, the adherence to the amateur principle of captaincy was reflected in regular changes at the top. There were few amateurs like the Winchester schoolmaster Rockley Wilson (who was good enough to play for England in Australia in 1920–21) who were able to play for Yorkshire as August amateurs and, for the first six post-war years, the captaincy was shared in turn by D. C. F. Burton and Geoffrey Wilson. Both had been useful batsmen at Cambridge but there was a sense in which their appearances for Yorkshire – generally batting at number eight – were seen as tokenism. It was at this period that the massively efficient Yorkshire professional cricket machine, with players of the calibre of Holmes, Sutcliffe, Oldroyd, Kilner, Rhodes, Robinson, Macaulay, Dolphin and Waddington, was seen at its most successful although, as the county historian J. M. Kilburn points out, this was often obtained at the cost of unpopularity with the other counties.

Nevertheless, Lord Hawke's influence in the matter of amateur captaincy remained supreme. There were, however, rumblings when it was announced that Major A. W. Lupton was to take over the side in 1925 at the age of forty-six, some seventeen years after he had first appeared for Yorkshire. Lord Hawke took this issue head on at the Annual General Meeting of the club that year with his famous and often misunderstood remark, 'Pray God no professional may ever captain England.' However, those who have sought to use these words in a critical social sense never complete the quotation, which went on: 'I love professionals, every one of them, but we have always had an amateur skipper. If the time comes when we are to have no more amateurs captaining England, well I don't say England will become exactly like League football, but it will be a thousand pities and it will not be good for the game.'

In the event, Major Lupton's captaincy and batting at number ten (where he achieved a career average of just over ten runs) were modest contributions as the county yet again emerged as Champions. However, it certainly added to the folklore of cricket when the impression was fostered (particularly by Neville Cardus) of the captain's dependency on the wise old Yorkshire professional

Emmott Robinson who, according to Cardus, on seeing the first ball turn while Yorkshire were batting would recommend an immediate declaration by simply saying, 'Bring 'em in, Major.' There can be little doubt that, for his part, Emmott Robinson had a high regard for the Major, for, as E. W. Swanton recalls, he was heard to remark, 'He's too nice a gentleman to 'ave to play cricket.'

Cardus's artistic enthusiasm in extolling the virtues of Yorkshire's professionals has led to charges of fantasy. There is ample evidence which suggests he caught the flavour of many of their great performers. Emmott Robinson was, indeed, the cricketing brain in the Yorkshire dressing-room with an independence of spirit which allowed him to chide Neville Cardus with the remark when they met, 'Mester Cardus – tha' invented me.' He also regarded himself as the heir to a great store of professional cricket wisdom. Bill Bowes, who came into the Yorkshire side as Emmott Robinson was nearing retirement, has described how the old pro took him aside as soon as he received his county cap:

> 'Congratulations, Bill. We're delighted for you. Now you can start to really learn about this game. Get a book and every team you play against, at night, write down all you remember about the day's play. Write down what you remember about the wicket. Put down the names of the batsmen and their best shots. Keep adding to this all through the season. Next year add to it again. In ten years' time, you'll still be learning something fresh in every match. And after that, you'll be playing from memory, anyway!'

If at this time Emmott Robinson represented the more vocal part of Yorkshire's professional cricketing wisdom, the county captain could still draw on the unparalleled experience of Wilfred Rhodes and George Hirst. Both played for the county through the twenties and although Hirst made only occasional appearances after he became coach at Eton in 1921, Wilfred Rhodes was in the county side from 1895 to 1930 before becoming the full-time coach at Harrow in the following year.

Bill Bowes has his own delightful recollections of the character

and personality of both men and their contribution to many generations of cricketers through their coaching:

> George didn't know anything like as much as Wilfred. But he had
> such wonderful enthusiasm and he could inspire the youngsters.
> He only played the odd match in my first season for Yorkshire
> but when we came in for the tea interval, he'd sit at the end of the
> table and we'd get him to reminisce. He was spellbinding and he
> made you feel you were part of a wonderful tradition.
>
> On the other hand, Wilfred was always very tight in his
> comments. I remember saying to him once, 'George must have
> been a very fine cricketer.' 'He was,' said Wilfred. 'Wasn't it
> really exciting when he first discovered that he could swerve the
> ball late into the batsman so that somebody said it was like a fast
> throw in from the covers?' I asked. 'Aye,' Wilfred said, 'he was
> very good. But he didn't know how to use it, you know. I had to
> set the field for him so that he got the best out of it.'
>
> When they were rivals as the coaches at Eton and Harrow
> respectively, it was rightly said that George's personality was
> part of the long run of success for Eton. Certainly, he would get
> the best out of people. On the other hand, what you've got to
> remember about Wilfred was that he could not relate to begin-
> ners. But if you were a Test match player looking to get advice,
> Wilfred was superb.

It was no doubt because of Wilfred Rhodes's cricketing brain
that, in his fiftieth year, he became a candidate for the Yorkshire
captaincy. The situation arose at the end of Major Lupton's tenure
in office when, in late 1927, a letter was sent to all members of the
Yorkshire County Cricket Club as follows:

Dear Sir or Madam:
   No doubt you are aware that there has been a good deal of
controversy in the newspapers as to next year's captaincy. This
being the case I think it is only fair that the members of the Club
should have an opportunity of expressing their opinions. I have
therefore decided to take a ballot of the members and should be

obliged by your filling in, signing and returning to me the enclosed postcard.

Yours truly,
S. E. Grimshaw

The following questionnaire was attached:

Yorkshire County Cricket Captaincy

1. Are you in favour of the appointment of an amateur or a professional?
2. If it is not possible to secure a suitable amateur, whom are you in favour of – Wilfred Rhodes or Herbert Sutcliffe?
   As it may not be possible to secure a suitable amateur will you please vote upon both propositions?

Bill Bowes describes the background to this early exercise in Yorkshire democracy:

Sid Grimshaw was a retired schoolmaster who was mad about cricket. He had only been a moderate player in the Leeds league but he came and helped George Hirst in coaching youngsters at Headingley. He got to know all the players and he felt it was wrong that Herbert Sutcliffe should be approached as the possible captain before Wilfred Rhodes. It looked, at that stage, as though the job might go to a professional, but Sid Grimshaw was determined to make sure that Wilfred's claims (and pride) were not overlooked.

Wilfred Rhodes represented the old school of professionalism with its hard but uncommunicative approach to getting the job done, while Herbert Sutcliffe was typical of a new breed of player who brought a certain glamour and style to their work (he would later write a generous, readable and unghosted autobiography simply entitled *For Yorkshire and England*). Sutcliffe's emergence as what today would be termed a media figure was part of a wider changing sporting scene which would soon make stars of golfers like Henry Cotton and tennis players such as Fred Perry.

'Our 'Erbert', as he was affectionately known to Yorkshire crowds, had gained their respect with his immaculate turnout and perfectly brilliantined hair which was the basis of a self-confident image that frustrated bowlers around the world as well as on the county circuit. It was not entirely surprising, therefore, when the Yorkshire membership voted in favour of Sutcliffe as captain for the 1928 season.

There followed a fascinating sequel which, to this day, is a closely guarded secret in the sense that no records are available for inspection of the Yorkshire committee's subsequent actions. Yet there was clearly a backlash in favour of amateur captaincy and pressure was put on Sutcliffe to withdraw his name. It is hard to believe that this did not reflect Lord Hawke's views, and it was certainly the case that there were voices within the Yorkshire membership calling for a more diplomatic and emollient style of leadership to improve both internal as well as external relations (since it was said that the price of Yorkshire's rare failure was an abundance of dressing-room recrimination). In the event Sutcliffe, who was coaching in South Africa, gracefully withdrew from the situation by sending a telegram indicating his willingness to serve under any captain appointed by the county committee.

With the appointment of W. A. (later Sir William) Worsley as captain, Yorkshire recommenced the process which, in all, would provide them with six short-term captains in fourteen years. This process ended in 1933 when A. B. Sellers took over the side. As the son of a committee man with nothing like the skill of the rest of his team, he faced a difficult task in asserting his leadership. Yet, through sheer force of personality, an ability to rise to the occasion in late-order batting, and fearless fielding, he was quickly seen to lead from the front. In addition, his physical toughness, which could match that of anyone in the side, meant that, in turn, he became as dominant a figure as Lord Hawke both as captain and committee man.

From his earliest days as captain, he showed a determination to maintain his authority without fear or favour. When Len Hutton returned to the Yorkshire side after making his maiden Test century against New Zealand in 1937, he was half an hour late in meeting

I. G. Crawley, ct Sheldon, b Coventry... 103

ABOVE: Lord's, 1921. The amateur training ground: Eton v. Harrow. L. G. Crawley (Harrow) is caught by H. D. Sheldon off the bowling of the Hon. J. B. Coventry for 103. Among the fielders are R. Aird (who would later play for Hampshire and become Secretary of the MCC – second on the left); G. O. Allen (later of Middlesex and England – third on the left); and Lord Dunglass (who would later play for Middlesex and, as Sir Alec Douglas-Home, become Prime Minister – fifth on the left).

BELOW: Eton v. Harrow, 1921. The fashion parade marked the height of 'the Season'.

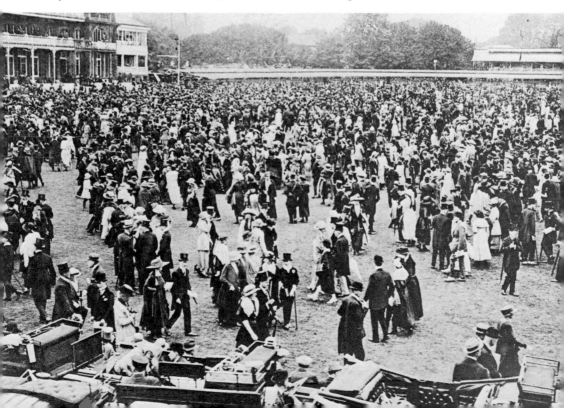

BELOW: 'Plum' Warner in his early playing days.

MR. P. F. WARNER

ABOVE: The Middlesex Championship Dinner at the Café Royal, 1921. At the top table in white tie and tails are Sir Pelham Warner (second on the left); Lord Harris (seated); and the captain of the championship side, F. T. Mann (standing, right). Others present include: P. G. H. Fender (top left of the middle table, in black tie) and G. O. Allen (top left of the nearest table) who is talking to his neighbour on the right, Patsy Hendren.

BELOW: The Oxford (dark blue) and Cambridge (light blue) teams at Lord's, 1922. Later first-class cricket appearances are shown in brackets. Front row, l–r: C. T. Ashton (Essex), V. R. Price (Surrey), A. P. F. Chapman (Kent and England), G. T. S. Stevens (Middlesex and England), H. Ashton (Essex), R. H. B. Bettington (Middlesex and New South Wales), A. G. Doggart (Middlesex) and T. L. Holdsworth. Middle row, l–r: P. A. Wright (Northants), T. B. Raikes (Norfolk), C. A. Fiddian-Green (Warwicks. and Worcs.), B. H. Lyon (Gloucs.), M. D. Lyon (Somerset), C. H. Knott (Kent) and G. O. Allen (Middlesex and England). Back row, l–r: L. P. Hedges (Kent), F. B. R. Browne (Sussex), M. Patten (Scotland), G. O. Shelmerdine (Lancs.), F. H. Barnard and W. W. Hill-Wood (Derbyshire).

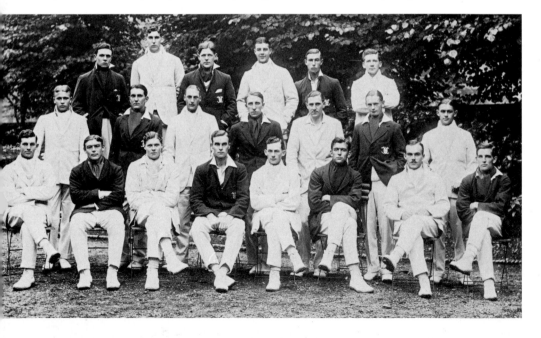

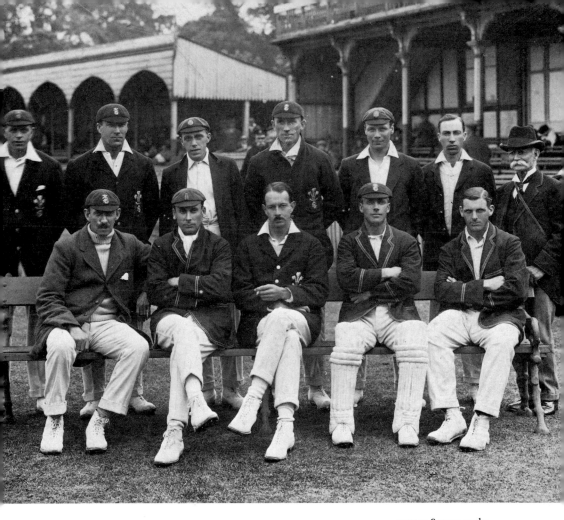

ABOVE: **Surrey at the Oval, 1921. Front row, l–r: T. Rushby, J. B. Hobbs, C. T. A. Wilkinson (captain), H. Strudwick and J. W. Hitch. Back row, l–r: W. J. Abel, A. Ducat, T. Abel, H. S. Harrison, H. A. Peach, A. Sandham and F. Bovington (scorer).**

LEFT: **Gentlemen's XI, Scarborough, 1922. Front row, l–r: E. R. Wilson, J. W. H. T. Douglas, H. D. G. Leveson-Gower, F. T. Mann and W. W. Leadbeater (secretary, Scarborough C.C.). Back row, l–r: A. W. Carr, A. E. R. Gilligan, V. W. C. Jupp, A. P. F. Chapman, G. T. S. Stevens, N. E. Haig, H. Ashton and A. H. Fawcett.**

LEFT: Major Lupton leads the 1925 Yorkshire championship side on to the field with Wilfred Rhodes and wicket-keeper Arthur Dolphin. Over Major Lupton's shoulder is his professional mentor Emmott Robinson and, to his left, the young Maurice Leyland.

BELOW: Part of the enormous crowd watching the Gentlemen v. Players match at Scarborough in 1922.

OPPOSITE ABOVE: The Yorkshire nursery. George Hirst coaches a young hopeful in the nets at Headingley.

OPPOSITE BELOW: A famous Yorkshire triumvirate at the match between Lord Hawke's XI and the 1929 MCC side in South Africa. From l–r: G. H. Hirst, who was one of the umpires; Wilfred Rhodes, who was making his last appearance in first-class cricket; and Lord Hawke.

The MCC tour of South Africa, 1923. Frank Mann's team with the celebrated Zulu rickshaw runners, in Durban. L-r: G. T. S. Stevens, P. G. H. Fender, W. H. Livsey, A. E. R. Gilligan, A. W. Carr, V. W. C. Jupp, F. T. Mann, F. Bond (manager), G. Brown, F. E. Woolley, G. B. Street, C. G. Macauley, A. N. Other, C. A. G. Russell, C. P. Mead, A. Kennedy and A. Sandham.

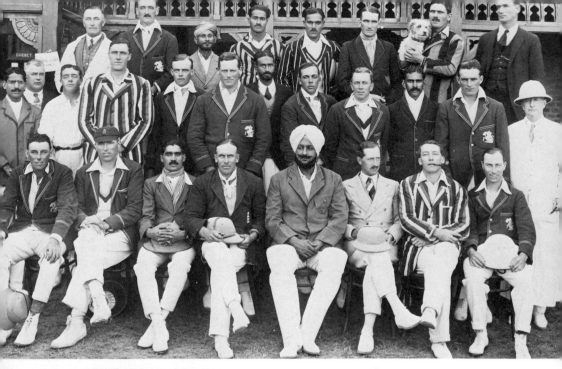

ABOVE: The MCC v. Northern India, Lahore, 1926. Front row, l–r: M. W. Tate, G. Geary, A. N. Other, A. E. R. Gilligan (captain), the Maharaja of Patiala, Major R. C. Chichester-Constable, M. Ll. Hill and A. Sandham. Middle row includes: A. Dolphin, G. T. Earle, P. T. Eckersley and J. Mercer (3rd to 6th from left), R. E. S. Wyatt, W. E. Astill and G. S. Boyes (8th, 9th and 11th from left). Back row includes: Rev. J. H. Parsons (2nd on left) and George Brown (last on right).

LEFT: Australian and England captains Armstrong and Douglas outside the England amateur dressing-room, Trent Bridge, 1921.

BELOW: The MCC tour of Australia, Sydney, 1924. Back row, l–r: H. Howell, R. K. Tyldesley, A. P. F. Chapman, F. C. Toone (manager), M. W. Tate, W. W. Whysall and J. L. Bryan. Middle row, l–r: F. E. Woolley, J. W. Hearne, J. W. H. T. Douglas, A. E. R. Gilligan (captain), J. B. Hobbs, E. H. Hendren and H. Strudwick. Front row, l–r: R. Kilner, A. P. Freeman, H. Sutcliffe and A. Sandham.

the captain's requirement to be present on the ground at least an hour before the start of Yorkshire's next home match. Thinking that perhaps this technical breach of the captain's rules might be overlooked because of his Test responsibilities, Len Hutton padded up and prepared to go out and open the Yorkshire innings only to be met at the door by his captain saying, 'What's tha up to, lad? It's the first time I've ever seen a twelfth man with his pads on.'

On other occasions Sellers's exercise in discipline over his professionals was seen as excessive. Early in his captaincy, he treated the team in a way which his senior professional Herbert Sutcliffe regarded as intolerable. There followed an embarrassing scene for the Yorkshire captain when, on entering the playing area through the amateur gate to lead his side out on to the field in an away match, he was kept standing in the middle with the two umpires and the incoming batsmen before Sutcliffe and the rest of the team, having made their point, joined their captain.

There was a sequel at the end of the season when Yorkshire once more won the Championship. The captain and his senior professional sat down to discuss bonus payments which would be paid to members of the team as a result of the Championship victory, and Brian Sellers opened the conversation by saying, 'Now let's talk about the share of the money and also about rebuilding the team for the future. But before we do that, let's get one thing straight. You are my senior professional but you are also the person who is leading the opposition to me. So you won't get a brass farthing by way of bonus.' Perhaps impressed by his captain's directness, Herbert Sutcliffe changed from that point on to become his greatest supporter. Together, they made a formidable combination which helped to guarantee Yorkshire's continuing success.

Bill Bowes, who came into the Yorkshire side in 1929, is in a unique position to sum up what can now be seen, in retrospect, as Yorkshire's last great Golden Age of cricket through the thirties. Living in retirement in a house which looks out on the glories of Wharfedale, his views are those of one of the most intelligent bowlers of his day as well as a distinguished cricket journalist:

When I came into the side Willie Worsley was captain but the first great influence on me was our senior professional, Herbert Sutcliffe. I remember that one of my early games was an away match against Hampshire at Portsmouth. In those days we went off to a marquee for lunch on the edge of the ground and the Hampshire side, which was dominated by amateurs, would walk off the field and go straight into the tent. When we were in the field and it came to lunchtime, I did the same and went into the tent in my shirt sleeves. I felt a tap on the shoulder and there was Herbert Sutcliffe saying, 'Can we have a word?' I got up and he said, 'Be a good chap, go and put on your blazer. I'll tell you why later.' Well, I did as he said and, when we got back into the dressing-room afterwards, he said:

'Look, I know you were following the example of the Hampshire amateurs. But the thing you've got to learn is that as a professional cricketer you must be better than the amateurs. You must be better as a player. You must be better in your dress. You must be better in your manners and you've got to show why you're a true professional.'

I've never forgotten that advice. It really was a question of setting standards and living up to them. Mind you, my first captains did set a high standard. For example, Alan Barber only led the side for one year but he was splendid. It was amazing how he managed to exert his authority. It wasn't easy with people like Wilfred Rhodes. Alan Barber was the boss but he wasn't bossy.

When it came to Frank Greenwood, we thought he was a bit unlucky in having to give way to Brian Sellers. Brian's father, Arthur Sellers, was a committee man and Herbert, Wilfred and I were all convinced that he had used his powerful influence to get Brian the job. I tackled Brian about this many years later and he told me, 'I'll tell you exactly what happened. My father came to see me one day and he said, "The committee have voted to make you captain next season. I told them not to do it. I said you'd be no damn good and when they went ahead I said it was against my advice." '

When it came to assessing the overall influence of Brian Sellers, Bill Bowes lays particular stress on his shrewdness:

Yes, it's true that, when we were fielding, he never asked anyone to do a job he wouldn't do himself and he fielded as near to the bat as any man in the side. The only thing which some of us slightly criticized him for was his tendency not to use an attacking approach when batting. He was a great striker of the ball but he tended to play a bit canny. If he'd given free expression to the bat, he might have been a real Test prospect. But the great thing about him was that, when he came into the Yorkshire side, he came, as I put it, in 'his stockinged feet'. He took advice. Before making the toss, if he wasn't quite sure what to do, he'd take out Hedley Verity and myself to inspect the pitch and, quite separately, he'd do the same with Herbert Sutcliffe and Percy Holmes. The final decision was his and we never knew whether we'd pushed it on to the batsmen or they'd pushed it on to us. But we knew that our advice had been taken into account and that was a very clever way to establish his authority and to build up the team spirit.

Just as Yorkshire had its personal connection with the Golden Age through Lord Hawke, Lancashire in the person of A. C. MacLaren had its own lordly survivor. Archie MacLaren, although lacking a title, brought to the game an autocratic splendour which led Neville Cardus to refer to his 'imperial pomp'. It was he who continued to dominate Lancashire thinking about the role of the amateur both when he became their county coach and even more dramatically when, in his fiftieth year, he fulfilled his boast that he could raise an all-amateur team under his captaincy which would defeat Warwick Armstrong's all-conquering 1921 side (see Appendix I).

With this background the Lancashire commitment to amateur captaincy was never in doubt, yet the story of Lancashire's consistent challenge for the County Championship could not be readily related to the ability of their leaders. M. N. Kenyon, who led the side until 1922, was an Etonian cricketer who batted at number nine and had a first-class career average of under fifteen. The appointment of his successor, John Sharp, suggested some desperation on the part of the Lancashire committee, for he was a former professional and although a fine middle-order batsman, good enough to score a Test century, he was forty-five when he was entrusted with the captaincy.

Yet in the seven years of the Kenyon and Sharp leadership, Lancashire were never lower than fifth in the county table, and soon after the all-round sportsman Major Leonard Green (who also represented Lancashire at rugby and hockey) made his début for the county at the age of twenty-eight in 1922, he led them to three successive years as Champion County from 1926 to 1928.

It is revealing that even those Lancastrians with the longest memories going back to cricket before the First World War tend to think only of A. C. MacLaren in terms of great captains of the county (and he last played for Lancashire in 1914). The one name which comes up regularly does so in other contexts, and that is the name of Peter Eckersley.

He was only twenty-four when he was appointed captain in 1929 and, as the period prose of *Wisden* recalls, 'This difficult position, with little amateur companionship, he held with honour for six years.' During this period, Lancashire twice more won the Championship and there is no doubt that Eckersley with his restless nature and enthusiastic fielding played his part. His image was that of the dashing cricketer-airman as he flew a plane to matches. He had given up a promising political career to take charge of the team, and he became Member of Parliament for Manchester Exchange in 1935 when he gave up first-class cricket. Thereafter his hospitality at the House of Commons for visiting Lancashire teams playing at Lord's or the Oval was legendary.

Cyril Washbrook, who came into the side half-way through the Eckersley captaincy, puts his finger precisely on his importance to the team:

> He was not a great player and that is putting it mildly. But he had the good sense to listen to his senior professionals, Ernest Tyldesley and George Duckworth. Ernest was enormously experienced, a wonderful judge of the game, and would give just the kind of quiet help that any captain hopes to get from his senior professional. George Duckworth as next in line was never slow to make himself heard – not just with appeals from behind the wicket that echoed round the world but also in aggressive counsel to his captain. But where Peter Eckersley scored most of all was in the fact that he was the kind of amateur who carried a lot of

clout with the committee. So he could and did go to bat for the boys. That was the big thing which set him apart from later professional captains – including myself – and that is one of the reasons why, like so many old pros, I greatly miss not just the spirit of adventure the amateur brought to the game but, frankly, his ability to deliver the goods for the rest of the side. If he thought he had to get an agreement from the committee whether in money or playing conditions or whatever, he felt strongly enough to tell them what they could do with themselves if they didn't support him.

Although Cyril Washbrook speaks strongly about the role of the amateur cricketer of his day (and his desire to see some of the same independence in modern cricket leaders), he is not slow to praise the outstanding professionalism he found when he first joined the Lancashire team:

I have mentioned Ernest Tyldesley. He was one of those batsmen who seem to get better and better in their maturity. And he was carrying on a great family tradition. His older brother J. T. Tyldesley was another fine strokemaker who had played for Lancashire until he was fifty and then became the county coach. He played a big part in bringing on the newer generation like Eddie Paynter and myself. In my own case, I succeeded openers like Makepeace, Hallows and Watson, who were sometimes known as the 'hair-shirt brigade' for their stubborn batting while I liked to get on with it.

Later on, when Charlie Hallows took over as county coach, I had a good opportunity to see how he could help even an established player. I had been given my County cap in 1935 but two years later I had a bad run early in the season for Lancashire and I was dropped. Charlie Hallows was always very tough on you when you were going well but if you were facing any kind of difficulty he would go to enormous trouble to help. In my case this meant that I would be playing for the club and ground on most days and for the second eleven, and Charlie Hallows would be down at the nets bowling to me for hour after hour. The result was that I regained my confidence and form and I played in my first Test match for England against New Zealand before the season was over.

Bill Bowes has his own perspective on both the batting and bowling resources of his Red Rose opponents. When he first came into the game, Cecil Parkin had left Lancashire. ('He was too forthright for his own good,' says his son Reg Parkin who followed him into the county team.) But Bill Bowes is keenly aware of the great bowling heritage which Cecil Parkin left with his county, together with what he describes as that other great import, the Australian Ted McDonald:

> Cecil came from Durham and actually played once for Yorkshire until it was discovered he was born literally a few yards the wrong side of the county boundary, and Ted McDonald was one of the greatest fast bowlers of his time. These two had a great deal to do with Lancashire's Championship-winning sequence in the twenties. And then there was the other Tyldesley. Just as Ernest Tyldesley was the backbone of Lancashire batting for so many years, so Richard Tyldesley (from a different family of four brothers who all played for the county) was their mainstay in the slow-bowling department. They were all fighters and we knew we had something on our hands in the Roses matches. Mind you, we always expected to win because we built up a lot of confidence. But we had some rare old tussles.

Cyril Washbrook's abiding recollection of playing cricket for Lancashire before the Second World War is also of the classic battles in the Wars of the Roses:

> I greatly admired Yorkshire in the thirties. They were not only immensely professional in their approach to the game but they showed enormous pride in their county and they had a dynamic leader in Brian Sellers. We played very hard on the field but we had great friends off it. The relationship between the counties at a personal level was brought home to me very early in my career. I was actually left out of the Lancashire side in my first season when we played Yorkshire because it was thought that I might

not be ready for the pressures. In those days you had a crowd of 20,000 in the ground on every day and people would be queuing up from nine in the morning to get inside. Well, you can imagine that I was very depressed and I sat on the Players' balcony as twelfth man feeling very sorry for myself. An elderly gentleman came up to me and said, 'You won't know me but my name is George Herbert Hirst.' Well, of course I knew that he was just about the greatest all-rounder that Yorkshire had ever produced and he went on, 'I hear you are on the verge of a very promising career. I hope you will not mind if I give you a word of advice. It is simply this. However well you are doing – never be satisfied.' I have often thought of those words. Indeed I have never forgotten them and it sums up for me what the true spirit of cricket between Yorkshire and Lancashire was all about.

For Bill Bowes, matches against Nottinghamshire were just as keenly contested as those against Lancashire, with one major difference:

You have to remember that, when I made my début for York-shire in the late twenties, Nottinghamshire in Larwood and Voce had the best-established new-ball attack in the country. In addition, they had probably the best coach in the country in the Yorkshireman Jim Iremonger and a really tough, long-established leader in Arthur Carr. Last, but by no means least, they had the commitment of as many as half a dozen miners who much preferred the chance to play cricket above ground to the poor prospects below in the coal industry in the Depression years.

Arthur Carr in his autobiography confirmed the Bowes analysis in summing up his time as Nottinghamshire captain from 1919 to 1934. He described how, when he first assumed the captaincy, he had been told the old Nottinghamshire professionals such as the Gunns and Joe Hardstaff senior would not want an amateur in the side. In the event, as virtually the sole amateur representative, he prided himself on the close relationship which he established with his players and his pleasure in their performance.

In the case of Harold Larwood and Bill Voce, he ascribed their success to both Jim Iremonger's coaching skills and his own ability in handling his two key bowlers. While it was said that Bill Voce was a naturally aggressive bowler who used his left-arm swing into the right-hand batsman's body to cause maximum physical discomfort, Harold Larwood had an easygoing temperament. Arthur Carr would bring out his aggressive instincts by using the tried and tested formula of suggesting that one of the opposing batsmen thought he was no longer as fast as he had been. However, he would recall ruefully that the same good nature did not seem to extend towards himself when he and Harold Larwood were in opposition in matches for the Gentlemen and Players, when it seemed as though his fast bowler was determined to show that he could not be accused of favouritism.

Harold Larwood, now living in retirement in Sydney and relishing the batting skills of his young Australian grandson, recalls today with affection but still with the longstanding respect of the professional of his day 'Mester Carr's' influence on him:

He was particularly helpful to me when I first started with Nottinghamshire. 'Now come on, young 'un – you do your best,' he would say. He'd give me five overs and then say, 'Do you want another?' He nursed me. He maintained the same approach even when I was at my best because both he and Mr Jardine would always like to bring me back for a burst before lunch.

Mind you, we needed nursing in some of those games. I remember on one occasion when we had a beautiful batting wicket at Trent Bridge and we occupied the crease for the first day and a half and we were kept in the field for the rest of the match. Our next match was at Cardiff and we didn't get to our hotel until two in the morning. When we did we found there'd been a mix-up over our rooms and Bill Voce and I had to sleep in the billiard room. We lost the toss to Glamorgan and fielded all day and the papers said that Larwood and Voce 'were not at their best'. Too bloody right, we weren't!

One of Arthur Carr's other contributions to the effectiveness of his pace attack has been well chronicled. He was not, as he put it, exactly teetotal and he was criticized by his county committee for his enthusiasm in sitting up late at night. But on the matter of drink his views were definite. He believed that, because of the physical effort required, it was essential for fast bowlers to have an ample supply of beer, and it was a familiar sight in the Nottinghamshire dressing-room to see the two opening bowlers sharing a bucket of ale between them.

Despite his easygoing attitude off the field, Arthur Carr was quick to exercise discipline during the course of the match. Joe Hardstaff junior, who made his début for Nottinghamshire in 1930, was soon made aware of the need to follow the old precept of keeping an eye on his captain:

Like Harold Larwood, I came from the mining community in the village of Nuncargate and, in one of my early matches for the county, I spotted a lot of mining friends in the crowd. I thought I had time to have a word with them when I was fielding in the deep while Harold or Bill went back to the start of a relatively long run. What I failed to notice was that my skipper had been trying to catch my attention when adjusting the field. When we came off the field at lunchtime, I apologized to him and said that I had seen a lot of friends in the crowd from Nuncargate. 'Oh, that's all right,' he said. 'You can carry on talking to them for the next three matches because I'm dropping you.'

Joe Hardstaff had the difficult task of following a famous father and today shows great pride in the achievements of both his father and his son. So far as his father was concerned, there was a certain rivalry which was highlighted when Joe Hardstaff senior would say to Joe Hardstaff junior, 'You may have beaten most of my records but I see you still haven't got a century in each innings like I did.' Young Joe comments, 'I knew how he felt and you can make what you like of it but the fact is that I did equal his record but only a few weeks after he died.'

Young Joe's son – another Joe Hardstaff – is a senior serving officer in the Royal Air Force who, by playing first-class cricket for the Free Foresters, has completed what must be a rare family triple. Young Joe Hardstaff, as his father will always be remembered, lives as a widower in a bungalow close to the Trent Bridge ground where he still shows the zest for living and the sense of humour which seemed a part of the personality which produced such stylish batting in his great days:

My father really didn't want me to go on the groundstaff at Notts. He felt they'd given him a rough deal over his retirement. So, although he took Harold Larwood to the nets at Trent Bridge, he tried to put me off. But he was wasting his time. When Jim Iremonger saw me and sent me over to the county secretary, I was a pushover. The secretary said, 'We have decided to offer you an engagement with the county', and I just said, 'Yes, Sir.' He asked me, 'Don't you want to know what you're going to be paid?' What he didn't realize was that I would have virtually done the job for next to nothing.

Mind you, seventy-five shillings a week, which was what I received, was more than many men were earning as miners on the coal face. But what I didn't realize was that going on the groundstaff meant being available to bowl at members of the club from seven in the morning till nine in the evening. I also didn't realize what a squire and peasant relationship existed between young professional cricketers and committee members in those days.

There was no problem with Arthur Carr. He was a team man. His father owned the famous racehorse 'Golden Miller' so he had a bob or two and he was a generous man. Every Saturday night, home or away, we'd meet for drinks at his expense. You didn't have to be a boozer – you could have a lemonade if you wanted. Once we'd got our drinks, Arthur Carr would say, 'Now, the gloves are off. You can say what you like. Let's hear what's on your mind.' And he would listen to any serious suggestions and deal with any grievances.

Of the matches in which he played for Nottinghamshire between the wars, Joe Hardstaff singles out three:

First, I shall never forget the match against Cambridge in 1930. It was my first full season for the county and I even remember the legside tickle with which I got my fifty. Arthur Carr gave me my County cap at the end of the match and I always say I got my colours at Cambridge.

The second match sticks in my mind only because it was part of the business of distinguishing between amateurs and professionals when it came to our travel arrangements. We were at Lord's and I got a hundred in the first innings and seventy-odd in the second. We travelled back to Nottingham by train that evening. There was plenty of room in the first class but the third class was packed out and I stood all the way. Next day, I got nought in the first innings and improved it to one in the second knock.

My third recollection is the match which decided the County Championship in 1937. Middlesex had to beat us to take the title. They got 600-odd and we were bowled out for about 270. We lost an early wicket when we followed on and, when I came in to bat, Walter Robins came out towards me and said, 'How does it feel to bat against the new Champions?' Now he was always a bit cocky and trying to put one over you and I'd had the odd tiff with him before. Anyway he really got my back up and I said, 'Never in this world.' I got my head down and determined to play a long knock. As the score mounted, Jim Sims and Jim Smith who were particular friends of mine kept saying, 'Come on, give it a go.' And I said, 'What and satisfy that bloody captain of yours – never.' I finished with 245 not out and the match was drawn.

This meant that Yorkshire won the Championship and Brian Sellers sent me a telegram saying, 'Well done South American Joe' (for some reason he always called me that). Walter Robins got to hear of this and said it was a northern conspiracy. So he sent a telegram to Brian Sellers saying that he was the luckiest captain ever and how would he like to have a challenge match with Middlesex. Brian Sellers sent him a telegram back saying, 'Name the place. Name the date and we'll be there.' In the event, Yorkshire made a big score, it rained and Middlesex were shot out twice for low scores. Walter Robins had it in for me for a long time afterwards but there was no question of a northern conspiracy. It was simply that you should never underestimate the stubbornness of those from mining stock.

*

Derbyshire, too, relied for much of its playing strength on the coalfields. But, unlike Nottinghamshire, it had suffered from the indiscipline which came from weak captaincy particularly in the years before the First World War when one professional received a jail sentence for brawling in a public house and another, one of the county's best bowlers, W. Bestwick (of whom we have already heard as the umpire who terminated Denis Compton's first innings for Middlesex), was dismissed by the county for drunkenness.

The problem of effective leadership was no easier in the post-war years when constant changes saw three captains in charge in 1919 and 1920. In the second of these years, the county lost all seventeen matches played. In the year following, G. M. Buckston, at the age of forty, took on the side for a single season and is well regarded for his work in bringing the side together (including the effective use of the rehabilitated and now teetotal Bill Bestwick who, at the age of forty-six, took 147 wickets). The process was continued by his successor, G. R. Jackson, who extended his support for the Bestwick family by including both father and son (William and Robert) as opening bowlers in his side. On one famous occasion, in June 1922, they found themselves bowling at the Warwickshire father and son combination of W. G. and B. W. Quaife in what must surely remain a unique first-class cricketing family occasion.

As for Guy Jackson, his influence is well summed up by the Derbyshire and England leg-spinner Tommy Mitchell, who joined the team in 1929:

> When I came into the side, he had already achieved the record of being Derbyshire's longest-serving captain of this century and he was great fun to play for because he believed in attacking cricket. He looked for results. If he thought we couldn't win, he wasn't worried about losing because he wanted us all to enjoy ourselves. What's more, he was very thoughtful about giving every member of the side the best possible opportunity. If you couldn't really play cricket, somehow he made you play cricket. So far as I was concerned, he soon showed what he thought about me and also some of his suspicions about the North/South divide. We were playing Middlesex at Lord's and by the close of play they had scored over 400 for six wickets and I'd taken all six. I was

down in the old professional dugout at Lord's and Guy Jackson was up in the amateur dressing-room at the top of the pavilion. Anyway, I got a message to go up and see him. 'What'll you have?' he asked me. 'A Pimm's Number One,' I said, knowing that it was a pretty expensive drink (I think about three shillings at that time). Anyway, I knocked it off and he said, 'Will you have another?' So I said, 'Thank you very much, Skipper. What about the others downstairs?' And he replied, 'They haven't earned it like you have.' He went on to tell me that he wasn't going to let me bowl again in that innings if Middlesex carried on batting again the following morning. I said that I might have a chance to get all ten. 'Yes, you might,' he said, 'but you've shown all the top people at Lord's what you can do. A lot of them didn't think you could bowl and I'm not going to let you get hammered tomorrow in a knockabout before a possible declaration.' You see, he thought I was good enough for England and happily I proved him right but I doubt I would have had my chance if it hadn't been for thoughtfulness like that.

Tommy Mitchell, like so many of his county contemporaries, came from the Derbyshire coalfields where he had been discovered by Guy Jackson while playing for a team of unemployed miners during the General Strike of 1926. Living today in the South Yorkshire coalfields, he reveals the same pride and occasional stubbornness that led to a love/hate relationship with his county captain:

When we first met, Guy Jackson offered me a pound a week less than I had been earning as a miner. I told him I wasn't prepared to take a wage cut to play cricket and that's how we started out – speaking frankly on both sides. I suppose the best-known row I had with him came when we were playing a match against Warwickshire. I bowled about forty overs for seventy runs and two wickets and as we were walking off for lunch Guy Jackson said to me, 'You weren't even trying to spin the ball this morning.' I said, 'Well, if I haven't been trying to spin, I'm no good to you, no good to myself and no good to the side. I'm going to pack my bag and I'm going home.' I set off from the ground and the County Secretary, Mr Taylor, caught up with me when I was half-way to the station in Derby. 'Mister Jackson didn't mean what he said,' he told me. 'He must have done or he wouldn't have said it,' I replied. 'Well, you're under contract,' said Mr Taylor. And I just said, 'I never signed over a postage stamp' (which was just bluff on my part as I couldn't really remember what the contract had looked like). Anyway, I came back to carry on playing but, for two weeks, I didn't really try to get a wicket. When we were away at Northampton, Mr Jackson came into our dressing-room and said, 'Good morning everyone' and then, coming over specially to me, said, 'Good morning Tommy.' I just sat tying up my bootlaces. Later, he came back in the dressing-room and said, 'I've lost the toss and we're going to have to work at it today.' Then, turning to me, he said, 'Tommy, I owe you an apology.' I said, 'Aye, I think you do.' Well, we shook hands and he said, 'Well, we're friends again, aren't we?' and I said 'Yes'. We went out into the field and we bowled out Northamptonshire before lunch and I got seven of their wickets. As we were coming off the field, the skipper said to me, 'There are those in this side who I have to kick up the arse but, with you, it's a matter of persuasion.'

At the Derbyshire Cricketers' Reunion in 1986, this story was recalled in the general praise which was accorded to Guy Jackson in building up the playing strength and spirit of the county for which he continued to play until the county's first Championship victory in 1936 under his successor, A. W. Richardson.

One of those attending the reunion was the Yorkshire-born amateur G. R. Langdale, who, after playing a few matches for Derbyshire, went on to an enjoyable career with Somerset and the Minor Counties. He recalled that Guy Jackson's policy in building up the strength of his side was clear and consistent:

In the twenties there had often been room for three or four amateurs, but Guy Jackson took me aside one day and said, 'I'm always willing to include an amateur in the side either if he is a good enough player or if he will help bring in the crowd because of his entertainment value. I'm afraid you don't quite fit into either category, old boy, but you should walk into several of those soft southern counties.'

Guy Jackson's positive approach to cricket made him a great favourite in Festival cricket and nowhere was this more apparent than at Scarborough. As Bill Bowes says:

Everybody wanted to play at Scarborough. The best description that I've ever heard was Jim Kilburn's comment that it was 'first-class cricket on holiday'. When you were given the ball, it was the end of the season and there was nothing desperate at stake. So you bowled as well as you could for five or six overs and then you could ease off from your top pace. Similarly, the batsman could get say twenty runs however he liked – no matter how slowly. But if they got to fifty they were expected to play every shot in the book and if they got to a hundred they would be barracked if they didn't hit every ball to the boundary.

There were occasional exceptions. In 1931, when Bill Bowes made his début for the Players, the match at Scarborough (see Appendix I) was dominated by a double-century opening stand from Hobbs and Sutcliffe which, after the first day had been washed out, meant that the Gentlemen had little hope of doing more than saving the match. Their captain, R. E. S. Wyatt, played a long defensive innings when his side was reduced to 35 for five. This was not simply a matter of upholding the Gentlemen's pride; the organizers of the Festival matches were always anxious to ensure that the maximum period of play was possible in the interests of gate money. It was around this period that Bob Wyatt acquired the reputation which he retains at Scarborough to this day as 'Third-day Wyatt'.

However, Bill Bowes recalls that there were occasions when he was thought to have carried his doggedness to excess:

Bob was playing for MCC against Yorkshire at Scarborough and he batted for an hour and a half before lunch and only scored twenty runs or so. During the interval Brian Sellers said to him,

'Bob, this is a Festival match. There are spectators out there from Birmingham as well as from Yorkshire.' Bob Wyatt replied, 'You look after your job and I'll look after mine.' So Brian said, 'We'll give you an over or two after lunch to settle in but if you don't get on with it, we shall do you.' 'What do you mean?' asked Bob. 'I'm just telling you, we shall do you,' said Brian. Sure enough, after lunch Bob went on playing his dogged stuff. Brian said to the team, 'Right. Next time he plays and misses, everyone but everyone appeals.' Sure enough, an over or two later, he played forward to Frank Smailes and the ball beat the bat by a whisker. We let out a shout you could have heard in Whitby. And the umpire gave him out. Well, he stormed off – he was livid. He came into our dressing-room at the tea interval. He was still furious and he said, 'You're a lot of bloody cheats', and Brian just said, 'Now then Bob, if you're going to talk like that, we shall do you again in the second innings.'

A year or two later, another amateur, T. C. Longfield, found himself on the receiving end of Brian Sellers's sense of humour. The late Tom Longfield (whose daughter Susan maintains the continuing family interest in cricket as Mrs Edward Dexter) was one of the recent or current Oxbridge undergraduates who were normally a standard part of the Scarborough invitation list. After playing for Cambridge and Kent, he spent most of his working life in India (where he led Bengal to their first-ever victory in the Ranji Trophy in 1939). Recalling his first outing at Scarborough, many years later, he illustrated the importance of a strong constitution both on and off the field:

I think Brian Sellers reckoned that I was a bit green. In the thirties, you were expected to keep up with everyone in the drinking stakes and the late-night activities and that was a bit of a challenge because some of them in the Gentlemen's accommodation at the Grand Hotel like Arthur Carr were real experts. Anyway, I found myself, at the end of the evening, with Brian Sellers, and I sensed that it was going to be a bit of a problem to find my room. 'Don't worry,' said Brian. 'I'll get you there.' So we made our unsteady way towards what I thought was my bedroom. Brian opened the door and pushed me inside, laughing like a drain. And lo and behold, who do I see in the room but Mrs Sellers who is in bed and not much amused at being woken up. My reactions might have been a bit slower than usual but at least I had the presence of mind to turn round and lock the door and shout, 'Thanks very much, Brian. See you in the morning.' At this point, he began hammering furiously on the door. Anyway, I think I could claim a moral victory and we certainly became great friends.

As we have seen, Tom Longfield readily accepted Arthur Carr's dedicated late-night activities. The Kent wicket-keeper, 'Hopper' Levett, recalls how these led to another cricketing challenge for the Nottinghamshire captain 'the morning after':

Arthur came in to bat low down in the order and it was obvious that he'd been hoping to have time to recover from his night out. One of the features of the Scarborough Festival has always been the brass band and, sure enough, it was playing full blast when Arthur came in. Well, you could see that the noise was like red hot needles going through his head and he said to me, 'I'm going to have to do something about those so-and-so's.' He proceeded to hit not one but two sixes in amongst them and they retreated in some confusion.

Although there was generally a lighthearted atmosphere in the matches at Scarborough, they played their part in cricketing history, including the Gentlemen v. Players series. In the Scarborough game in 1925 (see Appendix I), Arthur Carr hit two of the biggest sixes seen on the ground in his only century for the Gentlemen. His effort was, however, overshadowed by that of Jack Hobbs who, in the golden year in which he surpassed 'W.G.'s' record of 126 hundreds, made the highest score ever recorded in a Gentlemen v. Players match in his innings of 226 not out.

Another feature of the Scarborough game was the opportunity provided at the end of the season for farewell appearances by some of the giants of the game. This had special poignancy when the cricketer concerned had given long service to Yorkshire and England. In 1927 (see Appendix I) Wilfred Rhodes led the Players to a comfortable victory in his last appearance in the series. He had first turned out for them in 1898, but he still showed his all-round abilities in remaining undefeated as a batsman and bowling twenty overs for nineteen runs against the Gentlemen's stroke-makers.

In the 1921 match (see Appendix I) George Hirst made his farewell to first-class cricket in typical fashion by capturing the last two wickets in the match for ten runs. He did so on his fiftieth birthday and, in response to calls from the crowd, he appeared on the balcony to make a farewell speech which typified the modesty of the man and the best of the northern professional:

'Ladies and gentlemen, I'd like to call you the cricketing public. I thank you for your kindness to me. A person always knows his limitations and I am not such a good man as you make me out to be. If I've had any broad views on what they call the game of life, I've learned them on the cricket field. I've loved many games but I've been a bit more efficient at cricket. From an unselfish point of view, it's the best game. What can you have better than a nice green field, with the wickets set up, and to go out and do the best for your side? I leave first-class cricket to those who have yet to come. I hope they'll have the pleasure in it that I have had.'

4

THE SOUTHERN TOUR

One of the southern amateurs who appreciated invitations to Scarborough was Gubby Allen. As a Cambridge undergraduate, he had made his début for the Gentlemen there but his business commitments meant that he was rarely able to devote the time to the extended northern tour on the county circuit.

It was also the case that Gubby Allen and many other southern amateurs relished the particular flavour of the game on the southern tour. Its chief characteristic was that, in sharp contrast to the dominant professionalism in the northern counties, the southern counties had a strong amateur flavour. Extending the southern tour to the west country, Gubby Allen picks out Somerset and Sussex as counties where, in the twenties, it was possible to enjoy almost a country-house cricket atmosphere, and he adds to this list Kent, Hampshire and Gloucestershire because of the strong amateur direction of their sides.

In reviewing Gubby Allen's list, it may be helpful to work from west to east: from Somerset to Gloucestershire and through the solid southern counties of Hampshire, Sussex and Kent. Certainly, in terms of first-class amateur cricket, it is illuminating to look at the two sides in the match in which he took part at Weston-super-Mare in July 1922 when Middlesex with six amateurs found themselves opposed by Somerset with nine:

Somerset	Middlesex
Mr P. R. Johnson	Mr H. L. Dales
Mr J. C. W. MacBryan	H. W. Lee
A. Young	J. W. Hearne
Mr S. G. U. Considine	E. Hendren
Mr J. Daniell	Mr F. T. Mann
Mr T. C. Lowry	Mr N. Haig
Mr M. D. Lyon	Mr G. T. S. Stevens
Mr J. C. White	Mr C. H. L. Skeet
Mr W. T. Greswell	H. R. Murrell
E. Robson	Mr G. O. Allen
Mr J. J. Bridges	T. J. Durston

The outcome of this match – a win for the home county by two wickets – as well as their amateur dependence were both typical of Somerset in the twenties when they would frequently lose to the weaker sides yet, as in this case, beat the Champion county. Looking down the Somerset amateur list one is instantly reminded of the characters immortalized through the writings of R. C. Robertson-Glasgow, who made his first appearance for the county in 1920; the elegant Eton and Cambridge Blue Peter Randall Johnson; the spiky Jack MacBryan, who was a good enough batsman to play one Test for England; the England rugby international Stanley Considine; Jack Daniell, another rugby international and a tough captain; Tom Lowry, a New Zealand Test cricketer who was said to have qualified for Somerset due to a convenient misunderstanding about which Wellington he came from; 'Dar' Lyon who, while still a schoolboy at Rugby, agreed that he would go for Cambridge and Somerset while his brother 'Bev' Lyon would concentrate on Oxford and Gloucestershire; 'Farmer' White, whose left-arm slow-bowling skills we have already noted and who would captain both Somerset and England; W. T. Greswell, whose appearances like many other expatriates' were dependent on home leave when business took him to Ceylon where he became the island's leading cricketer; and J. J. Bridges, who had turned amateur after the war when he found a professional cricket career insecure.

There were many other Somerset amateurs in and out of the side in the twenties, especially when some of their team-mates received wider recognition (as, for example, in 1924 when MacBryan, Lyon, White and Robertson-Glasgow all appeared for the Gentlemen – see Appendix I). Among these were the twin Rippon brothers, A.D.E. and A.E.S. whose son, Geoffrey, better known in the political than the cricket world, has recalled how his father, a civil servant, would often play in club matches under an assumed name to avoid problems over 'time off' and, in the course of a long innings, would twist his cap round by degrees so that it entirely completed the full 360°. As for Raymond Robertson-Glasgow, or 'Crusoe', the many accounts of his eccentricities have sometimes obscured the fact that, as a fast-medium bowler, he was not far short of England selection and it is also a sad fact that his entrancing sense of humour hid the deep melancholy which led to his suicide.

'Crusoe' was a great chronicler of his amateur team-mates – as in a classic essay about R. J. O. Meyer, the first headmaster of Millfield School. Meyer, after limited first-class success in the early part of his career, went to work in India and returned to Somerset with a solid new batting defence and almost endless bowling variations of which he said, 'They work but, like the earlier models of the motorcycle, they need a lot of attention.'

'Crusoe' did not confine his enthusiasm to amateurs. In other writings he would recall the sturdy character of the Yorkshire-born all-rounder Ernest Robson who was fifty-two years old when, in a chase against the clock, he hit the winning six for Somerset off the last ball of the match in the county's 1922 victory over Middlesex. He also recorded the gradual shift in the Gentlemen and Players balance in the Somerset side with the replacement of the amateur Rippon brothers by the professional opening partnership of the former Middlesex players, the brothers Frank and Jack Lee; the emergence of bowlers like 'Bertie' Buse and Horace Hazell and the long-serving wicket-keeper Walter Luckes; and the virtues of Arthur Wellard as the schoolboy's dream of a fast bowler and big hitter. He was also one of the first to criticize the selectors' lack of daring in so rarely calling on the adventurous batting of Harold Gimblett for England.

But the Somerset professionals had their own chronicler in the shape of W. H. R. (Bill) Andrews. He paints another side to the glamorous picture of Somerset in showing how his own history with the club reflected its financial problems, which led to the concentration on inexpensive amateur selection and created uncertainty for their professionals. During an economy campaign, he was dropped from the side after three years in 1932. He returned in 1935 and continued as an all-rounder with the club until 1947 when he was again 'released', only to return again as the county coach.

In his autobiography delightfully entitled *The Hand That Bowled Bradman* (for 202!), he makes it plain that, like virtually every professional cricketer of his generation, he deeply regretted the passing of the true amateur from the game. But when it came to the competition for places in the Somerset side in the thirties, he spelt out how unfair the system could be. In the 1932 season when he was under pressure to retain his place, he played in only half the matches and these included the more difficult ones at the Oval and on the northern tour where, he implies, the Somerset amateurs were conspicuous by their absence. By contrast, he refers to the three games that season in the Weston-super-Mare Festival when only four, three and two professionals were included in successive matches when there was clearly no shortage of amateurs looking for a place in the sun.

What no doubt accentuated the bitterness still evident in his account, forty years later, was the effect such limited appearances had on professional cricket earnings. When Bill Andrews first came into the Somerset side, he was paid match fees of ten pounds for home games and twelve pounds for away matches. From this amount he had to pay for accommodation and, to avoid this, in the 1935 season he pitched a tent on the cricket grounds at Clacton and Maidstone. To supplement his early income, Bill Andrews would serve as a ground bowler for Somerset members. He was also required to bowl to the amateurs in the side at the start of a county match and complained that he was often tired by the time he had to bowl in the middle.

Bill Andrews felt that the fate of a young professional cricketer depended largely on his treatment by his captain and criticized 'Farmer' White for lack of encouragement, while praising both Reggie Ingle and 'Bunty' Longrigg, the Bath solicitors who succeeded him. (Ingle gave him a chance to move up the batting order and Longrigg knew exactly when a pint of beer would improve his bowler's morale.) It was also during these years before the Second World War when Somerset improved cricketers' pay by guaranteeing weekly year-round payments for all the professionals in the side (topped up with talent money), thus ending the constant worry of 'No play – no pay'.

Against Bill Andrews's critical but fairly balanced views should be set those of Harold Gimblett. In the tape-recordings he made before committing suicide in 1978, his views about the Somerset committee and its amateur players over the same period come across as paranoid and were perhaps part of the reason why David Foot's brilliant biography of this great cricketer is sub-titled 'Troubled Genius'. In his milder moments, the great Somerset opening batsman would refer to the amateur dressing-room as 'a rum lot', while Bill Andrews said the team as a whole had everything from 'DTs to round the bend'. But if Harold Gimblett suffered from cautious Test selectors, he could hardly complain about his success story with Somerset. The day of his historic début as the last-minute substitute who was to win the Lawrence Trophy for the fastest century of the season in 1935 began with the greeting in the professional dressing-room of: 'That's where you change. And speak when you're spoken to', and ended with press adulation, the immediate offer of a bat manufacturer's contract and a £300-a-year offer for an engagement with Somerset for the following season.

Yet for all his success, Harold Gimblett's story is a classic case of the insecurity which can affect the professional cricketer – particularly his less successful colleagues – in a side dominated by amateurs. For Gloucestershire in the early twenties, the widespread use of amateurs, as in the Grace era, was the policy followed by the county committee in the interests of economy. The captaincy also reflected the apparent need to find those who could afford the job. Of the county's first four post-war captains, the youngest was thirty-eight and none held the job for more than three years.

Stability and dash came with the advent of Bev Lyon. Coming from a wealthy family and into first-class cricket by way of Rugby and Oxford, he was only twenty-seven when he took over the captaincy in 1929. He brought to the job flair, imagination and a willingness to take risks, which is the reason why, today, the Gloucestershire and England opening batsman C. J. (Charlie)

Barnett recalls, 'Cricket under an amateur captain was much more fun.'

Charlie Barnett was well placed to judge. Living in the splendid stone-built house which he has created by converting a farmland barn, surrounded by the upland fields where he and his wife share an interest in horse breeding and in the Beaufort country where they both hunt, he is every inch the Gloucestershire yeoman. His father (C.S.) played for the county as an amateur, as did C.J. before turning professional in 1929. He vividly recollects the interest expressed in him by his first county captains:

> I was very young when I got my first chance to play for Glouces-
> tershire. In fact, when I turned out against Cambridge in 1927, I
> was only sixteen and I hadn't even got a full-size cricket bat. But
> when I started with the county in the following season, Harry
> Rowlands was our captain and he gave me the chance to play in
> matches early in the season when I was used mainly as a bowler.
> So I found myself bowling at the great Jack Hobbs at the Oval. I
> was convinced that I had him l.b.w. but the umpire was quite
> right. The crowds came to the Oval to see the Master bat and not
> to see me bowl. But Harry Rowlands showed great faith in me
> and I got my County cap after only three matches. When Bev
> Lyon took over, I was established as a batsman but I still liked to
> turn my arm over. I remember in one game I said, 'Can I have a
> bowl?' and he said, 'Certainly, if you can get a wicket each over.'
> Well, as it happened, I got a wicket in each of my first two overs.
> In my third over, I had two catches dropped. Despite this, I was
> taken off and he brought on Tom Goddard. The fact was that
> Tom was one of our greatest bowlers and he frequently had to
> put in a great deal of work on plumb batting wickets. So
> whenever there was a chance for him to pick up a few wickets
> cheaply, Bev Lyon would try to make sure that he got his fair
> share of the spoils.

Another giant in the Gloucestershire team between the wars was Walter Hammond, and Charlie Barnett does not hide the fact that they did not get on. Indeed, he reserves some of his severest strictures for what he saw as an attempt by the great English batsman to take over the captaincy from Bev Lyon:

Wally was a great player but he wasn't loyal to Bev. He copied his style in dress – the Savile Row suit, the trilby and so on – but at one point he tried to get me and the other senior members of the side to gang up for the removal of Bev. Well, we weren't having that and when Wally threatened Bev with his resignation, the Skipper called his bluff by just saying, 'You let me have it in writing and I'll be very glad to pass it on to the committee', and that was the end of that.

Perhaps the most rounded view of the county's cricket is that of Reg Sinfield, who is one of the great survivors from the inter-war years when Gloucestershire progressively built up a side which, by the thirties, was rarely out of the top half-dozen in the Championship. Still active in his eighties as a cricket coach at Colston's School in Bristol, the Gloucestershire and England all-round utility man sums up the strength of his team-mates:

We took our lead from the top and, for most of my time, we had an inspired leader in Bev Lyon. Whatever he did always seemed to come off. And we had such splendid bowling resources in our side and he knew how to handle them. For example, he was one of the few people who could get the best out of Charlie Parker. I am still convinced that Charlie was the best slow left-arm bowler in the country but he could be difficult, and he was very temperamental. He used to play hell with our fielders. I remember once I caught Bob Wyatt in the deep off Charlie. I had to run thirty yards to make the catch and it followed an earlier chance to me out in the deep which I couldn't quite reach. When I caught Bob, all Charlie said to me was, 'You should have caught him first time. Those two runs might cost us the match.'

Then there was Tom Goddard. He was a great workhorse but he liked to have things his own way. He wouldn't bowl into the wind or, if I was getting wickets at my end, he would want us to change over. But, as Charlie Barnett said, Bev Lyon knew how to encourage him by helping him to get his quota of wickets and he was the only man I ever knew who could persuade Charlie Parker to bowl another over after he'd decided he'd had enough, when he would normally simply take his sweater and march off into the field.

The one person whom Bev could not get to bowl was Wally Hammond. If Wally had bowled for us regularly we would have won the Championship. But he would say, 'You know better than that – the one affects the other and I'm here to bat.' The same rules didn't seem to apply to me, and for a large part of my time, I had to open the bowling as well as the batting. Wally would only bowl if something upset him. I remember once, we were playing Essex and when Wally came in to bat he hit the ball a real crack to Laurie Eastman in the covers. J. W. H. T. Douglas appealed and the umpire turned him down as it was a bump ball.

In the tea interval Johnny Douglas came into our dressing-room and said, 'Where's that so-and-so Hammond?' When he saw him, he said: 'You've got a bloody sauce. You know you were out.'

Next day, when we went out on to the field, Wally had a glint in his eye. He went up to Harry Rowlands, who was a Quaker and didn't like to see too much belligerence on the field, and just said, 'Skipper, I think I'll bowl today.' I'd never seen anything like his bowling to Johnny Douglas. Johnny had all the guts in the world as befitted an Olympic boxer but Wally had him backing away from the wicket and he knocked the bat out of his hands. He bowled him out in both innings and I'd have rather batted against Harold Larwood than Wally in that mood.

Reg Sinfield showed his all-round value to his side when, following the retirement of Charlie Parker, he gave up the new ball to bowl off-spin in partnership with Tom Goddard while maintaining his record as a consistent run-getter. Of the other Gloucestershire batsmen, he says:

You have to remember we were so strong that, in his early days, Charlie Barnett used to be batting at number nine. Wally could murder the best attack in the country and it's often forgotten just what a good batsman Bev Lyon was. What fascinated us was to see how he would respond to the challenge when we played Somerset captained by his brother 'Dar' Lyon. They were like cat and mouse with each other. They would always have a hefty side bet on the match and there was no quarter asked or given. I remember one year at Bristol, we lost the toss and Dar Lyon was dropped early on and got a double-century being cursed all the way by Bev. When it came to our turn to bat he said, as I went out to open, 'Reg, I want you to put on your heaviest spikes and bat as long as you like but get some wear and tear into that wicket for Charlie and Tom.' Well, I got my hundred not particularly fast but Bev said, 'That's just what I wanted.' He went in and got a hundred and so did Wally. They'd made 400-odd but we led them by 90 and our spinners bowled them out cheaply and we won by ten wickets. You should have heard Dar Lyon's conversation with Bev afterwards – there was nothing fraternal about it.

While Gloucestershire had mainly the appearance of a peer group, Hampshire, for much of the inter-war years, maintained the 'upstairs–downstairs' atmosphere of one of the very best country houses. This stemmed not only from the county captain from 1919 to 1933, Lionel, Lord Tennyson, but also from the tone set in the Players' dressing-room by such veterans as Kennedy, Newman, Brown and Mead.

Lionel Tennyson has often been described as a latter-day Regency buck. He certainly brought to the game a zest for life, a love of gambling and a genuinely outrageous quality which was summed up in his own view of the family succession from his grandfather the poet to his own time in his autobiography *From Verse to Worse*. Reading between the lines of the book, one can detect in the references to broken furniture, early departures to avoid the host's wrath and other extravagances the *enfant terrible* who never grew up.

For Hampshire, his hospitality was boundless. He would frequently invite one or two of the professionals for drinks and dinner after the match adding, 'Is there anyone else hard up or at a loose end?' When receiving an immediate suggestion for other names he would usually add, 'Oh to hell with it – tell 'em all to come.'

Despite his generosity, he could be a stern taskmaster as well as an inspiring leader. In 1922 two events illustrated both of these attributes. In the match against Nottinghamshire at Trent Bridge, Jack Newman, one of the county's longest-serving professional all-rounders, questioned one of his captaincy decisions and was promptly ordered from the field. In the same season it was said that, as was his usual custom, he made a bet on a Hampshire victory with the opposing captain, The Hon. F. S. G. Calthorpe, in the game against Warwickshire, despite the fact that his team had followed on over 200 runs behind. This led to a conversation in which Tennyson is reputed to have told the Hampshire wicket-keeper Walter Livsey, who was due to bat at number ten and who worked for him as a valet, to prepare his Lordship's bath and then go out and score a century. Livsey, who was a regular tail-ender, obliged by performing both tasks and was the architect of a famous Hampshire victory.

Downstairs in the Hampshire professional dressing-room, the same country-house rules were instilled by the senior pros. John Arlott, the county's greatest scribe, told how, as a very young man and a friend of one of the younger Hampshire players, he was taken into the professional dressing-room where – and he emphasized the words with relish – Jack Newman was carving the joint. The apparent noise of the interloper's arrival caused Newman to stop his conversation with Alec Kennedy, put down his carving knife and deliver a withering stare at the youngsters below the salt, before returning to his carving and saying loftily, 'You was saying, Alec?'

One of Lionel Tennyson's admirers was Freddie Brown who, at the start of his time with Surrey, envied the lifestyle of the Hampshire captain who was then nearing the end of his cricket career:

> Whenever he came off the field, his valet would have already laid out his day clothes. At the end of the day, his evening dress would similarly be ready for him and his bath would have been prepared. He never lifted a finger, but what a breath of fresh air he brought into the game.

Jack Newman and Alec Kennedy, who would bowl in tandem for the county over so many years, typified Hampshire's tradition of long service. So, too, did Phil Mead and George Brown. All four had come into the county side within a few years of each other before the First World War and would play on into the thirties. Two of the amateurs whose playing career with Hampshire cover this period were Ronnie Aird (1920–38) and R. H. (Dicky) Moore (1931–39).

Their collective memories are of the enormous work undertaken by Newman and Kennedy as professional all-rounders, of Phil Mead's reserved character (and his comment when, in the days of talent money, he would reach another fifty with the quietly satisfied observation, 'That's another bag of coal for the winter'), and of George Brown with his seemingly endless versatility as wicket-keeper, bowler, batsman and fielder. They also recalled Brown's role as the tough man of the side, deliberately 'chesting down' short-pitched deliveries with an unprotected body, as well as his reckless streak in commenting on the activities of the cricketing authorities.

One example occurred after George Brown toured South Africa with the MCC in 1922–23. He was asked by one of the team's senior amateurs, Percy Fender, if he would bowl to him. He obliged for over an hour, only to find that Fender was unwilling to return the compliment because he said it was too hot. In a match against Surrey in the following season, George Brown persisted in playing Fender's bowling with a dead bat for over after over. Eventually, Fender called out, 'What the hell are you up to, Brown?', only to receive the reply, 'I haven't forgotten that net which you owe me from South Africa.'

On another occasion, he was batting with Lord Tennyson and their appeal for bad light was refused. Subsequently, when his captain called for a possible run, Brown replied, 'I hear you, my Lord, but I cannot see you.' Sometimes, his Lordship rather than the umpire was on the receiving end. Ronnie Aird has recalled that Tennyson, as he got older, became more ponderous in the field, and George Brown would be heard to say when a lofted hit went in his captain's direction, 'That's it, my Lord. You've got it covered, my Lord. No problem there, my Lord,' and then 'Oh, Lord' when the catch fell to the ground.

Dicky Moore recalled one sad story in relation to the four Hampshire professionals which sums up the uncertainties of even the successful Test and county cricketer. With typical generosity he did not specify which of the four was concerned, but recalled that business failures meant that one of these Hampshire heroes would frequently meet the rest of the team 'on the train' or, in other words, would either use his well-known face or elusive skills in travelling without a ticket.

Sussex, too, was often concerned with financial matters. It had a long tradition of aristocratic patronage represented in the early twenties by the presidencies of Lord Leconfield, the Earl of Chichester and Earl Winterton, who gave direct financial support to the club. In the thirties they were succeeded by His Highness The Jam Sahib of Nawanagar – better known as Ranji, who gave practical expression of his support at a time of financial difficulty by presenting the club with new pavilion furniture. He was followed by the club's greatest patron, Bernard, 16th Duke of Norfolk, who held the club's highest office for over a quarter of a century.

When it came to Sussex cricketers, family links were evident to a degree which no other county could match; among the professionals, the Coxes, Langridges, Parkses and Tates stood out while, in the amateur ranks, the Gilligans set the tone for the side for almost a decade after A. E. R. Gilligan became captain in 1922. Percy Fender, who had played for Sussex before the First World War, assessed him thus:

> Until 1914, Sussex had been dominated by the great Ranji/Fry amateur partnership. After the war Arthur Gilligan was responsible for giving the professionals a new say in things, as did his brother Harold who succeeded him. There is no doubt that Arthur was one of the best-liked county captains on the circuit and he made Sussex into one of the finest fielding sides in the country by personal example. They used to call the Sussex off-side field directed by Gilligan at mid-off the 'ring of iron'. Generally, Sussex were a happy, if unpredictable side. They were usually short of bowling but for one brief period when they found that rare combination of an amateur and professional opening attack; with Arthur Gilligan and Maurice Tate they carried all before them. At that stage, Arthur was genuinely quick and Maurice was the best medium-pacer in the world.

Arthur Gilligan, who would serve Sussex County Cricket Club

as chairman and patron right up to his death in 1976, enjoyed an Indian summer as the county's elder statesman. In his last years he was a regular visitor at the Arundel Castle cricket ground where he would hold court with a host of his admirers and recall some of the highlights of what he said were 'truly, some of the happiest days of my life as Sussex skipper'.

He would, again and again, recall his debt of gratitude to his senior professional George Cox, who was in his forty-ninth year when he took over the side. Cox, known widely as 'The Governor' or 'The Old Warrior', ran the professional dressing-room with strict discipline and would insist on the highest standards of dress and punctuality. It was he, in the often recalled story of a match against Hampshire in 1922, who led over the professionals to their captain and said, 'Skipper, on behalf of the professionals, I should like to congratulate you most sincerely on your first victory.' Arthur Gilligan would later say:

> That action, so spontaneous in its warmth, will never be forgotten by me till my last hours. George set a very high standard for the other professionals, instilling in them the best traditions of an English gentleman.

There are other memories that Arthur Gilligan would recall with an infectious laugh: of the amateur he dropped from the side, saying, 'You may have scored fifty but you gave away thirty in the field'; of Maurice Tate, 'A big build and big heart who would have gone on bowling forever if I'd let him', and his own version of the famous story of one of his first experiences, while still an undergraduate, playing against Yorkshire.

The tale has gone down in Sussex history and has, no doubt, been improved in the re-telling, such as in Freddie Trueman's 1985 version:

> Arthur Gilligan came in to bat at Fenner's. Emmott Robinson was bowling and, as Arthur Gilligan neared the wicket, Emmott saw that he was apparently wearing new pads, he had a new bat, his boots looked brand new and he had just been awarded his Blue. So as Arthur went past him, Emmott said, 'Eh, Sir, you do

smell lovely.' Arthur Gilligan didn't last long before he got out to Emmott Robinson and as he went past him on his way out, he said, 'Well bowled, Robinson', to which came the reply, 'It were wasted on thee.'

Perhaps it was this early example of the supreme professional side's enthusiasm for putting one over on a 'Coloured Cap' that gave Arthur Gilligan such zest for the Gentlemen v. Players matches. Inevitably he would be asked about the game in 1924 (see Appendix I), in which his century made after injury so affected him that he was never the same fast bowler again. Yet it was typical of Arthur Gilligan that he would make runs, as on this occasion, late in the order when the professionals looked on top (his maiden first-class hundred had come when batting at number eleven) and it was equally typical that he should go on bowling until his retirement in defiance of doctor's orders.

One of Arthur Gilligan's few sadnesses was the unhappy ending to Maurice Tate's career with Sussex. Tate was aged forty-two and his wicket-taking had become expensive (although he was still a useful batsman who had scored over a thousand runs in each of eleven seasons) when, in 1937, he was called to the committee room at Hove by the chairman Brigadier-General D'Arcy Brownlow and told that his services would no longer be required. As the Sussex cricket historian John Marshall tells us, he was perhaps foolish in refusing to accept the inevitable and in airing his grievance to the extent of saying that he hoped his sons would never play for Sussex. Yet, although the county could not be accused of failing to give him adequate notice, there is still a sense, after all these years, of criticism of the committee of the day which has not been assuaged by a re-reading of the cold terms of the General's statement justifying the committee's decision:

An exceptionally strong selection committee considered that we shall have no room for Tate next season and their advice has been accepted (not unanimously) by the general committee. At the request of the committee, I, as Chairman, interviewed Tate and told him that we were not going to recommend him for re-engagement and further that unless casualties occurred, his services would not be required for the remaining matches. Our interview was a formal one but friendly. I told Tate that I was letting him know this decision at the earliest possible moment so that he should have ample time to look around. There was no possible misunderstanding and Tate, who left the room in a state of emotion, expressed his thanks to me for this timely information.

Yet if Maurice Tate's career ended on a sour note, he must have felt that he had long since made up for his father's single and unhappy Test appearance in 1902 (when, batting at number eleven, he was bowled with England needing four runs to win the match and the series). He had even exceeded his father's outstanding bowling deeds for Sussex.

For George Cox junior, the problem was how to follow a father who had been a fixture in the county side as an all-rounder for thirty-two years. Young George Cox was, from the first, an attacking batsman who, although a professional, played in what was generally regarded as the amateur vein. In his early years, varied form meant that he was in and out of the side and his confidence was not helped by his father – who had retired three years before his own début in 1931 – who regarded success as the natural expression of a professional cricketer's skill. He was reluctant to express admiration for his son's successful days and highly critical of the failures which came from what he saw as an excess of attacking zeal.

Young George was not alone in suffering from his father's critical approach. George Cox senior became county coach, and John Langridge (who was one of only four men to score more than 30,000 runs in first-class cricket without gaining a Test cap) describes the tough old professional's approach to coaching:

My God, how he worked us in the nets! We would be there hour after hour and you never got the slightest indication of whether or not you were making progress and you certainly got criticized for your mistakes. I simply didn't know where I stood with him until, one day, I happened to overhear him say that he thought I was the best of his young players. But he never ever said anything along those lines to me.

*

With this stern parental background it is to the credit of young George that, despite his great respect for his father, he continued to play the game in his own way, and he may truly be regarded as one of the 'amateur professionals' who gave enormous pleasure by his enthusiasm for attacking cricket. It seemed appropriate, therefore, that he should go on to become a country squire who, with his wife Betty, was a generous host at their country house in Sussex (complete with a cricket ground which was the scene of many summer-holiday schoolboy matches) as well as in their home in the wine-growing region of France.

If young George became a country gentleman, there remained a touch of acid in his comments on Sussex amateur and professional distinctions. One of the greatest cricketing raconteurs, he told stories which no doubt gained from poetic licence; he would assure his listeners that, at one stage, the subtleties of class distinction in the Sussex pavilion were so refined that butter was reserved for amateurs, mixed butter and margarine for the capped professionals, and plain margarine for the rest.

But if George could not resist a dig at the amateurs of his day, he showed his special affection for those who competed with him as fast scorers for Sussex: most notably Hugh Bartlett and S. C. (Billy) Griffith. Both were at Dulwich and Cambridge together and both had established a reputation for their rivalry in fast scoring while playing summer holiday matches on the Sussex coast at the Middleton Sports Club.

Billy Griffith, in pre-war days before he became a Test cricketer and MCC administrator (and later the driving force behind the Arundel Castle Cricket Club), was a typical amateur who recalls the Sussex dressing-room atmosphere with affection and enjoyment:

When I left Cambridge and started teaching I played for Sussex from July to the end of the season. I am often asked whether the regular Sussex 'keeper Tich Cornford objected to giving way to me. The fact is that Tich was my greatest fan. He would come and watch every game in which I played and advise me at the end of the day's play. He would come and help me when I was practising in the nets. As a matter of fact, I believe that the reserve wicket-keeper was just as helpful to him although he only played for Sussex something like nineteen times in twenty years on the staff.

Part of the reason why there was no obvious feeling of resentment was the fact that, in the late thirties, all the main Sussex professionals like Jim Langridge, Ted Bowley and Jim Parks were on an annual salary so there was no financial loss if one of them made room for an amateur. I remember asking Jim Langridge, 'What makes you want to go on playing?' (I suppose to me in those salad days he seemed a rather elderly gentleman, although he played for England and Australia after the war.) He just said, 'How lucky can you get to play for such a delightful county as Sussex by the sea in a game you love and get paid for it?'

Hugh Bartlett and I both came into the Sussex side after we had been up at Cambridge together and we found that there was the same atmosphere of fun and leg-pulling directed at both of us. I only had my Cambridge cap to wear and, as we went out into the field, George Cox and the others would say, 'Stand back there. Capped players first if you please.' He would also make fun about the whole business of getting a County cap, claiming that he had received his own in the gentlemen's lavatory at Loughborough station.

With Hugh Bartlett, he and the boys adopted a rather different approach. Hugh had burst on the cricket scene with a century as a freshman at Cambridge against Yorkshire (which incidentally only produced an offer to play for Surrey's second eleven, which is why he came to Sussex). After that, he got his famous centuries for the Gentlemen and for Sussex against the Australians and, from that point on, the boys would greet him with an exaggerated, 'Good morning, Sir', to which he would reply, 'I'm glad you appreciate who the hired hands are around here.'

He was a very nervous starter and in that match against the Players in 1938 I remember him chain-smoking before he went in to bat. For an over or two he was struggling, then – bang – he hit the ball through the covers for four and he was away. I know he told you he remembered very little of that innings or his hundred before lunch against the Australians – except for his concern when one of his sixes hit a small boy. But, at that time, he was the most exciting left-hand batsman since Frank Woolley. The tragedy was that so many of his best years were lost to the war.

The same might be said of Billy Griffith, who was good enough to emerge, for a brief period after the war, as an England player despite strong competition from Godfrey Evans. Although Evans had played a few matches for Kent in 1939, the man in possession pre-war was Les Ames who had come into the county side in 1926:

You have to remember that when I joined the influence of Lord Harris was total. There was even an instance when one of our professionals actually climbed down a drainpipe to get out of the Players' dressing-room rather than face His Lordship's wrath. So far as I was concerned, it was made pretty clear that, as a young professional, I should only speak when spoken to and for my first three years in the Kent dressing-room that meant hardly anyone.

The only person who was really helpful was Frank Woolley. When I went to report for practice before our first match for the county in 1927, Tich Freeman was just a name to me. Frank Woolley said to me, 'I'm going to bat against Tich in the nets. You can come and keep wicket behind me and I'll tell you what to watch out for.' As Tich bowled to him, he would say, 'This is the leg-break' or 'That's his googly', and so on. He batted for about an hour and it was a tremendous experience for me. This happened during our two weeks' pre-season practice at Tonbridge and was very helpful to me before I kept in our first match at Folkestone.

Les Ames's understudy 'Hopper' Levett, who played for Kent as an amateur, has his own special recollections of the social niceties of the Kent dressing-room:

Kent was and is a very social county. So, when I was first brought into the side, I was quickly made aware that, as a farmer's son, I wasn't regarded in the same light as the Oxbridge Blues. They were all seen as safe to put at the High Sheriff's table whereas, I suppose, they regarded me as a bit rough and ready – amateur though I was. My first captain, Geoffrey Legge, hardly said a word to me and, as for the committee, I knew that several of them would like to get me out of the side and replaced by a certain university Blue whose parents were likely to give them some stylish entertainment. I told some of those same committee people, years later, that it was precisely because I knew that that was how they felt I worked like mad to keep my place in the side whenever Les Ames was away.

Frank Woolley was more circumspect, though sharing the Kent wicket-keeper's view:

For many years, there was a definitely feudal feeling in the team's relationship with the county committee. Things did not change much until Percy Chapman came on the scene and he and later Bryan Valentine brought a breath of fresh air into our stuffy dressing-room. On the playing front, we were always short of bowlers. I had to do more bowling than I would have liked; otherwise, it was nearly all left to Tich Freeman. But we had a great batting linc-up and I enjoyed the competition with the attacking amateur batsmen in the side.

Of these, Percy Chapman had all too brief a period of success. In many ways the perfect example of the amateur, his appearances for Kent were limited by his business commitments and early success in Test matches. He only became a regular member of the side after he had taken over the captaincy in 1931 when alcohol was already affecting his once-great prowess. Yet Frank Woolley recalled:

He certainly was the Golden Boy. He had been an outstanding schoolboy cricketer and a great success at Cambridge. He was part of that apparently never-ending stream of glamorous young men who came in and out of first-class cricket as amateurs. When I first batted in partnership with him he was still a Minor Counties player for Berkshire who would soon be picked out for a short but in many ways brilliant Test career. We were both playing for the Rest of England against Yorkshire, the Champion County in 1924. I thought I could score quickly and I didn't like to be tied down, but when he came out to join me we put on 124 in fifty minutes of which he got 74. I remember we hit Wilfred Rhodes for three sixes in one over of which he got two and I got one.

Les Ames remembers Percy Chapman's contributions for Kent more off the field than on:

It's true that he was past his best when he became our captain. But he liked to keep the game on the move. I remember him sending a message out to Les Todd who'd been batting very slowly against Glamorgan to say that his innings was boring and he'd be dropped for the next two matches if he didn't get a move on. It certainly wasn't true that he left almost everything to Frank Woolley as the senior professional. But what he achieved, most of all, was an improved atmosphere in the dressing-room, particularly between amateurs and professionals. With him, it was all hail fellow, well met!

Les Ames expresses much the same sentiment about Bryan Valentine, who followed Percy Chapman as captain of Kent in 1937. For his part, Valentine – even in the eighties – still exuded a bonhomie and cheerfulness which had characterized his entry into first-class cricket:

I first came into the Kent side in 1927 before I played for Cambridge. I had trouble getting into the University side because there were ten Blues in residence when I went up, and as I played a lot of soccer and golf I had some trouble with the examiners even in those more easygoing days. So I was glad to get the cricketing experience with Kent. Luckily I had been at Frank Woolley's coaching school, and I always enjoyed playing attacking cricket. When I expressed anxieties to Frank about my forthcoming début for the county, he said, 'Oh, don't worry, you'll get a half-volley first ball and you'll just hit it for four.' Well, when we found ourselves in difficulty against Yorkshire – for that was my début game – I wondered about Frank's words. But, blow me down, Abe Waddington was bowling when I went in at something like 70-odd for 5, and whether he was kind to me as a new boy or what I don't know, but sure enough my first ball was a half-volley, and I did hit it for four. I thought to myself, 'There's nothing to this business', and I went on to make 60 or so. At the end of my innings I hit two successive sixes, but, attempting a third off a ball which was too low for the shot, I was caught. Anyway, I thought our captain, John Evans, would be well pleased, but not a bit of it. He said, 'We were in trouble when you went in, and having got a good start you should not have got out.' It was then that I realized that first-class cricket could be a serious business, but I am afraid I couldn't take it all that seriously. I did tend to get out rather more often than I should, going for the big hit. But I tried to make sure that everyone had some fun in the Kent side when I took charge of it, both on and off the field.

Hopper Levett, who played under Bryan Valentine's captaincy both before and after the war, sums up his role and that of other captains as well as the remaining amateurs in the side:

Percy Chapman certainly made us all enjoy our cricket. Despite the drink problem, he was a marvellous man and, for much of his time, a wonderful cricketer. He called me 'Hopper' not because of my antics behind the stumps but because I was a hop farmer. He was quite different in style to Geoffrey Legge, but when I got to know him through Percy I found he was really rather a shy man.

Our later captains like Gerry Chalk, Percy Chapman and Bryan Valentine were all much more affable and particularly good with our professionals.

The fact was that amateurs were expected to conform to a certain social pattern. If we were away in major cities like London or Leeds we would put on a black tie in the evening and always if ladies were present. It was a bit more relaxed if we went to, say, Northampton. But for much of the time, we amateurs would stay in the best hotels or in great country houses and the amateurs in the home team would entertain us and vice versa.

We would always find room in the Kent side for the good amateur who fitted in. This meant that when chaps like Tommy Longfield – who would have played for England if he hadn't gone to work in India – and C. P. Johnstone from Ceylon were home on leave, they'd get several games through us. And we had our share of schoolmasters, most notably 'Father' Marriott. He was a fine spin bowler who could make the ball hang in the air. He added a lot of fun to the proceedings because he was a terrible fielder and if the ball was hit in the air Percy Chapman would shout 'Get out of the way, Father' and name one of us to take the catch.

Above all, to be acceptable as an amateur in my day, you had to cope well with the cricket and the social pressure. It was no good if you couldn't play after a night out because we worked hard and we enjoyed our night life. We had our own Kent Festival at Folkestone and I can remember coming down to play there with Wally Hammond for two years in succession after burning the candle at both ends in the Scarborough Festival. We arrived in the middle of the night and, in both years, we lost the toss and I had to keep wicket all day.

But, so far as I was concerned, I felt that the social distinctions in our side simply reflected the way life was outside. It certainly gave me something to prove when I knew that there were committee men who would like to put their friends' sons in my place. You need to concentrate very hard keeping wicket day in and day out and, given Les Ames's presence in the side, I had to be prepared to go farming one day, play village cricket the next and raise my game for a first-class match afterwards. But the sense of fighting my corner kept me going as well as the great support of our professionals. They were a truly gentlemanly bunch, they knew the score and they reckoned I could keep to Tich Freeman as well as anybody.

And then there was Lord Harris. He was an autocrat but he was also an aristocrat. He was never snobbish and he was fair and, while he was around, there was no chance of a stab in the back. I shall always remember his attendance on Ladies' Day during the Canterbury Week. We would be bidden to lunch with the President and afterwards, when he left the pavilion, with that immaculate figure with the beard under the Panama hat, the crowd – men and women – just fell back deferentially and you had to be proud to be part of that Kent scene.

5

FROM WEST TO EAST

If the extended southern tour described in the last chapter took the reader from west to east, it may be helpful to repeat the process by considering the remaining counties as a midlands group involving Glamorgan, Worcestershire, Warwickshire, Leicestershire, Northamptonshire and Essex.

While there is inevitably a sense of the miscellaneous in looking at these counties, they had a common thread with others on the county list in the diversity of the role which both amateurs and professionals played in the inter-war years. For Glamorgan, the last team to join the Championship in 1921, economic necessity kept the use of professionals to a minimum, and one of the county's most famous captains, Wilf Wooller, is typically blunt in describing the majority of the early teams as 'a wide range of indifferent amateurs'.

An exception was Cyril Walters, who played for the county from 1923 to 1928 before going on to his greatest success for Worcestershire and England:

We were in the bottom three places in the table for half the time I was with the county and it really was very difficult to make progress. Funnily enough we always did well in the August Bank Holiday match against the touring side at Cardiff. I don't know what it was – perhaps an extension of the Welsh fervour for rugby internationals. But we were an unpredictable side largely because of unsettled captaincy. J. C. Clay did a pretty good job when he took over the county in my second season, but it was not

until Maurice Turnbull came onto the scene in the thirties that the
financial situation improved.

The success to which Cyril Walters refers relates to Maurice
Turnbull's untiring efforts in promoting fund-raising activities for
Glamorgan. He would take the team off to local dances and other
social events to build up the morale as well as the funds of the
county club and, little by little, it was possible to provide something like a fair reward for longstanding Glamorgan professionals
like Dai Davies, Emrys Davies and Jack Mercer.

Wilf Wooller who, as well as captaining the side, would become
the county's secretary and historian sums up the role of the captain
and his senior professionals:

> Maurice Turnbull came from a very well-to-do South Wales
> family and he was a bit of a martinet. He would think nothing of
> summoning one of his pros who had incurred his displeasure and
> keeping him waiting outside his room for over an hour. But he
> was a very fine player of fast bowling and the boys respected him
> for that. He was also totally dedicated to guaranteeing the liveli-
> hood of his team and they were devoted to him.
>
> Those long-serving Glamorgan professionals were great
> characters. Emrys Davies came from the tin plate mills of South
> Wales and Dai Davies from a mining village. I remember once,
> when we had to play out time to save a match, Emrys said, 'I will
> not get out until the last miner is above ground.' He was referring
> to a local colliery dispute where some of his family and friends
> were staging a protest by staying down the mine.
>
> Then there was Jack Mercer. He was a very fine medium-pace
> bowler with good control. He would close up one end by bowl-
> ing for hours on end. The trouble was that he rarely had a great
> bowler on at the other end. At the end of the day's play, we
> would coax him to perform his tricks in the dressing-room. He
> was a member of the Magic Circle (as was Bill Bowes) and Jack
> was brilliant. We'd all sit round him in the dressing-room and we
> still couldn't see how he did his tricks.

*

Of Glamorgan's pre-war county games, Wilf Wooller singles out those against Nottinghamshire:

We played some of our indifferent amateurs for economic reasons, and it has to be said that Maurice Turnbull liked to have a few cronies along with him as social companions. But most of them were never available when we went up to Trent Bridge to face Bill Voce and Harold Larwood.

I'll tell you a story which has never been made public about one of our games against Nottinghamshire. Funnily enough, it is the sequel to the story that Harold Larwood told you about his arrival in Cardiff at two in the morning. Our groundsman Trevor Preece knew what was required and the wicket had a low, slow bounce and I dare say Harold and Bill may have been a bit tired after their overnight journey. Anyway, Maurice Turnbull got a double hundred and, as Harold said, 'We kept them in the field all day.'

That evening, the Nottinghamshire players were pretty fed up with the pitch and they stayed a long time having a drink in the pavilion. The shortest way to get to their hotel was by going across the playing area and when they got out in the middle – not to put too fine a point on it – they expressed their feelings by relieving themselves all over Trevor Preece's pitch. When Trevor appeared at seven o'clock the next morning to get everything ready for the second day's play he found yellow patches all over his pitch. He went to see Maurice Turnbull when he arrived on the ground who, in turn, took Arthur Carr out into the middle with him. Maurice said, 'It's your turn to bat and I'm not proposing to take it any further. But we'd better have a word with John Morgan.' John Morgan was the Press Association man who, in those days, covered the general range of county matches. They told him what had happened and that they were not reporting it to Lord's because they wanted to protect their professionals. John respected their confidence. You couldn't do that kind of thing today. It would be all over the popular press.

When Cyril Walters left Glamorgan to go as secretary/amateur cricketer and later captain at Worcestershire, there was an adverse reaction within the professional ranks of his new county. As Cyril Walters explains:

> I had been fortunate, while I was playing for Glamorgan, that my father was a relatively well-to-do doctor. However, our family was very badly hit by the Depression and, unless I had been able to make the kind of arrangement I did with Worcestershire, I would have had to drop out of the first-class game. As it was, I only played until I was thirty when I felt I had to go and earn my living elsewhere.
>
> As a matter of fact, I was not at all unsympathetic to the reaction against my appointment because, when I came into the game, I didn't feel the difference between amateurs and professionals was right. However, I was just a young cricketer at that stage and I didn't think there was much that I could do, particularly when I found myself in economic difficulty.

The complaints to which Cyril Walters refers were largely created by one of Worcestershire's senior professionals – the long-serving opening bowler Fred Root. He particularly objected to the fact that the advertised salary of £1000 a year for the newly appointed secretary was more than three times his own earnings. Root, who had joined the county in 1921, would later write one of the most revealing of cricketing memoirs, *A Cricket Pro's Lot*, but he had no basic objection to the county's amateur connections.

When he first came into the side, Worcestershire were known as the House of Lords. Lords Coventry, Dearhurst, Sandy and Doverdale all served on its committee; Lords Cobham and Summers played for the county side, and Maurice Foster maintained the landed gentry's family tradition as the last in the line of seven brothers whose appearances for the county between 1899 and 1925 had made Worcestershire into 'Fostershire' during the height of its amateur strength.

The county had been so disorganized after the war that its re-entry into the County Championship was postponed until 1920, and thereafter it relied on its aristocratic patrons to bridge the gap in the annual deficit. Lord Doverdale gave even more direct help to up-and-coming members of the team. Soon after Reg Perks joined the county, His Lordship decided that he was too frail to last as a pace bowler. So he sent Reg Perks on an egg and sherry diet and a long holiday stay at Weston-super-Mare while keeping him occupied in the winters felling trees on his estate. The success of this support was evident when Reg Perks went on to play as an opening bowler for the county for over a quarter of a century.

Fred Root was appreciative of this kind of amateur patronage and, in playing terms, bemoaned the passing of the Golden Age amateur such as MacLaren, Spooner, Fry and Ranji. He also felt that their true amateur successors such as Maurice Foster (to whom he added many of the county and Test captains of his time, including Frank Mann, Arthur Carr, Percy Chapman, Bob Wyatt, Gubby Allen, Arthur Gilligan, Douglas Jardine and Percy Fender) were all 'twice blessed'. But, writing in 1937 after his retirement from the first-class game, he was among the first professional cricketers to express his resentment at the social distinctions in the game. He recalled the days when, in addition to separate hotel accommodation, there would be separate dining-rooms at the cricket with food for the professionals which was so bad that it would be left untouched.

In looking at the affairs of Worcestershire, Root was particularly critical in the matter of team development, contract terms and the abuse of 'shamateurism'. In his early days, the county still relied heavily on amateurs for purely economic reasons. There was a saying in the team's dressing-room that the side could well be completed by 'the first amateur to cross the bridge' from the town to the New Road ground (which perhaps explains the début and sole appearance for the county of the Reverend Reginald Heber Moss in 1925 at the age of fifty-seven). Moreover, in tackling its financial problems (aggravated by a position at or near the bottom of the County Championship), there was virtually no attempt to develop home-grown talent. When Root was playing with the county at the height of his powers there was only one Worcestershire-born player as a regular member of the side, which was usually referred to as the League of Nations because it included an Australian, a South African, a Welshman and professionals who had qualified from Surrey, Middlesex, Warwickshire, Kent, Gloucestershire and Derbyshire.

During the Depression, when he was earning £300 a year, it was suggested that the Worcestershire professionals should agree to a ten per cent reduction in line with similar proposals in other counties. As Root argued, this was in relation to a contract for twenty weeks' cricket a year against which he had to pay his hotel bills and for taxis, laundry and cricket equipment. In the matter of benefits, he obtained a £500 guarantee from Worcestershire only by threatening to leave for a job in League cricket which would offer the same amount annually, and he related this offer to the largest pre-war benefits of £4000 for Roy Kilner of Yorkshire and £2000 for Harold Larwood of Nottinghamshire.

At the bottom end of the benefit list there were many who refused offers of a second match since arrangements for such games required the beneficiary to bear all expenses with limited choice of the fixture concerned. This meant that, in the event of bad weather and a poor gate, the professional concerned might actually lose money on his benefit.

When it came to termination of contract, Fred Root argued that the system caused real hardship to many former leading players since, in the days when one-year contracts were the norm, no effective notice was given. The announcement was often made in the middle of winter when it would be too late to sign for a League club and the qualification rules prevented any opportunity of playing for another county in the following season. Richard Tyldesley of Lancashire and Tich Freeman of Kent were often cited as prime examples of those who suffered under this system, and Fred Root in another imaginative proposal put forward a scheme for transfer fees to enable both club and player to benefit from inevitable change as a cricketer neared the end of his first-class career.

It was on the matter of 'shamateurism' that Root reserved his most bitter comment. He implied that those playing as amateurs in the late thirties were effectively using the game to earn their outside living. He went on to suggest that many professionals would play as amateurs if they had their time over again and would expect to make more money.

Yet Cyril Walters, who was one of the main objects of Root's criticism, is not totally unresponsive to the views he put forward:

There is no doubt that Fred was right about some of the feudal aspects of the game. Of course you've got to remember that when he wrote his book – and Bill Andrews for that matter – they had both left their counties and there was always a feeling of grievance on the part of a chap who still thought he might have soldiered on and who didn't feel satisfied with his benefit arrangements and so on.

Certainly in those days real hardship was a possibility under the contract arrangements that Fred Root described and there was always the danger of ending a career early because of injury. I did what I could at Worcestershire, but it was very difficult for a county that was hard up and which had limited success in the Championship.

Gradually, a more solid professional basis gave Worcestershire some continuity and, in the last years before the war, the leadership of the side was in the hands of that popular figure the Hon. C. J. Lyttelton.

Charles Lyttelton (later Lord Cobham) was a prime example of the late developer. He had been unable to gain a place in the eleven while at Eton but benefited from the freemasonry of cricket when he went to South Africa in 1927. He would later describe how he spent two months with the great South African Test batsman Herbie Taylor, standing behind him in the nets so that, as he said, 'Anyone who could not play after that had to be daft or blind.'

As to his subsequent performances, Charles Lyttelton was always modest but, like the best amateurs, he took special pride in his best efforts against Yorkshire – in his case, an innings of 48 against them in 1937 made in twenty minutes with four sixes and six fours. Of his bowling, Charles Lyttelton said that he was willing to turn his arm over against anyone except Frank Woolley – 'That had to be a matter for Reg Perks.' As to his overall role in batting, he was 'willing to go in anywhere in the order except at number eleven – which was reserved for Percy Jackson, as of right'.

Charles Lyttelton was one of a number of amateurs who gave great service to Worcestershire in the thirties, and one of the post-war Worcestershire professional captains, Don Kenyon, puts Root's criticisms in perspective when he recalls:

Charles Lyttelton was certainly a colourful character who helped
pull in the crowd, whether it was to see his big hitting or to
follow his preoccupation with cricket theory which kept his own
team as well as their supporters guessing. I was just a teenager in
those last days before the war, but I later came to realize how men
like Charles Lyttelton and his amateur predecessors had kept the
club going through the Depression years. There were people like
Major Jewell who captained the side and became a long-serving
president who was a great financial benefactor in improving the
ground at Worcester and who, while he was still in charge of the
side, would take a group of his friends around the county with his
concert party to raise funds. Without people like that, I believe
that the county could well have folded up in the pre-war years.

Warwickshire's leadership between the wars was dominated by
two sharply contrasting captains. The Hon. F. S. G. Calthorpe,
who was in charge for the whole of the twenties, came to the game
via Repton and Cambridge as one of the laughing cavaliers of
cricket. R. E. S. Wyatt was a grammar-school boy, apprenticed in
the motor industry, who by sheer dedication made himself into one
of the most dependable players and shrewdest judges in the game,
so that he must be considered among the very best of the 'professional amateurs'. In looking back at his long career with Warwickshire, Bob Wyatt, now well into his eighties and jokingly referring
to the friends who send him bulldog postcards because of his
increasing resemblance to that fighting animal, feels that his reputation and the dedication which it implied were by no means to the
taste of his county committee:

I suppose it was inevitable that some kind of Cavalier and
Roundhead comparison should be made between Freddy Calthorpe and myself. But, from the first, I had difficulties with the
county secretary. And I faced constant interference in the matter
of team selection. I don't know why but the county coach Syd
Santall had some hold over the secretary and insisted that we kept
picking his son, who played as an amateur. While he was a gifted
cricketer, he was also a bit of a tearaway and whenever I tried to
discipline him I could not count on support from the committee.

Then there were the special problems in dealing with a couple of old soldiers in the persons of Tiger Smith and Canon J. H. Parsons, both of whom had made their début for Warwickshire before the First World War and went on playing into the thirties. Tiger Smith was a rough diamond and needed careful handling while Jack Parsons was always very conscious of his status. He had played for the county both as a professional and an amateur before finally settling on amateur status when he was ordained. I remember once that he complained I had criticized him in front of other members of the team (which wasn't really true) and after he'd gone off in a sulk and rested for a couple of matches I had to send him a telegram saying we couldn't do without him, where-upon he was delighted to return to the side.

While Bob Wyatt was appreciative of the long service of both Smith and Parsons, he reserves his greatest admiration for the contribution made by W. G. Quaife. Willy Quaife was forty-nine when Wyatt made his début for the county, and he saw the old Warwickshire and England batsman (who would continue with the county for another five years) as his mentor. He was also friendly with Willy Quaife's son 'young Billy' who played as an amateur (and with whom he played hockey in the winter), and it was not surprising therefore that a close friendship should spring up with the Quaife family. However, this led to yet another clash with the county secretary:

I was called in and told in no uncertain terms that, as an amateur, I should be more aloof from the professionals and that I spent too much of my time with Willy Quaife. Well, I wasn't having that and strong words were said on both sides.

With this background, Bob Wyatt's period as captain of War-wickshire from 1930 to 1937 was never entirely happy. What could not be denied was his value both to the county and in representative cricket as an effective batsman and a useful medium-pace bowler. Despite his reputation for gritty and solid batting, Wyatt was able to adjust his game to the needs of the situation at whatever level. Opening with Cyril Walters in the Gentlemen v. Players match at

Lord's in 1934 (see Appendix I), he scored a not-out century when his side got runs against the clock to achieve a rare victory.

However, Bob Wyatt feels that his success in these representative matches and his long Test career all added to the difficulty he had with his county committee:

> I had the feeling that they were always talking behind my back. On one occasion when I went in to a meeting with the committee the conversation stopped in a way which made it perfectly obvious they had been having a go at me in my absence. I said to them, 'Look here, if there are things you want to criticize me for, please do so to my face. I'm not perfect but I will always have a reason for decisions which I have taken and I will be happy to discuss them with you.' But they never took up the offer and it was no surprise to me when they eased me out in favour of Peter Cranmer.

Leicestershire's amateur instability is evidenced by the fact that they had ten captains in the inter-war years: several of them for a single year – one of them, C. W. C. Packe, playing so infrequently that the captaincy was shared by six amateurs in the same season. E. E. Snow, the county's historian, gave an engaging account of the procession which followed from 1922 to 1938 of G. H. S. Fowke, E. W. Dawson, J. A. F. M. P. de Lisle, A. G. Hazlerigg, W. E. Astill and C. S. Dempster:

> Major Gustavus Fowke was forty-one when he left the Indian Army to take on a six-year spell as a county captain who helped to build up team spirit. By contrast, he was succeeded by Eddie Dawson, who came to the county virtually direct from Eton and Cambridge. He was good enough to gain MCC and England honours and ran the side for most of the next six years. John Adrian Frederick March Phillips de Lisle made a rare regular appearance for us when he captained the side for a single season in his fortieth year in 1930. He was succeeded by A. G. (now Lord) Hazlerigg, who came to us from the same Eton and Cambridge stables as Eddie Dawson. He had to leave the game because of

family commitments (but like so many amateurs of his generation came back to help the county through administration and
as our current President). And then, in the last years before the
war, we were lucky enough to recruit the great New Zealand
Test batsman C. S. Dempster, who gave us some continuity
and class.

The odd man out in E. E. Snow's list, Ewart Astill, has a
particular significance as the first professional regularly to captain a
county side this century. His year of captaincy, 1935, saw Leicestershire sixth in the County Championship – their highest position in
the inter-war years – and it may well be asked why his captaincy
was not retained. E. E. Snow's answer is partly Astill's age, which
was forty-seven when he took over the side, and partly the availability of so good an amateur as C. S. Dempster in the following
season.

Nevertheless, Astill's recognition as captain was an appropriate
reward for one of the great old players who had served county and
country well – a Leicestershire list which would include both
George Geary and Les Berry.

The history of Northamptonshire leadership between the wars
was similar to that of Leicestershire. Nine captains followed each
other in quick succession. In the County Championship, the
general impression of Northamptonshire was as everyone's
chopping-block, and they finished in one of the last two places on
thirteen occasions. Apart from one brief period in the late twenties
and early thirties, when E. W. (Nobby) Clark was good enough to
bowl fast for England, and later when he was followed into the
England team by A. H. Bakewell as a batsman, the team was
heavily dependent on one man: V. W. C. Jupp.

Vallance Jupp played for Sussex as a professional, and Percy
Fender watched his post-war career with a certain wry interest:

He was known as 'Juppy' in his Sussex days and he was a very
fine all-rounder bowling off-spin and always showing tenacity as
a batsman. He was commissioned during the war and his old
professional colleagues did not take it too kindly when he came

back afterwards, turned amateur, and insisted on being referred to as Major Jupp. So it was perhaps as well when he made his move as secretary to Northants and later became their captain.

Vallance Jupp also became a regular choice for the Gentlemen, opening the batting at Lord's in 1920 (see Appendix I) and 1921. As county captain from 1927 to 1931 he had some success in taking the team from last but one in the championship table to thirteenth for two years. But his support was limited. He was constantly required to give a lead by personal performance as batsman or bowler, and he performed the double on ten occasions.

In 1934 he was joined in the Northamptonshire side by another player from outside the county who would become one of the team's stalwarts: the Yorkshire-born opening batsman Dennis Brookes. His association with the club both as a paid employee and, latterly, as President has lasted over half a century. In 1986, looking out over the county ground, this quietly spoken and self-effacing model professional gave an entertaining account of his early days with the county and its difficulties in the years immediately prior to the war:

> I had come down to Northampton in 1932 for a trial match in August when I was still only sixteen and I was out in the second over off a double bouncer. Anyway, the chairman of the cricket committee had been watching me in the nets and he thought he'd seen enough, so he invited me to return in the following April on a month's trial. There wasn't any second-team cricket as such for Northamptonshire at that time and we couldn't afford a coach. There were only about five regular professionals in the side and pay was only about twenty-five shillings a week. I sometimes wonder how on earth I managed to become a first-class cricketer while playing with Northants in those days. It wasn't easy to establish a place in the side. In effect, I had to learn the game the hard way by playing in the tough matches away against sides like Yorkshire while at home the chairman of the cricket committee would put in whichever amateurs might be available. But I have to thank Geoffrey Cuthbertson, who was captain in 1936. Like so many amateur captains at that time he wasn't available for a large

part of the season, but when he came into the side he said he
wanted me in his team and so I became a regular.

Earlier, when I first started, Vallance Jupp was still captain in
the odd match. He had been secretary of the club for a number
of years so that he could get an income to allow him to play as
an amateur without doing any real administrative work. He was
a difficult man and we youngsters used to make fun of him in
private. He wasn't the best-looking chap in the world as he got
older and very thin on top and he was very hairy just about
everywhere else, so we called him 'King Kong'. He was still a
fine performer but it wasn't an easy side to handle. We had a great
fast bowler in Nobby Clark, who might well have played more
often for England. He was a charming man off the field but a
red-headed temperamental performer on it. Mind you, his life
wasn't made any easier by the elderly slip fielders who never held
the chances off his bowling. And he was very unlucky with his
benefit which was rained off. Years later, he came back to watch a
match. The gateman tried to charge admission and he said, 'You
let me in that bloody gate. This club owes me a fortune in lost
benefit money.'

One of the saddest things about that pre-war side was the
terrible run of misfortune we had with motoring accidents.
Vallance Jupp was had up on a drink-driving charge and A. H.
Bakewell was only twenty-seven when he was so badly injured
in a car accident that he never played again. For a time the club
tried to prevent the team travelling by car and laid on a coach or
insisted on train travel.

In playing terms, the years immediately before the war were
terrible. I took part in a match in May 1935 which we won against
Somerset at Taunton when Nobby Clark and Austin Matthews
bowled them out for a low score in the second innings. We didn't
win again for four years until the match against Leicestershire at
Whitsun 1939. We had often been in a position to win matches in
years earlier but bad weather or misfortune seemed to affect us
and we began to think we were fated never to win again. I
remember when I arrived at the ground to play Leicestershire, I
met Frank Prentice, who was one of their middle-order batsmen
and, like me, originally from Yorkshire. Leicestershire had the

advantage of getting support from some of those who were retained by Sir Julian Cahn [the industrialist who ran his own private team] and one of them was the Australian left-arm spinner Jack Walsh. He was a great performer both before and after the war and I suspect that Leicestershire had got a pitch all ready for him. Anyway, when Frank Prentice saw me, he said, 'We've got Jack Walsh in the side today so it'll be a two-day match.' Our side was led by R. P. Nelson. He was a splendid cricketer who had just come down from Cambridge and was beginning to make his mark as a dynamic leader. We also had in our side Bill Merritt, the New Zealand leg-break and googly bowler, and, between the two of them, we managed to polish off Leicestershire in two days. We were all so overcome with our victory that even the teetotallers in the side came out and got drunk with us that night.

The history of Essex captaincy between the wars was typical of the role of amateurs in first-class cricket during this period. J. W. H. T. Douglas, a survivor of the pre-war side, had gained the captaincy in preference to the established Percy Perrin when Essex were in financial difficulty and his father, a wealthy timber merchant, was reputed to have offered assistance – provided his son was made captain. Despite this background, few would quarrel with Johnny Douglas's influence as a stern disciplinarian and leader of men. Cyril Walters recalls:

> He was particularly good in getting runs out of his lower-order batsmen. He used a combination of the carrot and the stick. On the way to the first fifty, he would be all coaxing and encouragement. After fifty, his lower-order batsmen would tend to get excited and want to start hitting out at everything. So he would say, 'Now, you must go on and get your hundred or there will be one hell of a row.'

Johnny Douglas had a long spell as captain in fourteen seasons on either side of the First World War and he was reluctant to retire despite the prodding of the Essex committee. When the committee forced his retirement in 1929 at the age of forty-six, H. M. Morris was officially nominated captain, but he could not always be available and when T. N. Pearce and D. R. Wilcox took over in 1933 it was on the basis that Wilcox, the schoolmaster, would lead the side as an 'August amateur' while Pearce, the businessman, was away. This formula worked well at a time when Essex became major contenders for Championship honours, but in 1939, when Pearce was unavailable, schoolmaster Wilcox shared the captaincy with the Army officer J. W. A. Stephenson and one of Essex's occasional amateurs, F. St. G. Unwin.

Tom Pearce, living in retirement in Worthing, still retains the amiable and light-hearted manner which made him so popular, if sometimes so absent-minded, a leader. He recalls that there were others entrusted with the county captaincy who caused the committee some concern:

When none of the official captains was available, Essex could turn to some of our brilliant 'occasionals' like Hubert or Claude Ashton but, more often than not, they relied on Percy Perrin. Well, Percy was a very solid batsman but he was always a passenger in the field and, as he played for the county in his fifties, he could hardly lead by example in that department.

When I came into the side in 1929, there was always a desperate desire on the part of the county committee to avoid asking Leonard Crawley to captain the team. He was a marvellous batsman – perhaps one of the most naturally gifted I ever saw – and those stories about his sporting versatility were true. He would come into the county side, immediately after playing in the amateur golf championship or vice versa. But as captain he was a terror. In those days, whoever was in charge for any away match had to pay the professionals' hotel bills and other expenses. The secretary would hand over a cheque to cover all this and ask for a refund on our return. With Leonard he always got the same answer: if we'd won – 'Oh, you owe me. I gave a party to celebrate our victory' or, if we'd been unsuccessful, it was still the same thing. He'd say that he'd spent extra money because we'd put up a good show.

When Tom Pearce took over the captaincy of the side, he found

that he also had to take into account Leonard Crawley's fascination
with technique:

> On one occasion we were playing Surrey and Jack Hobbs hit the
> ball for several boundaries through the covers quite close to
> Leonard. Now, he was a splendid cover-point and I went over to
> him at the end of an over and said, 'What's wrong? You made no
> effort to stop those shots', and he just said, 'Well ol' boy, I'm
> sorry but you know I was just fascinated by his footwork. Did
> you ever see anything like it?'

Tom Pearce shared Leonard Crawley's appreciation of the professional skills of 'the Master' but he was not slow to recall the
emergence of his own squad of pros who helped make Essex into a
real Championship contender in the years immediately prior to the
Second World War:

> For years Essex had relied on A. C. (Jack) Russell to give the
> batting solidity and I was delighted when Jack O'Connor became
> such a stalwart in the side. And I was even more delighted when
> we produced all-rounders of the calibre of Morris Nichols,
> Laurie Eastman and Ray Smith and I suppose I should add his
> cousin Peter Smith who was a marvellous leg-spinner and prob-
> ably the best number eleven we ever had.

For Frank Vigar, Peter Smith's success was a mixed blessing:

> I was trying very hard to establish myself in the Essex side in 1938
> but it was very difficult. Tom Pearce was a better player than
> many people realized and did a good job in ensuring that there
> was a happy atmosphere (although it often seemed as though his
> mind was wandering to matters on anything other than cricket).
>   My real problem was the comparison which was made be-
> tween Peter Smith and myself. I was a slower leg-spinner than he
> was and they reckoned he could tie the batsman down more than
> I would. Mind you, I always said that I was never normally given
> a chance to bowl until somebody had got their century and that's
> why my bowling figures weren't too clever. But I wouldn't want

to take anything away from Peter Smith. He was a fine performer and it gave me great pleasure when we had the record tenth-wicket partnership for Essex against Derbyshire in 1947, even though he scored 163 out of the 218 we'd put on together.

On the matter of occasional amateurs, Tom Pearce reflects:

It is not surprising that chaps like Frank Vigar were unable to get all that much bowling because apart from the people we've already mentioned we had, in those last years before the war, a unique trio of Gentlemen fast bowlers in 'Hopper' Read, Jack Stephenson and Kenneth Farnes. Hopper Read could only play occasionally and Jack Stephenson's cricket was more channelled through the Army than county cricket. Hopper was genuinely quick and Jack could be a very tough proposition and, as for Ken Farnes, he is one of the fastest I've ever seen if only you could get him worked up. Well, that certainly happened in the famous Gentlemen v. Players match at Lord's in 1938, but it is not often realized that he, Jack Stephenson and Hopper Read all gave the Players a lot to think about in those last few pre-war years.

An examination of several of the Gentlemen v. Players matches in the thirties bears out Tom Pearce's recollections (see Appendix I). Each of the three principal Essex amateur bowlers had an outstanding performance against the professionals: Read with nine wickets in the match on his début at Folkestone in 1934; Stephenson with nine for 46 on his first appearance in the 1936 Lord's match; and Ken Farnes's memorable eight for 43 in the 1938 Lord's match.

REPRESENTATIVE, TEST
AND TOURING CRICKET

The Gentlemen v. Players matches in the twenties and thirties served not only as Test trials for individuals but, increasingly, as an opportunity to identify a new generation of captains capable of facing the stern challenge of Test cricket.

The loss of a whole generation of leadership has often been described as one of the most far-reaching effects of the First World War. Perhaps no less significant was the questioning of Britain's authority within her Empire. Both aspects of such social and political change had their effect on Test cricket. There was an ever-growing sense of cricketing national pride, and the MCC saw its role as one in which a new generation of amateur leadership should be created which could meet this challenge and still maintain the high standards which set cricket apart.

Harold Larwood, looking back on the Gentlemen v. Players matches from the standpoint of the eighties, is in no doubt as to their significance:

The public used to think that, for a bowler like myself, playing against the Gentlemen would mean picking up easy wickets. By George, it was different! It wasn't even easy pickings at the university level. My brothers used to say that I ought to do well against them – that they were no more than a bunch of glorified schoolboys. But there were some fine mature cricketers in those games. They were brought up on good pitches and they didn't yet know the pressures of failure. Certainly, in the Gentlemen and Players matches, you couldn't relax. They were a better test than the so-called Test trials when one professional was rarely going to go all out to do down another. But I thought that the amateurs who came through that Gentlemen and Players trial into Test cricket had to be good 'uns.

An examination of the Gentlemen and Players representation in Test matches at home and overseas shows how the selectors took every opportunity to blood amateurs at the highest level. The argument was that from the ranks of these leaders of men would come the future Test captains. For Test captaincy between the wars was the Gentlemen's monopoly and, of the forty-seven amateurs who represented England during that time, sixteen captained the side.

The relationship between Gentlemen and Players in Test cricket was thus governed by the tone set by this amateur leadership. J. W. H. T. Douglas had established a good reputation as captain of the successful England touring team in Australia in 1911–12 and in South Africa in 1913–14. However, the task which faced him in captaining the first England teams to play against Australia after the First World War was an unenviable one. Wartime years had taken their toll of the seasoned Test players of the Golden Age, and Douglas was thirty-eight when, in September 1920, he embarked for Australia with two other amateurs (P. G. H. Fender and E. R. Wilson) together with thirteen professionals on the RMS *Osterley*.

Percy Fender recalled some of the circumstances of this, his first tour for England overseas, over sixty years later:

The first thing you have to remember is that, allowing for several weeks' travelling time by ship on the journey out and back, we were away from England for eight months. So it was a big slice out of one's life – sometimes called 'the divorce trip' – as well as an expensive operation. This was the reason why Rockley Wilson and I both took on writing engagements for the newspapers. Rockley was one of those remarkable schoolmasters who showed his quality as a spin bowler when playing for Yorkshire as an August amateur or, as in this case, in making his only Test appearance when he bowled very well for us in the last match of the series. But, like me, he had only limited funds. It was unfortunate therefore when some of our reports for the English papers were used for selective and misleading quotation when cabled back to Australia. This led to some difficulties for us with the authorities at Lord's, which was another of the reasons why I was never given a chance at the England captaincy. However, as amateurs we were wined and dined everywhere we went and made honorary members of all the best places like the Melbourne Club and so on. I must say that I was a bit uneasy about the class distinction which looked after us in this way but excluded great professionals on the tour like Jack Hobbs and Frank Woolley.

As for Douglas's captaincy, Fender felt that he attempted to do too much:

He was a wonderful all-round athlete but it was asking a lot to go in for his 'Johnny Won't Hit Today' dogged rearguard batting efforts as well as opening the bowling and taking on all the cares of captaincy in a losing side. Of course, I felt that he made the task harder for himself because, as was often the case in those days, he did not have an official vice-captain. But the amateurs were listed in order of seniority and, as the senior of the two, it would have been sensible to let me take charge of the side away from the Test matches. But Johnny did not like delegating responsibility. In addition, he didn't believe in slow bowling. This meant that Rockley Wilson and myself were forced to see far too much of Australia when we weren't picked in most of the Tests. But the fact was, we were outgunned by the enormously strong resources Australia had at that time.

One of the additional difficulties which Douglas had to overcome was the traditional problem of the bowler captain in determining how much of the attack he should undertake himself, and he found criticism directed against him both from the professional and from the amateur ranks. This went back to his first Test match as captain of England in Australia in 1911–12 when he insisted on taking the new ball in preference to S. F. Barnes. But in the early post-war

Test matches against Australia, Douglas had little option but to utilize himself as an opening bowler when there were few other effective alternatives to counter the awesome power of Gregory and McDonald.

In the matter of bowling resources generally, his task was not made easier by selectors who, apparently, were unwilling to persist in selecting professional cricketers who showed any signs of temperament. C. W. L. Parker of Gloucestershire was just such a case, and Percy Fender recalls his selection for the 1921 home series against Australia thus:

> At that time he was far and away the best slow left-arm bowler in the game but he was a highly intelligent man who could be difficult with amateurs he did not respect. He was also physically a very strong man and a dangerous man to cross. It was really ridiculous that he only played in one Test match for England when we were short of top-class bowling and I believe that the story of the later fracas he had with Plum Warner when he verbally and physically threatened him may well have been true.

After losing seven Test matches in succession to Australia, it was not surprising when the Hon. Lionel (later Lord) Tennyson was appointed captain. Percy Fender recalled his attributes thus:

> Lionel Tennyson was no great thinker about the game but he was a tough nut who lived life to the full. His great moment came in the Test match in 1921 when he went out to bat one-handed against the Australians and scored 36 and 63. There's no doubt that this gesture of defiance, at a time when Gregory and McDonald were consistently sweeping away English batting, lifted the whole tone of the game. Moreover, it was seen as a classic example of the amateur leading from the front and it's often forgotten that part of the problem which England faced in playing Australia in 1921 was the illness which kept Jack Hobbs out of the Test matches so there was an even closer interest than usual in trying to determine how far the amateur could produce results against the odds. This was all reflected in the build-up to

the match between Archie MacLaren's eleven and the Australians
when Archie vowed that he could raise an all-amateur team
which would end the Australians' undefeated run.

As the scorecard shows (see Appendix I), the defeat of the
Australians by MacLaren's eleven after being outplaycd for much
of the match has its own place in cricket history. One of the
Australian touring party (although resting in that match) was
H. S. T. L. Hendry. Still an upright figure in his late eighties,
holding court at the Sydney Cricket Ground, 'Stork' Hendry vividly recalled not only the match but also his general impression of
the role of English amateur cricketers:

Some of our side tried to imply that we weren't taking the match
too seriously but I can't go along with that. Warwick Armstrong
always demanded and got the best out of us. There's no doubt
that we did perhaps underestimate the opposition when we were
well on top early in the match. Nevertheless, there were some
very fine cricketers in MacLaren's team and he ran his side in the
same old lordly way that we had been used to seeing in Australia
so many years before. Of course, he was in his fifties and well
past Test cricket but I remember that he came to Australia and
New Zealand with his own side in 1922–23 and got a half-century
at Sydney and a double-century in New Zealand. He was a great
tactician and we Australians had a sneaking regard for his autocratic ways. However, the other great cricket brain who really
should have been the amateur leader for England at that time was
Percy Fender. We thought he was brilliant but I gather that he
was never quite accepted by the powers that be.

Percy Fender was invited to tour South Africa in 1922–23 but,
almost certainly for the reasons suggested by Stork Hendry, he
went under the captaincy of F. T. Mann. Frank Mann was another
amateur leader who believed in leading by personal example. For
the 1922–23 tour, he was supported, in addition to Percy Fender, by
four other amateurs (Gilligan, Carr, Stevens and Jupp) and eight
professionals. Hobbs and Sutcliffe among others had declined an
invitation to tour and this strong amateur representation was, on

this occasion, less a case of extending the search for future leaders than a prime example of the selectors' sometimes mistaken assessment of the lesser challenge of playing countries other than Australia. It was also a typical expression of the establishment of the day's enthusiasm for providing amateur 'tone'.

Such social considerations were highlighted by the accompanying party, which included several of the amateurs' wives. This relatively recent innovation created its own special difficulties so that, in the great majority of subsequent tours, the presence of wives was strongly discouraged. The problems arose in part from the effect which team selection had on social relations among the camp followers and, perhaps in a more subtle way, in the establishment of seniority which carried over to players' families. Frank Mann's son George has recalled how his father would often say that one of the most difficult parts of the whole tour was meeting his team-mates at breakfast when he knew that he would receive complaints channelled through them from one or more of the team wives about the seating plan at some official function the previous evening.

Percy Fender also recalled some of the other social problems which could arise within the team itself:

> It wasn't the easiest of tours for George Mann. One of our amateurs – who should have known better – was always trying to get the young professionals to keep up with him in the drinking stakes. He was one of those people who could hold a lot of alcohol without, apparently, affecting his performance, but he did a great deal of harm to at least one young player.

Frank Mann's vice-captain on the tour of South Africa was Arthur Gilligan. His preference over Percy Fender both on that tour and as captain in the home series which followed were further examples of the selectors' consistency in looking elsewhere than in the direction of the Surrey captain. But there could be no doubting Arthur Gilligan's selection on merit as an opening bowler. He and his Sussex Colleague Maurice Tate were at the height of their powers and, in the first Test at Edgbaston in 1924, they bowled out South Africa for 30. Gilligan's dream début as bowler/captain continued, and he had taken sixteen wickets in two Tests when he went to the Oval to play for the Gentlemen at the beginning of July (see Appendix I). On that occasion, it was his late-order batting which enthused the crowd when he made a century batting at number ten after following on. However, during the course of that innings, he received an injury from the fast bowler Harry Howell and his bowling was never the same again.

When he came to captain England in the 1924–25 tour of Australia, Gilligan was handicapped not only by his own loss of form but also by the lack of two professional bowlers, Parkin of Lancashire and Macaulay of Yorkshire, who might have affected the outcome of the series. Parkin had been the main wicket-taker on the 1920–21 tour of Australia and Macaulay had shown good form against South Africa in 1922–23. Both, however, had been critical of Gilligan's captaincy and, in particular, of his bowling. In the case of George Macaulay, it was said that words had been exchanged during the Lord's Test match in 1924 so that, as Lord Hawke said, 'It was nobody's fault but his own that he was not on the boat.' Parkin's criticism of his England captain had been even more public. After the first Test against South Africa when Gilligan had enjoyed such remarkable success with Tate, Parkin wrote a piece in a national newspaper which criticized his captain's handling of the attack in the second innings – despite the fact that England won the game by an innings and 18 runs. After so public a difference, he was dropped from the England side and, soon afterwards, retired to play League cricket.

Whatever criticism might be made of Gilligan's captaincy (and he was the first to compare himself unfavourably with others), he was a universally popular leader both with his 1924–25 touring side and the Australian public. He also set a fine example in the field at mid-off so that, under his captaincy, England was seen as an outstanding fielding side. Moreover, despite losing the series 4–1, there was a feeling that the luck had gone against England so that the series might have been closer, and the lone victory at Melbourne over the old enemy was seen as the turn in the tide of relentless Australian supremacy.

All this gave special significance to the choice of captaincy for the series against Australia in 1926. In his splendid study *The Captains of*

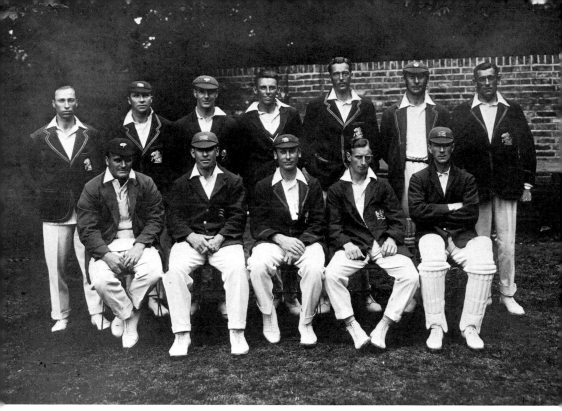

ABOVE: Players XI at Lord's, 1923. Front row, l–r: R. Kilner, E. H. Hendren, J. B. Hobbs (captain), H. Smith and J. W. Hearne. Back row, l–r: A. Sandham (12th man – the nearest he came to representing the Players at Lord's), H. Howell, H. Sutcliffe, M. W. Tate, F. E. Woolley, C. P. Mead and C. H. Parkin.

BELOW: Gentlemen's XI at Scarborough, 1925. L–r: K. S. Duleepsinhji, G. T. S. Stevens, D. R. Jardine, N. E. Haig, Hon. L. H. Tennyson, F. W. Gilligan, Hon. F. S. G. Calthorpe, V. W. C. Jupp, J. W. H. T. Douglas, A. W. Carr and A. E. R. Gilligan.

ABOVE LEFT: Players XI at Scarborough, 1926. L–r: H. A. Peach, H. Strudwick, J. Mercer, J. Newman, G. Geary, G. E. Tyldesley, J. B. Hobbs, C. W. L. Parker, A. Kennedy, A. Sandham and W. W. Whysall.

ABOVE RIGHT: Gentlemen v. Players, the first match at Folkestone, 1925. Back row, l–r: A. Young, Major Edwards (camp-follower), A. C. Gore, M. Kiddey (camp-follower), J. J. Thorley, G. E. Livock and K. S. Duleepsinhji. Middle row, l–r: F. Chester (umpire), G. M. Louden, A. Waddington, W. R. Hammond, T. F. Shepherd, Capt.

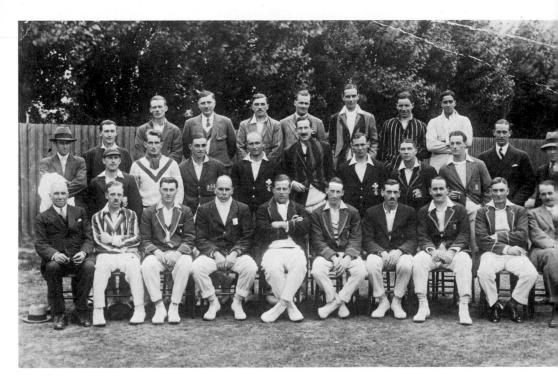

T. O. Jameson, H. A. Peach, H. Howell, L. T. A. Bates, A. H. H. Gilligan (not playing) and A. E. Street (umpire). Front row, l–r: Folkestone official, G. R. Jackson, E. H. Bowley, Rev. F. H. Gillingham, Hon. L. H. Tennyson, Hon. F. S. G. Calthorpe, R. R. Relf, G. W. Stephens, C. W. L. Parker and Folkestone official. Above G. R. Jackson is W. L. Cornford.

BELOW: Players XI at Scarborough, 1927. L–r: M. W. Tate, J. B. Hobbs, H. A. Peach, J. Mercer, G. Duckworth, G. E. Tyldesley, A. Sandham, H. Sutcliffe, P. Holmes, W. Rhodes and G. Geary.

LEFT: Master and valet, captain and wicket-keeper: Lord Tennyson and W. H. Livsey (Hampshire).

BELOW: A Gentlemen's batting line-up in the 1920s. L–r: N. E. Haig, E. W. Dawson, K. S. Duleepsinhji, F. W. Gilligan and V. W. C. Jupp. In front, M. J. Turnbull.

OPPOSITE ABOVE: MCC v. Yorkshire at Scarborough in the early 1930s. The batsman, A. Mitchell of Yorkshire, takes the traditional tea on the field with, among others, to his right, E. W. Dawson and T. J. Durston. F. R. Brown can be glimpsed with hands on knees on the ground while, standing to his right, N. E. Haig has a drink and a cigarette.

OPPOSITE BELOW: The Gentlemen during a stoppage for rain at Scarborough, 1931. Their captain, R. E. S. Wyatt (back to camera), seeks divine guidance while, taking a breather, to his right are: E. W. Dawson, V. W. C. Jupp, umpire D. Denton, R. W. V. Robins, G. T. S. Stevens, H. J. Enthoven and G. D. Kemp-Welch.

GENTLEMEN
v.
PLAYERS

Lord's 1932

This match was seen as a Test trial for the 1932–33 tour of Australia.

TOP LEFT: A famous Indian partnership for the Gentlemen: the Nawab of Pataudi (left) and K. S. Duleepsinhji during their stand of 161.

LEFT: G. O. Allen beats W. R. Hammond with a ball which comes back so far from outside the off-stump that the wicket-keeper W. H. V. Levett has to take the ball down the legside. The other batsman is E. Paynter. K. S. Duleepsinhji is at first slip and M. J. C. Allom is at second. Hammond went on to score 110.

BELOW: Gubby Allen's revenge: Wally Hammond plays on for five in the second innings.

Of those shown on this page, Pataudi, Duleepsinhji, Allen and Hammond were chosen to tour Australia, but ill-health forced K. S. Duleepsinhji to withdraw and to retire from first-class cricket.

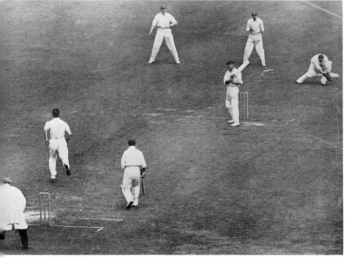

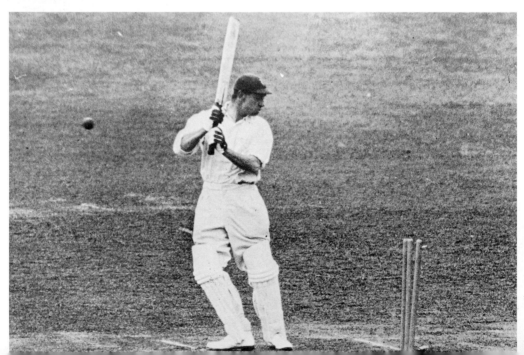

GENTLEMEN
v.
PLAYERS

The Oval and Lord's 1934

RIGHT: 1934. This was the last match in the series to be played at the Oval. A portly Lord Tennyson, nearing the end of his career, skies the ball off the bowling of Wellard and is about to be caught by Alex Kennedy. Typically, he made top score for the Gentlemen in their second innings.

INSET: At Lord's, 1934. A light-hearted and stylish start to a famous partnership: R. E. S. Wyatt and C. F. Walters about to commence their first-wicket stand of 160 in 87 minutes which gave the Gentlemen their first victory in twenty years. Wyatt is wearing Gubby Allen's grey top hat and Walters the black silk hat of A. E. R. Gilligan. Both Allen and Gilligan had been attending the wedding of R. C. Robertson-Glasgow.

BELOW: At the Oval, 1934. J. Arnold of Hampshire, who made top score for the Players of 125 out of their highest-ever score of 651 for 7 declared, is about to be caught off the bowling of A. D. Baxter by P. G. H. Fender. R. S. Machin in the Cambridge Quidnuncs cap is the wicket-keeper and Errol Holmes is at first slip.

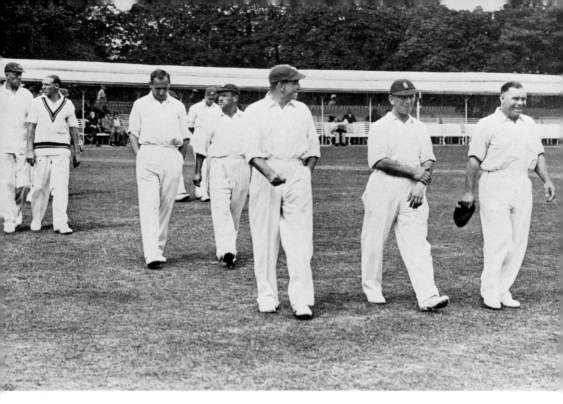

ABOVE: Gentlemen v. Players, Lord's, 1934. The Players take the field led by their captain, Patsy Hendren, and (from the right) Maurice Leyland, Walter Hammond, Jack O'Connor, Arthur Mitchell, Hedley Verity, Morris Nichols and Jim Smith.

BELOW: Gentlemen v. Players, Lord's, 1934. The successful Gentlemen's XI: front row, l–r: B. H. Valentine, C. F. Walters, R. E. S. Wyatt, G. O. Allen and M. J. Turnbull. Back row, l–r: W. H. V. Levett, E. R. T. Holmes, A. Melville, F. R. Brown, J. H. Human and A. D. Baxter.

England, Alan Gibson describes how the field of county captains from whom the choice was likely to be made was, by the standards of the Golden Age, thin. Leaving aside those who had already held the job, the field effectively came down to a choice between Arthur Carr and Percy Fender. Fender recalled the situation thus:

> Arthur was a tough chap and did a fair job. There was one revealing moment during his captaincy which tells you a lot about those days and the character of the people concerned. Arthur Carr was taken ill during the fourth Test at Old Trafford and Jack Hobbs was asked to take over the side. 'But what about Mr Stevens?', he asked, pointing to the only other amateur in the side. Well, Greville Stevens was a fine all-rounder but he was new to the Test scene. So Jack, quite properly, took charge. But how typical of the man and the deferential view towards the amateur of England's greatest batsman! Another interesting thing about Jack Hobbs in that series was that he and Wilfred Rhodes were co-opted as selectors – the first professionals to take on the job. So they were involved in the decision about the captaincy when, with the Ashes depending on it, we came to the final Test at the Oval. There were rumours that Arthur Carr might be replaced and it was said that I was waiting by the telephone. But the plain fact of the matter was that I knew the people at Lord's would never pick me. So it was no surprise to me when the captaincy went to Percy Chapman.

Chapman became first choice for the job over the next five years. It is interesting however that, despite the successful outcome of the 1926 series, the one-year experiment of adding professional cricketers to the panel of England Test selectors ended, except when Hobbs and Rhodes were once more co-opted in 1930. Meanwhile, Percy Chapman fulfilled the selectors' and the public's hopes in a successful series at home against the West Indies and, even more satisfyingly, in retaining the Ashes in Australia in 1928–29.

When he was unavailable for overseas tours, the selectors, who now included Arthur Carr as well as Shrimp Leveson Gower and J. W. H. T. Douglas, reverted to Arthur Gilligan for the MCC 'B' Team tour of India in 1926–27 and brought in Col. R. T. Stanyforth

– an Army wicket-keeper who had never played for a county – to lead the side in the drawn Test series against South Africa in 1927–28. One of those who took part in both tour series was R. E. S. Wyatt. On these, his first overseas tours, he quickly became aware of some changes in attitude on the part of senior professionals once they were on tour:

> In my very first game for MCC overseas, I had a long partnership with Andrew Sandham at Karachi. Quite early in the stand, I called Sandy for an easy single towards the end of the over. He made no response but as I had hit the ball into the deep there was almost time for two runs so I continued on my first run. When I got down to his end, there he was just looking at me with the flicker of a smile as he said, 'If you don't get back quickly you'll be run out.' I still had time to scamper back but at the end of the over I thought I'd better have a consultation. Before I could say anything, Sandy just said to me, 'Look, I spend year after year letting Jack Hobbs monopolize the strike. Now it's my turn!'

After two winters away Bob Wyatt was unavailable to make the 1928–29 tour of Australia, and he recalls that it was only possible for Chapman to make the trip through some private commercial sponsorship. This was borne out when, for business as well as social reasons, he stayed on in Australia for part of the season in 1929. In his absence, the captaincy at home passed to 'Farmer' White of Somerset who was ironically dropped after three Tests in favour of the previously deposed Arthur Carr. For the parallel tours of New Zealand and West Indies in the following winter, the selectors brought in Harold Gilligan and the Hon. F. S. G. Calthorpe.

These choices reflected the pattern of amateur availability. Harold Gilligan took the side to New Zealand when his brother Arthur was unfit, and Freddy Calthorpe, who had substantial private means, had taken the MCC 'B' Team to the West Indies in 1925–26. But despite the increasing challenge from other cricketing countries, success against Australia was still the yardstick by which England's captains were measured, and even the schoolboys' idol, Percy Chapman, had to give way when it seemed that the Ashes might be lost to Australia.

Just as Chapman had been brought in as captain for the last Test in 1926, so in 1930 he was replaced by another leader. With the series at one-all and Donald Bradman increasingly in the ascendant, the teams went to the Oval for the final Test in August 1930. Chapman, like Carr, was unlucky to be superseded, but his successor, R. E. S. Wyatt, was unable to emulate Chapman's example and had the misfortune to lose the match and the series. Despite this setback, Bob Wyatt's gritty performances and shrewd assessment of the game made him an actual or likely choice for captaincy over the next few years.

But first came the Jardine interlude. Plum Warner was back as chairman of the selectors and with P. A. Perrin and T. A. Higson set about the quest for a captain who could regain the Ashes in 1932–33. Douglas Jardine was successfully blooded as leader in the Tests against New Zealand and India in 1931 and 1932, and the subsequent history of his adoption of bodyline to check Don Bradman's run-getting requires no repetition.

What is of more immediate interest in the context of this book is the relationship which Douglas Jardine established with his team and the degree to which he was capable of inspiring loyalty. To Gubby Allen, 'he appeared most aloof with the professionals, and I was the only person he spoke to regularly even though he knew I was opposed to his overall policy'. Harold Larwood, on the other hand, still refers to him as 'Mester' Jardine adding, 'He stuck to me and I stuck to him.' Perhaps Bill Bowes's experience explains why Jardine was capable of inspiring great loyalty as well as criticism from those with whom he toured:

Early in the tour when I was bowling at Vic Richardson I asked Douglas Jardine if I could have an extra fielder on the legside. He refused. I was angry about this because Arthur was a great hooker but, to make my point, I fed him with several deliveries on the legside which he kept hitting to the boundary. At the end of the day's play the skipper said, 'I want a word with you' and I said, 'And I want a word with you.' I told him that I did not understand what he wanted from me and it was going to be well-nigh impossible for me to perform if I could not get the support I thought I needed in the field. I went on to say that it would perhaps be better if I took the boat home if we had such a fundamental difference in view.

I could see that Jardine was sizing me up and I think he realized I wasn't bluffing. Anyway, he then said, 'You can't have just one more fielder on the legside but you can have several.' He then explained to me his ideas about the legside attack and, once we understood each other, I thought he was a fine skipper.

I think perhaps the answer was that he took a lot of getting to know. But, gradually, he won the side over with his courage and determination so that the players used to say that if they had to be part of a team which was fighting for its life they'd always vote to have Douglas Jardine on their side. Hedley Verity, who had only limited Test opportunities on the tour because of the emphasis on fast bowling, nevertheless named his son after Douglas Jardine, and Tommy Mitchell, who'd played in only one Test match in the series, has always been full of praise for him.

What is totally ridiculous is the suggestion in the recent Australian television series on bodyline which suggests that Jardine and Harold Larwood were both filled with hate against Australians. That's absolute rubbish. They were in fact two of the kindest people you could meet.

Gubby Allen also has strong views on the recent Australian fictional account of the tour:

The whole thing was riddled with inaccuracies, particularly in the way it tried to portray those who were for and against the use of bodyline bowling. Plum Warner as the manager was certainly against it but it is absurd to suggest that he took to the bottle over it. Bob Wyatt as vice-captain and I had agreed that we were against this form of attack but we also agreed that we could not say anything which would create a split in the side. Certainly, the suggestion that I publicly refused to field in the leg-trap during a Test match is absurd. The same goes for Pataudi. He has been ill served by some of his friends who try to make out that he was dropped after the second Test match because of his opposition to bodyline, whereas in fact he was having some difficulty with the spinners and Eddie Paynter came in and played very well for us.

The TV series was also adrift in suggesting that there were endless team meetings to discuss the issue. In fact, there was only one team meeting which was relevant and that came quite late in the tour after the third Test at Adelaide. The reason for holding the meeting was nothing whatever to do with bodyline. There had been some story put about that Maurice Tate had thrown an egg at Douglas Jardine and this had been built up by the press into talks about splits within the team. When we had the team meeting, Douglas Jardine obviously was not present and Bob Wyatt was away. So Herbert Sutcliffe conducted the meeting as the senior professional in rather a heavy-handed way. He suggested we should all sign a statement of support for the captain. I said, 'I never sign a document which I haven't read.' He seemed to take offence at that but, eventually, when I read through the document I said, 'There's no mention of the bowling in the statement and so I will sign.' I then left the meeting.

It was after that meeting and the reference to bowling right at the end which set up a kind of conversation between me and other members of the team. For reasons I've given, I had not previously said anything openly although it was well known that I would not bowl bodyline myself. But after that meeting, both Les Ames and Wally Hammond came up to me and said, 'I don't think this is quite right.'

When Douglas Jardine returned to England in 1933, he continued as captain in the first two Test matches against the West Indies. In the game at Old Trafford he scored a century despite the bodyline attack which was particularly directed against him by Martindale and Constantine. He also showed his ability to motivate another occasional England fast bowler, E. W. Clark.

For Nobby Clark, Douglas Jardine was the best captain under whom he had played. Dennis Brookes recalls:

Nobby told me that the secret of Douglas Jardine's success in getting the best out of him was that he knew when to pull his leg and when to crack the whip. He had first played under his captaincy in the series against the West Indies at Old Trafford in 1933 when Jardine made a great century despite being hit by the

West Indian bodyline attack. When England took the field, Jardine almost bowled Nobby into the ground for fifty-five overs which was far more than any of the spinners, Verity, Robins and Langridge. Nobby was a pretty indifferent fielder but he had hardly been seen in that role since he was virtually keeping one end going by bowling through the match. As they came off the field at the end of the West Indies second innings, Jardine said to Nobby, 'I want to congratulate you, Clark, on your improved fielding.'

When Jardine led the MCC to India in 1933–34, Nobby Clark was also in the team and it was here that he saw the other side of Jardine's captaincy. Again, he told his Northamptonshire team-mate Dennis Brookes of this part of Jardine's 'stick and carrot' approach:

Nobby found it pretty hard work on some of the featherbed wickets on which they had to bowl in India. He was always a temperamental performer who quickly got 'sore shins' if things were not going his way. On one occasion, it was clear that he was not over-enthusiastic about continuing to bowl. 'What's the matter, Clark?' asked his captain. 'I've got a sore shin, Skipper,' Nobby replied. Douglas Jardine just said, 'You remember when we were out shooting the other day and we saw a buck wounded? What did it do then?' 'It got up and ran away on three legs, Skipper,' Nobby replied. 'Well,' said Jardine, 'you can bloody well bowl on one leg.'

However, the Jardine approach in handling his bowling did have its critics. Freddie Brown felt that he was an excellent captain of fast bowlers but had limited knowledge and appreciation of the value of spin.

'Hopper' Levett, who was one of the two wicket-keepers in the side which went to India, had further criticisms of the Jardine approach even when it came to fast bowling:

Douglas Jardine had got used to the idea of demanding and receiving support from his fast bowlers in leg theory which depended upon the exceptional accuracy of people like Larwood, Voce and Bowes. When we went to India, he failed to appreciate that a bowler like Morris Nichols was a natural in the sense that he could swing the ball both ways but he could not be sure which way the ball would move. As a wicket-keeper, I could see the problem which Jardine created by insisting that Morris should bowl on one side of the wicket all the time whereas, if left to his own devices, he could cause the batsman difficulty precisely because he varied his attack. Jardine didn't take kindly to it when I pointed all this out to him.

When Australia came to England in 1934, Douglas Jardine decided to retire from first-class cricket and diplomatically withdrew from the position of England captain in favour of cricket journalism. It was under these circumstances that R. E. S. Wyatt – who had been his vice-captain in Australia – took over the side. However, despite his intense study of the game and all-round ability as a player, the loss of the series against the old enemy followed by defeats at the hands of the West Indies and South Africa meant that the selectors were once more looking for a new leader for the forthcoming Australian tour in 1936–37. Their choice was Gubby Allen:

I was keen to go. I had not yet been made a partner in my stockbroking firm but they were very good to me and as we did some Australian business they thought the England captaincy would put me on the map down under.

So far as my choice as captain was concerned, I think I was the roaring favourite at the time. As Jim Swanton has pointed out, I am one of the few men who played reasonably regular Test cricket who never got a hundred wickets or a thousand runs in a season. The fact was that, as a genuine amateur, I simply could not spare the time away from my business. The problem, therefore, was getting enough cricket at the highest level. As I've explained to you, I was able to keep fit by regular training so that my bowling did not suffer. The problem of batting for an occasional amateur was that you need to get opportunities to play a long innings against the best bowlers.

In fact, in 1936 I managed to play more first-class cricket than on almost any other occasion and I was made captain for the home series against India (although I was never able to play regularly enough for Middlesex to captain the side except for the odd match when the regular skipper was away). Overall, that season, I took seventy to eighty wickets and was averaging forty-seven with the bat.

So it came as a great surprise when I heard that one of the selectors was querying whether it was reasonable for me to open the bowling and to captain England in Australia. Claude Ashton's name was put forward as a possible alternative but I didn't think he was really up to Test cricket at that point. We had been in the Cambridge side together but he had subsequently played even less cricket for Essex than I had played for Middlesex and he had no Test experience. I said I wasn't prepared to go under him as captain. The selectors and I talked very frankly about all this. In the end, I think that Plum's view carried a lot of weight. He was still chairman of the home selection panel and, as manager of the 1932–33 tour, he knew better than anyone the problems which we had to overcome in 'mending fences' in Australia.

The fact that I had been born there was an obvious help and I think it was this together with my good form and being the man in possession which all led to my choice rather than thanks to any re-hash of the argument over bodyline and my known opposition to it. However, there was one further snag I had to overcome before we left England after my appointment had been announced. Sir Stanley Jackson was one of the enhanced panel which had appointed me and he said, 'We must appoint your selection committee for the tour – I suggest yourself, Robins and Wyatt.' Walter Robins was officially appointed as my vice-captain and I think they were grooming him as a possible Test captain when Bob Wyatt had rather had his turn but I said I wanted to add Leyland and Hammond. 'No, you can't have professionals on your committee,' Sir Stanley said. So I said I wouldn't have a committee and this was agreed. When I got out to Australia, I just formed my own informal committee and included Leyland and Hammond.

I saw this as part of the process in getting the amateurs and professionals closer together than they had been. In the event, I think we had a happy side although, naturally, I was disappointed when we lost the series after winning the first two Tests.

This was something for which I've had to take stick ever since. But looking back on that third Test when we had bowled Australia out cheaply only to find ourselves on a sticky dog after torrential rain, I can't accept the argument that I should have declared to get the Australians in while the wicket was at its worst. They might equally well have declared after the briefest of innings and still left us with too much to do before the close of play and, in any case, it could have poured with rain at any time.

For two of the professionals in his side, the loss of this match had a different but lasting effect. For Charlie Barnett:

Up till then, the Australian crowds had written their team off. The Aussies don't turn out to see a losing side. Suddenly, the grounds were packed and people were climbing over the gates. I still think Gubby might have won the series by declaring earlier at Melbourne but, in the wider interests of cricket, he did the right thing because he certainly restored goodwill between England and Australia. And, I have to admit, I wouldn't have my house today if we'd won the series. You see, my earnings with Gloucestershire were £250 a year in 1936 (we had never had match money and I much preferred this guaranteed salary). In addition, pay on the tour was £400 and, with the high earnings coming from the big crowds at the end of the tour, I got a bonus of £350 and that's how I came to live in reasonable comfort in my home county.

For Joe Hardstaff, the loss of the third Test caused particular difficulties in his relationship with Gubby Allen:

It made life very difficult for me. I was in good form on the tour but, once the Australians began to claw their way back into the series, Gubby said to me, 'I don't want you to score centuries in two and a half hours. I want you to take five hours to get them. A draw will be enough for us to clinch the series.' I said, 'I can't play like that,' and it created a difference between us which was to make life difficult at later stages in my career.

However, there was one lighter moment arising from the tour which I will always remember. My father and I shared the unique record of being the only father and son to play for England in Australia and when I got back after the tour I went and had Sunday lunch with him and my mother. Naturally, they asked me many questions about the tour and, at one point, I said to my father, 'You know, Dad, it was remarkable. Wherever we went – whether it was to Sydney, Melbourne, Adelaide, Perth or Brisbane – a lot of little old ladies kept coming up to me and asking me for my autograph. Then they would ask me how you were and ask if I would give you their kindest regards.' My father said, 'I want you to come outside and give me a hand with a little job I've got in the greenhouse.' When we got outside, he turned to me and said, 'You bloody fool! Don't you know better than to tell stories like that in front of your mother!'

Back in England in 1937, Joe Hardstaff continued his Test career under the captaincy of R. W. V. Robins. Walter Robins had established a great reputation as an imaginative leader of Middlesex and did well as the England captain against New Zealand. However, like his predecessor, he found it difficult to make himself available for the increasingly non-stop demands of Test cricket. Moreover, it was clear that the growing media coverage and national prestige associated with success or failure called for continuity in captaincy of the side.

It was under these circumstances that Walter Hammond made his decision to change from professional to amateur status. Apart from the obvious fact that this could lead the way to the England captaincy, his move was also a practical one. He found a London-based company, Marsham Tyres, who were willing to guarantee him an annual salary which was well in excess of his probable earnings as a cricketer and, as expected, he captained the side at home against Australia in 1938 when the series was drawn.

Walter Hammond also led the MCC team on its tour of South Africa in 1938–39 without any officially appointed vice-captain, and his impact as a leader on tour was recalled by two of the other amateurs in the party. For Hugh Bartlett:

> As it turned out, this was my only overseas tour for MCC and, like everyone else, I did not see much of our captain. He was a great one for taking off in a car and driving great distances while leaving the rest of us to follow by train. Eventually, this got to such a pitch that I joined up with Ken Farnes, Paul Gibb, Bryan Valentine and Norman Yardley to organize some hired cars. The next time that Wally was about to set off on his own he found himself as part of a convoy which raised clouds of dust and made the whole journey tough going. As a matter of fact, I think I saw more of him in that notorious final Test match in Durban which had to be abandoned after ten days so that we could catch the ship to come home. The problem was that we seemed to have rain overnight on most days of the match and as the pitch was rolled every morning it came up good as new, but I could tell that Wally was getting very impatient and although we might easily have found a bit of time on the eleventh day to win the match, he just said we'd had enough and we were off.

Bryan Valentine also noticed a change in the captaincy from the more carefree true amateur leadership, such as that which had been given by Percy Chapman, to the more lacklustre methods of his successors:

> Wally always lived in a world of his own. He was such a wonderful player that he could always lead by example, but there was a feeling that we were into a new era of the businessman-cricketer form of leadership, and although South Africa was a marvellous place to tour we were conscious of being part of the kind of grinding-down process which we had seen in the previous year with the timeless Test at the Oval and at Durban in 1939. So far as I was concerned, touring cricket which involved Test matches was becoming damned hard work and many very good amateurs much preferred to take part in the private tours which still took English cricket of a high standard to many parts of the world in

the sides organized by H. M. Martineau, Lionel Tennyson and Sir Julian Cahn. I went to Jamaica with Tennyson's side and I went to Egypt on several occasions with Martineau's team. Technically, most of this cricket did not qualify as first-class but it was often played to a very high standard and, above all, it was great fun.

Martineau's teams which visited Egypt were all amateur and included club cricketers as well as those who played in the first-class game. Sir Julian Cahn's teams were usually combined amateur and professional sides. Although Sir Julian was listed as captain as well as organizer, he would rely on a leading cricketer to direct the side on the field. The most famous or (in the context of what follows) the most infamous of these was Lionel, Lord Tennyson. His Lordship was permanently in debt and, on one occasion, cunningly arranged for his creditors to slap a writ of debt on the ship's mast. Cahn, faced with the prospect of losing his effective team leader, settled the debt.

Because of the strength of the opposition, Lionel Tennyson's own teams in Jamaica and India were virtually Test sides. Alf Gover, who took part in Tennyson's tour of India in 1937–38, has vivid memories of the trip:

I suppose that the best-remembered match on the tour was the one in which I found myself in special difficulty. Like most of the side, I had been suffering from dysentery early in the tour, but I told Lionel Tennyson that I had got over it.

When we got to Indore, I was all set to play and to open the bowling when we took the field. I shall never forget the wonderful setting. We came out of the marble pavilion and there was the Maharaja of Indore's hunt silhouetted against the skyline as they set out at just the same moment when we took the field. I took the new ball and prepared to bowl to the Maharaja's opening batsman Nimbalkar. The umpire called play and I went into my usual run-up to the wicket which critics have rather unkindly called my cocktail mixing action. I suddenly realized my difficulty and I went straight on past the umpire without delivering the ball down the wicket towards the batsman. He looked positively alarmed as I got closer to him and gave a sigh of relief when I swerved past him and went straight on into the pavilion where, as Ian Peebles later wrote, 'There emitted the sound of primitive plumbing.'

For Alf Gover, as for the rest of the team, Lionel Tennyson exerted a special fascination:

He was a very powerful man: squat with the kind of creases in his face which women found attractive. I noticed on the ship coming out and on the tour that he had a way of charming them by moving in when others had done all the chatting up.

He had that easy confident manner that you find in an Old Etonian aristocrat. He really should have been at low ebb. He had just lost £40,000 through gambling and one of the reasons he had agreed to bring the side to India was to keep away from his father who was furious. Meanwhile, he just breezed round India addressing Lord Linlithgow the Viceroy by his Christian name and claiming that he had been his fag at Eton. On one occasion, I heard the Viceroy say, 'You know, I'm the Viceroy – the Queen's representative. In public you really must refer to me as Your Excellency.' This had seemingly little effect and he continued to live in style. When we got to Bombay, the Governor Lord Brabourne had him to stay. We were getting a little fed up not seeing him and it was getting near to Christmas. We hinted, therefore, that the captain might put in an appearance. When he did we got him well organized with drink and, when he went to sleep, we loaded him into the Governor's barge and told the captain to take him out on a tour of Bombay harbour. That harbour is something like ten miles wide and he woke up at four in the morning feeling distinctly chilly. When we were presented to Lord Brabourne in the match at Bombay in the stadium which now bears his name, he said to Arthur Wellard, Stan Worthington and myself, 'I understand you are the three rascals who ensured that the captain had a trip round the bay.' We all thought that he might be about to tell us off but he just said, 'I thought it was damned funny.'

*

For Joe Hardstaff, the tour was also an occasion in which he took full advantage of his own aristocratic connections:

I had become very friendly with the Maharaja of Cooch Behar. He was a more than useful cricketer and in those days what I suppose you would call a bright young thing and man about town in London as well as in India. Anyway, he invited me up to his palace when I had a rest before one of our unofficial Test matches. I had a marvellous time being wined and dined and with every kind of entertainment but my stay developed into a challenge into who could drink the most mixed and numerous drinks. To cut a long story short, when I rejoined the team Lord Tennyson took one look at me and said, 'Get him under the shower.' We won the toss and, when it came to my turn to bat, I managed to score a century. I do not remember any of the innings now and I could not remember anything of it when I got out. I can only assume that I played it entirely by instinct.

Joe Hardstaff's other great friend on the tour was Jim Sims:

One of the great joys of touring was the friendships you made with those you had never really known well at home. Jim and I became like brothers on that trip. He had a marvellous sense of humour. I remember on one occasion he jibbed a bit when Lionel Tennyson told him to field close in on the legside. 'Sims, you are a coward,' his Lordship roared. 'A coward, Skipper,' replied Jim, 'never a coward. Just a trifle apprehensive.'

Back home, opportunities for professional cricketers to appear in representative matches other than Test matches were limited. There was a famous example of this in 1934 when the MCC played the Australians (see Appendix I) and the club was represented by ten amateurs and one professional, Patsy Hendren. On the first day of the match, the ten amateurs came out on to the field through the Long Room and down the centre steps of the pavilion while Patsy Hendren emerged from the Players' dugout at the side of the pavilion. The popular press took pictures of this unusual convergence and Percy Chapman invited Patsy Hendren to join with the rest of the team so that they could all come out together in the later stages of the match. Patsy Hendren made light of this when writing in *Wisden* on his retirement in 1937:

> When on tour, amateurs and professionals mix splendidly. They are all part of one team: all live together, all change together. A lot has been said and written from time to time about separate exits on grounds at home for amateurs and professionals. So far as Lord's is concerned, professionals have the option of going through the centre gate on to the field if they care, but they probably think it is too much trouble to walk along there from the dressing-room.

However, for Fred Root writing in the same year, it was all part of the sharp distinction between amateur and professional which, he suggested, still lingered on at Lord's as a diehard policy which had begun there and which he hoped would finally die there.

While reaffirming the importance for a professional cricketer in playing well at Lord's because of the opportunities it provided for wider recognition, he emphasized that matches there were not popular among professionals because of the rules and restrictions which bound them and the general feeling of under-privilege. He added that, if the authorities knew what both sides privately dubbed the snobbish title of Gentlemen versus Players, the match might well be cancelled.

Fred Root's resentment of those in authority at Lord's went back to the time in his early days when an official had told him he should get on with his bowling in the nets, adding, 'You are nothing more or less than a hired labourer in the game.' Perhaps for this reason, he was one of the first to urge that all the names on the scoresheet should be put in the same form – a proposal which would only be adopted with the abolition of the amateur in 1962.

Certainly, in what proved to be the last Gentlemen v. Players match between the wars at Lord's in 1939 (see Appendix I), there was no such thought of any radical change. However, the amateurs were made to suffer for the ferocious bowling of Ken Farnes which had given them a rare victory in the previous year by an even more menacing display from Bowes and Copson on a rain-affected wicket. Some of the amateurs also found themselves on the receiving end of Wally Hammond's peculiar sense of humour. As Billy Griffith recalls:

Wally laughed at the oddest things but I couldn't help wondering whether there wasn't just a touch of getting his own back on some of those whom he had played against when he was a professional only a couple of years before.

When we went out to field, he said to John Brocklebank, 'You must be Brocklebank. Where would you like to field?' John was playing in his first match for the Gentlemen, as I was. He was a nephew of Sir Stanley Jackson and later became a great ship-owner in Liverpool. Before getting down to business he was hoping to play some cricket for Lancashire as a leg-break and googly bowler. However, his greatest friends wouldn't have claimed that he was an outstanding fielder. Anyway, he replied, 'Anywhere you like except close in.' So Wally put him at silly mid-on to the bowling of Ken Farnes on a wicket which was soft on top and hard underneath where all the batsmen were likely to struggle and perhaps resort to some desperate shots. After he had been fielding there a short while, Wally called out, 'Are you all right there?' John tactfully replied, 'I have never fielded here before', to which Wally's response was, 'It's not a bad match to learn in, is it?'

When it came to our turn to bat, it was very hard going but Jack Stephenson and I put on thirty-odd runs for the eighth wicket before the rain came down. We fully anticipated that we should need to bat on at least for a while when play resumed on the third day but, to our amazement, Wally declared at the overnight score. While Jack Stephenson had taken a nasty knock on his arm, I was still not out and we had Ken Farnes and John Brocklebank to come and I couldn't help suspecting that Wally declared because he knew that Freddie Brown, Bryan Valentine and one or two others had gone off shopping and, in the event, we took the field with several substitutes.

Billy Griffith also recalls the match in its wider context:

I suppose looking back on it one inevitably sees a greater significance in that game than one would have felt at the time. Nevertheless, we all knew the war was coming. I'm not sure whether it was during this match or later that we heard that the bust of W. G. Grace had been removed from the Long Room for safe keeping but I always thought that, if the reported remark of one old member to another, 'You see that? This means war' was not true, it deserved to be. Certainly, so far as we were all concerned, it was a tough match between the Gentlemen and the Players but there was a marvellous spirit between the two sides. We could not have known that the war would rob us of chaps like Ken Farnes on our side, who would be killed in the RAF, or of splendid professionals like Eddie Paynter on the other side who would be too old after the war. But, somehow, we knew things would never be quite the same again.

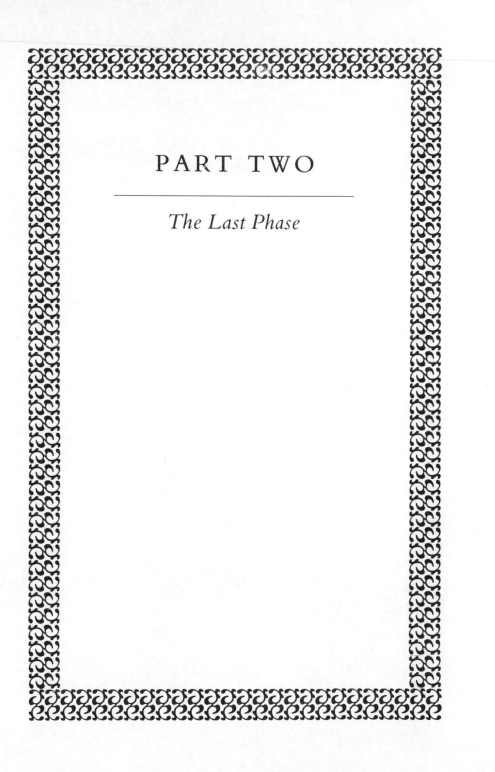

PART TWO

The Last Phase

7

WARTIME AND EARLY
POST-WAR AMATEURS

The changing social patterns which had allowed so established a professional cricketer as Walter Hammond to turn amateur and take over the England captaincy were accelerated by the simple fact that, in wartime cricket, all the participants were effectively amateurs. Although some counties agreed on small token payments for their professionals, cricket activities for first-class players between 1939 and 1945 were almost entirely devoted to charity. Moreover, unlike the First World War when cricket was regarded as unpatriotic, it was now widely encouraged by military and civil authorities.

Thus, in addition to those counties which maintained a fixture list (for example Derbyshire, Lancashire and Nottinghamshire arranged their own local competition and Northamptonshire played fifty-five matches between 1940 and 1945 against other county, Service and makeshift sides), there also appeared the time-honoured MCC teams which toured the country, together with such intriguing cricketing combinations as the British Empire Eleven, the London Counties Eleven and the Buccaneers (who continue today as an invitation touring team). All these teams provided cricket at or near first-class level without any amateur or professional distinction. It was perhaps not surprising, therefore, and certainly in keeping with the reduced mood of the times when even such a traditional journalist as Hubert Preston, who had been concerned with the preparation of *Wisden* since 1895, wrote in his 1943 'Notes by the Editor':

Under the word professional in the *Concise Oxford Dictionary* you will find the words 'Playing for money'; under amateur you will find 'One who is fond of' and 'One who cultivates a thing as a pastime'. You will also find, but not in the dictionary, that as regards modern cricket, these respective definitions are to a remarkable degree interchangeable: for all professionals whom I have known are fond of cricket and regard it as a pastime as well as being a living, and many amateurs, besides being fond of cricket, play it for the equivalent of money, namely for the publicity which attracts clients to themselves or to the business for which they may be working. The only difference here is that professionals' pay is direct and the amateurs' indirect. To both cricket is in fact, whatever it may be in law, their source, partly or entirely, of livelihood. To distinguish between these two sorts of cricketer, on any commercial consideration, is surely humbug.

In the season of 1939 there still existed in county cricket a few, a very few, amateurs who earned no money, directly or indirectly, from the playing of their game. They received only their travelling and hotel expenses, and in some cases, not even these. Long may cricket encourage and be encouraged by such men. Their unbiased leadership and natural generosity have served cricket honourably and long, and they have given to the game from half-legendary times, many illustrious players, many great captains, and many prudent legislators. But they are survivors of an almost lost society of an age that is nearly gone. For these reasons, with whatever feelings of pleasure or regret they may be regarded, I would welcome the total deletion of all distinction between professionals and amateurs in first-class cricket. To me at least such questions as the position of a cricketer's initials and the precise gate from which he is to enter the field have long seemed vastly absurd.

There was another factor in wartime cricket which gave added strength to Hubert Preston's call for the ending of social distinctions in the game, and that was the social mobility of many of the professional cricketers. Just as Walter Hammond with his immaculate Savile Row suiting and trilby had modelled himself on his county captain Bev Lyon and had shown that the modern professional could break into the Gentlemen's cricket world by becoming an amateur, so in military terms had many of his professional colleagues obtained the status afforded by an officer's uniform.

The international matches organized to entertain wartime Bank Holiday crowds in August 1943 and 1944 (see Appendix I) clearly illustrated the reduction of the social divide. Pre-war professionals like Captain J. D. Robertson (who created his own wartime legend in keeping with the amateur spirit when he hit a six shortly after throwing himself flat on the ground during a doodle-bug bombing raid over Lord's), Squadron-Leader L. E. G. Ames, Squadron-Leader W. J. Edrich and Lieutenant D. V. P. Wright now joined such fellow-officers and pre-war amateurs as Flight-Lieutenants W. R. Hammond and R. W. V. Robins in competition with their Dominion opponents (see Apendix I).

Others, like Lt.-Colonel S. C. Griffith, did their part to support cricket as the war neared its end. Billy Griffith had been one of the first glider pilots to land in Normandy on 'D'-Day when, after failing to find signs of the expeditionary force for several hours, he was heard to remark, 'Do you think we have come on the right day?' Back in England, commanding officers at Royal Air Force and Royal Navy airfields were subsequently puzzled and impressed to receive messages warning them of forthcoming tours of inspection by Commander, British Glider Pilots. They would subsequently find that the CBGP concerned was Billy Griffith, piloting an army aircraft, who would conduct the briefest of inspections before inviting promising cricketers on the station to join him at a cricket match which, by chance, was taking place nearby.

Dennis Brookes would later reflect on some of the lasting effects as well as the other folk tales of wartime cricket:

> In many ways it could never be the same again. So many of us had got used to changing in the palatial surroundings of the upstairs dressing-rooms at Lord's which had formerly been the restricted preserve of the amateurs. And there were marvellous stories going the rounds about some of our pre-war professional colleagues. Denis Compton was in great cricketing and social demand when he was stationed in India. On one occasion, when he was batting for the Europeans in the Ranji Trophy at Eden

Gardens in Calcutta, there was a major riot. The mob stormed on to the ground with every intention of stopping the match. Fortunately, when their leader got out into the middle, Denis just offered him a cigarette from his back pocket (how like Compo batting with fags in his trousers) and the whole riot dissolved in laughter and requests for autographs.

There were also stories about the less than reverent wartime attitude of some of the professionals. There was my old adversary the batsman – and now Major – Frank Prentice, who would turn amateur after the war, trying to put one over (just as he had tried it on with me in the match against Leicestershire in 1939) in hauling up so dangerous a quick bowler as Private Dick Pollard of Lancashire for failing to salute him. They were both taking part in a charity match and Dick just showed him his fist and said, 'I've a damn good mind to salute you with this but in any case God help you when I get you up at the other end at Old Trafford after the war.'

Even at Lancashire where they were renowned for their discipline, there was a famous exchange when the secretary called in Freddie Cooper in 1946 to tell him that his services would no longer be required. Freddie had been a Flight-Sergeant in the RAF who had broken his leg when parachuting into Germany but he was still only twenty-five. The secretary said to him, 'Now then Cooper, I'm afraid you'll have to collect your cards', only to receive the reply, 'Thank you very much, Howard.' So Rupert Howard said, 'Are you aware that my name is Major Howard?' and Freddie said, 'I'll tell thee what, Major – thee call me Flight-Sergeant Cooper and I'll call thee Major Howard.'

There were some other new professionals entering first-class cricket after the war who also fell foul of authority. One of the most notable was Surrey's Yorkshire-born bowling genius, Jim Laker, whose dedicated professionalism and periodic clashes with the cricketing establishment all added to his later enjoyment in having a dig at administrators and amateur cricketers alike:

I'd always said that my reputation for 'being difficult' was unfairly based. Take the example during the war when I first began to bowl reasonably well. I had been essentially a batsman and quicker bowler when I was just starting before the war but, when I experimented with off-spin in Egypt, I found I could spin the ball, and before I knew where I was I was playing representative cricket. We played one match against an Australian Services Team on a club ground called El Alamein in Cairo and, after the match was over, I hitched a lift a little way from the ground from an officer who was driving past. 'Where have you come from?' he enquired. 'El Alamein,' I replied. 'How are things going there?' he asked, and I said – all innocent – 'Well, we missed several chances and the Australians made a big score.' He ordered me out of the car and said I was damn lucky not to be on a charge.

That's how you can get an unfair reputation. Mind you, after the war, it is true that I had an early clash with authority but I felt that I had right on my side. I was invited in 1948 to go up and play in the Scarborough Cricket Festival [see Appendix I] which was still run by Shrimp Leveson Gower as his own private party. He had his favourites but he was our president at Surrey and I thought I had been given the presidential blessing. Unfortunately, I had a bit of an up and a downer with Shrimp. There were eight amateurs in the side in which I played and when lunchtime arrived on the first day they put on their blazers and set off for the president's marquee. So did Bill Edrich, Tom Pritchard and I only to be stopped in our tracks and told in no uncertain terms by Shrimp that we were not welcome with the nobs. I think I may possibly have made a few critical comments and the fact of the matter is that I was never asked to play in the Festival again.

For the amateur considering a cricket career in the early post-war years, life on the surface remained much the same in the opportunities provided for public-school and Oxbridge entrants. One of these, Trevor Bailey, has described how his own cricket education followed closely those of pre-war amateurs such as Freddie Brown:

I was exceptionally lucky. When I went to prep school I received excellent coaching from Dennis Wilcox who had just come down from Cambridge where he had captained the University side. I caught him at the right time because he later became an excellent headmaster, but when he first took up teaching he was still able to devote a good deal of time to encouraging young cricketers.

By the time I went on to Dulwich at the age of thirteen I was completely coached so far as my batting was concerned with the exception of the hook shot. So far as bowling was concerned, I learned how to improve my steadiness but I had all the basic technique. Where we were again fortunate was that facilities at Dulwich were first class. We had extremely good nets and an excellent middle and our old professional, Bill Brown, gave you ideal practice by his ability to bowl line and length. Moreover, we had a number of masters who gave us a good deal of encouragement. There was Grahame Parker, who had played for Gloucestershire as an amateur and was an England rugby international, and 'Father' Marriott, who was still one of the best leg-break bowlers in the country.

The thing which wins school matches is good bowling, and the most effective attack would include a good leg-break bowler and a couple of quickies. Father Marriott was helpful in encouraging both and, moreover, he taught me everything I know about playing leg-break bowling. He would bowl slowly in the nets to you when you could play back and he would bowl flat in the middle where you had to play forward. Consequently, when I got into first-class cricket and a leg-break bowler came on, I regarded this as my dream time.

When I went up to Cambridge we had limited coaching but there was really little need. I had decided what I could and could not do and, in a sense, I was my own coach from that time onwards. I had played for Essex before I went up to Cambridge and in the early post-war University sides there were a number of us who were relatively mature. We had nearly all of us spent at least some time doing military service – I had been in the Marines – and we were physically more mature than the equivalent University side today. My first captain at Cambridge was Guy Willatt, who went on to be an excellent captain for Derbyshire, and I suppose he must have been twenty-six or twenty-seven at that time. He certainly demonstrated a highly professional approach and I learned to look at things in very much the same way.

When I went up to Cambridge, I had already been teaching and

I was thinking of a career as a schoolmaster. Things began to go pretty well in cricketing terms and I made a good decision when I turned down an invitation to tour with the MCC while still at the university. Certainly, the offer to go to the West Indies was very tempting but, as it turned out, I would have probably been bowled into the ground because of our shortage of quicker bowling at that time and I decided to complete my degree.

I was also lucky to come into the first-class game when I did. There were those enormous post-war crowds; money was pouring into the game and it was all tremendous fun. Another factor was that the standard of bowling was low – almost as low as it is in the 1980s. Mind you, virtually every county had a high-class leg-spinner like Jim Sims, Doug Wright, Roly Jenkins or Eric Hollies, but fast bowling was almost as rare as it had been after the First World War. That certainly helped a quicker bowler like me.

I was fortunate again when I saw there was an opportunity to join Essex as assistant secretary, which would give me a reasonable year-round salary and allow unlimited opportunities for cricket. I realized, by then, that I was on the threshold of an international career and that I could make it, so, when further invitations to tour came along, I took them and decided to go on playing and for over a decade I played international and county cricket virtually non-stop.

We shall see how Trevor Bailey's approach as a 'professional amateur' would influence English cricket at the highest levels in the post-war years, but equally, for some of the new professionals entering the first-class game after the war like Don Kenyon, wartime service had provided both valuable experience and an unusual maturity in recruits to the county sides:

You have to remember that there was a new breed of young professional cricketer coming into the game. I'd only played for Worcestershire club and ground before the war at the age of fifteen but, by the time I came back, I'd had several years of wartime service and you grow up rather quickly in those circumstances. Moreover, I'd been lucky enough to play a great deal of cricket for the RAF towards the end of the war and, just after, prior to my demobilization, I made it my business to ensure that I was playing virtually non-stop. Northern Command, Eastern Command, RAF sides – you name it, I'd be there. So when I came into the Worcestershire side, I didn't feel overawed in the way that most young professionals would. The people who had the most difficult time were the old professionals who'd played for the county before the war and who had lost six years of first-class cricket. For quite a while after the war, we had two factions in our professional dressing-room at Worcester. This was still an old wooden shack attached to the side of the pavilion which housed both the old and the new professionals and some of the old-timers felt threatened by the new intake.

Another factor which you have to take into account is that professional cricketers weren't too badly off in relative terms in the immediate post-war years. We weren't in the Denis Compton super-star league. I believe he got £5000 a year for the Brylcreem advertisements, which was a lot of money in those days, but we didn't do too badly. When I began playing full-time with Worcestershire in 1947, I was getting £350 a year plus £4 home and £6 away match money and, in addition to that, a bonus when we won. You have to relate that to average wage earnings just after the war of perhaps £5 to £7 a week. There was such enormous popular support for cricket at that time, the counties could afford to pay reasonable money and I could even run a car without recourse to my winter earnings. Some of the other professionals liked to simply take time off in the winter but, if you were ambitious as I was, you got yourself organized in some work outside cricket. I started in the motor trade but decided I wanted something more solid so, coming from the Black Country, I went into the steel stockholding business and was involved with that for the next twenty-six years. Given the reasonable pay and opportunities outside the game, it is not surprising that we had a steady flow of new recruits coming into the game who were more mature than the traditional intake.

As Don Kenyon implies, the military connection did not stop with the end of the war. In place of wartime service came National Service, and the military selectors for inter-Service matches in the forties and early fifties were able to call upon (indeed, to command) the talents of such future cricketing stars as Aircraftsmen R. Illingworth, F. J. Titmus, F. S. Trueman and J. T. Murray for the Royal Air Force; Second Lieutenant D. B. Carr, Gunner G. A. R. Lock and Signalmen D. B. Close and F. H. Tyson for the Army; and Sub-Lieutenant J. G. Dewes and Writer P. B. H. May for the Royal Navy.

Another of those who did National Service was Colin Ingleby-Mackenzie. As Midshipman Ingleby-Mackenzie he appeared for the Combined Services against the 1953 Australian touring team. His account of the match is both revealing as well as entertaining:

The match was played at Kingston, Surrey, in September. I had played for Combined Services in a couple of matches earlier in the season but they were obviously seeking to strengthen the team to play the tourists and they brought in Aircraftsman F. S. Trueman who had had a sensational début for England in the previous year. So far as I was concerned, it looked as though the last place in the side would go to Jim Pressdee or myself, and I said to my father, 'Look, Admiral' (I called him that because he was an Admiral), 'they may give me the boot in this match.' Well, that really set him going. He came down to Kingston and got hold of our captain Lt. Cmdr. Mike Ainsworth and gave him the works. Mike Ainsworth had served under him in the Navy and he was a bit overwhelmed when the Admiral wished him luck with the toss and asked him if he had made his team selection. So poor old Jim Pressdee was made twelfth man, which was outrageous. Fortunately I made top score for our side in the match so the family honour was saved.

However, before that happened we had to field while the Australians got almost 600 in quick time when Keith Miller and Jim de Courcy both got double centuries. In the course of their stand, they hammered Freddie Trueman and he made it pretty clear that he was not particularly interested in the proceedings by sitting on the sightscreen for much of the time.

After the game, there was a kind of disciplinary tribunal headed by an Air Vice-Marshal. We were all given a rocket for losing in two days but the real bollocking was directed at Freddie

Trueman, who was told that his performance in the match was appalling, that he had bowled all over the place, and that he had appeared completely uninterested in the field. To this, he gave the immortal reply, 'Well Sir, firstly, I knew that there was really not much chance in shifting those two on that wicket and, second, I was appalled when you put that bloody Major Parnaby at short-leg. I'm supposed to be a specialist fieldsman there for England and yet you expected me to give way to an old gentleman like that.' At this, the Air Vice-Marshal gave him a further rocket and said, 'You will never play for the Combined Services again.' 'Too bloody right,' replied Fred, 'I'm being demobbed tomorrow.'

Even those professional cricketers who had achieved commissioned rank were not necessarily accepted as part of the brave new post-war world. At the Oval, Major A. R. Gover found himself refused service in the members' tearoom where, only weeks before, he had been welcome as captain in one of the wartime games organized by the Surrey County Cricket Club. Later, when he gave up playing and became a sporting journalist, he was elected as one of the first professionals to follow Jack Hobbs on the county committee, only to find that he was treated as untrustworthy by some of the senior members who suggested that, as a journalist, he should withdraw from certain meetings.

At Bristol in 1948, Second Lieutenant T. W. Graveney, who had recently completed his National Service with the Royal Gloucestershire Regiment, was awarded his county cap by his skipper, B. O. Allen, who, in front of the whole team, threw it across the dressing-room with the remark, 'You'd better have this. You'd have got it much sooner if you weren't so big-headed.'

Basil Allen, who had played for the Gentlemen before the war, was one of the old school who were determined to reassert the traditional values of amateur leadership and who resented moves towards egalitarianism in the county game. He believed that professional newcomers, however talented, should be kept in their place, and he made an even more public demonstration of his views so far as his newly capped colleague was concerned a couple of years later. In congratulating David Sheppard on his century for Cambridge University against Gloucestershire at Bristol, Tom Graveney called him 'David', whereupon his skipper rounded on him with the remark, 'He's Mister Sheppard to you.' He later went into the Sussex dressing-room and said to David Sheppard, 'I must apologize for Graveney's impertinence. I think you'll find it won't happen again.'

Basil Allen was one of the pre-war amateur captains who resumed control after the war. Most of them, like him, were determined to maintain the old distinctions. In 1939, all the counties had amateur captains. In 1946, the old order was virtually restored when all but one of the counties had amateur leaders.

Those counties which followed a different pattern did not do so out of choice. Leicestershire, which in 1946 had the sole professional county captain, Les Berry, selected him because no suitable amateur was available. Although the side achieved reasonable success under his leadership and although he was still a mainstay of the county's batting, it was clear that his committee was determined to find an amateur captain. Major S. J. Symington was tried in 1949 but the appointment of a regular army officer was not a success, and long-term amateur leadership only came when the – by now – increasingly general practice of appointing a secretary/captain produced the Bromsgrove schoolmaster C. H. Palmer in 1950:

I think I allowed my enthusiasm at the prospect of playing more first-class cricket than I could as a schoolmaster to overcome some of the obvious snags in joining Leicestershire. At that stage they were bottom of the Championship, the accounts were in deficit and there was virtually no capital available to the club. I had been brought up in the atmosphere at Worcestershire of 'upstairs and downstairs'. While I saw myself as more of a downstairs chap, there had been genuine regard between the amateurs and professionals, and one advantage of the old system had been the ability to call on the aristocratic patrons to meet the club's financial needs. Thus, at Worcestershire, the secretary would have an annual conversation with the president in which he would say, 'Good morning, Your Grace' and our aristocratic president would reply, 'How much do you need this year?' before writing out a cheque.

At Leicestershire, we were saved by two factors. The first was that, in place of an aristocratic benefactor, I was fortunate in having a dedicated self-made businessman as chairman in Frank Smith. I learned from him the value in having a small committee and, sometimes, the use of a little dictatorship. Second, we managed to persuade the doubters in our committee that we should follow Warwickshire's example in having a supporters' club football competition and this transformed our revenues.

Gradually, we were able to do more to help our players. In his benefit in 1936, that great Leicestershire and England stalwart George Geary had actually lost money, and Les Berry, my senior professional, received a lower benefit in 1951 than those which had been paid to less established players in the immediate post-war years when there had been more money in the game with the initial enthusiasm for the resumption of first-class cricket. The problem which shortage of money imposed on us was restricted recruitment but, gradually, we were able to build on a nucleus of such good professionals as Maurice Tompkin, our Australian spin pair of Vic Jackson and Jack Walsh, Gerry Lester, Paddy Corrall and Jim Sperry, with successful new recruits such as Maurice Hallam, Jack Firth, Gerry Smithson and Terry Spencer, so that, by 1953, we were up to third in the county table.

For Lancashire, the search for new leaders proved a reaffirmation of their amateur faith as the county enjoyed considerable post-war success. They first tried the unknown J. A. Fallows, whose batting average in his single season as captain was just over eight. Yet as *Wisden* reported, 'Whatever his limitations as a batsman, the new captain proved shrewd in the field and inspiring everywhere. Willingness to go out for victory and keen finishes assured maximum interest and enjoyment.' He was followed by the even more swashbuckling figure of Ken Cranston, captain in 1947 and 1948, an outstanding all-rounder who was good enough to gain a Test cap. He was also one of those wartime survivors whose zest for life was obvious to all who met him:

I suppose I was the sort of amateur equivalent of Don Kenyon's mature professional entrant into the first-class game. I was twenty-nine when I took over the Lancashire side and I had had a good deal of cricket with the Navy and the Combined Services towards the end of the war.

The great thing about taking over Lancashire was that, in many ways, it was a going concern. You had a kind of ring of discipline into which the captain could slot. Our chairman Tommy Higson and the secretary Rupert Howard kept their cards pretty close to their chests. Cyril Washbrook was a tough senior professional and Harry Makepeace, as our coach, kept the youngsters very much in order. I was lucky, therefore, to have a side which ran itself to a degree and allowed me to make the most of my limited time in first-class cricket.

My father was a dentist and I was due to follow him in the practice. He kept things going for me during the war and in the period immediately after it when I had my big cricket opportunity. But I knew that it could only be for a limited period. I was determined to enjoy it and make the most of it – and I did.

Cyril Washbrook adds his own comment on Ken Cranston's brief appearance in first-class cricket:

It was a classic case of the true amateur of high quality. After all, in only two years he played for England against South Africa and Australia and went on tour to the West Indies as vice-captain where he actually led England in one match. Although he is very outgoing with a great sense of humour, he soon acquired a bit of Test caution and I wouldn't say he was an adventurous captain. But I was close to him and we got on well and he is still one of the most popular figures whenever we get together at our annual cricketers' reunion.

Nigel Howard, who succeeded Ken Cranston in 1949, had the difficult task of overcoming the image of 'the committee's man'. His father was still secretary of the club when he made his début and, as captain, he had the added disadvantage of constant advice from his chairman, Tommy Higson, who, as a former Test selector, was not slow to express his views.

Cyril Washbrook assesses the Howard captaincy in the following words:

The stories that the chairman would send instructions for bowling changes out to Nigel Howard on the field are much exaggerated. But it was difficult for him not only because of his obvious links with the county establishment but also because the boys in the side had bowled at him in the nets since he had been in short trousers. It made it difficult for him to be taken seriously – especially as he had a rather retiring nature. But he would take advice. I would say to him in the field, 'I'll tell you what I think – particularly what I would least like if I were batting against us at this point. It's entirely up to you as to whether or not you take my advice and I shan't be offended if you ignore it.' Nigel always responded very sensibly and he established himself as a player and a captain, and it's only fair to point out that he led Lancashire to a share of the Championship in 1950.

Surrey's search for a new generation of amateur leadership has become the subject of one of cricket's best-known after-dinner stories. Like most after-dinner stories, it has no doubt improved in the telling. Certainly, no one told it with more enjoyment than Jim Laker, although a willingness to be fair emerges in his 1985 recollection:

Immediately after the war, Surrey were scratching around trying to find an amateur captain. The matter was one which was determined by the president, Shrimp Leveson Gower, and the secretary and they had in mind A. C. L. Bennett who was a well-known club cricketer for the BBC and others. The story goes that, while they were debating this matter, news came through that Major Bennett was in the outside office enquiring about club membership. It was said that they invited him in and offered him the job on the spot. The only snag was that the man to whom they made the offer was Nigel Bennett. He had just left the army with his post-war gratuity and was wondering what he might do with it. It was said that his previous cricketing experience had mainly been with Wimbledon's second eleven but, nevertheless, he was delighted to accept the offer.

I think this version of the story is probably a bit unfair to all concerned and I prefer the version that suggests that the letters got mixed up in the wrong envelopes. Moreover, it has to be said that, in his one season as captain in 1946, Nigel Bennett scored over 800 runs for Surrey. But I think the whole story shows that there was a slightly desperate approach to finding amateurs at the time.

The search for new amateur leadership was not confined to Leicestershire, Lancashire and Surrey. For Derbyshire, there was an unsettled period with four captains in five years before G. L. Willatt brought stability to the scene:

I was lucky in having an opportunity after wartime service and Cambridge to take on the captaincy before I was fully committed to my career as a schoolmaster. Later, it would have been more difficult for me to finish up as headmaster of Repton but, in those early post-war days, there was a certain degree of flexibility. I like to think that I made my own particular contribution to Derbyshire's social development by abolishing the separate amateur and professional dressing-rooms for our home matches.

I felt this was in keeping with the changing times and, in any event, the Derbyshire professionals were a grand bunch of blokes who were willing to speak their mind to anyone. I remember a classic example of this when we were playing Sussex. Their president was the Duke of Norfolk and he came into our dressing-room during the match and said, 'The Sussex team are a useless lot. They know nothing at all about racing. Is there anyone here who has ideas about backing a horse?' And Cliff Gladwin replied, 'Well, where I come from, the only 'orses we know about backing are between t'shafts.'

We have already noted the reintroduction of pre-war amateur leadership in Gloucestershire when, after his unsuccessful tour of Australia in 1946–47, Wally Hammond handed over the county captaincy to Basil Allen. When he, in turn, retired the search for a new generation of amateur leaders began. Allen's successor for the seasons 1951 and 1952, Sir Derek Bailey, deserves especial note as perhaps one of the few 'true amateurs' to appear in the post-war game. While many counties were increasingly using the device of secretary/captain appointments to overcome the difficulty in finding amateur cricketers who could afford to play the game, no such consideration affected Sir Derek. Son of the South African gold-mining magnate and cricket patron, Sir Abe Bailey, he possessed the private means which enabled him to enjoy a brief cricketing interlude in his life. The following late-night exchange occurred while he was entertaining the Derbyshire amateurs Donald Carr and Richard Sale:

Sir Derek: 'Why are all you schoolmasters so dreary, Richard? It's hard enough being reminded of our schooldays without having to put up with you every August.'
Richard Sale: 'And who are you to talk – a mere commercial traveller!'

Donald Carr would later become secretary/captain of his county and in doing so was following the most notable post-war example of E. D. R. Eagar who, as a new amateur recruit to Hampshire, combined both roles from 1946 to 1957. Others who followed the same path included Trevor Bailey for Essex and Wilfred Wooller for Glamorgan.

For Northamptonshire, the day of the stop-gap amateur captain ended with the special registration of F. R. Brown in 1949 thanks to industrial sponsorship by the ballbearing company British Timken. Freddie Brown had been a prisoner-of-war and had virtually dropped out of first-class cricket when he was persuaded to take over the Northants side. He was appointed to a position on the public relations side of British Timken, where he was soon joined by several other members of the Northamptonshire team so that, at one stage, more than half the county side were available to play for the company's team.

Dennis Brookes, then the side's senior professional, describes how Freddie Brown generally made it clear who was boss:

The chairman of the Cricket Committee at that time had been used to running things his way, particularly when it came to team selection. Soon after Freddie Brown joined us, this official wrote down a list of names and said to him, 'Here you are. That's the team I think you ought to have for the first match. What do you think?' And Freddie Brown, who was drinking a pint of beer and watching some team practice going on in the nets, said without even glancing at the piece of paper, 'Bloody awful!' So from that day on the battle was joined, but Freddie Brown always got his own way in having the side he wanted and quite right too.

Freddie Brown's own view on how the amateur was maintained in the game in the first years after the war is direct and open. He relates his own experience and that of others in response to the charge of 'shamateur':

British Timken came to me and said, 'How much do you want?' I named a figure and they didn't quibble. They just said, 'We'll give you a job in the winter and we'll pay you all year round, whether you're playing cricket or not.' Mind you, by then many of the leading amateurs were working all kinds of dodges. Reg Simpson, for instance, was virtually full-time with Gunn & Moore and, if he'd been a golfer, he'd have been a professional. Similarly, as captain of Kent, Bryan Valentine had a sporting equipment deal with Slazenger.

There were some other companies who were still willing to help leading amateur cricketers. Walter Robins was in insurance and so was Bob Wyatt with Sun-Life of Canada (although I believe they put him on a commission so that if he didn't get any business he didn't earn). Gubby Allen was one of the few remaining true amateurs then nearing the end of his career and it had taken him some time to become financially independent as a stockbroker. All in all, when I took on the job at British Timken, I suppose I had unconsciously accepted that the end of the amateur was only a matter of time.

One of the new generation of amateurs who came into county cricket soon after Freddie Brown took over the Northamptonshire side was Colin Cowdrey, who recalls:

I went up to Northampton with Godfrey Evans in May 1951. Godfrey had just come back from the best tour of his career in

Australia under Freddie Brown's leadership and I was curious to see what I would make of the England captain in my first full season with Kent.

When I came in to bat, I was immediately made conscious of the larger-than-life approach of the Northamptonshire captain. 'Morning, young Cowdrey,' he said. 'I hope you have a good season.' He was a big man: sixteen and a half stone with a red face and his particular trademark the white knotted scarf round his throat.

I made a few runs and whenever I hit a good shot he never failed to applaud with the remark, 'Shot'. It was all so different to the general approach which I found in county cricket. I suddenly realized that I was in the presence of the old-style amateur.

After the day's play, Freddie invited Tom Crawford, our captain, for dinner and said, 'Ask young Cowdrey to come if he's not already committed.' Godfrey Evans was thrown into the foursome as a kind of court jester and we had a very amusing evening. Freddie oozed bonhomie and it was then that I realized what an evening with the amateurs was all about.

Colin Cowdrey had earlier received a great deal of help from a professional source while he was at Tonbridge School:

Our coach was Maurice Tate. He had a great gift for building up your confidence. If someone said, 'I don't know if I can cope with their leg-spinner,' he would immediately say, 'Oh, you'll just hit them through here on the offside and there on the onside' and it was all most encouraging.

He always called me Mister Cowdrey. There I was – the school captain a twit of seventeen talking to that great England player. And he would bowl specially for your benefit. He would say to the master in charge of the nets out of the side of his mouth, 'Watch this cover-drive' and then he would feed your pet shot. He'd let out a yell of apparent surprise when you hit the ball well. It all helped to build up your confidence.

After a coaching session we would love to get him going about his battles with the Don in Test matches, and his versions always suggested a wonderfully adventurous approach. We would look

up the records and say, 'What was in your mind? You'd just got
the second new ball and the Don had already got 200 against his
name', and he would say, 'Well, I'd got Wally at first and Patsy at
second with Percy Chapman at short extra-cover.' And we
would say, 'But hadn't you thought it necessary to set a defensive
field with that big score against you and a full house of Yorkshiremen all thinking you were a Sussex no-hoper?' 'I didn't
worry about them,' he would reply. 'I could see that there was a
bit of rough which had been created by the bowlers' follow-
through at the other end. I'd got a new Duke's ball in my hand
and I reckoned if I could hit that spot, I'd knock his off-stump out
of the ground. You see, it was all a matter of attack. I never
bowled a ball to keep him quiet and that's the way I think you
should all try to play the game.'

Colin Cowdrey also gives a fascinating picture of the way in
which county captains catered for the 'occasional amateur':

When I first started with Kent in 1950, the captains of the Kent
first and second elevens were each given an address book. I remember it was a long, narrow book and the secretary had one as
well. The captain was entirely free to pick his team but he would
have to grapple with the amateurs' social and business commitments as well as trying to bring some new boys in from the
second eleven. So, if he was interested in trying out an amateur,
he might well say to the captain of the second eleven, 'I think I'll
give young so-and-so a game or two. He's got a month's holiday
but he's got to be abroad when we go down to Somerset. He can
play for me at Maidstone and Canterbury and I'd be grateful if
you could give him a knock with the second eleven in the games
just before that.'
  The game really was geared to help amateurs in counties like
Kent, and captains like Bryan Valentine would pick those he
considered great triers and still feel free to drop them if they did
not come up to scratch. All this went back to Lord Harris who
had no time for using selection committees. Of course, some
counties used the committee route but, in Kent, it was very much
left to the captain's discretion and he had quite a tricky time

co-ordinating all those diaries. You couldn't imagine Mike
Brearley or one of the modern captains coping with that.

I was fortunate that my business interests allowed me time to
play cricket for large parts of the season and, as an ambitious
cricketer, I could reasonably hope that the captaincy might come
my way.

Reg Simpson was another post-war amateur cricketer for whom
business sponsorship made an extended spell of captaincy, in his
case for Nottinghamshire, possible:

I have never been a great believer in coaching and I did not receive
much at Nottingham Grammar School. But I do believe in the
influence of leading players and, in my case, I learned a lot from
watching Walter Keeton. He was one of the first Nottinghamshire cricketers I saw who made me understand about the value of
playing to the onside for runs. When I saw Don Bradman, I saw
the same skills plus a killer instinct in making sure that when he
hit on the onside it went for four.

I also remembered how Dodge Whysall had scored 240 against
Gloucestershire when he constantly swept Charlie Parker on to
the onside much to that temperamental bowler's fury. I also
remember seeing the great George Gunn showing his amazing
capacity for giving fast bowlers the charge even when he was a
veteran, although, sadly, his retirement from the game was
hastened when he was laid out by Alf Gover. The other batsman
who stayed in my mind when I began to develop as a player
myself was an old professional, Willis Walker, who managed to
keep his score moving along with tremendous rapidity by virtually cutting out all shots in front of the wicket and scoring with
the most delicate late cuts and legside tickles.

So far as captaincy was concerned, I felt that George Heane did
an excellent job as our immediate post-war skipper. It was obvious that he tried to model himself on Brian Sellers but I think he
got a lot out of our side. It was a mystery to me why he was
dropped. I did hear that this may have been due to complaints
from one of the senior professionals who objected to being
shouted at. I thought he handled the side pretty well but, when I

took over in 1951, I tried hard to run things with a relatively light touch, recognizing that we had a number of real characters who often gave of their best if they were left to get on with it.

By modern standards, some of the characters in our team simply would not survive in present-day cricket. Take Charlie Harris. He started out as a tailend batsman batting at number ten or eleven. By not moving his bat he acquired a run of not-out scores and gradually moved up the batting order. Later he turned himself into an extremely good player and if he had not been such a joker and apt to cock a snook at authority, he might have become an England player.

You never knew what he was going to do next, whether it was appearing stark naked in the amateur dressing-room saying, 'I just thought I'd see if you were all alright,' or taking out his false teeth and handing them to the umpire saying, 'I'll just get rid of these. I'm going to bowl in my fastest style.' Perhaps his most outrageous effort was when we were playing Surrey and he skied a ball up towards mid-off where their skipper, Michael Barton, was fielding. As he moved underneath it to take what should have been a comfortable catch he heard a voice shouting, 'Mine, I've got it covered, Skipper.' Michael Barton, being an extremely nice, well-mannered Cambridge Blue, moved aside and the ball fell to the ground. It was only then that he realized the voice he had heard was that of Charlie Harris.

I certainly had my hands full in coping with some of our characters like that, and we had one or two 'old soldiers' when I took over the side. I was fortunate when I established a long-term relationship with Gunn & Moore that allowed me to play as an amateur, but in the early days I was helped by the county when they made me assistant secretary. I think I can admit, after all these years, that they didn't see very much of me in the office.

In looking for new amateur leadership, Somerset had eight appointed captains in the first ten post-war seasons. Oddly, this continual uncertainty seemed only to add to the county's longstanding reputation as a team of surprises. In 1950, when the county had one of its most successful seasons finishing equal seventh under the 25-year-old Londoner S. S. Rogers (who was yet another appointed via the secretary/captain route), *Wisden* reported: 'The appointment of an inexperienced player to lead a side forced to make experiments seemed like a leap in the dark but . . . in the end, deeds spoke louder than words.' Rogers received valuable amateur support that season from one of the county's outstanding 'August amateurs', the Sherborne schoolmaster M. M. Walford. He headed the batting averages in 1949 and 1950 and generally showed that it was still possible for the gifted occasional amateur to make his mark in first-class cricket.

Worcestershire, too, had their own crop of schoolmasters. Before he became captain of Leicestershire, Charles Palmer turned out regularly for Worcestershire in the school holidays, as did the Malvern schoolmaster George Chesterton, who recalls his introduction into the Worcestershire dressing-room with particular pride:

> When I first appeared, Reg Perks as the senior professional took me in hand. I'd hero-worshipped him for years and now here he was, offering me his own peg in the dressing-room to hang up my clothes, and he couldn't have been nicer or more encouraging. I suppose it's just possible that he was quite glad to have a bit of bowling support by that stage of the season even from an amateur like myself who reckoned to bowl tidily at medium pace. But I think it went deeper than that. He had been brought up in the old school which accepted the amateur as a welcome addition to the side.

Don Kenyon shares George Chesterton's assessment of Reg Perks's approach to the use of amateurs. However, he recognizes the problems which were created for some professionals and sees them in a typically balanced way:

> The difficulty was not for well-established professionals like Reg but for some of those who I describe as marginal cricketers in the side. They were the kind of people who had to drop out when an amateur came in and, if you talk to them today, they are still ticking away on the subject. Although people like Charles

Palmer and George Chesterton were good enough to hold their place in the side, occasionally we included amateurs who weren't quite up to it and that did cause resentment. When it came to the captaincy, the same situation applied. My first county captain was Sandy Singleton and he was a very fine player who did great things for Rhodesian cricket after he left us in 1946. But we had an awful lot of chopping and changing with five captains sharing the leadership in the first ten seasons after the war before Bob Wyatt brought some stability into things.

R. E. S. Wyatt had joined Worcestershire after severing his connection with Warwickshire in 1946 and, despite the need to earn his living and his work as chairman of the Test selectors, he left his mark both as a solid performer and as a successful captain. Don Kenyon learned a great deal from him:

Bob Wyatt was a very mellow gentleman when he came to us. He was over fifty when he captained the side and I think he found the atmosphere here a good deal more congenial than he had latterly with Warwickshire. I'm quite certain that everyone who played with him in the Worcestershire side respected him. Perhaps they didn't all like his old-fashioned amateur ways, especially when he had one of those non-jobs as assistant secretary to the county. But everyone respected Bob because he was such a fine player. I spent many hours watching him from the other end when we were batting together and I studied his footwork just as I did when batting with Len Hutton. We also spent a long time together talking – especially on how to play slow bowling. He was a magnificent player of off-spin and the turning ball and influenced me in getting into the habit, one winter, of working on one thing alone. That was to move one pace to the right in front of the mirror as my first movement until it became second nature. I found that this gave me more room for both quick and slow bowling. Reg Simpson did the same thing quite naturally but I learned how to become a good back-foot player by emulating Bob Wyatt. He maintained his form splendidly right up to the end. I remember him winning a match for us

at Taunton when we had to get five off the last ball and he hit
Bertie Buse for a magnificent straight six. You'd've thought he
was thirty years of age, not fifty.

At the Edgbaston Test match in 1986, Bob Wyatt summed up his
thoughts on captaincy as follows:

> I think that some of the amateur captains in my early days were a
> bit overrated. Percy Chapman was good up to a point but he was
> no tactician. Wally Hammond was a lucky captain – at least in his
> early days – but things had to go right for him. I took as my
> model Percy Fender. Now there was a chap who communicated
> his ideas to the side. That's what I always tried to do – to discuss
> both before and during the match how we could get some of the
> best players on the other side out. When I was with Warwick-
> shire, Eric Hollies always said I helped him a lot and I was
> delighted to find the Worcestershire boys were responsive to my
> ideas – especially 'Roly' Jenkins. Mind you, he could be a bit of a
> handful and I had to crack the whip from time to time. I
> remember once I thought I'd given him a particularly hard time
> and the next day my wife met his wife on the train and she said,
> 'Oh, you know my husband is devoted to your husband.'

Bob Wyatt, who maintained his dedicated 'professional amateur'
approach to the end of his playing career, had more claims than
most to be described as the professional's friend. All his life he had
shown his enthusiasm for the company of professionals and his
fascination for those who could add to his knowledge of the history
of the game. We have noted his debt to Willy Quaife when he first
went to Warwickshire, and of his early touring days he would say,
'I preferred to spend an evening talking with one of the giants of the
game like Wilfred Rhodes rather than going to the pictures or out
on the town.'

Now at the end of his playing career and from the influential
standpoint of chairman of the Test selectors, he did his best to help
improve the lot of the professional cricketer. In his autobiography
published in 1951, *Three Straight Sticks*, he called for a major review
of unreasonably low cricket salaries and for the abolition of the

amateur/professional distinction. In this, as in his call for broken-time payments, intended to keep part-time cricketers in the game, he was ahead of his time. Before change could come, it would first be necessary to see some signs of wider acceptance of professional status in the first-class game.

8

PROFESSIONAL
TEST CAPTAINCY

The ultimate recognition of the professional contribution to the game came in 1952 when Leonard Hutton was appointed captain of England. Bob Wyatt played a major part in this choice as a selector. Earlier, as chairman, he had shown his own inclinations by adding Les Ames to the panel – the first professional selector since the brief experiment of co-opting Jack Hobbs and Wilfred Rhodes in the twenties and the thirties.

It is also significant that the other selectors in 1952, N. W. D. Yardley and F. R. Brown, had direct experience of the difficulty in providing a challenge to Australia's cricketing strength. For Hutton's appointment in the series against India was clearly designed to test his suitability to lead England against Australia in the following summer. As after the First World War, so England had been made to suffer in the battle for the Ashes both in Australia and at home, and it was this continuing state of defeat which hastened the selection of England's first twentieth-century professional captain.

Yet the earlier post-war selectors, Sir Stanley Jackson, A. B. Sellers, A. J. Holmes, R. W. V. Robins, J. C. Clay and T. N. Pearce (of whom all but Sir Stanley were current or recent county captains), had all shown continued faith in amateur leadership. After Wally Hammond's disappointing farewell tour of Australia in 1946–47, the captaincy at home passed naturally enough to his deputy, N. W. D. Yardley. Norman Yardley was almost certainly a better Test than county captain. The most likeable of men, he brought a friendliness to the task which suited an international peer group. He also displayed an astute judgment – particularly as re-gards the likely behaviour of wickets – which served England well.

He obtained the respect of many of the current England side by his willingness to trust in their judgment. Trevor Bailey recalls:

He was the best captain I ever played under. He wasn't the kind of captain who would try to set a field for you. I didn't want that – it was my job, my life. What I did like was his ability to encourage me with suggestions as the game progressed. He might say, 'Would you like another slip?' or 'How about a gully now?' and I would feel free to say, 'Good idea' or, perhaps, 'No, I'd rather leave things as they are for the moment.' Yes, he was an excellent captain and I wish he'd been free to tour with us as well as to captain the side at home.

When Norman Yardley's business interests ruled out further touring, the selectors turned to the 45-year-old Gubby Allen to lead MCC in the West Indies in 1947–48. Today, he is the first to admit that he was mistaken in allowing the selectors to persuade him to come out of virtual retirement (he had only played twice for Middlesex that year).

There is little doubt that he faced a well-nigh impossible task. From their earliest days in Test cricket, the West Indies had been formidable opponents in the Caribbean and the England touring party lacked several of their senior Test cricketers. Gubby Allen's problems were compounded by a series of illnesses and injuries which affected his side, beginning with one which he sustained himself while leading his team in physical training on board the ship carrying them to the West Indies. Godfrey Evans has vivid recollec-tions of the voyage:

There were difficulties with arranging travel by sea in those early post-war days and the only accommodation that MCC could find for us was aboard an old tub called SS *Tettela*. We left just before Christmas in that dreadful winter of '47 and the first part of the trip was terrible. Most of the team were laid up with seasickness and there wasn't much competition in sharing out a pretty greasy pork lunch on Christmas day. Gubby Allen did not find much enthusiasm, either, when he tried keeping some of the older members of the side up to the mark with his keep-fit classes. We were three days late in arriving in Barbados and for much of the tour we were pressed to produce twelve fit men from whom to choose a side.

Gubby Allen's difficulties were increased by problems in personal relationships with some of the senior members of his side. He and his vice-captain Ken Cranston did not work well together, and his relationship with the senior professional, who, until Len Hutton came out as an emergency replacement, was Joe Hardstaff, still suffered from the differences in view they had had in Australia in 1936–37. Dennis Brookes, who was making his first and only tour for England, outlined the problem thus:

> Ken Cranston and Joe Hardstaff were unlikely to tour again and, when Gubby Allen tried to exercise discipline by checking what time people got to bed and so on, Joe just said, 'Listen. I didn't come through six years of war to be treated like a schoolboy', and both he and Ken Cranston decided to enjoy themselves.

Old West Indian players like Jeffrey Stollmeyer and Allan Rae recall with a chuckle how the amateur and the professional subsequently created records of unparalleled social endurance including, on one occasion, the consumption of rum punch on an epic scale while making the journey from Montego Bay to Kingston. Billy Griffith, who made his Test début on this tour as a makeshift opening batsman, played his part both by scoring his maiden first-class century in the match at Port of Spain and as a peacemaker between the team's warring factions:

> It had its lighter side. I remember once having to divert Gubby when we were on our way to the ground for early morning practice and I bumped into Ken Cranston returning to the hotel in his dinner jacket. But, in a way, it was all rather sad and we finished the tour without a single victory.

There was, however, one outcome of the tour which would have lasting significance. When Len Hutton joined the side halfway through the tour, he asked Gubby Allen, 'Why don't the MCC make some of the professionals members, particularly those who have played in many parts of the world on the Club's behalf?' Gubby Allen describes subsequent developments:

I thought about this a lot and it seemed to me Len was on to a very fair point in suggesting that professionals who had played for the MCC over very many years should be members. So I put it up to the Committee and I must say that I found that opposition came from some very surprising quarters who had better be described as the old guard. It took me a year, but happily when the Duke of Edinburgh became our President in 1949 it was decided that we would offer membership to a select number of English professionals. It was made a condition that they should have retired from the game (and Paul Gibb, for example, had his membership put in abeyance when he turned from amateur to professional in 1951). Looking down that first list of ex-professional honorary life members unanimously agreed at the 1949 AGM, you can see we were restricting it to the really great players, but it was a step in the right direction: S. F. Barnes, C. J. Barnett, L. C. Braund, W. E. Bowes, G. Duckworth, A. P. Freeman, G. Geary, G, Gunn Senr., J. W. Hearne, E. Hendren, G. H. Hirst, J. B. Hobbs, H. Larwood, M. Leyland, C. P. Mead, E. Paynter, W, Rhodes, A. C. Russell, A. Sandham, E. J. Smith, H. Strudwick, H. Sutcliffe, M. W. Tate, E. Tyldesley, W. Voce and F. E. Woolley.

Back home again in 1948, Norman Yardley resumed charge of a side which was easily defeated by Australia and, when he was unable to tour South Africa the following winter, the search for a suitable replacement was on again. One possible candidate was Bill Edrich who, following Hammond's example, had turned amateur in the obvious hope of captaining his country. In this ambition he was unsuccessful – in large measure because he, too, was seen by the selectors as a man of enormous social appetite. No one enjoyed recalling his extra-curricular activities more than Bill Edrich himself:

Yes, I set out to have a good time and it's true that Denis Compton had covered for me many times in Australia when Wally Hammond came round checking the team's movements. (Denis's best effort was to tell him that I had just slipped out to get some oysters for breakfast when I was off on one of my jaunts.) And, yes, it's true that I enjoyed my drink. But the story that I dived overboard on the ship going to Australia for a bet so that the captain threatened to put me in irons is quite untrue. For a man who has had as many marriages as I have, it's been really quite a quiet life.

Despite his zest for life away from cricket, Bill Edrich's record as a fearless performer and his remarkable physical stamina allowed him to play at the highest level after a night on the town, and he might still have been seen as a possible captain. However, the selectors were looking for a safer choice and he was not invited to tour South Africa in 1948–49. Instead, his county team-mate, the Middlesex captain George Mann, was selected. He had strengthened his claims with a fine innings on a difficult wicket at Lord's in a Gentlemen v. Players match (see Appendix I) and he was delighted when he was asked to follow his father's example by leading the side to South Africa. This was a happy choice. Senior professionals like Len Hutton and Denis Compton recall it as one of their most enjoyable tours. George Mann led the side in the unselfish manner of the best of the old-style captains. Always willing to play for his side at number six, he had the satisfaction of making his maiden Test century in the final Test which clinched the series for England.

Asked how he engendered such good team spirit, Mann – the most modest of men – replied initially with the charming if uncommunicative response, 'I did what you'd have done, old boy.' But on more considered reflection he feels that there were certain elements present which made for a happy and successful tour:

The first thing was that I got the side I wanted. MCC had cracked down on those counties who had effectively discouraged some of their leading players from touring. Then I had some personal luck. I knew Len and several of the pros wondered why I had been chosen. Fortunately, I got a hundred in the first match at Cape Town, and Len came up to me and with that quiet smile of his said, 'Aye, well, I can see why you're out here.' And, you know, you need a bit of luck. The first Test could have gone either way but we won by a whisker with Cliff Gladwin's famous leg-bye and it really isn't too difficult to keep a winning side happy.

George Mann's successful tour was rewarded by the captaincy of England at home against New Zealand in 1949 but, recognizing the need to identify another leader for the tour of Australia in 1950–51, he shared the captaincy in this series with F. R. Brown. Freddie Brown was also given the opportunity to lead the side in the last Test against the West Indies in 1950, although he recalls that it was his performance in the Gentlemen v. Players match earlier that year (see Appendix I) which really gained the captaincy for him:

Once I heard that Norman Yardley and George Mann were not available I knew there was a chance, but there were those who questioned whether, in my fortieth year, I would stand the pace as an all-rounder and captain. Fortunately everything went right for me in the Gentlemen and Players match. I got a hundred, took some wickets in a long bowl, and I was sitting in my bath with a large whisky and soda when Walter Robins came in and said, 'I think the selectors will want you to take the side to Australia.' Well, I had some reservations about it. I had already planned to take a British Timken side to South Africa for a splendidly social tour but you don't turn down the England captaincy in a hurry and by the end of the second day's play I was sitting with the selectors in the pavilion at Lord's discussing who should be in my team.

Freddie Brown's wholehearted approach to the game (vividly illustrated when he bowled 44 eight-ball overs of mostly medium pace when his side were down to three regular bowlers in the Test match at Sydney) was such that Australian street vendors would offer lettuces for sale 'with hearts as big as Freddie Brown's'. His endeavours were rewarded when he led the England team to the first post-war victory over Australia in a Test match, and there were many who thought that, with a modicum of luck, the result of the series would have been closer than the four-to-one result in favour of Australia. From Freddie Brown's recollections today it is clear that he was one of those who, while still maintaining some of the amateur and professional distinctions, nevertheless really believed in the value of consultation:

> The chaps I talked to were Len Hutton and Godfrey Evans. Len is a great thinker about the game and Godfrey, like all great keepers, knew more about the bowling than anyone else. But I also said to the whole team, 'Look, if you've got ideas, come and talk to me. I can't see everything.' I think this helped team spirit, although I didn't always take the advice I was given.

Freddie Brown achieved more success when England defeated South Africa by three matches to one in the 1951 series, but neither he nor fifteen of those who had toured Australia were available when the selectors came to make their choice for a visit to India and Pakistan in 1951–52. The team was seen as barely an England second eleven, and the job of captain required special diplomatic skills in these newly independent countries. Nigel Howard certainly showed the necessary tact in dealing with local sensitivities but had a difficult tour due to his poor batting form. His vice-captain, Donald Carr, gives an interesting insight into the process of team selection on tour:

> By the time we got to the fourth Test there was a real problem about strengthening the batting. I had effectively stood down after the first Test and I was showing good form in the matches outside the Tests. So when we had our discussion about the team for the fourth Test and the question of who should be dropped to find room for me came up, I was a bit embarrassed when the senior professional Alan Watkins said, 'Well, I think the skipper is the natural person to leave out.' I learned later that Nigel Howard had been told at Lord's that whatever he did he was on no account ever to drop himself. So I didn't play in that match

but, as it happened, he wasn't fit for the final Test so I got my opportunity to lead England for the first time.

Clearly, the captaincy of Nigel Howard and Donald Carr had been in the nature of stop-gap appointments, and so it was that the selectors took the plunge in opting for a professional captain in 1952 as a preparation for the greater challenge from Australia in the following year. Sir Leonard Hutton's present-day comments on his feelings at that point are instructive:

I was totally surprised when they offered me the captaincy. I never even considered the possibility as I thought they would continue to choose amateur leaders. But when the offer came I couldn't refuse – it was too great an honour. At first it was suggested that it might help matters if I considered becoming an amateur, but I said that I couldn't be true to myself in doing that. It would be going against my whole background and upbringing. But when it came to doing the job I hadn't reckoned on the full extent of the limelight. I had never enjoyed the business of being in the public eye. What many people don't realize is how much I had suffered from the effects of that 364 score against Australia in 1938. It made me a so-called celebrity overnight while still a very young man and I really hated that. I felt forever afterwards that I was being looked at by the standards of that score and expected to perform accordingly.

Sir Leonard's wife, Lady Dorothy Hutton, who comes from the Dennis cricketing family in Scarborough (and whose brother and nephew both played for Yorkshire), adds her own perspective to the pressures which faced her husband:

You have to remember that Len was born in the Moravian community of Pudsey. They are a religious group who originally came to this country from Czechoslovakia and, in Len's case, they gave him a somewhat gloomy view of life. This meant that – even when things were going well – Len would be looking for the down side and I think all this makes his ability to cope the more admirable.

Despite the added pressures of captaincy, Len Hutton's success as England captain is simply stated by the fact that he never lost a rubber and, above all, that he regained and retained the Ashes. At home, his batting remained dependable as ever and he directed the regular bowling squad of Bedser, Bailey, Laker and Lock and reserves like Wardle, Jenkins and Tattersall with skill. But perhaps his chief success both at home and overseas was in the development of the English fast-bowling attack of Statham, Trueman and Tyson after the long years of suffering at the hands of the Australians Keith Miller and Ray Lindwall.

The emergence of this trio was by no means straightforward or consistent and each has his own recollection of the influence of Len Hutton's captaincy. Brian Statham was the first on the Test scene when he flew out to join the 1950–51 touring party to Australia but, as he says, 'It was really Len Hutton's faith in me on the West Indies tour of 1953–54 which got me going.' Similarly, Frank Tyson recalls Len Hutton's encouragement on the tour of Australia in 1954–55 when, after a disastrous début, he adopted a shorter run and destroyed Australian batting during the rest of the series. But it was with Fred Trueman that Len Hutton had the most difficult and complex relationship.

After his dream début in 1952 (including the Test match at Leeds when he took three of the first four wickets to reduce India to a score of 0 for 4) Trueman was a natural choice for the next MCC overseas tour to the West Indies in 1953–54. There were problems on that tour with arguments over umpiring decisions and the riots which followed, but the young Yorkshire and England fast bowler felt that he had a raw deal in the accounts of his own part and his relationship with his captain:

> I needed someone I could turn to for advice and help. After all I was only twenty-two, but Len found it very difficult to communicate with the younger generation. And most of the stories about me were ridiculous. I never said 'Ay up, pass the salt, Gunga Din' to one of the West Indian officials. And when one of the Government House wives complained I had been rude to her it turned out she had mistaken me for someone else. But somehow I got the reputation of being a bad boy. Of course I wasn't a

plaster saint but I felt that there was no sympathy to be had from the captain or Charles Palmer, the manager, and I suppose it gave me a bit of a chip on the shoulder. In any event, it meant that I didn't go on another MCC tour for five years and that robbed me of a lot of Test cricket.

There is no doubt that the wear and tear of the 1953–54 West Indies tour, with its bottle-throwing and strained personal relationships, took its toll of Len Hutton, who would later say that it probably finished his career two or three years earlier than would otherwise have been the case. However, his Test captaincy finished on a high note with the Tyson and Statham destruction of Australian batting in 1954–55. Again, however, his personal relationships suffered when he felt obliged to drop Alec Bedser.

The decision, clearly justified by events when Australia were decimated by genuine pace, was one which Trevor Bailey considers could have been softened.

Len just found it impossible to have a quiet talk with Alec. He was very much aware of Alec's great service to England – especially when he had been the only real threat to Australia as well as the workhorse who bowled vast numbers of overs against them. He knew what his decision would mean to a great professional like Alec and he couldn't bring himself to talk it over. So the first Alec knew was when he saw the team sheet in the dressing-room and that hurt him all the more.

It was argued at the time that such problems and the earlier difficulties with Freddie Trueman were the inevitable outcome of putting a professional captain in charge of other professionals. It was also said that Len Hutton's approach was that of a cautious captain who must not lose at any cost, and he was criticized then, and since, for substantially reducing the number of overs bowled by his faster bowlers if there was any danger of losing the match.

Such views gave ammunition to those who, while accepting that his success in regaining the Ashes at home entitled him to a run of Test captaincy, yet argued that there was a different case for bringing back an amateur captain to lead England on tour. The two men

most generally identified with such a move were Walter Robins and
Errol Holmes. Walter Robins was then a Test selector and Errol
Holmes had been on the panel before the war. Both were famous
for their risk-taking captaincy, and their choice of the man to follow
in the same tradition was David Sheppard, who had led Sussex to
second place in the Championship in 1953 but who had given up
regular first-class cricket to study for the Church. The Bishop of
Liverpool (as he is today) takes up the story:

There were all kinds of cloak-and-dagger activity over the choice
of captain for the side to go to Australia in 1954–55. And, after all
this time, I think I can be rather more indiscreet than I was when I
wrote about it. Errol Holmes made much of the running over
this. He was one of the old brigade who thought that leadership
should be a matter for the amateur first, last and all the time, and
he was also a natural backstairs intriguer. He even infected the
secretary of MCC, Ronnie Aird, with the atmosphere of conspiracy. Ronnie was a natural cricket bureaucrat – discreet and
bending over backwards to be fair to all concerned. However, I
got various mysterious messages from him, including one that I
should come to a meeting at his house when, he said, 'I will leave
the door open so that you can come straight in without too much
chance of recognition.'

I was devoted to Len. I had first got to know him well on the
1950–51 tour of Australia when, like most of the youngsters in
the side, I was keen to learn as much as I could from him. It was
on that tour that, in response to the question, 'How do you build
the big innings?' he replied, 'You just keep boogering on.' Later,
when my future was firmly committed to the Church, I introduced him to Norman Sykes who was a great figure in Church
affairs in Yorkshire. He knew a great deal about the Moravian
sect in Yorkshire and he and Len became great friends. When
feelers were put out to me about the possibility of taking on the
England captaincy, I went for a talk with Norman Sykes and
asked him how he thought Len would feel. 'I think he'd be
relieved,' he replied.

Len and I maintained the best relationship despite all the
machinations going on around us and it was he who said to me, 'I

think they're going to ask you to captain England in Australia.' Typically he added, 'I very much hope you agree and we'll tell you what to do.' I told Norman Sykes about this and he said, 'That proves it.'

For his part, Len Hutton reacted then and now with great dignity to suggestions that he should give way to an amateur leader overseas. Indeed he goes out of his way to distinguish between the backstairs plotters and the authorities at Lord's with whom he had to deal 'and from whom I got absolutely fair treatment so that at no time did I feel that I was treated any differently from my amateur predecessors'. He also pays handsome tribute to the new generation of amateur Test cricketers who came into the side under his leadership:

> With the pre-war change in the leg-before-wicket rule, I thought we would see the end of the classical off-driving amateur but, to my great joy and delight, I found that a whole new post-war generation of amateur batsmen came on the scene with genuine claims for England recognition and leadership.

When Len Hutton retained the captaincy for the 1954–55 team to Australia despite the intrigues, it was clearly felt inappropriate to include David Sheppard in the party, and the vice-captaincy went to P. B. H. May. Significantly Peter May was preferred over the longer-serving Test amateurs in the side – Trevor Bailey (who had been vice-captain in the West Indies), Bill Edrich and Reg Simpson. May was therefore seen not only as the finest batsman to emerge since the war but also as a potential successor to Len Hutton and, as he explains today, he made it his business to study 'the Master' closely:

> Len had and has a superb cricket brain. He would put himself in the incoming batsman's place: think about his worries and decide what he would least like to face at that point. When it came to his own batting, he would lead from the front with his magnificent performances and I tried to follow his example in both the mental and playing sides of the game when my turn came to lead

England. When you consider the wartime injury which had shortened one arm and his slightly frail physique it's remarkable how well he performed despite the physical and mental wear and tear.

Another of the new group of amateurs about whom Len Hutton enthused was the baby on the 1954–55 tour to Australia, M. C. Cowdrey:

I had tried to model myself on Len Hutton ever since I started playing serious cricket. I really came under his influence when I got a hundred for the Gentlemen against the Players at Scarborough in 1951 [see Appendix I]. I had travelled up to the Festival in Godfrey Evans's Bentley and Len Hutton was the other passenger. When it came to my turn to bat, I was trying desperately hard and Len made it perfectly clear that he wanted to help me. In concentrating, I was crouching too much and as he passed me, he said, 'Stand up higher and play straight.' We talked about it later that evening and although I did not have much success in the next two years while I was still up at Oxford, I am convinced that it was that innings and our talk which got me my place on the tour to Australia under Len's captaincy in 1954–55.

Colin Cowdrey has also paid handsome tributes to his first touring captain's thoughtfulness and help particularly after the death of his father soon after he had arrived in Australia. Thereafter, the captain's care and concern for the youngest member of his team was legendary and he was rewarded by Colin Cowdrey's success at critical stages in the Test series. However, looking back on Len Hutton's overall influence, Colin Cowdrey has some reservations:

Len was an enormous help and he took a great interest in me. The only problem was that he was so defensive in his approach. From his viewpoint, I can well understand the reasons but if I had toured under a captain like Bryan Valentine I'd have been a different player. With Len it was a case of 'Keep the game within you'. His whole idea was to control the game and I tried to follow that pattern. The trouble with these things is that you can overdo it, as I did at later stages in my career. If I had my time again, I would give it more of a go and, funnily enough, Len has since told me that if he had his chance again he would be more adventurous.

Whatever reservations he may have in respect of his first Test captain's general approach, Cowdrey's memorial to Hutton is nowhere more telling than in his description of his captain's skill in dealing with the Australian press in a way which showed all the Yorkshireman's ability to master even the most difficult situations:

At the first press conference which was held on board ship before we landed, Len gave one of his greatest-ever displays of dead–bat play. 'Noo, we 'aven't got mooch boolin'. Got a chap called Tyson but you won't 'ave 'eard of him because he's 'ardly ever played.' 'Ah, yes, Lock and Laker. Aye, good boolers but we 'ad to leave them behind.' 'Batsmen? Well, we 'aven't got any batsmen really. We've got these youngsters, May and Cowdrey, but we 'aven't really got any batsmen.' 'What it comes to is that we're starting out all over again. We're 'ere to learn a lot from you.'

These and other similar replies absolutely took the wind out of their sails. Of course he was highly admired for his batting and I think that there was a general feeling of sympathetic support for him as the first professional to captain England, which fitted nicely in with some traditional Australian prejudices about the English class system. I think he was playing the unsophisticated cricket professional to win them over, and my word it worked.

On the field, one of the most entertaining compliments to Hutton's cricket brain was that paid by Tom Graveney, whose graceful forward play was in the best 'amateur professional' mode. He had been struggling to find form in Australia and was included in the final Test after Len Hutton had found it difficult to establish an effective opening partnership. Bill Bowes, who was covering the tour as a journalist, gives his account:

Although England had already won the series, you never got a relaxed Test match against Australia and, at Sydney, they'd been put in to bat. As they walked out, Len said to Tom, 'What are you thinking about, Tom?' Tom said, 'Oh, nothing much. Nice day. It would be good to get some runs and end the tour on a high note.' 'Well,' said Len, 'I tell you what I'm thinking. I'm looking at the wind to see whether it will help Lindwall or Miller or Alan Davidson when he comes on as first change. Then I'm going to check the wicket to see whether the moisture is drying out because Ian Johnson is hoping that he and Richie Benaud may get some turn. Then I'm going to check what they've been thinking about in field placing since the last Test match. You've got to think of these things you know, Tom.' Well, as it happened, Len got out early and Tom made his only Test century against Australia – a beautiful hundred in just over two hours. When he came back to the pavilion, Len said, 'Well played, Tom. You really thought that through.' And Tom told me later, 'I didn't dare admit to him that I hadn't had a thought in my head the whole time I was out in the middle – but you can see why I, too, regard him as the Master.'

Despite his criticism of Len Hutton's difficulties in handling personal relationships, Freddie Trueman is among the most eloquent voices in praising his batting skills. In addition he gives an appreciation of Hutton's great professional contemporary, Denis Compton:

They were the two greatest professional batsmen of my time and they made a fascinating contrast. One thing they had in common was that they both played under severe physical handicap in the later part of their careers – Len with that shortened arm and Denis with his continuing knee problem. As a bowler who reckoned he could trouble the best of them, I can only say that Denis was a genius. He had every shot in the book and some that weren't. Off-spinners found it virtually impossible to bowl at him and he could demoralize an attack to such an extent that, by the time they had recovered, the lesser players had been making half centuries at the other end.

It used to amaze me how he could roll up at the start of the season, hit half a dozen balls and go out and get a hundred with virtually no practice. I've never seen anyone in my life who could get so far down the wicket to the medium and fast bowler and hit them on the full toss and, when the mood took him, the bowlers didn't know where to bowl at him. He would hit you for four from outside leg-stump through the covers and he would pull you from outside off-stump behind square-leg. As far as the famous Compton sweep was concerned, I've seen him let the ball go past him before hitting the ball almost directly behind the stumps to the boundary.

Oh yes, Denis was a world-class player and so was Len. I think Len was the greatest player I ever saw on all types of wickets. What you have to remember is that, unlike the defensive batting of someone such as Geoffrey Boycott today, he could score faster than anyone in the side. He still says that he doesn't understand why so many young cricketers hit the ball so well straight to fielders. He was brought up to put the ball where the fielders weren't. He could play the ball early or late. He was like a ballet dancer on his feet in deciding whether to look for the ball or let it come to him. I've seen him get inside the ball and hit it like a cover-drive down to third man. When they tried placing a field to him and they moved a man two yards this way or that Len would hit it just a bit later and it would go two yards past the fielder's left hand or he'd hit a little bit early and put it two yards past his right hand.

I have to regard Len as the greatest batsman I've played with in English cricket, and his efforts are all the more staggering when you realize the enormous pressure he felt in taking on the Test captaincy. I've had my words of criticism to say about him but, all in all, my admiration for him is unbounded.

At Scarborough in 1986, Sir Leonard Hutton's services to Yorkshire and England cricket were recognized when he was made president of the Festival in its centenary year. His reflections on his cricketing career were, as ever, typically modest and philosophical:

I sometimes look back and wonder, 'Did this really happen to me?' No one expected the England captaincy less than I did. When Norman Yardley told me that the selectors wanted to give me the job, I sat down and thought, 'What's happened? It can't be true.'

In county cricket in England I was kidding people into paying me for playing a game I loved. When it came to Test cricket as a batsman it was a different proposition. When I went to Australia in 1946, I'd beaten Don Bradman's highest-innings record and they were out to do me. And no one could really say that they enjoyed batting against Lindwall and Miller at Sydney getting up to three or four bouncers an over.

As captain of England, I became even more strongly aware of the difference in pressures when playing overseas as opposed to at home. I think that this aspect of human nature is often over-looked not just by the critics but also by the general public. In the days when we went on tour by ship, you had a pretty good idea of who would be successful even before you arrived. For example, when I first went to Australia, we sailed on the *Stirling Castle* which was only about 12,000 tons with sixteen cabins. So you were very much thrown together. Similarly, when we were travelling through Australia we would spend days at a time on the train. You would find yourself sitting in the observation car at the back of the train after a long hard day in the field with a glass of cold beer in your hand looking out at miles and miles of bugger-all. It was at times like these that you discovered those who didn't take to the country or to its beer or – even more basically – those who suffered emotionally from long periods away from home.

As captain, I had to try to understand these problems and to help where I could. It wasn't made easier by the increasing external pressures. When I went out as an emergency replace-ment to Jamaica in 1948 we had five weeks there and the pace was leisurely. When I went back as captain in 1953–54 we were made aware of an intense feeling of nationalism and the move towards independence and it was desperately hard to avoid giving unin-tended offence.

That side of the game has settled down but the media pressure which was growing in my time has become intense. Cricket for me was always an art and not a science. You cannot write a cricketing script in advance that will have any real comparison with what actually happens. I always felt, therefore, that as cricketers we were artists and not scientists and I think this was what gave the game so much of its appeal. The game has changed a lot in the last twenty years and I suppose you could say that, today, they are all businessmen. When we had amateurs, they contributed – even at Test level – to the richness of the artistry and I hope that the modern player will not ignore that aspect which is what sets the game apart.

9

CHAMPION COUNTIES

When Leonard Hutton returned to county cricket from Test duties, it was to serve under an amateur captain. In 1946, Brian Sellers had resumed his pre-war captaincy of Yorkshire in the same authoritarian but totally committed way and taken his side to the first post-war Championship.

Norman Yardley, who succeeded him as captain in 1948, described his contribution and their partnership thus:

> He was certainly tough and he would have a go at anything. He once, for a bet, hit a golf ball from the front of the pavilion at Bramall Lane over the Sheffield United football stand on the other side of the ground. And the stories about him having Guinness with a raw egg for breakfast were true. In the early post-war years we were together a good deal. There were three dressing-rooms at Headingley – two large and one small – and so we would make the two large rooms available to the professionals on both our own side and the visitors' while Brian and I would change with any other visiting amateurs who might be on the other side. When we were away on tour we would stay in our own hotel. Brian would always say, 'The boys see enough of me on the field all day, I think we should leave them to let their hair down' but at least once in every away match he would say, 'Come on, let's go down and see what the lads are up to.' Off we would go to the professionals' hotel and spend long hours talking

THE FINEST PLUM IN THE BASKET

Sportsmen, journalists, businessmen and actors pay tribute at
a dinner in honour of Sir Pelham Warner's knighthood in 1937.

ABOVE: D. R. Jardine (in hat) and Herbert Sutcliffe about to launch a boat belonging to one of Gubby Allen's Australian relations, which had been christened during the first Test at Sydney in 1933. (G. O. Allen is in the background on the left.)

LEFT: Patsy Hendren goes in to bat at Lord's in 1937 in one of his last appearances for Middlesex.

BELOW: Family and overseas links at Scarborough, 1936. Tom Longfield of Cambridge, Kent and Bengal (whose daughter is Mrs Edward Dexter) goes out to bat for the Gentlemen with Errol Holmes of Surrey and England (who was born in Calcutta)

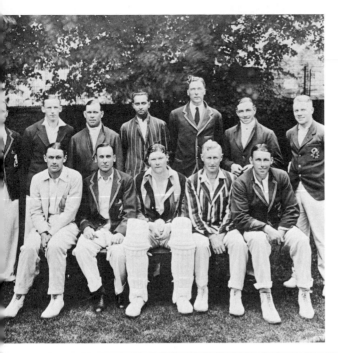

LEFT: The England XI at Lord's v. Australia in 1930 contained five amateurs (with initials) and six professionals (without). Front row, l–r: G. O. Allen, Hobbs, A. P. F. Chapman (captain), J. C. White and Tate. Back row, l–r: Sandham (12th man), R. W. V. Robins, Hendren, K. S. Duleepsinhji, Woolley, Hammond and Duckworth. In this match (which is often seen as the last Test where the amateur spirit of refusing to play for a draw was evident), the amateurs provided a splash of colour with Duleepsinhji in Quidnunc colours; G. O. Allen (Cambridge); J. C. White (Somerset Stragglers) and the captain in his Uppingham Rovers blazer.

BELOW: G. O. Allen hooking a bouncer from Bill Bowes in a match between Middlesex and Yorkshire in the 1930s.

Gentlemen's Gallery

(Dates indicate length of first-class career).

1. T. N. Pearce (Essex, 1929–50), for many years the post-war organizer of the teams for the Scarborough Cricket Festival.
2. H. T. Bartlett (Cambridge and Sussex, 1933–51).
3. S. C. Griffith (Cambridge, Sussex and England, 1934–54).
4. K. Cranston (Lancashire and England, 1946–50) and N. W. D. Yardley (Cambridge, Yorkshire and England, 1935–55).
5. W. Wooller (Cambridge and Glamorgan, 1935–62).
6. G. H. G. Doggart (Cambridge, Sussex and England, 1948–61).
7. D. B. Carr (Oxford, Derbyshire and England, 1946–68).
8. A. C. D. Ingleby-Mackenzie (Hampshire, 1951–65) and M. J. K. Smith (Oxford, Warwickshire and England, 1951–75).
9. Rev. D. S. Sheppard (Cambridge, Sussex and England, 1947–62).
10. Raman Subba Row (Cambridge, Northamptonshire and England, 1950–68).
11. M. P. Donnelly (Oxford, Warwickshire and New Zealand, 1936–60), batting for the Gentlemen at Lord's in 1946.
12. R. G. Marlar (Cambridge and Sussex, 1951–68).
13. A. R. Lewis (Cambridge, Glamorgan and England, 1955–74).

1

2

3

4

6

Players' Parade

(Dates indicate length of first-class career).

1. John Langridge (Sussex, 1928–55).
2. J. Hardstaff Jr. (Nottinghamshire and England, 1930–55).
3. C. J. Barnett (Gloucestershire and England, 1927–54).
4. A. R. Gover (Surrey and England, 1928–48).
5. George Cox Jr. (Sussex, 1931–61).
6. L. Hutton (Yorkshire and England, 1934–60) and E. I. Lester (Yorkshire, 1946–56).
7. W. Voce (Nottinghamshire and England, 1927–52).
8. H. E. Dollery (Warwickshire and England, 1934–55).
9. D. Brookes (Northamptonshire and England, 1934–59).
10. L. Harrison (Hampshire, 1939–66), Colin Ingleby-Mackenzie's 'model senior professional'.
11. R. T. Spooner (Warwickshire and England, 1948–59).
12. R. Illingworth (Yorkshire, Leicestershire and England, 1951–83).
13. A. Wharton (Lancashire, Leicestershire and England, 1946–63).
14. D. Kenyon (Worcestershire and England, 1946–67).

ABOVE: Yorkshire wartime Officers and Gentlemen and Non-Commissioned Officers who all became amateurs 'for the duration'. L–r: Captain H. Verity, Sergeant F. Smailes, Major H. Sutcliffe, and Sergeants M. Leyland and L. Hutton.

BELOW: A wartime cricket gathering at a bomb-protected Lord's. Back row, l–r: Captain S. C. Griffith, Sub/Lt. G. T. S. Stevens, Flt/Lt. R. W. V. Robins, Major G. O. Allen, P/O R. L. Taylor and Sergeant L. Hutton. Front row, l–r: G. H. Heane, O/Cadet B. H. Valentine, Lt. F. R. Brown and L. N. Constantine.

cricket with the odd jar or two. I learned a lot from him but his style of leadership was not the same as my own.

Bill Bowes, who was nearing the end of his career with Yorkshire in 1946 and 1947, comments on the differing styles of Yorkshire's first two post-war captains:

Brian Sellers used verbal abuse to motivate people and he sounded equally offensive to friend and foe. When Colin Cowdrey got his first hundred for the Gentlemen at Scarborough he was told by Brian Sellers that he could well understand why he was not stopping on for the final match of the Festival after getting out to such an appalling shot. When he realized that Colin was upset by this he added, 'It'll be nobody's fault but your own if you're not playing for England and on the next boat to Australia.' He was very much like that, his bark was far worse than his bite and, above all, he cared passionately about Yorkshire and England cricket in that order.

Norman Yardley cared equally for both and of course gave tremendous service as an England Test captain as well as captain of Yorkshire. But in those early post-war years Brian Sellers treated him with the same total disrespect as he did the rest of us.

Although Norman was a useful change bowler wobbling the ball about for England, he hardly ever got on to bowl for Yorkshire while Brian Sellers was in charge. 'You may be good enough to bowl for England,' he would say, 'but you're not good enough to get on for Yorkshire.'

Brian Sellers would exert a stern influence over the character of Yorkshire's cricket. Thus, when it came to matches against Lancashire, he was quick to stamp on anything which suggested frivolity. Gerry Smithson, one of the most attractive left-hand batsmen to appear for Yorkshire for many years, sought to play an attacking game at all times. In the match against Lancashire at Bramall Lane in 1947, he hit Dick Pollard for four fours and a three in the last over before lunch only to be called in by his captain and the cricket committee and told to behave himself.

When Norman Yardley took over the Yorkshire side in 1948, his more easygoing style might have been seen as an opportunity for change in the Yorkshire camp. However, Brian Close, who made his début for the county in 1949, felt that such an approach created problems:

I never played under the perfect captain. There is no such thing. But Norman Yardley knew the game and, in many ways, was a splendid captain. He is also a super bloke but he is a quiet man and he didn't like rows. So he found it difficult to discipline the senior players in our side. We kept coming second to Surrey and I felt that a major part of the problem was the fact that too many senior chaps got their own way.

Although well into his fifties, Brian Close takes perverse pleasure in turning out once a year to lead his team against the touring side at the Scarborough Festival because it means the statisticians have constantly to update his career record on the basis of one appearance. He also plays regularly for Baildon and in his house nearby, high in the Yorkshire Dales, he recalls the early influences on him in the Yorkshire side as well as his first experience of Sellers's discipline:

Bill Bowes and Johnny Wardle were the two people who helped me most. By then, Bill was a press man but he did a bit of part-time coaching and he was a sort of father figure to me. Johnny Wardle could be difficult but, for some reason, he took to me. He was an exceptionally deep thinker about the game and his ideas influenced me a lot when I later became Yorkshire captain.

So far as discipline was concerned, I've said that Norman Yardley was too easygoing. But I got a sample of the Sellers influence soon after I made my début.

I was in good form that year [1949] and I played in the Gentlemen v. Players match at Lord's [see Appendix I]. It was a great honour and it was certainly as good as a Test trial and I was only just eighteen. I really hadn't taken on board all the social niceties of the game – I was only just out of school and, as far as I was concerned, I was surrounded by my cigarette-card heroes. Anyway, I got the highest score on our side in the first innings and, when I got to fifty, the Gentlemen's wicketkeeper, Billy Griffith, said, 'Well batted, Brian,' and I just said, 'Thank you, Billy.'

Ten days later I got word that Brian Sellers wanted to see me. By now, he had gone from the captaincy to the committee room. He gave me the most tremendous rocket, finishing, 'In future, when you address an amateur, you will call him Mister.' Bill Bowes heard about this and said to me, 'I know what's happened. If you have to address an amateur, just say what you have to say. Don't say Mister, Sir or anything else.'

Norman Yardley's instincts were in favour of breaking down some of the old social barriers. As vice-captain of the England team to Australia in 1946–47 he had been on Christian-name terms with all the professionals in the side. His period as captain of Yorkshire for eight years was not without success when the county shared the Championship once and was runner-up four times. Fred Trueman is one of those who feels that criticism of his old captain has been overdone:

When I came into the Yorkshire side in 1949, Norman Yardley was a great help and encouragement to a new young fast bowler. As far as I'm concerned, I still call him Skipper and I always shall. Then, again, his abilities as a player are sometimes overlooked. There were not many better onside players than Norman, he could wobble a new ball and he was a fine slip and close-in fielder.

You also have to remember that Norman had to contend with quite a lot of problems. He was leading both his county and England when they were rebuilding. Then he had the problem of Brian Sellers still running Yorkshire cricket from the committee room and, finally, he inherited an awkward squad in the dressing-room. If you have to criticize, I suppose it is that his reluctance to involve himself in arguments within the team led to an increase in some of the off-the-field problems which continue up to the present day.

Ted Lester, who had first played for Yorkshire as an amateur and who retained his aggressive approach to batting when he made

his professional début for the county in 1948, has described how
internal dissension in the side affected him:

> After a while I really got to hate the atmosphere. When we were
> travelling by train as we often did at the start of my career, I have
> seen a pack of cards flung out of the window in the compartment
> next door where the prima donnas were having yet another go at
> each other. When we played sides like Kent and Gloucestershire
> there was such a different atmosphere in their dressing-room that
> I longed to up sticks and join them.

Ray Illingworth, who joined the side in 1951, has described how
the old guard made life for the newcomer thoroughly unpleasant:

> In one of my first games for the county, I hung a shirt on what I
> thought was a spare peg only to have it thrown across the
> dressing-room by Johnny Wardle. He could be a real so-and-so.
> Behind that marvellous clowning act which the public loved, he
> was an insecure and difficult man. He once refused to let me have
> the ball when Norman Yardley wanted to bring me on as a
> change bowler. Johnny mellowed a good deal after he gave up
> playing but in the early days he was only one of several of the
> senior pros who made our lives a misery.

Fred Trueman also felt the pressures imposed on a newcomer to
the Yorkshire side:

> It's true that you were thrown into the deep end with Yorkshire
> and there was a bit of jealousy over my early successes and all the
> press comment about 'Fiery Freddie'. So some of the team would
> urge me to have a go at the great players – perhaps hoping I
> might come unstuck in the process.
>
> I remember in my early days this was particularly directed
> against Denis Compton. There had always been needle in our
> games against Middlesex and I responded to suggestions that I
> should keep bouncing the ball at Denis. At the end of the day's
> play in one of our games, he got hold of me and said, 'Come and

have a drink.' He sat me down and explained how people would egg me on to live up to my image and this might not be best for my long-term prospects. He did it all in the friendliest way – making it clear how I could come unstuck if I was permanently seen as 'the bad boy of cricket'.

I thought a lot about it and there was no question of Denis simply protecting himself – he had the courage of a lion. I came to realize how he had my best interests at heart and we became great mates. Mind you, it didn't stop my natural aggression but I started to learn how to use it with discretion.

The Warwickshire wicket-keeper, Dick Spooner, was one of those who saw how this discretion would work in practice:

I must admit, I wasn't above trying to put Fred off a bit. In one game I got down to his end and said, 'Why are you bowling off-spinners today?' Well, it was like the famous red rag. He really tore in at me and I had a rough time of it. But when we walked off the field, he put his arm round my shoulder and said, 'Well, where are we drinking together tonight?'

The rivalry with Middlesex to which Fred Trueman referred had existed before the war and continued after. Middlesex were runners-up five times consecutively to Yorkshire from 1936 to 1946 and the reason for their breakthrough as Champions in 1947 – and for the contrast between the two sides – was summed up by their leading batsman, Denis Compton, as follows:

Walter Robins carried us all along with his spirit of adventure. Whereas Yorkshire seemed to need the Sellers discipline to keep the side together, Walter would always show the greatest confidence in our ability to deliver. In many ways he seemed to cope in just the same way as it was always said Percy Fender had done with Surrey. We, too, had limited bowling resources, and when we won the toss Robbie would say to us, 'Right, I want 400 on the board fastish so that we can get at them tonight.' Happily, in those golden summers of the forties, Jack Robertson, Sid

Brown, Bill Edrich and I were usually able to oblige. And if we needed any help, Walter himself and George Mann could come in for the run chase before the declaration.

Despite his cavalier approach to the game, Walter Robins was a stern disciplinarian who maintained his influence on the young Middlesex professionals in spells as captain of both the county's first and second elevens. Much of the Middlesex success in the Championship was based on the strength which Robins built up in the Middlesex second team to provide the reserves required when there were Test calls for Edrich, Compton and other first-team players. Ron Hooker, who made his first-class début in 1956, recalls how the Robins influence was still felt when he exchanged the role of captain for that of committee man:

Walter Robins would summon a young player into the pavilion and tear him to shreds if he thought you were idle (for instance, if you had been sitting on the ground after the fall of a wicket). But he would also forgive almost anything if you were a trier so that if you were out of form but kept working in the nets, he would be right behind you. Above all, he would always try to get you included in the side if you were good in the field.

For J. T. Murray, who would become a stylish wicket-keeper for England as well as Middlesex, Robins's interest took another form:

He was the first person who ever suggested that I should think long-term about money matters. He insisted that we put part of our earnings into an insurance savings plan. I collected mine in the eighties. It wasn't worth much but it reminded me of Robbie's advice and how he'd made me think of my future. I also remember how he insisted on making cash payments direct to the hotel for our meals when we were on tour so that we had to eat in. He knew that, otherwise, any food allowance would be blown on drinks, smokes and inadequate food.

But Walter Robins was not always able to exercise total control over other members of the side if they happened to have the independence of the amateur. Ted Jackson, today a leading Middlesex committee member, was, in his early days as a second-team bowler, notorious for entrances into Lord's on a bicycle in sweater and jeans. Walter Robins was determined to make him conform to the standards of dress he insisted upon but found it difficult to know what to say when Jackson was seen to enter Lord's on the day following Robbie's rocket, still on his bicycle but this time in top hat, white tie and tails.

George Mann adopted a more relaxed approach to captaincy:

Middlesex was a happy side and you just had to take the foibles of some of our team in your stride. Denis Compton was always vague. He would frequently lose his gear and on one occasion he got a marvellous hundred with the bat which Fred Titmus was just about to discard as a piece of dead wood. Then, Denis was always late and it was quite a relief when you actually saw him out on the playing area. As for Bill Edrich, well, we all knew he enjoyed his night life.

Often, when the pair of them were deep in conversation at the wicket, I knew that they were much more likely to be talking about the day's racing rather than the problems of the match in which we were engaged. But you couldn't crack the whip with chaps like that – you had to give them their head and they – and the others – never let me down.

George Mann's reference to the Compton/Edrich interest in racing is one which is well illustrated by Colin Ingleby-Mackenzie who, in 1951, was making his second appearance in first-class cricket at the age of eighteen:

We were at Portsmouth and I had just started doing my National Service in the Navy. I walked into the dressing-room at Portsmouth with my little Etonian cricket bag and a *Sporting Life* under my arm. There were my great heroes, Bill Edrich and Denis Compton. So I said, 'Good morning, Sir' to each of them. Bill gave me a friendly reply but Denis said, 'Come here, young man. What is your name?' I said, 'Colin Ingleby-Mackenzie.' 'That's a very long name,' he said, and went on, 'Can I say two

things to you?' 'You certainly can, Sir,' I said. 'That's the first
thing,' he said. 'You will never call me Sir again – you will call me
Denis,' to which I replied, 'Yes, Sir,' and he said, *'Denis.'* 'Yes,
Denis,' I said. 'Second,' he went on, 'could I borrow the *Sporting
Life?'* We've been the greatest friends ever since as I was with
Bill Edrich. The three of us had three doubles and a treble on the
horses that day and I knew that, from that moment on, I was
going to lose thousands in their company but it has been worth
every penny to be a friend of the Middlesex twins.

When Bill Edrich took over the Middlesex side in 1951, it was at
first on the basis of shared captaincy with Denis Compton. Reg
Simpson comments:

It was a tragedy that the idea of using Denis as captain was not
really pursued. He had such an adventurous approach which we
saw when he captained the Players. If he had been given a chance
of leading England instead of Len we might have had a wholly
different story in encouraging attacking cricket at a time when
England were growing in strength.

Bill Edrich sees the exercise as having a dual purpose in the minds
of the England selectors:

The idea that we should somehow work in harness was always a
non-starter. I think the fact was they wanted to try me out as the
newly turned amateur captain in case I could go on to higher
things, but also I believe they were keeping Denis up their sleeve
in case he got the choice as professional captain for England. In
any event, Denis always found it hard enough to look after
himself in getting from A to B and his late arrivals on cricket
grounds were legendary. It didn't therefore make much sense
expecting him to exert much discipline. As for his running
between the wickets, someone once said that his calling was
merely a basis for negotiation but to be fair he never seemed to do
much wrong when we were batting together; but some of the
others used to say that Denis's calling always consisted of 'Yes,
no, yes. Oh Lord, sorry!' But I couldn't have had a better

supporter when I took over the captaincy full time in 1953 and I enjoyed pitting my wits against some of the other captains of the Champion counties.

One such was Wilfred Wooller. The giant Welsh rugby international resumed his cricket-playing career with Glamorgan when he accepted the post of assistant secretary in 1946 under the captaincy of the veteran J. C. Clay, whom he succeeded as captain in 1947. He would combine the roles of secretary/captain for the next fifteen years but, inevitably, his chief and happiest memory is of leading Glamorgan to their first county Championship in 1948:

I came into the game full-time in 1946 and I learnt a lot from Johnny Clay. At the end of that year I went up to the Scarborough Festival. I spent hours talking about the technical aspects of cricket with Bob Wyatt. He was a great friend and, as has often been said, he has forgotten more about the game than most professionals ever learn.

When my time came to lead Glamorgan, I knew I was a good analyser of the tactical approach to the game and I tried to think how we might use our limited resources. Before the war, most counties attacked the offside edge of the bat. In Glamorgan, we had always been familiar with off-spin bowling and I decided that we should concentrate on attacking the legside edge of the bat. Other counties had tried it occasionally like Fred Root for Worcestershire but not as a consistent tactic. I decided that we must build up our leg-trap and one of our Yorkshire imports, Arnold Dyson, was very helpful in working this plan of attack out. We had another import, 'Pete' Hever, who could duck the ball in to the bat at medium pace, and we still had Johnny Clay available to bowl orthodox off-spin. Even at the age of fifty he was still pretty useful. To support him, we took on Len Muncer from Middlesex. He was a great thinking cricketer who was then a leg-spinner but I told him, 'Forget leg-breaks. I want you to bowl off-spin but flatter than Johnny Clay.' And he did with great accuracy.

I then developed my legside field for Hever, Clay and Muncer. There is a big difference between fielding on the legside and in the slips. At slip, you watch the ball all the way down. But at leg-slip, you watch the bat and you don't move. Too many people rock and move. You shouldn't move until you see the ball in the air.

We were not a great batting side but we could make enough runs on rain-affected wickets to be in with a chance – particularly when we began catching everything in the leg-trap. Soon afterwards, other counties followed our example – particularly Surrey when Tony Lock made a name for himself at leg-slip. But in '48 we got going before the others caught on.

Warwickshire, too, obtained their first Championship victory in the post-war period in 1951 but, unlike Glamorgan's, their success came under a professional captain. H. E. (Tom) Dollery had shared the captaincy with the amateur R. H. Maudsley in 1948 but had sole charge of the side from 1949 to 1955:

When it was first suggested that I should share the captaincy – with Ronnie Maudsley taking over the side in August – I felt rather badly about Eric Hollies who was senior to me in the side. So I told the committee I must talk it over with him. When I did, I found he couldn't have been more pleased. What's more, he went to the committee and said, 'If we are in the first three places at the end of Tom's spell, he should be allowed to go on as captain for the rest of the season.'

Well, we were in the first three at the end of July but the committee honoured their commitment to Maudsley. Nevertheless, I got the captaincy full-time in the next season. The committee were pretty good to me – they asked me if I wanted to keep the captain's dressing-room but when I said I would like everyone to change together they agreed. I think I had something of an advantage in learning about leadership when I was at Reading School but I did wonder how the other county skippers would treat me as the first full-time modern professional captain. In fact, they received me as one of their own. Nobody tried to come the high hat with me and, in any case, I felt the old barriers were beginning to come down.

*

Warwickshire's wicket-keeper, Dick Spooner, feels that a key ingredient in his team's success was his captain's understanding and successful use of Eric Hollies:

I loved keeping wicket to him. He wasn't what you expect from a leg-spinner. He was so accurate – he was almost like a stock bowler. And what a character! I remember when he was bowling and Dai Davies was standing as umpire – there would be endless cross-talk. Once, Eric became so excited that he got his false teeth jammed. Oh yes, there was always laughter about when Eric was performing but he was a wonderfully successful bowler for us and Tom Dollery did a splendid job in pacing and encouraging him.

One of those with whom Tom Dollery felt a special affinity was Stuart Surridge:

He was a tough competitor but he always gave the impression that he was one of the boys so far as the Surrey team were concerned. There is a bit of a tendency to dismiss his captaincy as one which, with four England bowlers – Bedser, Loader, Lock and Laker – in the side, was simply a matter of putting them on and taking them off in a reasonable order. Well, you can turn that argument right round because Surrey had to manage for so much of the time without those bowlers when they were playing for England, and Stuart Surridge's leadership at the start of Surrey's long Championship victory sequence was very clear to me in getting the best out of his side whether or not they were at full strength.

One of those who followed the absence of Surrey's Test players with close interest was Roy Swetman:

I was on the edge of the side because Arthur McIntyre was a marvellous wicket-keeper – particularly in his ability to take Alec Bedser standing up. As a result, I spent a good deal of time in the Surrey second eleven and, after I made my first-team début, I was very much aware of the playing strength of our reserves. Stuart

Surridge had come up through the second eleven route himself
and Arthur McIntyre did a great job with them after he became
county coach. I always had the impression that we had a lot of
second-eleven players like bees buzzing round the honey-pot
desperately keen to get into the Championship side.

One of the young hopefuls of this period was John Edrich:

My father had a small farm in Norfolk and I was originally
destined for agricultural college. But after one season playing for
Norfolk my cousin Bill [W. J. Edrich] and his father suggested
that I should try my hand with Surrey. So, in 1954, at the age of
seventeen, I arrived at the Oval and came under the strict code of
Andrew Sandham. As a young professional you were told what
to do and that was that. I was expected to turn out in most of the
club-and-ground games. If you were not playing, you would
have a net between nine and ten in the morning and then you
were expected to sit and watch the county side in action.

You didn't move unless a county member wanted someone to
bowl at them. Otherwise, Andrew Sandham would check that
you were there and he would question you at the end of the day.
'What did you think of so-and-so's field placing?' he would ask
you, or 'What did you notice about the way X paced his innings?'
The only real break we got was at lunchtime when we were given
a lunch voucher and we would all go off to the Horn's Tavern
near the ground and talk more cricket.

Alec Bedser, who has never been slow to criticize modern cricketers for anything less than a hundred per cent effort, is in no doubt
about Stuart Surridge's flair and contribution:

The great thing about Stuart was that he was literally one of the
boys and yet he was his own man. We had all played together for
the Young Players of Surrey as teenagers and his succession to the
captaincy was just like one of the family achieving something in
which we could all share. There was no awkward period of
establishing a relationship between the captain and his team as
could often be the case. And Stuart had this amazing self-

confidence. He wrote in his diary in 1952 – the year in which he took over the side: 'Surrey will win the Championship for the next five years.' Well, we did precisely that under his captaincy.

It's true that he had complete faith in our attack. This meant that he would often do the most unconventional things which rattled the opposition used to the familiar pattern of county cricket. A classic example was our match against Worcestershire in 1954 when we bowled them out for 25. We were 92 for 3 with Peter May and Ken Barrington then both at the height of their powers batting well on an improving wicket when suddenly, out of the blue, Stuart declared. Whereupon, we bowled Worcestershire out for 40 to win by an innings and 27 runs all in the one day.

On another occasion, I remember Stuart going all round the dressing-room and asking what we thought about a decision as to whether or not we should bat. We all agreed that the wicket was a beauty and we should. 'Right,' said Stuart, 'we'll put them in.' The fact was that he was really happier leading in the field as a bowler himself and shock decisions like this frequently put the other side off.

The other thing about him was that he was such a fearless fielder close in on the legside. I take some credit for getting him to agree that we should build up a team of specialist close catchers with himself, Ken Barrington, Tony Lock and Mickey Stewart instead of the old idea of resting the bowlers near to the bat. On one occasion, one of our reserves wasn't keen on the idea of having to field in close and Stuart simply took over the position himself.

Alec Bedser played a key part in the Surrey success story. Not only was he a tireless bowler for his county as well as for England but, as senior professional, he showed himself to be a shrewd judge of the game. Indeed, it was said that on the rare occasions when Surrey faced a long stand against them, the captain would occasionally depart from his accustomed close-in fielding position to the deep to ponder on wider cricketing matters affecting the county leaving Alec Bedser in charge. However, it was also said that it only took the fall of a wicket to bring the Surrey captain back into the middle in a rush saying, 'Right lads, we're in amongst them.'

Mickey Stewart, who, with Stewart Storey, served an apprenticeship as junior professional, saw his captain and the senior professional in the traditional light of new boys. As the England manager of the eighties, his recollections are of particular interest:

It wasn't just that we thought of Stuart Surridge as the boss but with Alec and Eric Bedser, Jim Laker and Tony Lock and so many long-serving professionals, we were certainly kept firmly in our place. The Surrey bowling squad was sometimes referred to as the Surrey moaners and I think Stuart Surridge did a great job in getting them all to pull together. So far as we were concerned as junior players it was mainly a matter of making sure they got their equipment in good time from one match to another. I remember on one occasion Stewart Storey and I actually had to get all the team cricket bags down the tube at the Oval because there was a taxi strike. He would load them on at one end and I'd be pulling them off at the other. That went quite well but you can imagine what panic stations it was both in getting them on and off the tube trains before the doors closed.

Stuart Surridge today, still deeply involved with cricket through his sports equipment business, plays down his own role both as captain and bowler and insists on giving the credit to his team for their long run of success:

You couldn't go far wrong with the talent I had at my disposal. It's true that our bowlers were temperamental artists in their own way. But when the chips were down, I knew I could rely not only on Alec Bedser, Jim Laker, Tony Lock and Peter Loader, who all competed like mad to get on to bowl, but also I could turn to stalwarts like Eric Bedser with his off-spin. He would have performed the double many times if he'd played for another county and he was an invaluable chap to have in reserve. And I think that Arthur McIntyre was often underestimated because he kept brilliantly to all our great bowlers. And I had some pretty fair batsmen to turn to – not least Peter May, who played as hard if not harder than any of my pros. I knew, too, that he would run a tight ship as captain and so it proved.

10

THE MAY AND ALLEN
TEST ERA

Just as Peter May established himself as the natural successor to Stuart Surridge for Surrey, so his emergence as England captain following Len Hutton seemed in the natural order of things. Similarly, his partnership with Gubby Allen, as his chairman of the Test selectors, was one which was to provide the Gentlemen with their final spell of authority. But this restoration of amateur leadership came at a time when Test cricket was undergoing major change.

With the increase of new Test-playing countries expecting their full share of home and away series, the intensity of international competition grew so that there were fewer breaks from the game. Peter May led England in a record forty-one matches in only seven years. With the growth, too, of increased media attention through radio and television, as well as an ever-growing press corps, came added pressures for the captain and his team-mates. Yet, despite these pressures which in large measure led to Peter May's early retirement from the game, his tenure as England captain was marked by what may now be seen to be a final flowering of amateur batsmanship.

In this process he was undoubtedly helped by a new generation of Test selectors when, in 1955, Gubby Allen became chairman and Brian Sellers and Wilf Wooller joined the long-serving solitary professional, Les Ames. Gubby Allen assesses the selectors' role and that of Peter May thus:

With Len's retirement and the end of the Test careers of Bill

Edrich and Reg Simpson we were looking for some new batting talent. Peter May maintained marvellous form despite the cares of captaincy and Colin Cowdrey gradually became an automatic choice – although for much of the time as a makeshift opener, since he really preferred to bat in the middle of the order. Trevor Bailey remained as the great all-rounder and utility man who frequently opened the batting as well as the bowling on tour. But when looking for others in the batting line-up, we did not consciously go after amateurs – it is just that, as Len told you, there was this wealth of amateur batsmen coming forward in what we now know were the last days of the Gentlemen.

I suppose the fourth Test at Old Trafford in 1956 really summed it up. Usually this is remembered as Jim Laker's match, but it is often overlooked that England at the end of the first day had over 300 on the board for the loss of three wickets, all scored by the amateur batsmen in the side: Peter Richardson, Colin Cowdrey, David Sheppard, Peter May and Trevor Bailey. That was a rate of scoring that we thought had gone out of the game. Then, at Edgbaston in the following year, May and Cowdrey showed the modern amateur could play with as much discipline as the most dedicated professional with their match-saving partnership of 411 against the West Indies. And we seemed to have similar success with our choice of amateurs during the May captaincy: Doug Insole had a highly successful tour of South Africa and we progressively brought into the side at home Mike Smith, Raman Subba Row and Ted Dexter.

Gubby Allen is entitled to take much of the credit together with his fellow selectors for the effective consolidation of the amateur batting line-up which served England so well in the late fifties, including the successful recall of David Sheppard to Test cricket in 1956. Moreover, the selectors showed an uncanny touch in their equally successful recall that year of some of England's senior professionals. In the final Test at the Oval, Denis Compton, who had recently had a series of knee operations and was mainly a passenger in the field, nevertheless scored 94 in the first innings and took part in an undefeated partnership with his captain in the second innings which ensured that England retained the Ashes. Earlier in the series, in the third Test at Headingley, England had been 17 for three when Cyril Washbrook came out to join his captain:

> I had just become a Test selector myself that year and, when we were considering the side for Leeds, Gubby said, 'Cyril, I think we want to talk about the possibility of bringing you into the side', and I said, 'Surely things can't be as desperate as that.' But Gubby just said, 'Well, you go and order the drinks for the rest of us', and to my amazement, when they came out to join me in the bar, I heard I was back in Test cricket. I know Peter May wasn't entirely happy at the choice and I had my own reservations. But you don't refuse to play for England. Well, we put on 187 and I got 98. Afterwards Peter May came up to me in the dressing-room and said, 'It was marvellous to see you coming out to join me when England were in trouble and I'm so glad that the selectors persuaded me.'

One of those selectors, Wilf Wooller, recalls the Washbrook appearance as one of his greatest cricketing experiences:

> He looked so cocky. He was almost strutting when he came out with his cap a bit on one side. Then he got a marvellous reception from the Headingley crowd – a great Yorkshire tribute to a great Lancashire hero. He took guard, looked round the field and then checked his guard again and just nodded to Archer who was waiting to bowl as if to say, 'Whenever you're ready.' You could see the Australians saying to themselves, 'We've got a great batsman out here against us who scored a lot of runs against Australia. There's another good one at the other end.' You could almost feel it. It was like a bromide – the game settled down.
>
> To be immodest, I think that Les Ames and I had a strong influence in persuading Gubby and the captain that this recall was a good idea. We were both still actively involved in playing the game and I think that this gave us the feeling that Cyril would have the capacity to treat this Test match as just another game.

The selectors, too, played a part in building up the formidable England attack during Peter May's era, particularly in the success-

ful partnerships of Lock and Laker and of Trueman and Statham.
But it was perhaps in this area of selection that Peter May played his
own distinctive role since, unlike the chosen batting line-up, the use
and direction of bowlers depended heavily on their captain.

Freddie Trueman is in no doubt about the role of his captain in
ensuring his Test recall:

> You have to remember that I had been out in the cold for a long
> time after my first tour of the West Indies in 1953–54. I wasn't
> picked for the next two MCC tours to Australia and South Africa
> and, when I came into the side for Australia in 1958–59, Freddie
> Brown was the manager. He obviously saw me as a potential
> trouble-maker and he said to me on the ship, 'One spot of bother
> from you and you're on the next boat home.' But I had played in
> all five Tests under Peter May's captaincy the previous year
> against the West Indies and once I got into the Test side against
> Australia, I willingly bowled more overs for him than any of the
> other England quick bowlers. Thereafter, unless I was unfit, I
> was a regular first choice along with Brian Statham to open the
> England attack.

Peter May puts his own thoughts on the matter very simply:

> I always wanted F.S.T. in my side. He was such a trier. And we
> did evolve a good relationship so that even today when we meet
> he still calls me 'Skipper'. In fact, when I was made chairman of
> the selectors, Fred came up to me and said, 'I know you'll find it
> difficult to get round seeing as much cricket as you'd like. If
> there's anyone you want me to look over on my cricket travels,
> you've only to say the word.' Now that's the generous side
> of Fiery Freddie, and he did a great job for me in the England
> side.

As Freddie Trueman implies, a major part of the England success
story during Peter May's captaincy came from the fast-bowling
combination of Brian Statham's nagging accuracy at one end and
his own explosive skills at the other. In conversation today, he
reveals more details of the tricks of the trade:

Brian Statham and I were complete opposites. He moved the ball into the right-hander and I moved it away from him. Even the greatest players find it more difficult to play the ball moving away and many times we would give a run away so that he could bowl at the left-hander and I could bowl at the right-hander.

The equally famous slow-bowling partnership of Jim Laker and Tony Lock (together with the continued all-round skills of Trevor Bailey) ensured that the England attack at this time was as well balanced as ever in its history. Jim Laker's assessment in 1985 was typically to the point:

You should never underestimate the part that Trevor Bailey played in our best Test match efforts. He was always such a great trier and it did not surprise me in the least when he tied the Test series against the West Indies in 1953–54 virtually singlehanded by bowling them out for a low score on a good batting wicket. So far as Tony Lock and I were concerned, people always talked to me about the Old Trafford Test match in 1956 when he got one of the wickets and I got the other nineteen. The fact was that Tony is a great competitor and I know it was agony for him to see all the success coming my way on that occasion. But if you look up the records you will find that he did a great job of containment and there may be a little bit of a parallel between Brian Statham helping Fred Trueman to get wickets at his end and Tony helping me. Perhaps if he had relaxed a bit he would have picked up a few wickets, but he was trying too hard to keep up with me. I do recall that Tony used to get really mad when we met yet another person who had been present at Old Trafford in 1956 who would remind him of his one wicket and me of my nineteen. I ought to add that we met many people like this – in fact, at my rough estimate, I think there must have been half a million people in the ground judging by all those who have claimed they were at Old Trafford on that day!

Freddie Trueman also sees the strength of the England bowling reserves as part of the reason for success during both the Hutton and the May captaincies:

What you have to remember is that even those of us who were regarded as well established were still competing for places because of the strength of our reserves. The really fast and quicker bowlers like Frank Tyson and Bob Appleyard had great success during their relatively short Test careers. As for the spinners, you could not ignore the claims of Johnny Wardle – particularly on hard wickets overseas. He was not a great spinner but he could bowl a consistent line and length and turn the ball the width of the bat which, as he often said, was often better in getting an edge than turning the ball too much and beating everything. Then, on the good batting tracks overseas, he could go over the wicket and bowl his Chinaman and googly with great effect.

Freddie Trueman is also appreciative of the part played by the two leading amateur batsmen in the England side during most of his Test career after the retirement of Len Hutton:

I never ceased to be amazed at Colin Cowdrey's ability to stroke the ball so effortlessly. You would see the cover fieldsmen saying to themselves, 'No problem there – I can gather that in all right', and the next thing you knew the ball was past them and into the boundary. Peter May, on the other hand, hit the ball pretty hard but he was so correct that he rarely gave a chance.

For a long period Peter May's captaincy followed the same successful pattern as his predecessor's and he equalled Len Hutton's record of five successful series before the disaster in Australia of 1958–59. Gubby Allen describes the significance of that ill-fated tour:

It was ironic that the England side which we chose to go to Australia that year was considered to be the strongest ever to leave England. In the event, a controversy over chuckers in the Australian side put a bit of a blight on the whole business and in some ways I see that series as an aberration in the general run of a long spell of general success for English Test cricket at the time.

So far as the throwing problem was concerned, Don Bradman

came over to England in 1960 as chairman of the Australian Cricket Board. He wouldn't budge an inch and neither would I. He said the Australians had no chuckers and I said that was rubbish. We agreed not to mention names. I had film of some of the worst offenders and of course we were far from blameless ourselves but Don and the other Australians wouldn't look at them. But deep in his heart he knew they had a problem and within a year or two of his return to Australia they'd cleared the chuckers out.

There were other facets of the 1958–59 tour which highlighted some of the social and economic changes affecting cricket at this time. Colin Cowdrey sums these up by comparing his experience of his first and second tours:

> I only played under Len Hutton in one series and when Peter May took over there was little apparent change in the sense that he played it just as professionally and perhaps even tougher than his predecessor.
> When I first went to Australia in 1954–55 I took all my Oxford colours: my Harlequin cap, my Vincent's tie and also my Free Foresters tie. I was specially fond of the Free Foresters tie – it seemed to bring me good luck. I was wearing it on the day I got my first Test century in Melbourne. So I suppose I provided the conventional appearance of the public-school, Oxford-educated amateur. I realized that some of the team members looked at me a bit sideways when I was sporting these colours but I didn't think much about it at the time.
> Certainly, I never even thought about any distinction between amateurs and professionals in Test cricket, but I was reminded of the old values when we were in Australia in 1958–59. Freddie Brown came as our manager and he was a great enthusiast who was happy to bowl at us in the nets and who retained enormous popularity from his time in Australia as captain. He came to me one day and said, 'Look, they're having the Oxford and Cambridge dinner at the Melbourne Club when we play the Test match there. Get your dinner jacket out and come along with me.' Well, I knew there was a long tradition of Australian

Oxbridge graduates getting together but I also recalled there had been a time when the amateurs got invited to the best clubs while the professionals were left out, and I suppose in effect that this was still the case. So I had a word with Peter May, who discouraged me from going because he said it did not help team spirit. I felt myself torn between the pull of the old and the new amateur. Anyway, I went to the dinner and had a thoroughly good time. But, from then on, I began to think deeply about the illogicality of differing status within an international side.

Another of those who had been on the same successive tours to Australia was Frank Tyson. He reflected a growing cynicism among the established England professionals with the increase in shamateurism:

There had been a steady increase in the amount of money paid to amateurs for out-of-pocket expenses which, in turn, developed into broken-time payments for loss of earnings. As far back as the 1950–51 tour of Australia, Reg Simpson and Trevor Bailey had held out for increased expenses saying that they could not afford to tour otherwise.

Then there was an obvious difference in view between the old- and new-style amateurs. I had a great regard for Freddie Brown as a captain and a player, but when he came as manager to Australia he got very agitated when I called Peter May by his Christian name. 'For heaven's sake, call him Skipper,' he said. But the fact was that I thought of Peter May as the first among equals. He was the first England captain of modern times to emerge having played under a professional captain. Moreover, in my time in the Test side you had some very dominant established professionals like Denis Compton and Godfrey Evans. So our manager in 1954–55, Geoffrey Howard, and assistant manager in 1958-59, Desmond Eagar, were seen essentially as administrators. I felt that, with the appointment of Freddie Brown as manager, there was an attempt to crack the whip and this at a time when the amateur status seemed likely to disappear.

*

Frank Tyson's assumption is almost certainly correct, for, as Wilf Wooller says:

I was with Gubby Allen during the whole seven-year period of his chairmanship of selectors. It was probably as successful a Test period as we have had at almost any time and we had a good balance of players. But there was undoubtedly a need to instil a bit of discipline in the England dressing-room. Denis Compton, Godfrey Evans and Bill Edrich were all delightful characters but they could be real blighters and laws unto themselves. This is where Gubby was so good. For example, Denis Compton had missed practice at Lord's during the series against Australia in 1956. There was another of the famous Compo excuses about missing a plane and so on but Gubby just said, 'If you're not there in time to practise before the start of the final Test, you won't play at the Oval.'

Aside from the question of discipline, however, there was an element of mounting discontent within the professional ranks, which had come to a head in the challenge to authority when invitations were extended for the 1958–59 tour of Australia to two of the best spin bowlers available for selection: J. H. Wardle and J. C. Laker. Johnny Wardle had been the most successful bowler in the MCC's previous tour to South Africa in 1956–57, with his varied mixture of left-arm wrist and orthodox spin. He had let it be known that he was disinclined to tour again but changed his mind and accepted the selectors' invitation. Shortly thereafter he wrote a series of articles critical of his county captain, and the invitation to tour was withdrawn under the MCC's blanket sanction of 'bringing the game into disrepute'.

Jim Laker had similarly indicated his reluctance to tour but also accepted the invitation. In 1985, he described the background to his reservations:

I knew that the Australians felt they had been done on pitches to suit Tony Lock and myself in 1956 and I think they reckoned they could take me apart Down Under. Although I say it myself, I bowled very well in Australia and, in any case, it wasn't that aspect that really worried me. I felt it was time to end the unfair financial disadvantage which was beginning to favour the amateurs. I went to see Gubby Allen about this (of which more anon) but, most of all, I was getting fed up with shamateurism.

I had no complaints about the skipper, Peter May. He had been fixed up by Lloyd's and, similarly, Colin Cowdrey was taken care of by his father-in-law. But Trevor Bailey had been working a flanker for years as the supposed secretary of Essex. Similarly, Raman Subba Row had just left Surrey to go to Northampton-shire as captain and assistant secretary. Finally, I disapproved of the selection of Ted Dexter, who was called upon as a late reinforcement. I didn't think then and I don't now that he was ready for a full Test career at that stage. Of course he became a great player and he was honest about getting every penny he could out of the game. But at that stage I didn't think he was really up to Test match cricket. Of course, we became good friends later and no one appreciated his splendid batting for England – once he had become established – more than I did. But, at that time, he was a sort of final straw in what I thought was becoming an intolerable situation over shamateurism and the unfair money differential available for amateurs through expenses compared to the low payment for professionals.

Ted Dexter's view on his late selection for the tour of Australia does not differ substantially from that of Jim Laker's – except in one important respect:

I think Jim was right about the doubts over my selection at that particular stage. First of all, I was whistled out in the middle of a tour which was already in trouble. I had an appalling trip because of winter flying problems which took over five days and I had to go straight into a match. On top of that, I was in poor batting form and there was therefore very little chance of settling down.

However, where I think Jim was wrong is to ignore the inevitable benefit which you get from a tour of this kind if, as in my case, you are supposed to have been picked out because of your potential. There were three people who all, in their various ways, made it possible for me to develop as a Test player.

The first was Cyril Coote. He was our groundsman while I was up at Cambridge but he liked to do a little private coaching when he spotted someone he thought was worthwhile. He was a great judge of the game and he came to me one day and said, 'What you are doing is fine but if you want to be a great player you must learn to play off the back foot.' He came out to the nets and threw the ball so that I learnt to hit the ball as hard off the back foot as off the front. That made me into a potential England player.

Second, Gubby Allen as a selector was a tremendous encouragement. He took the view that I was the right sort of material. Early in my career, he came down to Worthing and I scored 20 or so and got out. I said, 'I didn't cover myself with glory', and he said, 'I didn't come to see how many you made. I wanted to see if you were still going about it the right way.' What he was checking was that I was playing off both front foot and back and, in effect, I felt he had given me a clean bill of health and I was selected for my first Test match soon afterwards. He didn't leave it there, he was genuinely interested if you had a lean patch and he would come and bowl at you in the net. I remember when I pulled a muscle bowling, he arranged to take photographs to see what I was doing. He was the kind of guide and mentor I was lucky to have at that stage in my career.

Third, when I was having a difficult time in Australia, it was a good old professional, John Mortimore, who put me right. Freddie Brown, Peter May and Trevor Bailey had all tried to help but nothing seemed to click. I simply could not get going with the bat. One day, towards the end of the tour, I was batting in the nets when John Mortimore was bowling and he just said, 'Turn your bat in – you're opening the face too much.' Suddenly the ball really began leaving the bat and I got my first Test hundred in New Zealand soon afterwards.

That's where – despite what Jim Laker said – there was value in picking an inexperienced player for a tour of Australia. Although I think he was right in the sense that, if you were blooding a youngster, you should give him a chance to play throughout the whole tour rather than bringing him in as an emergency replacement. On the other hand, as it happened, I did get a lot of experience from that tour and, above all, I got the feel of what Test captaincy was about by watching Peter May.

Peter May's own recollections of the tour present a somewhat different interpretation to what was seen at the time as a major setback after a long run of success for England under his captaincy:

I don't think we realized that Jim Laker was so exercised over the question of shamateurism: what was of more concern was how he would fare as a bowler in Australia. He proved to be our most successful performer.

What really bedevilled the tour was the problem of chuckers and that is why, unlike my critics, I regard this as one of my most successful tours. The problem was that we had our own suspect bowlers – particularly my Surrey team-mates Tony Lock and Peter Loader – and even though we thought they were minor offenders compared to people like Meckiff and Rorke, Freddie Brown and I were in a difficult position in lodging formal complaints which could have been written off as the response of the 'whinging pom' to our loss of the series. But it did lead the way to removing the chuckers from the game and that is why I regard this as a successful tour although, when we came back from Australia, I didn't realize this would be my last full series as captain of England.

Peter May's reference to his last full series for England reminds us of the abdominal operation which brought his Test career to a premature close. Wilf Wooller is convinced that there was another factor:

As selectors, we had to recognize that Peter May did not like the press and PR side of the job. He therefore left this to Gubby Allen when captaining the Test side at home and that worked reasonably well. On tour, it is much more difficult. All the press want to have access to the captain.

The problem was that Peter May had really had such a remarkably untroubled and successful career. He had come straight into

Test cricket with a century against South Africa and he had been part of a virtually non-stop success story ever since.

When you are up against it in playing terms on tour the press start scratching around for a scapegoat. On this particular occasion, they compounded the pressure on Peter May by hounding him over his private life. He was engaged to Virginia Gilligan (Harold's daughter and Arthur's niece) and it was perfectly natural that she should be in Australia as the Gilligan family were regular supporters of the England touring side out there. What Peter found totally objectionable – and I don't blame him – was people on the lookout for a story who rang him up at three in the morning from London to ask whether it was true that he had been secretly married. All this, and the inevitable blame heaped on him for defeats in Australia, proved hard to take. He had been a solid and sensible captain who exerted a natural authority. What is more, he had had the great ability to lay aside the cares of captaincy when he went out to bat so that he was a most successful performer. But I think that the newspaper pressure towards the end of his career really got to him and made him disillusioned.

Just as Peter May had been seen as the natural successor to Len Hutton, so it now seemed that May's own successor was clearly established in the person of his regular vice-captain, Colin Cowdrey. Yet, with Peter May's retirement from Test cricket in 1961, Colin Cowdrey was to find that the job of stop-gap Test captain in earlier years had sown the seeds of doubt about his suitability for holding the job on a permanent basis. These doubts were, in many ways, inherent in the work of a captain 'holding the fort' for odd matches and compounded by a degree of ill fortune and difference in view between the old and the new guard of English amateur cricketers which was to deny him long-term opportunities in Test captaincy and also the appointment – which he sought above all others – to captain England in Australia.

Yet when Colin Cowdrey took over the England captaincy from Peter May for the last two Tests against India in England in 1959 he was only 26 years old, and he led his side to further victories which completed a five-nil clean sweep in the series. But his appointment had been clearly intended as temporary and he was happy to revert to the role of vice-captain when Peter May led the touring party to the West Indies in 1959–60. When illness forced the captain to return to England after the third Test, Cowdrey once more found himself in charge of the side for the crucial last two games. England were leading one-nil in the series but faced a ferocious challenge from the fast bowling of Wes Hall and a suspect chucker in Charlie Griffiths. As a makeshift opening batsman on the tour, Cowdrey had achieved great personal success by revising his batting technique and by protecting himself with massive foam rubber padding. But the challenge to his leadership was not confined to the opposition:

One of the most difficult things about the tour was the clash of generations – between, if you like, the new-style amateurs like Peter and myself on the one hand and our manager Walter Robins on the other. He made his prejudices clear from the start of the tour: pressing us as a former leg-spinner himself to use that kind of bowling as a key element in our attack and, above all, arguing that we must always play to win even if it meant the risk of losing. All this came to a head in the final Test at Port of Spain, Trinidad. We had been battered black and blue by the West Indies attack; we'd lost a major batsman in Peter May's withdrawal and, because of injuries, we had to call up Jim Parks who was coaching in the West Indies to play in the Test match side. So when we found ourselves fighting a rearguard action to save the match in our second innings, I was absolutely delighted with Jim Parks and Mike Smith and their long if slow partnership which ensured that we drew the match and won the series. To my amazement, I found that Walter Robins was furious about my unwillingness to make a sporting declaration. On the final day, he made a sort of flamboyant entry on to the ground just before the lunch interval and proceeded to give me a personal rocket in front of the whole team in the dressing-room. We never saw eye to eye from that moment on and later, when Walter Robins became chairman of the selectors (ironically, in part because of his success in managing the winning team in the West Indies), I knew that my appointment as England captain was far from certain.

*

In recalling these differences between the manager and the stop-gap captain of the England side, it is hard to ignore the genuine differences which divided them. For Walter Robins, Test cricket had deteriorated from a sporting encounter to a win-at-all-costs game. He was one of those who felt that the last sporting gesture by an England captain had been Percy Chapman's refusal to play for a draw in the Lord's Test in the 1930 series against Australia. He had also been on the receiving end of a drunken selector's disapproval when he got out hitting in the same match. Now he was urging upon English captains an approach which they and the rest of their side felt was no longer possible in the high-pressure world of international competition.

For Colin Cowdrey, the problem was compounded not only by the temporary nature of his captaincy and by the feeling that he was on trial match by match; he was also, as a batsman, facing what many now see as the start of the intimidatory bowling which bedevils the game today. As he put it, 'I did not feel I had been given charge of the side only to throw away a series which we had sweated blood to win.'

On behalf of Robins, it may be argued that Gary Sobers was able to show that a sporting declaration was still possible in Test match cricket when, only a few years later, he gave an England team under Colin Cowdrey the chance to come from behind and win the 1967–68 series in the West Indies. However, apart from receiving a famous telegram from the Duke of Norfolk congratulating him on his sportsmanship and giving Test cricket a new lease of life, Gary Sobers was to face massive criticism in the West Indies which persists to the present day. Moreover, it brought to an end what many shrewd judges like the president of the West Indian Cricket Board of Control, Allan Rae, today calls 'the danger of falling into the trap of living up to our old reputation as carnival cricketers'.

All this lay in the future, however, and Colin Cowdrey took charge of the England side for the whole of the 1960 home series against South Africa, when Peter May's illness kept him out of Test cricket. He led his team to a three-nil victory in the series and was re-appointed captain against Australia in the first two Tests of 1961. However, when Peter May returned to lead the side for the last

three Tests in the series, it seemed that the stop-gap nature of his
captaincy had been reaffirmed.

After England lost the fourth Test (and with it the series) at Old
Trafford in chasing a victory which had only been made conceiv-
able by a swashbuckling innings from Ted Dexter, they were
widely criticized although, again, there was a certain irony in the
fact that this attacking approach was one which the selectors had
encouraged. Peter May's opposing captain, Richie Benaud, recalls
not only that Test match but also the general state of amateurism in
the early sixties:

> In some ways, I think that Old Trafford Test match was one of
> the last occasions on which you could see the effect of amateur
> leadership on both sides. Peter May was a very tough captain but
> he was responding to the selectors' encouragement to play attack-
> ing cricket.
>
> On our side, I suppose I was probably the last of the amateur-
> style captains from Australia. I must emphasize that I didn't like
> the distinctions when I came into the game – there was a sort of
> myth about the amateur and the need to call him mister and so on
> but, so far as I was concerned, anyone who received payment of
> any kind was effectively a professional. In my time, many of the
> English amateurs were paid through a job with their county or in
> some under-the-counter arrangement. So far as I was concerned,
> once the Australian team was on tour we were certainly profes-
> sionals because we got expenses.
>
> However, this thing about the amateur was essentially a matter
> of leadership. Just as Peter May was willing to go for the win at
> Old Trafford in 1961, I decided we had to bowl England out and
> not play for the draw. I'm not sure that my team understood
> when I told them this but they knew that I was always willing to
> take full responsibility for losing as well as winning. It came off
> for me but I can't help thinking that, if we had had professionals
> in charge on each side, or if we were thinking of the situation
> today, there would inevitably have been a tendency for the
> captains to say to themselves, 'I think I'd better play safe.'
>
> Mind you, when it came to the question of Australian and
> English amateurs, it's important to understand the differences in
> the approach of our two countries. I think in Australia we have

always thought in more down-to-earth terms about cricket. In England there was and still is an image of cricket with tea and cucumber sandwiches taken in a nice pavilion with the setting sun. It doesn't work that way in Australia where we are likely to be playing on matting on grounds with rough outfields surrounded by dead gum trees with a rough hut as the pavilion in many country areas.

The other big difference is in the numbers game. When I led the Australian team out on to the field I was aware that it represented the best eleven which our selectors could put together from a choice of 300,000 to 400,000 cricketers. I would have had no major part in choosing that team but I was very much aware of the wider pool of talent from which we could draw compared to the English selectors. They were looking at the playing staffs of the seventeen counties and this meant, at the most, they were considering eleven cricketers from a pool of perhaps a hundred at the most. Given this restriction, I thought that the partnership of Gubby Allen as chairman of the selectors with Peter May as Test captain was one which produced excellent results.

Gubby Allen sums up his partnership with Peter May as follows:

It is a remarkable thing that Peter and I started together when I became chairman of the selectors and he became captain, and we went on over seven seasons before we both gave up our jobs. I can honestly say that we had a marvellous relationship. I couldn't be present on all five days of the Test matches at home but I was there for at least three days. In every interval, whether we were batting or bowling, I used to pop into the dressing-room and we'd talk over the situation together. I would say, 'What about that?' or Peter would say, 'What do you think about this?' We hardly ever disagreed and his only black day was at Old Trafford in 1961.

By then, I think he was feeling the media pressure and he had quite a difficult time with illness. Still, I was very sorry to see him leave the Test scene at the age of thirty-one, but I was so glad that he was able to go on in county cricket for a couple of years afterwards.

11

AMATEUR AND
PROFESSIONAL CAPTAINS

The start of the May Test era in the mid-fifties was also a time of major changes in county captaincy with a greater mix of professional and amateur captains. Yet, in most of the successful counties, the amateurs still led the way.

Surrey, as the long-standing Champions from 1952 to 1958, experienced a relatively smooth transition from Surridge's captaincy to that of May, although Peter May recalls that the job was not without its immediate challenges:

> When I took over the county side in 1957, I was already established as the England captain. But in one of my first matches I gave one of my two England spin bowlers a short spell and, when I saw the wicket wasn't doing much, I said, 'All right, I think we'll bring you on again later at the other end', and he said, 'That's the worst bloody bit of captaincy I've ever heard.' So I walked him across the field and said, 'Look, for good or ill, I've been entrusted with the captaincy of this side. I'll always listen to your suggestions but if you ever question my captaincy on the field I'll do my damnedest to see you don't get picked again.' After that we got on famously.

In telling this story almost three decades later Peter May, who retains the boyish diffidence which hides the man of steel beneath, also showed his sense of humour by quoting the spin bowler's dialogue in a Yorkshire accent. Jim Laker, for he it was, confirmed the basis of this first clash by commenting simply, 'I thought I'd see what he was made of.'

Peter May is also quick to relate his own and Surrey's success to the support which he received in two important directions:

> I was lucky with both my predecessor and my senior pro. Stuart Surridge eased my way into the captaincy in the most helpful way. Having taken Surrey to the Championship, he wasn't an easy man to follow. But he was the greatest help and it gave him as much pleasure as anyone else in the side when we retained the Championship in the first two years of my captaincy. Alec Bedser, our senior pro, played a great part in this. I insisted that he be made official vice-captain as a form of recognition and I like to think that this helped him on his way both as a future Test selector and a Surrey committee man. Both he and Stuart have remained life-long friends and godfathers to my children.

Alec Bedser gives his own impression of the May/Bedser amateur/professional partnership:

> He was a different style of captain to Stuart Surridge but he was shrewd and tough and far-sighted. Obviously, I am biased but I thought that his insistence on having me as his vice-captain was typical of his thoughtfulness both towards me and the team. We'd never had an officially appointed professional captain or vice-captain before and I was very proud to take on the job. But, more important, Peter had realized that he couldn't follow in Stuart Surridge's shoes by being available throughout the season for the county and, when he was away on Test duties, he wanted someone in charge with whom he saw eye to eye so that there was the minimum disturbance when we took over from each other.

Surrey's main rivals and successors as county Champions in 1959 were their old enemy Yorkshire. After Norman Yardley's easy-going captaincy, his successor in 1956, Billy Sutcliffe, had difficulty in ending the internal dressing-room dissension which was high-lighted when as good a player as Willie Watson left the county for

Leicestershire at the end of the 1957 season. Sutcliffe had a difficult job in following a famous father (particularly as he had been 'one of the boys' in his early Yorkshire career), yet Peter May thought that he was under-estimated both as a captain and as a player.

Brian Sellers played a leading part as Yorkshire's newly appointed chairman in ensuring that Ronnie Burnet took over the captaincy in 1958. Burnet, who had been captain of the second eleven, was thirty-nine when he took charge of the senior side and he had obvious limitations in making his first-class début. His difficulties in his first season were compounded by the public row with Johnny Wardle which led to the left-arm spinner's departure from both Yorkshire and England cricket at the end of the 1958 season. Yet, as Ronnie Burnet recalled at the Scarborough Festival in 1984, there were advantages in being a former captain of the Yorkshire second eleven:

> Obviously, I had some difficulty with those who were in a negative sense the old pros and trouble-makers. But I had known most of the up-and-coming players in the Yorkshire side when they were colts under my captaincy and they were used to me keeping them in order. Gradually, I felt that the old hands who were opposed to me like Brian Close and Ray Illingworth were people I could turn to as they both had excellent cricket brains and could be immensely helpful. As for Freddie Trueman, once we discovered we could get along together, he was still as great a trier as ever.

Freddie Trueman sees the Burnet influence as a classic example of Yorkshire's need for impartiality at the top:

> I've always said that I never objected to an amateur in any side during my playing career so long as they were good enough in playing terms. Ronnie Burnet was rather a special case because we needed someone at that stage who was tough enough to sort out the trouble-makers and get us back on course. He achieved that and took us to the Championship in his second year and I was glad to give him all the support I could.

*

Brian Close describes how the captaincy and the direction of Yorkshire's cricket affairs evolved after Ronnie Burnet's spell in charge:

We were really back to the one-man band of Brian Sellers running the show from the committee room. He liked to have his way and so did I when I got the Yorkshire captaincy in 1963 (my wife says the trouble was we were too much alike and I'm not sure that either of us would have accepted that as a compliment). But before my time came, Brian Sellers and the committee had put Vic Wilson in as the first Yorkshire professional captain this century. His form had been rather inconsistent and he was very much under the Sellers thumb.

Ray Illingworth concurs with this view:

About this time, Brian Sellers had rather a fixation about statistics. I would see Vic Wilson on his way into the committee meeting with the team's latest averages and I told him it was ridiculous to go by results on paper – it should be up to the captain to say how people were performing based on his understanding of what had been happening both on and off the field. I know that Bill Bowes always said I was making the bullets that Brian Close, as senior professional, was firing at Brian Sellers. In the event, it didn't seem to do him much harm when he succeeded to the captaincy, but there were the first rumbles of discontent which would lead to both Brian and I leaving the county. Still, you must give Vic Wilson his due. It was through him that we made the breakthrough in getting Yorkshire's acceptance of a professional captain and he led us to two Championship victories in 1960 and 1962 and we were a bit unlucky that we didn't make it three in a row.

When Hampshire won the Championship in 1961, the legend was created that they had done so despite their activities off the field. Their captain, Colin Ingleby-Mackenzie, had fostered this myth in a famous interview with a BBC reporter who asked him what was his personal recipe for the team's success, only to receive the reply, 'Oh, I always insist on the boys being in bed by dawn.'

Trevor Bailey has always said that he could not imagine Colin Ingleby-Mackenzie playing as a professional in a million years but that the rest of his side were by no means imbued with the same cavalier spirit. Indeed, he argues that it was the blend of adventurous amateur captaincy with dedicated professionalism which gave Hampshire their first Championship victory. Early in 1987, Colin Ingleby-Mackenzie, who retains the debonair spirit and sense of humour which make him such a popular figure in the cricketing world, summed up his relationship with his professionals as follows:

I would not quarrel with Trevor Bailey's assessment. In people like Derek Shackleton, Butch White, Vic Cannings, Dennis Baldry and Jimmy Gray we had fairly tight professional bowlers. Certainly, in the case of 'Shack' I had the perfect professional foil for a captain. Although he was the bowling star of our side, he made absolutely no demands. He didn't know if it was Wednesday or Friday – he simply knew what he had to do. With that economical action of his he would come on and bowl for as long as I needed him. He would bowl into the wind and he would run uphill or downhill as needed. He didn't mind. He just got on with it with great success. On the other hand, Butch White was aggressive and a potential matchwinner but like many quick men he could be temperamental and you had to jolly him along.

Of our batsmen, Harry Horton and Roy Marshall were both tough guys and I had my difficulties with Roy. The only lighter approach came from spinners like Peter Sainsbury and Mervyn Burden and, above all, my first senior professional, our wicket-keeper Leo Harrison. He was superb. He was the professional dressed in amateur clothes. I took him with me everywhere we went by car and, when we were in a stately home, he would appear in his dinner-jacket and play poker with the best of them. He had all the social graces and we had a lot of fun together.

With this background, Colin Ingleby-Mackenzie describes how he was groomed for the captaincy of the side and how he had to overcome certain difficulties before winning over all his professionals to his approach:

It was Desmond Eagar who made it possible for me to take over the side at the age of twenty-four – the youngest member of the team. I shall never forget my first appearance for Hampshire against Sussex at Bournemouth in 1951. It was clear that, when he invited me, Desmond Eagar wanted to see how I might develop as his potential successor. When I went in to bat, Oakman was bowling. He is a very nice person who later became a great friend. The match was rain-affected and we were unlikely to get a result and, in any event, he obviously decided to give a new boy one off the mark. So he bowled me a juicy half-volley which I nervously pushed to silly mid-on. It was the kind of delivery which – if bowled to me at Eton where I had been only a few weeks before – I would have expected to hit not only out of Agar's Plough but into Slough. 'Oakey' could not understand this – but he kindly gave me another gift. When I did nothing with that, he told me later, 'I'm not going on with this rubbish' and he bowled me one on leg-and-middle which hit the top of the off-stump.

It was hardly the most auspicious start for the new Hampshire amateur hopeful. But Desmond Eagar talked and cajoled the professionals into accepting me only a few years later. I think his willingness to do this was helped by the fact that we became great friends. I suppose that if he had decided that I was just an Etonian upstart, he would never have felt able to organize things as he did. In the event, we became joint captains in 1957 which was not a good arrangement. He led the team with great personal enthusiasm. I was perhaps rather more laid back – relying on the support of my professionals.

But I suppose that my natural gambling instinct was evident as soon as I had sole charge of the side, and we should have won the Championship in 1958. We played Yorkshire very early in the season and rain reduced the match to one day. We made 240-odd and I set them the target of getting the runs in 110 minutes. Freddie Trueman went mad that day and hit Shackleton all over the park in a way which I have never seen before or since and they got the runs. Some of the old professionals who were writing on the game, like Bill Bowes, were highly critical of this tomfoolery and implied that I might be God's gift to gambling but I was wrong for cricket. But I felt we'd had a marvellous match and I decided to keep up the business of setting the other side a target and encouraging them to do likewise. We lost a couple of matches and won one when Roy Marshall and I each got a hundred and we made runs against the clock to beat Kent at Canterbury. It was on this occasion that the so-called famous interview took place. I suppose I have been asked about it at all 2846 cricket dinners that I have attended ever since but it was really not the premeditated gag that is often suggested. The odd thing about it was that the reporter who interviewed me was an Irishman who obviously knew very little about cricket, and when he asked me about my recipe for the team's success I gave him an off-the-cuff reply which just came out. Over the years, the reply has been quoted and misquoted but I think what I actually said was that I insisted on the team being in bed by breakfast. But the background to the remark was simple. I was in good form, we had just won an important game and I was elated.

As it happened, we had a pep talk with the whole team afterwards when some of the professionals suggested that this approach of sporting declarations had got us so far but we ought to get down to serious cricket if we wanted to win the Championship. I argued that, if we did that, we would have no chance. I even said that if we didn't go on enjoying ourselves by staying up late and going to nightclubs then we'd lose our way. I argued that we would naturally try like mad out on the field but we should still enjoy ourselves off it. That way we could maintain team spirit and enthusiasm and, as it turned out, we were only ruled out of the Championship during the last three matches of that season.

In 1961, my father died at the beginning of the year and I felt I had to do something to make my mark. Perhaps I had toughened up a little. As it turned out, everything went right for us. We won nineteen matches out of thirty-two and lost only five, which was ridiculous with the side we had. The whole process really got under way when we played Gloucestershire at Portsmouth early in the season. I was convinced that I had to open the game up because we lost time due to rain. Gloucestershire made about 240 and we only had a day and a half left. Jimmy Gray and Roy Marshall put on about 160 for the first wicket and were still out there when I declared. It was all a bit embarrassing because they refused to come off but eventually I got them off the field and, when they came in, Roy Marshall threw his bat at me. Fortunately, there was a happy ending. The Gloucestershire captain, John Mortimore, was a good chap and he gave us a very fair declaration. Butch White went in and scored forty in a couple of overs and we won the match and this set us off on a high.

We really were not natural champions. But other sides entered into the spirit of our willingness to declare. Chaps like Reg Simpson and Wilf Wooller were prepared to keep the game going on an attacking basis. They would continue their run chase all the way down the batting order. They would not give the match away but they gave us a chance for a decision when a draw might have been easy. This came down to a certain mutual respect among the amateur captains but I think it was also a matter of seeing Hampshire as the under-dogs who might deserve to have their day. They did not mind losing to us as they would to Yorkshire or Surrey.

It was not always plain sailing. I've indicated that I had my difficulties with Roy Marshall. He had a good cricket brain which is why I later made him senior professional. I've already mentioned the bat-throwing incident but we had another little set-to at Canterbury when I wanted him to bowl and he threw the ball back at me. I decided the time had come to exercise discipline and I dropped him for the following match. On my way back to Canterbury the secretary said, 'You do realize that you've ruined Jimmy Gray's benefit match at Portsmouth, don't you?' Well, of course, I hadn't realized. I had to go round to Roy Marshall's house at two in the morning and get Shirley Marshall out of bed and say, 'Tell your delightful husband that I'll be talking to him in the morning but he will be playing in Jimmy Gray's benefit match.' That was the sort of thing you had to do to keep the side pulling together.

   Colin Ingleby-Mackenzie also pays tribute to the support which
he received from the Hampshire committee:

> You have to remember that the county's fortunes had been
> rebuilt by Desmond Eagar as secretary/captain, and both he and I
> received great support from Harry Altham as our president. He
> was not only a great cricket historian and cricket coach at Win-
> chester but he was the kind of person who took a friendly and
> keen interest in me. Then, we had Charles Knott who had played
> as an amateur spin bowler for the county for years although his
> approach was more that of the amateur by bank balance because
> he had essentially a professional approach. They both kept an eye
> on me and, as long as I did not go over the top, I was given
> complete discretion in getting on with running the side. I was
> certainly fortunate in having this kind of support which allowed
> me to become, as we now know, the last amateur captain to lead a
> county to the first-class Championship.

   The almost total commitment of Surrey, Yorkshire and Hampshire to amateur leadership at this time (for Hampshire the Eagar
and Ingleby-Mackenzie reign extended for twenty years) was
shared by half the remaining counties: Derbyshire, Essex, Glamorgan, Kent, Middlesex, Nottinghamshire and Sussex.
   Guy Willatt's successor as captain of Derbyshire from 1955 to
1962 was D. B. Carr. Donald Carr brought a style and vigour to the
traditionally stolid Derbyshire batting and a humour and love of the
game which would serve him well when he later became a leading
administrator with MCC and the Test and County Cricket Board.
   Essex, too, had their own long-serving captain and administrator
in the person of D. J. Insole. Doug Insole, who led the side through
the whole of the fifties, was a highly effective batsman who became
a Test selector and chairman of the Test and County Cricket Board.
As a grammar-school boy who had shown his leadership potential
at Cambridge, Insole was seen as one of the new generation of
businessmen amateurs. In his autobiography published in 1960,
Cricket in the Middle, he made a strong case for retaining the amateur
in first-class cricket, although, talking in the England dressing-
room at Sydney in 1983 where he was managing the England side,

he made it clear that he had been opposed to the old distinctions within the Essex dressing-room:

One of the greatest compliments paid to me was when Roy Ralph, who had been a useful medium-pace bowler for us as an amateur, came to me in 1958 and said, 'Would you mind if I turned professional?' 'Of course not,' I replied, and he said, 'There's no difference playing as an amateur or a professional in this team. I may as well earn the money.'

Where I think the amateur brought his particular contribution to bear was in the captaincy. In my time in the job with Essex, the captain had total responsibility for paying the players, sorting out who travelled with whom and so on. I was particularly fortunate that we had a small committee which included several of those who had played for the county.

It wasn't all that easy to maintain my amateur status. I worked for Wimpeys but they paid me on a part-time basis. It was a very pleasant life but it did involve a lack of financial security.

Trevor Bailey recalls the Insole captaincy thus:

Doug was a very tough and determined leader. I remember once this led to a splendid clash of wills in a match between the Champion County and the Rest when he first asked and then ordered Robin Marlar to go in as nightwatchman. Robin was clearly very cross about this and when he went in he hit the first ball he received for six and was stumped off the second by a mile. When he got back to the pavilion he just said, 'As I was saying, I'm not a nightwatchman.' But Doug usually had his way – certainly in county cricket – and, so far as I was concerned, he was good at getting the best out of me because he knew me inside out from Cambridge days onwards.

When Doug Insole gave up the Essex captaincy in 1961, Trevor Bailey succeeded him while continuing to serve in the role of county secretary (as he had been doing since 1954). He describes some of the features of Essex cricket at that time:

We were always a very happy side. Whatever the merits of the various individuals, I believe that one of the factors in this was that, bringing the story virtually up to date, there have been only five Essex captains in fifty years. This gives you an opportunity to build good relations and a certain stability into the team, but we were up against it in financial terms when I became captain. Having been assistant secretary when I first came to the county, it is perhaps fair to say that I was relatively free to get on with my cricket when there was plenty of money about. But by the early sixties we were struggling. Our nets were twenty miles away from the county ground, out in the middle of nowhere, so we had very little opportunity for practice. At the start of the season we would play matches against London University followed by Cambridge University. The trick was to get in the middle and bat for say thirty or so runs and this would be worth ten nets. Mind you, once the season got under way we played so much that we really didn't need that much practice, and I agree with Harold Larwood's comments about the absurdity of too much practice before matches, particularly at Test level. I would only bowl one or two overs at the most before the start of a game but as I bowled over a thousand overs in the season and had to bat a lot this was hardly surprising.

Glamorgan's amateur captaincy was still in the tough and determined hands of Wilf Wooller (he would retain the job until 1960). He had been part-time secretary as well as captain of the county for many years and there was a major row when he insisted, towards the end of his playing career, on becoming full-time secretary of the club. Wooller was successful in his battle with the committee, which was replaced at the next Annual General Meeting, and it became clear that he was increasingly concerned with preparing the way for his successor. Tony Lewis recalls:

Almost as soon as I came into the side, he made it clear that he was grooming me for the captaincy. He made me sit with him at the committee table away from the rest of the team, just saying, 'You might as well get used to it – it's part of the job', although he knew I'd much rather be with the boys. And he'd test me in other ways by hurling the odd marble clock at me in our hotel after dinner to see if I could take a heavyweight rugger pass. When I managed to get it straight back to him he was as pleased as if I'd scored the winning hit or a try against England at Cardiff.

Wilf Wooller's other method of testing cricketers, particularly those in the opposition who were new to the game, was to gauge their response to verbal abuse. Don Kenyon recalls how the Glamorgan captain tested the mettle of the young amateur Peter Richardson and what advice he, as an old professional, gave to meet the situation:

I think it was the first time that Peter had played against Glamorgan and Wilf Wooller stationed himself very close in at forward short-leg and began to give him his famous tongue-lashing. After an over or two, Peter came down the wicket to me and said, 'What do I do with this chap? He's talking non-stop and cursing me up hill and down dale and suggesting that I'm lacking in many things as well as my batting.' So I, knowing Wilf, just said, 'There's only one way and that's to give it straight back to him. If he curses you, you curse straight back at him and make it worse. On top of that, you might apologize to him in advance by saying that your hands get rather sweaty when you're batting and it's quite possible that you may lose control of the bat and if it should come flying out and hit him in a vulnerable spot you know he'll understand.'

Wilf Wooller, of whom Ray Illingworth said, 'He was a hard man on the field but one of the first to buy you a drink when you got into the pavilion', has his own amused recollections of several of his personality clashes, most notably those which involved Reg Simpson and Robin Marlar. Both of them are tactfully vague as to the origins of the keen personal rivalry which developed with the Glamorgan captain, but Wilf Wooller is happy to recall the details:

The Simpson/Wooller saga started in a curious way. In 1951, the Trent Bridge wicket was very hard and glassy. You couldn't make a mark on it if you slipped. For most of my time, they had a very good batting line-up with chaps like Walter Keeton, Charlie Harris, Joe Hardstaff and Reg himself, and they reckoned they could normally get the runs in any reasonable declaration.

On the occasion when Reg and I fell out, we batted solidly but slowly to get about 220 by the tea interval. I suppose, by comparison, they might have got 300. Reg suddenly did his nut. He put himself on at the pavilion end and announced, 'I'm going to bowl underhand.' As sometimes happens with rubbish bowling we almost made a mess of it. I nearly got out and Willy Jones was very upset and lost his wicket. We finished up with about 280 by the close.

On Monday, we batted till lunchtime as I had decided to teach the blighters a lesson! When they batted, we had no limitation in the number of legside fielders in those days and I could bowl in-duckers. So I had short third-man and cover, and everyone else on the legside. I started bowling my slow in-duckers and Reg Simpson kept stepping away to leg and hitting through the offside. He got twenty-odd in no time at all and the crowd loved it. But he overdid the stepping away and got caught. Then when Reg got out, I tightened up the field and they began to play defensively. So I kept saying, 'I thought you boys were supposed to be strokemakers.' They got so mad we dismissed them for 170-odd. Trying to rub it in, I made the mistake of asking Reg to follow on but they batted out time comfortably enough even though I gave everyone on our side a bowl.

Reg Simpson obviously decided to give us a taste of our own medicine and in a return match a year or two later, by lunch on the second day, they'd got 490-odd. I was knackered because I'd done a lot of bowling. I often felt that that was the best thing I could do to protect my regular bowlers from getting too much stick when they would still have a lot of bowling to do through the season.

Anyway, at lunch as I went past the players' table on my way to the top table I said out of the side of my mouth to Joe Hardstaff, Wally Keeton and Charlie Harris, 'I'm going to keep you so-and-so's in the field for the rest of this match.' Joe said, 'I told you he'd get mad if we batted on.' When we went in to bat after lunch, I told my openers, 'Fifty an hour is what I want for the next ten hours. No more and no less.' Emrys Davies was the ideal man for this situation. Once he got over the new ball he knew they couldn't get him out and he was the sheet anchor while the others responded to my fifty-an-hour instruction. If the rate fell below fifty I would give them a signal to speed it up but if they were going faster than the required rate I would signal them to slow down. At the end of the match, sure enough, we were 500-plus.

Wilf Wooller, in concluding this story, exploded with laughter by adding, 'But these things get exaggerated out of all proportion.' He went on to recall his clash of wills with Robin Marlar:

It was set fair at Hove when we played Sussex in 1956. We included a fast bowler called Hugh Davies. He didn't play a lot for us but at Hove that day there was still just a trace of sea fret. What often happened there was that Sussex would lose early wickets and still finish up with 300-plus. Anyway, I went out to look at the wicket with my senior 'professors' (I always did that if I was considering putting the other side in) and I invited Robin to bat. When they were 210 for 0 my fast bowler fell in the deep and broke his ankle and they finished up declaring with 379 on the board. All this put Robin in rather an uppity mood. We were going through a bad patch at that time and we had to bat in a sea fret when the ball moved about. I went in first with Gilbert Parkhouse with the intention of battling it out until conditions improved. Gilbert and I both batted a very long time for single-figure scores, but we were still all out for 64 and Robin was even more cock-a-hoop when he asked us to follow on.

I said to Gilbert Parkhouse as we went out to open the batting in the second innings, 'I'll take my bat to you if you play a shot.' What had also got me going was not just Robin's needling but there were two archetypal old Sussex members sitting near the pavilion gate who had been highly critical of my slow scoring in the first innings in voices which they fully intended I should hear. As we went out in the second innings, I said to them, 'See you at tea.' Then when we were still there and came back after tea I said, 'See you at the close of play.' Gilbert and I were not out overnight and, sure enough, there they were the following morning and I said to them, 'See you at lunch.' So it went on and I was undefeated for 79 made in six and a half hours. We saved the match but by the end Robin was doing his nut. He was reduced to bowling donkey drops, which are actually quite difficult to play.

It went on from there and whenever we played Sussex Robin and I would have a bit of a go at each other. It didn't always go my way. When we played them again at Hove only a year or two later, I made a sporting declaration after we had had the edge throughout the match only to see them get the runs against the clock. I was very fond of Robin and we had a lot of fun playing against him. I remember, once at Horsham, we had been having a very difficult time getting wickets and even Robin was scoring runs against us. I went down on my knees and prayed to the east and, sure enough, he hit a long hop straight to a fielder. That was the way it was. There was a lot of fun involving everyone on the field and spectators really didn't know what we were up to half the time. But we always had a beer or two with the opposition afterwards – always.

So far as our own team spirit was concerned, I shall always recall the marvellous evenings we had together when we were away on tour. Glamorgan never really had separate dressing-rooms and nor did the other smaller counties, so we saw a good deal of each other. But we made a ritual every Saturday night of getting together in our hotel for drinks. I would give the boys the opportunity of asking why I had done this, that or the other. As the pints went down, so the talk would move, inevitably, to rugby, and Willy Jones, with three pints inside him, would declare that the three longest kickers in Wales had been Sullivan, Wooller and Jones. By the time he'd downed five pints it was Sullivan and Jones and by the time we got him to bed he could only tell us about Jones.

When Wilf Wooller gave up the captaincy in 1961, Tony Lewis was unavailable and the leadership of the side was entrusted to Ossie Wheatley, a Cambridge Blue who was only twenty-six and who had played for Warwickshire. He was another Glamorgan import who became a lifelong supporter of the Welsh club. His chief recollection of his early days as captain was of the continuing influence of Wilf Wooller, especially when it came to sorting out those hotels in which the team were still welcomed from those with long memories of damaged furniture occasioned on a previous Wooller visit. As county secretary Wilf Wooller continued to exert a Brian Sellers-like grip on the affairs of the club, and it is no secret that his retirement as secretary in 1977 was hastened by differences of view over recruitment policy. Looking back on his long involvement with Glamorgan, he sums up:

I believe our strength, like so many things in Wales, came essentially from a certain national pride. In my time we never had more than two or three imports and we soon had them imbued with Welsh fervour.

But for a team like Glamorgan, captaincy was all-important. It is so much more than just doing the job on the field. You can't really run a good side if you don't gain their respect. It's a bit like the army where it is nearly always the case that a popular colonel leads a bad regiment. In my view the captain should be responsible for decisions on behalf of the whole team and above all for relationships with the committee. In my time, the senior professional fulfilled the sergeant-major role and a very important one it was in taking responsibility for team discipline. With that went arrangements for nets, financial matters and a sympathetic ear to players' emotional and private worries. He would involve me in these matters only when necessary. This was the strength of the system of which I was able to take advantage, and it has to be said that in some of the other counties there was a certain amount of scratching about in looking for new captains all the time. Not only could you con a number of them but we also had the great advantage of continuity.

Kent's post-war commitment to amateur captains was not total but it was clear that, from his début in 1950, Colin Cowdrey was destined to lead the side. Meanwhile, in their search for a stop-gap captain, Kent approached their senior professional, Les Ames:

They asked me if I would consider becoming an amateur and I

said I couldn't do that – it would just not have seemed right after
so many years in the professional ranks. But I was delighted
when they invited me to become cricket manager and later on
when I became both county secretary and cricket manager.

When Les Ames declined the captaincy, the Kent committee
approached Doug Wright. It is no secret that Wright found the
cares and responsibilities of captaincy from 1954 to 1956 onerous
and was happy to hand over the side to Colin Cowdrey in 1957. The
new captain was only twenty-four and he has described how he had
considerable misgivings before accepting the appointment while
still touring with MCC in South Africa. He reflected on all those in
the Kent side who had already had long-established international
experience, such as Arthur Fagg, Fred Ridgway, Jack Pettiford and
Godfrey Evans. However, when Colin Cowdrey asked Godfrey
Evans how he thought the senior players would respond to him, he
received a typical response: 'We're all behind you, Master – give
everything you've got and we'll all give you a hand.'
Colin Cowdrey later described the one exception:

I realized that Arthur Fagg as my senior professional was miffed
that the job had gone to someone almost half his age and I
suppose he thought it ought to have come to him. In any case, I
made a point of seeking his advice in one of my early matches as
captain. He just said, 'You've been made the captain so you can
get on with it', but he didn't put it as politely as that.

You have to remember his background. He was embittered.
He went to Australia on tour in 1936–37 and came back early
because of rheumatic fever. He only played in one more Test and
lost some of his best years during the war.

I think he felt really sore when I was picked for Australia in
1954. I was having a bad time that season while he was still
batting like a genius. It was all very embarrassing and my selection for that tour had to be seen as an investment for the future,
but it was certainly one in which I didn't have the senior professional's blessing.

While Colin Cowdrey felt there was no way in which he could

get through to Arthur Fagg, he found that it was possible to win over some of the other professionals – although it was often a slow process:

> When I first started with Kent, the professionals were not particularly well disposed towards me until the point they realized that I could play. That was the time when the amateur and professional distinction and the feelings about a public-school and Oxbridge background faded away. You were seen as there on merit and, in some ways, it must be a bit like politics. You are competing but there comes a point when you decide that a certain person is essential in your team.
>
> There were one or two hard cases who, when I was batting with them, made it pretty obvious that they did not wish me well. They were the kind of people who, if you nicked one to the 'keeper early on, could almost be heard saying, 'That'll take the wind out of his sails for a bit.' So you had to try and find a way to win them over. All sorts of things could help – some of them quite small. You might find that you could help a colleague in some aspect of his private life but, day in, day out, it was what happened in the middle that counted. Here, I was lucky. I'd never felt worried about the type of bowling one had to face. Naturally, I got out to all of them but I never felt that I had a particular concern for off-spin or pace or whatever. So, if you had a rival with you at the wicket or someone who you could tell didn't much like you, it was good to be able to say, 'What do you make of these two?' If, in modern terms, he replied, 'I've got no bother with Phil Edmonds – he can't bowl a bloody hoop down a hill – but John Emburey is making my life difficult as a left-hander by turning the ball away from the bat,' you could say, 'Why don't you play Phil Edmonds and I'll take John Emburey?' Then, as you went off at the next interval if you'd been able to put on some runs together, you could say, 'That seemed to work all right. They'll probably have to take the new ball after tea and if we can see that off we might have some fun.' You obviously had to make sure you weren't too obvious about this kind of tactic but over a month or two you began to build up a different kind of relationship.

Looking back on his early years as captain, Colin Cowdrey sees
his partnership with Les Ames as a crucial factor in building up the
team spirit which eventually led to Kent's Championship victory in
1970 – their first in over half a century. Part of the Les Ames success
story was in recruiting playing strength from outside the county,
and an interesting example of an amateur turning professional to
join them was that of Peter Richardson, formerly captain of Worcestershire. When he left his old county under unhappy circumstances in 1959, he retained his sense of humour:

> I suppose I had built up a certain amount of self-confidence
> playing as an amateur at Worcester, although my father had said
> to me, 'Why don't you earn some money out of the game?' But
> Worcestershire wanted to groom me as an amateur captain and so
> I was made assistant secretary which was really just a fiddle. In
> many ways, I felt happier playing as a professional for Kent as it
> was all open and above board and I still felt able to have a go at
> people. For example, after my baptism of fire with Wilf Wooller,
> I was always happy to mix it with him. He was a real character
> and I thought he was superb.
>
> Off the field, I had long been fascinated by Jim Swanton's
> ability to seemingly be in charge of everyone in sight, particu-
> larly when we were touring overseas. He has done a lot for Kent
> cricket and he has become a leading figure in the Band of
> Brothers and of that great Canterbury Week scene. Nevertheless,
> I thought it might be fun to have a go at the famous Swanton
> grand manner. We set him up during Canterbury week. I was
> opening for Kent and we got the umpire Bill Copson in on the
> act. I arranged that we would have a signal from the television
> commentary box when Jim was broadcasting and, as soon as he
> began, I complained to Bill Copson about the blooming noise
> which was distracting me when I was trying to bat. He went over
> to the commentary box and passed on the complaint. Colin
> Cowdrey was also in the box and he pretended he couldn't hear,
> so Bill Copson had to repeat the complaint very loudly which set
> the crowd off in gales of laughter. I'm told that Jim had to pull out
> all the stops as the best summarizer in the game to explain to the
> viewers what the problem was.

The Middlesex leadership also acquired a reputation for wit and humour when J. J. Warr took over the side from Bill Edrich in 1958. There are many splendid stories linking the two. Perhaps the most famous concerns one of Bill Edrich's weddings at which it was decided to have a church blessing. Johnny Warr, entering the church, was asked if he would like to sit on the bride's or the groom's side only to reply, 'Put me wherever you like, old boy. I've got a season ticket for all these matches.' Less well-known is the story of the Middlesex committee meeting at which the question of wedding presents for first-team players was discussed. The meeting was disrupted by what the Minutes should have shown as 'prolonged laughter' when J.J. said, 'Well, thinking of Bill Edrich, for heaven's sake let's not make it retrospective.'

Peter May considers that this off-the-field wit (which is still evident today in J. J. Warr's after-dinner speeches) detracts from his undoubted playing and tactical skills:

> I think his reputation suffered unfairly from his unsuccessful tour of Australia in 1950–51 when he was still a Cambridge undergraduate. He was always a good bowler in England and specially at Lord's when the ridge was still in evidence, and he and Alan Moss made life difficult for visiting batsmen. Moreover, he was a very shrewd captain and I always found it one of the tougher encounters to match wits with him when Surrey played Middlesex.

Charles Robins, who had the difficult task of following so great an all-rounder as his father into the Middlesex side, describes how J. J. Warr's use of gamesmanship helped him:

> The fact is that my leg-spin bowling wasn't in the same league as my father's but J.J. would say to the batsman as he put me on, 'If you can't score runs against this rubbish you shouldn't be playing first-class cricket', and, you know, this helped me because it didn't seem to matter if I bowled the odd bad ball; the batsman wasn't sure what to expect so I picked up a few wickets with his help.

*

Middlesex's continued commitment to amateur leadership was, in part, due to the remaining influence of both Walter Robins and Gubby Allen. But a new kind of young professional was emerging with J. T. Murray, P. H. Parfitt and F. J. Titmus, whose confidence was built up by their success in Test matches. Nevertheless, Fred Titmus recalls the effect Gubby Allen had on them:

> I can remember occasions when I was with J.T., Peter Parfitt and some of the boys and Gubby would come walking by. We would all freeze and it was all we could do to get out, 'Good morning, Mr Allen.' I can only remember, in my early days, one variation on that, and this was when we were practising for a Test match and Freddie Trueman, who was with us, just said, 'Morning, Gubby, and how are you today?' As a matter of fact, I still call him Mr Allen, and now it will have to be Sir George.

Fred Titmus also recalls how the authorities at Lord's maintained the old amateur and professional distinctions:

> I have often been asked about the announcement over the public address system in the late fifties when the message came over, 'Ladies and gentlemen, there is a correction to your scorecards. For F. J. Titmus, read Titmus, F. J.' Yes, it's true that they still insisted that amateurs had initials in front of their surnames and we had them after the surname. But that itself was progress from the old days when amateurs were denoted by 'Mister' and we were generally referred to simply by our surname. By the time we came to the fifties and initials in front or after the surname, there were several cases of confusion. When a relatively unknown player appeared for the other side at Lord's, we quite often had to change the initials depending on whether or not he turned out to be an amateur or a professional.

Despite – or perhaps because of – these reminders of status Fred Titmus retained his regard for cricket authority so that, when he succeeded J. J. Warr and was made the first full-time Middlesex professional captain in the mid-sixties, he began by telling his assembled team, 'If you think democracy's arrived, you've got another think coming.'

Nottinghamshire, too, maintained its traditional hierarchy through the fifties with Reg Simpson normally the only amateur in charge of ten professionals. Apart from a brief period when the Australian leg-spinner Bruce Dooland joined the county and helped the team to the top half of the table, the captain had a difficult time as Nottinghamshire fortunes slumped.

Reg Simpson received some further overseas support when Gamini Goonesena of Ceylon came down from Cambridge:

I had played a few games for Nottinghamshire as a professional before I went up to Cambridge and I later had the opportunity of playing for them as an amateur which suited my part-time availability. It also gave me the opportunity of appearing for the Gentlemen.

I only saw the amateur and professional business towards the end. There was no separate gate but we still had separate dressing-rooms at Trent Bridge and there was an upstairs and downstairs arrangement. The opposition were downstairs and we were upstairs with a captain's room for Reg Simpson. He didn't have the luxurious room with soft chairs and so on they have at the Oval but he invited me to make use of it. I preferred to change with the boys because I felt we were together and, in away matches, I went to great pains not to use amateur dressing-rooms there either. There was a case for the captain being away from the rest of the side, but I never captained Nottinghamshire so it never arose. In any event, we were a happy side despite our limited success.

Reg Simpson tried to improve the team's fortunes by a willing-ness to offer or accept challenges from other county captains. While he had some success with this approach, he had – as we have seen – personal clashes with Wilf Wooller and, seemingly by extension, with Robin Marlar:

It is hard now to understand why some of the grudges which

arose were carried over from season to season but I think they
usually centred on arguments about whether or not there had
been a reasonable declaration. You heard Wilf Wooller's account
and I don't think I need re-fight that particular battle. As for
Robin Marlar, I was sometimes mystified by what he had in
mind and I always think of him as one of those amateur captains
whose team followed him if only out of curiosity.

Robin Marlar became captain of Sussex in 1955. He was part of
the amateur restoration after early post-war difficulties. Billy
Griffith had found the task of serving as both captain and secretary
an excessive load and Hugh Bartlett's spell in charge ended in his
own resignation as well as that of the entire committee. In the
ensuing chaos, James Langridge emerged as the county's first professional captain, but this was seen as no more than a stop-gap
arrangement. David Sheppard's appointment in 1953 seemed once
again to make the classic case for amateur leadership when the side
became runners-up in the Championship. Part of the county's
success was due to the return of attacking batsmanship led not only
by the captain but by another Cambridge Blue, Hubert Doggart
(who would follow him for a single year as captain), and the veteran
professional George Cox, who competed in fast scoring with the
two young amateurs as he had done with Hugh Bartlett in pre- and
post-war days.

Yet, despite the success of these amateur captains, it was from
among their ranks that some of the most significant stirrings
against the concept of Gentlemen and Players emerged. For David
Sheppard:

No one could afford to play cricket for six days a week unless
they were getting paid by somebody. It was hard to justify the
logic which said if you were paid by the county as a player you
were a professional but if you were paid as assistant secretary
who also played you were an amateur. Some of us were able to
play as amateurs while we were single and at university but,
inevitably, we had to earn a living. When it came to the argument
that you needed amateurs to perform the independent captain's

role, I can think of some who were complete slaves to their committee and one professional who seemed totally independent from his county committee.

I was strongly influenced in my thinking on these matters by George Cox. He had, as you have seen, always been one for getting a bit of a dig in about the amateurs. I think he felt the social divide even more intensely when he went as cricket coach to Winchester and was told that, as he was not a member of the formal teaching staff, he could not be found a place in the school chapel. He went on playing for Sussex for most of my time with the county and he was a great influence on me. We talked about the increasing absurdities of the shamateur and George encouraged me to press for changes.

Hubert Doggart, too, as a true amateur able to captain the side for only one year before becoming a dedicated schoolmaster, had his own reservations about the system:

The fact was that I was lucky to have my opportunities in playing at the highest level. I had just made something of a name for myself at Cambridge when I was given my Test cap but I was perhaps unlucky in gaining it against the West Indies when we first began to see the rise in their great post-war strength. On the other hand, the system was tilted to a degree because the selectors were always willing to give an amateur an opportunity in the hope that he might show leadership potential.

Robin Marlar had to suffer much leg-pulling when the Duke of Norfolk appointed him librarian at Arundel Castle and charges of shamateurism were widely heard but, as he says:

I was a young schoolmaster with a wife and children to support. The county tried to help me by giving me £500 entertainment allowance on top of my normal expenses. But I hated the whole idea of having to fiddle. So I was certainly looking for the end of the old system.

*

Ted Dexter, who succeeded Robin Marlar as captain of Sussex in 1960, believes that the contribution of his predecessor has often been underestimated:

Those stories about Robin's eccentricity are greatly exaggerated and, on occasions, I think we did not back him up perhaps as well as we should have done. I can remember at least one occasion when we threw a match away when Robin's instinct – quite rightly – was to deny the other side the points. And he was a fine bowler – you only have to look at his performances against the Players to see that. I certainly learnt from him when it came to my turn to captain the side and I shared his view that it was becoming increasingly difficult to justify the means by which amateur leadership was maintained as a matter of principle.

In the remaining counties – Gloucestershire, Lancashire, Leicestershire, Northamptonshire, Somerset, Warwickshire and Worcestershire – the system had already changed in the sense that the traditional commitment to amateur leadership had given way to a more pragmatic approach (although the temptation to revert to amateur leadership was never far away in the minds of several of these counties' committees).

For Gloucestershire, professional captains in the persons of Jack Crapp, George Emmett and Tom Graveney had charge of the side from 1953 to 1960. The county finished third in the Championship under George Emmett and runners-up in 1959 under Tom Graveney, and it seemed that the case for continued professional leadership had been firmly established. However, some committee members were critical – more of the Graveney style of leadership than of its end result – and there were major splits in the county membership as well as the committee when, in 1961, Tom Graveney was relieved of the captaincy and replaced by the Old Etonian C. T. M. Pugh, who would make a greater name for himself as a rackets player than as a first-class cricketer. Looking back on his dismissal today, Tom Graveney finds there were several consolations in what at the time was a distressing experience:

I must say I was very depressed about the whole business, particularly as I had to spend the year kicking my heels. However, as it turned out, the Gloucestershire committee had really done me a good turn. Once I went into the Worcester side, I seemed to get a new lease of life and I certainly found life a lot more relaxed without the problems which I'd faced as a captain dealing with a committee which did not seem able to make up its mind about whether or not it wanted amateur or professional leadership.

Lancashire's change to professional captaincy was evident when Cyril Washbrook began his six-year spell in charge in 1954. We have seen that he had always been an admirer of the amateur style of leadership:

> I tried to carry on the amateur tradition. I'd loved to have played as an amateur but I couldn't afford it. Mind you, I was a stern disciplinarian. Right or wrong, out there, I wouldn't have any opposition. Anyone who wanted to argue with me on the field would be out of the side. I was always willing to listen to suggestions but, once I had made up my mind, I expected to be supported.

Alan Wharton, who opened the Lancashire innings on many occasions with Cyril Washbrook, was known in his early days as 'the Shop Steward' because of his tendency to criticize and challenge those in authority. At the Lancashire players' reunion in 1986, mellowed with the years and rejoicing at the sight of hundreds of young schoolboys receiving coaching in the middle at the annual Old Trafford Schools' Cricket Week, he recalled his first experience of the stern Washbrook code:

> I was batting with Cyril and he had already got his hundred. I was on 99 and looking for my maiden first-class century. I called Cyril for a quick single and he sent me back. I only just got in by measuring my length. Soon after, he called me for a quick single and I sent him back and he had to make a dive to get in in time. At the end of the over, he called me into the middle and said, 'Young man, I've had a great deal more experience than you and I'm the best judge of a quick single.' And I said, 'Well, Mr Washbrook,

when I'm on 99 I reckon I'm the best judge of a quick single in the game.' And, you know, I was dropped for the next six matches for disrespect to the senior professional.

Although Lancashire under Cyril Washbrook's captaincy had several successful seasons in the County Championship, he was criticized as too authoritarian and Lancashire made further experiments with amateur captains after he had retired from the game. R. W. Barber led the team in 1960 and 1961 and J. F. Blackledge in 1962. However, neither appointment was regarded as successful. Blackledge had never played in first-class cricket until he came to Lancashire as captain, and Bob Barber was a very dour player until, after arguments with the Lancashire committee, he moved to Warwickshire. Here, without the strain of captaincy, he blossomed as one of the best attacking left-hand opening batsmen in the county and Test match game. Before he left Lancashire, however, his adherence to the amateur privileges which went with his job left an indelible impression on the mind of Richie Benaud, the visiting captain of the Australians at Old Trafford in 1961:

> Bob asked Neil Harvey as my vice-captain and myself whether we'd like to change in the captain's dressing-room which had very spacious accommodation in the top of the pavilion. We looked at him in amazement and I said, 'If we were to accept your invitation, we'd be torn limb from limb by the rest of our team.'

Leicestershire's adoption of professional captaincy also resulted from the move of a discontented player when Willie Watson left Yorkshire at the end of the 1957 season and succeeded Charles Palmer as captain of Leicestershire from 1958 to 1961. Charles Palmer, who retains a life-long interest in Leicestershire as their chairman, assesses the role of his two successors as captain:

> In a way, I am not sure that it is really fair to give a considered view on the last of our amateur captains, David Kirby. He had played the odd game for us as a Cambridge undergraduate and had just come down from university in 1962. It was a tall order thrusting him in as captain at the age of 23, and I wouldn't put too

much significance on our bottom place in the table at that stage. Indeed, we were going through a difficult time and we had finished bottom of the Championship in both of my own last two years as captain. We were much affected by the retirement of several of our most experienced players like the Australian stalwarts Jackson and Walsh and by the tragically early death of Maurice Tompkin. Under Willie Watson, the side had proved unpredictable – either half-way up the table or at or near the bottom. But from a personal point of view, there was a parallel between Willie Watson and Tom Graveney's change of counties since Willie also re-established himself as an England player and showed splendid form for the county in his last years in first-class cricket.

Northamptonshire, too, had come under Yorkshire professional leadership when Dennis Brookes became captain in 1954. It was typical of the loyalty which he showed to his adopted county when he stayed on to play under Raman Subba Row after the Surrey and England opening batsman was specially registered to become captain of Northamptonshire in 1958. Subba Row recalls:

I didn't realize it at the time but Dennis Brookes had rather a rough deal. I was approached by one of Northamptonshire's contact men who also acted as a talent scout for football teams and asked if I would consider joining the side. It was implied that this would be on the understanding that I should take over the captaincy. I was quite happy with Surrey but the offer of a captaincy was a different proposition and, I can reveal after all these years, there was also a financial package on offer including support from outside the club by a local industrialist. I think some word of these arrangements got out because this is why there was a certain amount of resentment against shamateurism which seemed particularly directed at me. But no one could have had a better senior professional than I had in Dennis Brookes. He had led the county in the season before I came, to be runners-up for the first time ever in the Championship. Yet he batted as well as ever and was a great help to me. He was the best of the old-style professionals and it was interesting to contrast him with other chaps in the side like Frank Tyson, who I saw as the new-style professional. Frank and I were on tour in Australia together and there was little thought in my mind of amateur and professional differences when we were playing together for Northamptonshire.

For his part, Frank Tyson gives an interesting illustration of this 'new professionalism':

I suppose in an earlier period I might have played as an amateur, particularly in the days when Sir John Pascoe of British Timken had as many as fourteen of the Northamptonshire groundstaff on his company's payroll. But I didn't like the suggestion that, because I was a university man, therefore I must play as an amateur. I was probably one of the first to go straight from university into a professional cricket career but I had played in League cricket before I went up to university as a professional and, being a northerner, I suppose I accepted the old adage about a labourer being worthy of his hire. I certainly didn't like the sycophancy of some of the pseudo-amateurism which I found when I came into the game.

On the other hand, I admired the approach of the old-style amateur like Freddie Brown. I rated him highly as a captain with Northamptonshire because he would do anything himself whether batting, bowling or fielding, and as captain he was a law unto himself. When he told the committee, 'That's the team I want for the next match', that's what he got.

With Raman, it was much more the feeling of a peer group. He did a sound job for us and we had a good season when he first took over the side. I suppose I had acquired a certain independence because of my successful Test breakthrough in Australia. (I had in fact been given my Test cap before my County cap and I got this when we came back from Australia together with a tankard commemorating my Test performances, on the stage of the Northampton Repertory Theatre.) As Raman and I had been on tour together for MCC in Australia, I felt we were part of what was increasingly a peer group of cricketers rather than amateurs and professionals, and he seemed to reflect that view.

Soon after he took over the side, we were playing at the Oval where the professionals were crowded into a small changing room. Raman came up to me and said, 'For heaven's sake, come and change in my room. I don't want to be rattling around there on my own.' So, with the appointment of someone like Raman as captain, I could see very little difference between the amateur and the professional captain and it was no surprise when Raman resigned to pursue his business interests and Keith Andrew took over as professional captain in 1962.

The appointment of Maurice Tremlett as the first professional captain of Somerset in 1956 was seen as an obvious response to widespread unease among the club's members after the side had been led by eight amateur captains in the first post-war decade and finished bottom of the Championship table in the previous four years. The county's historian Eric Hill who, after a distinguished wartime career flying with the RAF, played for Somerset as a professional until the early fifties, has described the rise of Maurice Tremlett from office boy in the club's headquarters to the captain who took them to their highest-ever third place in the Championship in 1958 as typical of the romance and charm of his county's story. It was perhaps a sign of the changing times that Somerset, the county with the greatest record of amateur predominance, should now feel that its future lay with professional leaders like Maurice Tremlett and his successor, the Durham-born wicket-keeper H. W. Stephenson, supported by overseas professionals like the West Indian P. B. Wight and the Australian trio of McCool, Alley and McMahon.

Warwickshire after their Championship victory in 1951 continued with professional captaincy for the next five years, four of them under Tom Dollery, with a brief single year 'lap of honour' for Eric Hollies. In 1957, the captaincy reverted to an amateur when M. J. K. Smith was appointed for what proved to be a decade as county captain.

Mike Smith's appointment was made possible when he was given financial support as the club's assistant secretary. This led to an entertaining mix-up with his namesake, E. J. 'Tiger' Smith, who was then serving as the county coach. The old professional was one of those who had long complained about the financial distinctions which had increasingly begun to favour the amateur, and the story went round the club membership of his delight when he opened his pay packet to find a cheque with a substantially increased amount. It was said that the old Tiger's eye lit up – only to become glazed again when he discovered that the cheque had been intended for M. J. K. Smith.

Mike Smith, after a brilliant cricket career at Oxford, had played a few games for Leicestershire and he was to prove one of those amateur leaders who gave the Gentlemen a good name at a time when criticism was mounting of the shamateur. He proved an exceptionally popular leader not only of his county but also in twenty-five Tests for England. He was one of those whose style, like that of George Mann, was relaxed. A fine attacking batsman and, despite his glasses, a fearless close fielder, he gives the same disarming kind of reply as did George Mann when asked about his formula for getting the best out of his side:

> I found that you could build a good side and make the most of the skills available to you if you had harmony, and that means having a team of nice chaps. All I can say is that I was lucky to have both for Warwickshire and England.

One of M. J. K. Smith's 'nice chaps' who played a great deal under his captaincy for England was D. A. Allen of Gloucestershire:

> He was one of the best captains I played under and he was part of a change in the game which brought a new kind of amateur to the fore. Although he was an Oxford graduate, he was not an Establishment figure and he proved it was possible to be 'one of the boys' in the dressing-room and still be an effective leader.

Worcestershire's first long-term professional captain, Don Kenyon, has some reservations about David Allen's enthusiasm for a captain who is one of the boys:

> He may have a point so far as the Test captain is concerned but I

think you need a bit of 'arm's length' relationship in a county team. That was the basic justification of the true amateur but, by the early fifties, they were hard to find. Of my immediate pre-decessors, Ronnie Bird had played for Warwickshire as a profes-sional but he came back after the war as a war hero who did not take too kindly to the widespread use of military rank of those who had never seen a shot fired in anger. When Reg Perks got the job in 1955 at the age of forty-three, it was widely recognized that he was holding the fort until Peter Richardson could be available to us full-time in the following season. He was only 24 when he took over the side in 1956 and, playing as an amateur, it seemed that he might have the job of captain for a very long time. He had tremendous application and made the most of his run-getting ability to establish himself as a Test batsman, and I was sorry when he unexpectedly left the county and joined Kent.

When I took over as captain as a professional, I was lucky in a number of respects. You can play the game for many years at the highest level but it is quite a different proposition when you are in charge. I was fortunate in three ways. First, I was a very successful player and the rest of the team knew that I would perform. Second, I had always been seen as a steady sort of bloke who didn't stay drinking at the bar all night. Third, I was never a great mixer and I never had the problem of picking or getting rid of a special friend in the team.

That's the problem for so many today who take over the side having been 'one of the boys'. On the other hand, I was also lucky in the sense that I was raised in the Black Country, born and bred. My best bowler, Jack Flavell, was another. There were one or two people in the side and on the committee who were a bit inclined to make fun of his broad accent, but he and I were on the same wavelength and he gave his all for me. We had to build up our side – particularly when we had lost a major batsman in Peter Richardson – but gradually we achieved some success so that we went on eventually to win the Championship.

I did not need to crack the whip. I was a determined sort of chap and if I said something they knew I would stick to it. In general, they only had to look at me to know what I had in mind. I certainly didn't interfere with their private lives but, if I felt that someone was letting the county down, I made it pretty clear that they could earn their passage by showing they were prepared to pull their weight through a performance on the field or they must be prepared to make way for someone who would.

So far as my bowlers were concerned, I had an easy answer. I was always determined to make sure that they did their fair share of the work and, if they misbehaved, I would simply say to them, 'Now, here's the ball. You can go on at this end and you will bowl until I tell you you can bloody stop.' They always seemed to understand that message.

Don Kenyon, today, reflects on the difficult problem facing most professional captains:

As I said, I was lucky in being that little bit remote from the team. Nowadays, they tend to bring in someone who has been a member of a peer group. This inevitably makes it difficult for him to exercise discipline. That was the case for the old amateur and I, like my contemporaries, never minded playing against the likes of Peter May, Colin Cowdrey and Mike Smith, who were all good enough to represent their country under whatever label. What became more difficult to accept in the fifties was the shamateur. When Peter Richardson came to us he was the son of a farmer who was given the job of joint assistant secretary. It was a nonsense and it was not necessary. The days of the old amateur were gone or were going. In the fifties virtually no one could afford to be an amateur and that was what gave some added needle to the last matches played between the Gentlemen and the Players.

ABOVE: Scarborough, 1949: a return to old standards as footmen bring tea to the cricketers on the field while the President's guests dine in style in the marquee. The brass band which played throughout the game was to the right of the President's marquee.

LEFT: Yorkshire in 1946. The nucleus of the championship-winning side: front row, l–r: W. Barber, W. E. Bowes, A. B. Sellers (captain), P. A. Gibb and M. Leyland. Back row, l–r: E. P. Robinson, L. Hutton, A. Coxon, T. F. Smailes, W. Watson, H. Beaumont and A. Booth.

BELOW: Glamorgan Championship side, 1948. Front row, l–r: A. Watkins, E. Davies, W. Wooller (captain), H. Davies and E. L. Muncer. Back row, l–r: W. E. Jones, P. Clift, J. Pleass, J. Eaglestone, W. G. Parkhouse, N. Hever and G. Lavis.

LEFT: Gentlemen v. Players, Lord's, 1951. L. Hutton hits R. V. Divecha for four. The wicket-keeper is D. V. Brennan and W. J. Edrich is at first slip.

CENTRE: Gentlemen v. Players, 1953. P. B. H. May pulls R. Tattersall for four. The wicket-keeper is T. G. Evans and A. E. Moss is in the gully.

BELOW: Gentlemen's XI at Scarborough, 1952. From left: D. J. Insole, D. V. Brennan, R. W. V. Robins, N. W. D. Yardley, P. B. H. May, R. T. Simpson, T. E. Bailey, C. H. Palmer, W. J. Edrich, C. N. McCarthy and M. C. Cowdrey.

RIGHT: M. C. Cowdrey makes his début at Scarborough in 1951 wearing his Tonbridge School blazer.

CENTRE: Gentlemen v. Players, Lord's, 1956. C. Washbrook plays a shot off J. M. Allan. The Cambridge wicket-keeper is M. E. L. Melluish and M. C. Cowdrey is at first slip.

BELOW: Gentlemen's XI at Scarborough, 1955. From left: G. Goonesena, E. J. Lewis, J. J. Warr, N. W. D. Yardley, W. J. Edrich, P. E. Richardson, T. E. Bailey, W. S. Surridge, D. J. Insole, R. T. Simpson and W. H. H. Sutcliffe.

LEFT: Surrey Championship County, 1952. Front row, l–r: D. G. W. Fletcher, A. V. Bedser, L. B. Fishlock, W. S. Surridge (captain), P. B. H. May, J. F. Parker and B. Constable. Back row, l–r: A. Sandham (coach), G. A. R. Lock, A. F. Brazier, R. C. E. Pratt, T. Clark, G. J. Whittaker, E. A. Bedser, J. C. Laker, P. J. Loader, G. N. G. Kirby, A. J. McIntyre, D. F. Cox, H. Strudwick and J. S. Tait.

BELOW LEFT: Surrey 2nd XI, 1954. Among the rising stars receiving guidance from Andrew Sandham were: M. J. Stewart (at right end, front row); behind him, the young John Edrich; and, in the middle of the back row, Ken Barrington.

RIGHT: E. R. Dexter of Cambridge makes his début for the Gentlemen at Scarborough in 1957.

BELOW RIGHT: MCC in Australia, 1954–55. Front row, l–r: T. E. Bailey, W. J. Edrich, P. B. H. May, L. Hutton (captain), D. C. S. Compton, A. V. Bedser and T. G. Evans. Middle row, l–r: J. H. Wardle, R. T. Simpson, J. V. Wilson, R. Appleyard, J. McConnon, J. B. Statham, M. C. Cowdrey and C. G. Howard (manager). Back row, l–r: G. Duckworth (baggage-master), K. V. Andrew, P. J. Loader, T. W. Graveney, F. H. Tyson and H. W. Dalton (masseur).

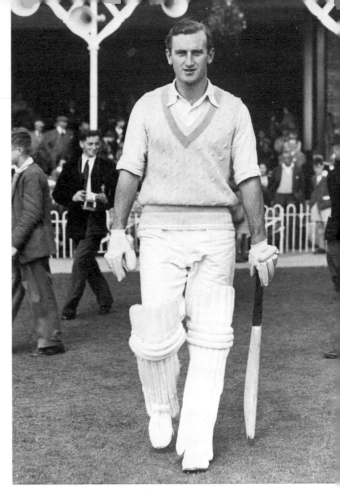

ABOVE: Gentlemen's XI at Lord's, 1961. Front row, l–r: O. S. Wheatley, E. R. Dexter, P. B. H. May (captain), T. E. Bailey and M. J. K. Smith. Back row, l–r: E. J. Craig, J. M. Brearley, R. M. Prideaux, R. W. Barber, C. D. Dryborough and J. D. Piachaud.

LEFT: J. R. Burnet, captain of Yorkshire's championship side in 1959.

RIGHT: W. S. Surridge, captain of
Surrey's championship side in 1952–56.
BELOW: Players XI at Scarborough,
1960. L–r: P. J. Sainsbury, B. R. Knight,
W. E. Russell, H. Rhodes, A. E. Moss,
T. W. Graveney, K. F. Barrington, R. E.
Marshall, R. Swetman, D. A. Allen and
J. H. Edrich.

ABOVE: Gentlemen v. Players, 1962 – the last match at Lord's. E. R. Dexter, captain of the Gentlemen, pulls a ball from F. J. Titmus for four. K. V. Andrew is keeping wicket, P. J. Sharpe is at first slip, P. Walker at leg slip and D. A. Allen at short square-leg. Dexter went on to score 55 and was rewarded with the captaincy of the MCC side in Australia.

LEFT: Gentlemen v. Players, 1962. F. S. Trueman leads out the last Players side to appear at Lord's. He is followed by T. W. Graveney and D. Shackleton. Behind them are N. Gifford, P. Walker and K. V. Andrew (largely obscured). In the final group are J. Edrich, P. H. Parfitt, P. J. Sharpe (largely obscured), F. J. Titmus and M. J. Stewart.

THE LAST GENTLEMEN
AND PLAYERS

The needle to which Don Kenyon referred in the Gentlemen v. Players matches was increasingly evident in the fifties as the pressures to end the amateur and professional distinctions grew. Yet the records of the Gentlemen v. Players matches from 1946 onwards (complete scorecards appear in Appendix I) now have a special nostalgia as the last battles in a campaign which had lasted for more than a century and a half, and, for most of those taking part in the early post-war years, there was little evidence of the end of amateurism.

True, on the resumption of the series in 1946, Plum Warner recorded how six years of war had greatly reduced existing or potential amateur talent, and there were those who took a pessimistic view of the future of the Gentlemen's team. But from 1947 onwards, there was the appearance of business as usual with first-day attendances at the Gentlemen v. Players match at Lord's up to an estimated 16,000 in that year and 23,000 in 1948. Plum Warner had resumed his role as match patron and selector. Right up to the last game in the series in 1962, he not only took a keen personal interest in both sides but also would go into the two dressing-rooms and congratulate those who, during the match, had been selected to tour with the MCC overseas during the following winter.

Certainly, the Gentlemen v. Players games at Lord's were seen, once again, as the most effective form of Test trial. After his brief reappearance in 1946, Walter Hammond's retirement left the way open for a choice of amateur captain whch was reflected in the leadership of the Gentlemen. Norman Yardley captained the side on a number of occasions both at Lord's and at Scarborough but, as we have seen, when it came to giving opportunities for potential MCC leaders overseas, he was happy to give way to others such as George Mann, Freddie Brown and Nigel Howard.

Amateur playing strength was topped up by some outstanding overseas players of unusually mature vintage who came from Oxbridge cricket in the early post-war years. Perhaps the most notable was Martin Donnelly:

We were all amateurs in New Zealand and I had been made aware of the subtle distinctions in England when I first came over on tour in 1937. I had just left school and we were brought up on the concept of showing respect for our elders. So, in my first match against Lancashire, when I asked for guard I called the umpire 'Sir'. George Duckworth behind the stumps said, 'You don't call him sir. You are an amateur. He calls you sir.'

After the war, I felt that the atmosphere was somewhat lighter but I noticed that the old distinctions still applied in the case of separate dressing-rooms in counties like Hampshire. If you were at Oxford or Cambridge, you had a unique opportunity to measure your skills against the counties. On the other hand, we thought it was sad that there seemed to be no way in which one could keep a door open to club cricketers. Therefore many of the very good university cricketers would be increasingly ruled out because they could not spare the time for six-day cricket, and the idea of turning professional was still not attractive in relation to other career opportunities – quite apart from the lingering social divide.

My chief recollection of playing in the matches for the Gentlemen was of my good fortune in putting together some scores. I also realize, looking back, that we did not have the challenge they faced a few years later of some really quick men. The professional bowlers who stick in my mind are Doug Wright and Jack Walsh. I always thought that Doug bowled just a little bit too quickly. With the spinner you are looking to get down the track but you couldn't do that with Doug. So you played him as a medium-pacer waiting for the occasional loose ball or his quicker one, but he was still capable of producing the unplayable delivery.

Jack Walsh was a fascinating bowler who spun the ball as much as anybody. I had played against him in New Zealand when he came across from Australia before the war. He was the kind of bowler who you have to get down the track to play or he would tie you up in knots.

I had a good opportunity of taking a long look at both Doug and Jack when I got my century for the Gentlemen in 1947. The significance of that innings from a personal point of view was that it was part of a Lord's treble. I got a hundred for Oxford at Lord's in 1946, then one for the Gentlemen in the following year, and a Test hundred for New Zealand in 1949. The only other person who has achieved all three was Percy Chapman for England, Cambridge and the Gentlemen. He sent me a telegram in which he pulled my leg about the ghastly coloured New Zealand club cap I was wearing, finishing up his message with G.D.B.O. which, for the uninitiated, is the time-honoured message, 'God damn bloody Oxford'. Yes, I was certainly fortunate to have that opportunity to appear for the Gentlemen.

But Martin Donnelly was by no means a lone overseas star in the early post-war years. A. H. Kardar (Pakistan), C. B. Van Ryneveld (South Africa) and R. V. Divecha (India) all made their mark, and they were part of the great tradition of Oxbridge reinforcements for the Gentlemen (see Appendix II). Progressively, too, the return of home-produced amateur batting skills which so surprised and pleased Len Hutton became a feature of the Gentlemen's playing strength.

Over the same post-war period, the Players had demonstrated not only their technical bowling skills but also the emergence of rising batting stars and of a new confidence in captaincy. Cyril Washbrook made centuries in each of his first two appearances for the Players at Lord's in 1946 and 1947, and Brian Close showed his all-round skills on his début for the Players in the game at Lord's in 1949. For much of the time, professional captaincy was entrusted to Denis Compton rather than Len Hutton – a more adventurous choice. But the professionals continued to show their greatest strength in bowling – particularly at Lord's in an era when, seemingly, hardly a year went by without their skills being seen to best advantage on the uncovered, often rain-affected wicket at Lord's – with its notorious ridge at the Nursery end. It was under these conditions that the Players gained their victories in 1948, 1949 and 1952.

This last match was one of the epic contests between the amateurs and the professionals, in large part because the amateur bowling was unusually strong. Apart from Trevor Bailey, who showed consistent steadiness in opening the Gentlemen's bowling, Freddie Brown was enjoying an Indian summer with bat and ball and the professionals always seemed to bring out the best in Robin Marlar's off-spinning talent. But the Gentlemen's real threat, in 1952, was provided by a lean 23-year-old blond South African pace bowler, C. N. McCarthy.

Cuan McCarthy, until his later difficulties over a suspect bowling action, was a formidable proposition. He had already played Test cricket for South Africa in 1951 and developed his experience of English conditions while gaining his Blue at Cambridge in 1952. D. G. W. Fletcher, who with Len Hutton opened the batting for the Players in 1952, recalls:

> Yes, I was the Surrey cricketer who riled Andy Sandham so much because he never represented the Players at Lord's and I had several games there. But in 1952 I knew I had to earn my match money. As Len and I went out to bat, I said to him (and after all he was captaining the side): 'This chap McCarthy's a bit quick and it's hard to pick up his delivery with that bent elbow. What do you think is the best way to cope with him?' 'There's only one way,' replied Len, 'and that's from the other end.' Well, as senior partner, he took first strike against McCarthy and, sure enough, he called for a quick single in the first over. As it happened, I got a half-century and Len, for him, made a low score. When we went out to bat again, I said, 'Will you take first strike again?' and Len said, 'Well, you got the runs first time around, I'll give you the honour!'

In the event, Hutton got a half-century in the second innings

despite leaving the field for attention to his hand after being hit by
McCarthy, and David Fletcher fell not to McCarthy but to the ever
reliable Trevor Bailey. The match was also memorable for a century by Charles Palmer for the Gentlemen on a drying pitch. This
was in keeping with the long amateur tradition of producing a big
innings against the professionals despite, as in this case, Palmer's
relatively poor batting record at Lord's. For another amateur in the
Gentlemen's team, G. L. Willatt, the challenge of batting on a
difficult wicket against the best professional bowling caused anger
in even as easygoing a person as the Derbyshire captain:

Alec Bedser and Derek Shackleton were not going to let us get
away with much after Cuan McCarthy had given their batsmen a
torrid time. And there was no let-up when Jim Laker and Johnny
Wardle came on as the change bowlers. We had to get over 300 in
the last innings and I decided to try and play a sheet-anchor role,
so I batted a very long time for 26 while Palmer was going great
guns at the other end. And, you know, when I got out, having
done, I thought, a fair job, I was abused by one of the MCC
members as I went up the pavilion steps. When I say abused, I
mean the four-letter variety. I was so angry, I insisted that he
come out of the pavilion, and I followed him almost to the Grace
gates still with my pads on demanding and finally getting an
apology.

The end result, a win for the Players by two runs, was the closest
finish between the two sides since the First World War. Later in the
year there was another exciting finish in the drawn game at Scarborough. As in many of the Gentlemen v. Players matches here at
this time, the battle was one of leadership between the two Yorkshire cricketers who had captained England, Norman Yardley and
Len Hutton. Norman Yardley recalls:

Len and I were charged with the responsibility for trying to
ensure that the match lived up to its old prestige. We were
appointed captains of the two sides for the first time in the game
at Lord's in 1948, which was in celebration of W.G.'s Centenary,
and the president of MCC, Lord Cornwallis, who was a former

captain of Kent in the twenties, took us quietly aside and said, 'This game is being downgraded and seen as a bit of a beanfeast. I hope I can count on you to restore it to its rightful place in the cricket calendar.' It's true that the contest had become somewhat one-sided in favour of the Players, and the fixture was dropped from the Scarborough Festival for three years. As it happened, we made the 1948 match into an exciting contest and although Plum Warner criticized me for a declaration which allowed the Players to win the match after we had been in the driving seat for most of the game, I believe that, in the context of the series, we got it back on the kind of basis which made it, once more, into a genuine Test trial. That was certainly true of the game in 1950 when Freddie Brown established his claim to take the side to Australia and again in 1951 when Nigel Howard was given his chance as captain before taking the side to India.

We were also able to get things moving again at Scarborough, and Len and I were responsible for some very close finishes in the matches during the early fifties.

The year 1953 marked a turning-point in the fortunes of the Gentlemen's team when the Players were beaten at both Lord's and Scarborough. Their side benefited from Bill Edrich's move from the professional ranks (he scored three centuries for the Gentlemen between 1953 and 1956) and from the realization of Reg Simpson's potential at the highest level. But perhaps even more exciting was the emergence of the new school of amateur batsmen. Peter May had scored a century on his début for the Gentlemen in 1951, as did Colin Cowdrey at Scarborough in the same year, and they shared a partnership of 205 against the Players at Scarborough in 1953.

This year also saw the return of the Gentlemen's historic fixture against the Australians and for much of the match (see Appendix I) it seemed as though the amateurs might gain their first victory since 1878. In the event, the bowling of Miller and Lindwall prevailed. In the next match in the series, in 1956, J. J. Warr – always so effective at Lord's – took revenge for the hammering he had received in Australia in 1950–51 when he made heavy inroads into the Australian batting line-up and disconcerted the Australian captain Keith Miller by giving him a black eye and ensuring his dismissal 'hit wicket'. At a lunch in Sydney in 1983 given by the New South Wales Cricket Association under the chairmanship of the former Test opening batsman Arthur Morris, Richie Benaud, who took part in both the 1953 and 1956 matches and captained the 1961 Australian touring side, outlined his views on the relevance of these contests:

When I first came to England in 1953, I had heard about the business of the underling professionals and the true blue amateurs. Bill Brown said that people like Bryan Valentine and John Human had never played back in their lives. So I was quite curious to see what was involved when we played an all-amateur side.

The 1953 match was quite a low-scoring game. And, for much of the match, the Gentlemen of England as they were listed had something of an edge. I was very impressed with Colin Cowdrey who got two half-centuries and I think that these innings did a lot to ensure that he came to Australia in the following year. He played Lindwall, Johnston and Archer extremely well and I particularly recall how well he was hooking on that occasion with a lovely graceful all-in-one-movement hook which beat long leg on a number of occasions.

When we came to bat, I was second top scorer at number six and my score was exceeded only by Bill Johnston batting at number eleven. Robin Marlar bowled beautifully against us to take five wickets for next to nothing. So far as I was concerned, I was bowling with a new action and I used this game to try it out. It didn't really work and I gave it up but I did get four wickets. Then, when we needed to get runs quickly, Arthur Morris who, for him, had had a very thin time of it hit his only first-class century of the tour. I heard him telling you it was all due to his protracted courtship of an English girl who later became his wife but, in any case, he came good that day and we won quite easily in the end. The other thing which stays in my mind about that particular match was the selection of both Wilf Wooller and Robin Marlar in the same side. They were deeply involved in all-out warfare at that time and I think it showed the selectors must have had a good sense of humour.

I do not remember much about the 1956 game because it was virtually washed out by the rain except that J. J. Warr obviously loved every minute of having us on the receiving end for a change. By the time we came to the 1961 match, I tended to regard it as a bit of an anachronism and I gave myself a rest in that game. I wouldn't have minded so much if we had played a match against the Players as well as the Gentlemen as they used to do in the old days. But, by 1961, there was a lot of talk that this might well be the last game of its kind and I wasn't really sorry to see it go. On the other hand, while the amateur and professional categories remained, I could see that there was keen competition between the two when it came to finding places in the Test match side.

As Richie Benaud implies, through the fifties the Gentlemen v. Players matches at Lord's were seen increasingly as a Test trial for both amateur and professional. So far as amateur batsmen were concerned, Peter May always thought that runs scored against the best professional bowlers in the country helped to ensure an amateur batsman's Test selection, and his century for the Gentlemen in 1951 was seen as a prelude to his Test début. On the other hand, for Colin Cowdrey:

Those matches at Lord's for the Gentlemen became something of a nightmare. I felt I had a lot to lose and if you look through the records you'll see that I rarely made a worthwhile contribution. On the other hand I did well for the Gentlemen at Scarborough. Apart from the hundred which I got there in 1951, I recall the century I got there in 1953. Bedser, Tattersall and Wardle were all bowling well but I kept moving it on and I felt I had played really well. However, in the year up to the tour of Australia in 1954–55 I had a very poor season and my confidence was not increased when, in the Gentlemen and Players match at Lord's in 1954, when all eyes were on the hopefuls for Australia, I was clean bowled by Peter Loader for a duck. He was really swinging the ball and, for an ambitious amateur, there was a lot at stake.

For the professionals, the general resurgence of amateur batting of high quality meant that there were opportunities for bowlers to show their skills against several of those who became major Test batsmen. The inclusion of Peter Loader, to whom Colin Cowdrey refers, followed an agreement by Alec Bedser to stand down so that his Surrey team-mate could – as it proved – successfully stake his claim for inclusion on the tour of Australia. In the same match, the Test selectors showed that they were directly concerned in trying out possible candidates for captaincy when David Sheppard was asked to lead the Gentlemen as part of the continuing process by which he was encouraged to return to international cricket.

In 1955, the needle to which Don Kenyon referred earlier was evident in the match at Lord's – a needle which was sharpened by experiments recently introduced to assist the bowlers. Don Kenyon, who played in that match, recalls:

That was the year when it was decided to leave more grass on the wicket and to add stitches to the seam of the ball. It certainly had its effect. When I arrived for the Test match at Lord's, I genuinely could not see where the wicket was, and the whole ground was shining like glass. When I faced up to the first ball of the match bowled by Heine, it took off from just short of a length and went straight over my head. Peter May got a hundred in the second innings for us but he was battered black and blue. So, with that background, it was likely that the Gentlemen and Players match would be a tough affair and, sure enough, we had a spate of injuries on both sides.

In 1956, the selectors once again looked at the Gentlemen v. Players match to check on the performance of leading professionals like Frank Tyson, who came back to representative cricket after a longstanding leg injury, as did Denis Compton. This match was notable not only as the 150th anniversary game in the series but also for a ferocious assault by Tyson and Trueman on the amateur batsmen. Frank Tyson recalls:

I was getting very cynical about the shamateur business. There were a lot of assistant secretaries about and Trevor Bailey had told me when we were in Australia, 'You know Frank, I couldn't afford to be a professional.' I understood the dilemma of some of

the post-war amateurs who had to choose between £700 or £800 a
year as a professional and the better-paying job opportunities
outside, but it was hard to accept that those who stayed on to play
in the game as amateurs should earn more than we did through
expenses and fake jobs. So Fred Trueman and I certainly put our
backs into it when we saw that the wicket could help us to get
after some of those shamateurs.

Freddie Trueman recalls that this element of aggression was a
continuing feature until the end of the series:

I remember that Frank and I also gave them a rough ride at Lord's
in 1957, and Brian Statham and I repeated the dose the following
year. Those were rain-affected wickets and we had some trouble
when it came for our turn to bat and, with the amount of rain we
had, we had a series of drawn matches. But in 1961 we were right
back on top at Lord's when we won comfortably. I remember it
well because we were told that the Gentlemen would be strengthened by two Cambridge undergraduates who had scored a
tremendous number of runs at Fenner's that year. One of them
was E. J. Craig, who played a few games for Lancashire but
dropped out of the game quite early on. The other was the
Gentlemen's wicket-keeper by name of J. M. Brearley.

Mike Brearley recalls:

It was a pretty formidable proposition coming in to cricket at that
level and both Eddie Craig and I were quickly made to realize that
we were out of our depth.

In what proved to be the last match of the series at Lord's in 1962,
the choice of England captain in the post-May era was wide open. At
Lord's, Colin Cowdrey, Ted Dexter and David Sheppard were all
invited to play and, when Colin Cowdrey withdrew because of
injury, David Sheppard scored a hundred which took him to
Australia – but under Ted Dexter's captaincy. David Sheppard was
then Warden of the Mayflower Family Centre in Canning Town

and today, as Bishop of Liverpool, recalls the intrigue which surrounded this final attempt to bring him back as England captain:

Of all people, the first person to make a move was the cricket journalist E. M. Wellings. He had run a consistently critical line in his column about unfair advantages given to amateurs like me, so I was very surprised when he asked if he could come and see me. He came over to Canning Town and said, 'I want to persuade you to go to Australia as captain.' The next thing that happened was that Walter Robins, the chairman of the selectors, rang me up and, with shattering indiscretion, virtually offered me the job. I'd been through all this before when they wanted to put me in to replace Len Hutton and I wasn't going to play that game again. But of course the press built it up into the big shootout between Colin Cowdrey, Ted Dexter and myself in the Gentlemen v. Players match at Lord's. Meanwhile I had been through an appalling patch of failures in county games. What made it worse was that the press exuded sympathy which made it clear they were supporting me. So when we came to the Gentlemen v. Players match and I got a hundred pretty well, I thought I must be in with a chance to lead the side to Australia. But I had no regrets when Ted was chosen and we had a happy tour together, particularly because our wives became great friends as well.

Ted Dexter also recalls the background to the 1962 game at Lord's and his earlier appearances in the series:

I rarely got big scores at Lord's in those games and I hated the place. Fortunately, on my first appearance there in 1957, the wicket was drying to just the right consistency. I was always a good polisher and when I had a go with the ball I managed to get it to come up in cherry-blossom style and it was swinging and doing all kinds of handy things. Then when we went up to Scarborough later that year for the Gentlemen I got out cheaply to Brian Close. This seemed to be the start of a bit of rivalry between us. To some extent we were competing for an England place and we always enjoyed doing the other down.

For his part, Brian Close chuckles when he recalls some of their early encounters:

> You remember how Ted would pace up and down at the batting crease even between deliveries. I realized quite early on that what he really hated was losing the bowling. So we would give him a single and he would find he had to watch the bowling for another five balls in most overs. This led him to take risks by hitting across the line and so on. He was not good at that. He was a great straight player. He would say to me, 'I don't know how you managed to get me out with that rubbish', and I'd say, 'I'd get you out with an orange if you play shots like that.'
>
> He could be pretty handy when conditions were right for his bowling but I remember that Ray Illingworth and I enjoyed taking a lot of runs off him and the other amateurs in the Gents v. Players match at Lord's in 1959 when we had our record partnership of 184 for the seventh wicket, but Ted was just getting into his stride around that time and I certainly didn't begrudge him the England captaincy.

Ted Dexter believes that Walter Robins chose him as captain because he had more of a gambling instinct than either of his immediate predecessors, Peter May or Colin Cowdrey. He adds:

> That was probably true but I didn't always get it right. I think Robbie marked me up when I got runs and tried to make a game of the 1962 match with a declaration.

There was another factor which one of the new breed of professionals, Peter Parfitt, had noted when Ted Dexter led the MCC team in India and Pakistan during the winter of 1961-62:

> I found then, and subsequently, when Ted had a run as the established Test captain that he was the most unselfish international performer in my career. When you get to Test level, you are apt to look after number one because the price of failure is so high. But, with Ted, he was always willing to take on the more difficult of the bowlers if you were going through a bad patch and

he would help and encourage you all the way. Funnily enough, that was true in Test cricket, but in county cricket Johnny Wood-cock always argued that Ted was selfish because he would get out if he wanted to go and watch the 3.30 at Ascot on the television. Tony Lock always said that, if Ted had been a professional, he would never have been picked for England. But, for my money, he was the least selfish player of my time and that, in part, must have stemmed from his amateur status.

Ted Dexter gave his own unconscious illustration of this quality in comparing Gentlemen and Players matches at Lord's and at Scarborough:

Towards the end of that series, the amateurs were suffering because so much of the fire power was on the Players' side. I didn't do much at Lord's but in the match at Scarborough in 1957 I got 80-odd in the second innings. There were some members of our side who'd had a heavy night out before we were due to begin our second innings and no one seemed very keen on facing Fred Trueman and Frank Tyson. I was young and keen in those days and volunteered to go in high up the list. I think that perhaps helped me too when the selectors were thinking about me for the captaincy later on.

In the earlier post-war years at Scarborough the mood had remained essentially lighthearted. Tea was still served on the field to the not-out batsmen and the fielding side by waiters in tail-coats carrying silver trays with china cups and saucers. Len Hutton, asked about his record 241 for the Players in 1953, when he com-pleted his hundred with a six just before lunch, is apt to write it off as 'knockabout stuff': 'I really wasn't happy unless I had to do my damnedest to succeed.' On the other hand, Norman Yardley, whose leadership of the Gentlemen in this match enabled them to complete a double over the Players, adds:

It is typical of Len to play that innings down. It was mag-nificent and there was a bit of background to it because he had had some kind of row with Robin Marlar, who finished up with one for a hundred and plenty. So the competition was more intense than might have appeared judging by the declaration and it was almost twenty years since we had last beaten the Players. So to do it twice in one year meant a lot to us, even if it was Festival cricket.

Trevor Bailey (who, as we shall see, had his own reservations about the value of the Gentlemen v. Players match and who normally preferred cricket the hard way) was always prepared to enter into the festival spirit:

On one occasion I won some bottles of champagne by going out to bat against F.S. [Trueman] wearing a yachting cap and I once bowled an orange at Len Hutton. This trick had to be accomplished with a full toss, first ball after lunch. I managed that all right and he was covered in the stuff. The crowd loved it but there were some fairly terse comments from Len including references to cleaning bills. You could only do that kind of thing infrequently and sometimes it was overdone. The main thing was to ensure we got a finish as near to the last over of the match as possible and it was remarkable how well some people managed to perform considering the way they had punished their system the night before.

As soon as the day's cricket was over, we would repair to the pavilion bar to have drinks with all the Players. Then it would be off to the Grand Hotel for a quick bath and change into black tie before descending to have drinks with the ladies who were all in long dresses. It was all quite formal and we were expected to circulate and be rather grand. I remember the consternation there was on the part of Shrimp Leveson Gower when Billy Sutcliffe demanded that he had his pint of beer before we went in for dinner.

That meal was taken in the Cricketers' Room with the portraits of amateurs round the walls. Until his death in 1954 Shrimp would preside and, as a former wartime transport officer whose bedtime reading was *Bradshaw's Railway Guide*, he would invariably succumb to put-up questions such as, 'What is the best way to get from

Nether Wallop to Cockermouth?' Across the road, the professionals and their ladies would gather in more relaxed fashion at the Balmoral Hotel (inevitably referred to as 'The Immoral') and progressively, in the post-war years, the two streams of Gentlemen and Players and their ladies would merge to drink and dance at the Spa Pavilion.

Just occasionally there was a rare outbreak of cricket conflict to upset the relaxed atmosphere. Billy Sutcliffe remembers:

> Denis Compton hardly ever came to play in the Scarborough Festival and I think I am right in saying that he only once appeared there for the Players. This was when he came to captain the side in 1956. I think he thought that we ought to let him make a few as he was clearly nearing the end of his career. But after he had got a single, Doug Insole bowled it wide and Denis was out stumped. He was upset at coming all that way without showing the crowd anything. So when I went in to bat with Bill Edrich for forty minutes that evening, we found Frank Tyson bowling at one end and Alan Moss at the other, and we were surrounded by packed-in close fielders in a way which would have made Keith Carmody proud. We didn't half get some hammer in that last session.

Such 'needle' was rare at Scarborough; and social change was generally subtle and unlikely to spoil the atmosphere of a party which had been in progress for over half a century. When more direct challenges to Scarborough's social distinctions came in the late fifties and early sixties, they came not from the professionals but from the amateurs.

Charles Robins, who followed his father into the Gentlemen's team at Scarborough in 1959, puts it very directly: 'By the time I came on to the first-class scene, the amateur was more of an embarrassment than an adornment.' His fellow Middlesex teammate, Mike Brearley, who played in both matches for the Gentlemen in 1961, was even more blunt in his rejection of the Festival's traditions:

> When I went up to Scarborough that year, no one told me about

all the dressing-up and so on and I didn't have a dinner jacket and therefore I was in a bit of a jam when it came to dining in the Cricketers' Room at the Grand Hotel. All this seemed pretty anachronistic to me and I felt that the sooner we saw the end of the distinction between amateurs and professionals the better.

Mike Brearley, whose intelligence would make him an outstanding leader at Test and county level, was a key figure in bridging the gap between the old amateur and the modern cricketer of today. Certainly, his forthright views helped to expedite the end of amateur cricket. In this he was following in the footsteps of the Reverend David Sheppard, who had been pressing for the abolition of the amateur and professional distinction for some years.

Even at Lord's there were increasing signs of impatience with the historic fixture between the Gentlemen and Players. For one of the Gentlemen's most regular performers, Trevor Bailey:

The match did not mean as much as when I started in the game. In my early days it was a genuine Test trial. However, I suppose my position was a bit special as the Gentlemen were always short of bowling and so I got picked a lot for them. I enjoyed the matches but they lacked the challenge of, say, Essex v. Yorkshire when there was really something at stake. One year, I declined an invitation to play for the Gentlemen. I'd pulled a muscle in my back and I played instead for Essex against Sussex. I did not bowl in the first innings but I batted and had a turn with the ball in the second innings. I think I got a few wickets. Anyway, I remember that Robin Marlar, who would have been captaining Sussex in that match but who had been chosen as my replacement for the Gentlemen, was livid. I suppose this illustrated the way we approached the Gentlemen and Players match with less reverence than in my early days.

In 1954, David Sheppard recalls that someone came into the Gentlemen's dressing-room and announced that the first day's attendance (which had progressively fallen after the balmy days of 20,000-plus in the early post-war years) was sufficient to ensure that the match could be played again in the following year and, more facetiously, that it would even be possible to meet the expenses claim made by Reg Simpson in travelling from as far afield as Trent Bridge.

In the 1958 match, the Players' captain Godfrey Evans made his point when he told his team, 'Gentlemen, it is time for the Players to take the field.' Later, when Raman Subba Row came out to bat, he found the Players' captain in even more waspish mood. At that time Subba Row was on the receiving end of much of the criticism of shamateurism. Cheerfully relaxed on the subject today, the current chairman of the Test and County Cricket Board recalls:

> I remember that particular match pretty well because after I had been batting a short while Godfrey Evans said to me, 'Well, before you came in, I knew you were no Gentleman. Now that I've seen you batting a bit, I realize that you're not a Player either.'

Typically, Raman Subba Row did not add that he went on to score a century in the match, and there is little doubt that this innings ensured his selection for the tour of Australia.

For a time it seemed that this 'Test trial' opportunity, together with the general arguments in favour of the independent cricketer as a leader, might ensure the continuance of some kind of unpaid first-class performer. The matter was considered directly by a special committee of the MCC in 1959 which was constituted to consider the role of the amateur in first-class cricket. It was chaired by the Duke of Norfolk and comprised H. S. Altham, G. O. Allen, M. J. C. Allom, Col. R. J. de C. Barber, F. R. Brown, E. D. R. Eagar, C. A. F. Hastilow, C. G. Howard, D. J. Insole, P. B. H. May, C. H. Palmer, Col. R. S. Rait Kerr, A. B. Sellers, Rev. D. S. Sheppard and R. Aird (secretary).

The committee arrived at a number of conclusions which were subsequently accepted by the Advisory County Cricket Committee. These included:

> The wish to preserve in first-class cricket the leadership and general approach to the game traditionally associated with the amateur player.

The rejection of any solution to the problem on the lines of abolishing the distinction between amateur and professional and regarding them all alike as 'cricketers'.

The reaffirmation that the distinctive status of the amateur cricketer was not obsolete, was of great value to the game and should be preserved.

David Sheppard describes how even he found himself having to give public support to these recommendations:

Within the committee, only C. A. F. Hastilow, the chairman of Warwickshire, and myself had argued that it was dishonest to pay amateurs on the side through mechanisms such as the assistant secretary. However, when I saw I was heavily outnumbered, I had to decide what to do and I decided not to voice my opposition publicly but to try and work the change from within.

A few weeks later, I appeared by previous arrangement on a BBC Sportsnight programme on television. When my interview began, I was immediately attacked on the grounds that I had changed from my previous opposition to the distinction between amateur and professional. So I found myself saying, 'I think that what the committee had in mind was this or that', but I felt very uncomfortable about the whole thing.

It seemed that matters might have been left in this state indefinitely, were it not for growing embarrassment over the question of amateur expenses. Billy Griffith was among those working behind the scenes as assistant secretary at Lord's who hoped that a way could be found to resolve the problem fairly:

I, too, was fed up with the hypocrisy. Several of the counties had made stupid arrangements by which they gave funds to the amateur and asked that they be reimbursed any unutilized expenses. Obviously they got nothing back. I suggested the better way would be for counties to pay employees for the time spent playing cricket beyond the agreed level for each individual and their company. This way, a number of amateurs could have played on holiday if they so wished and added extra days which the county could make up. But we seemed to get into a jam when we tried to work out practical arrangements.

Part of the problem to which Billy Griffith referred was illustrated by the examples of both David Sheppard and Ted Dexter. As David Sheppard says:

I went to Australia on the so-called broken-time payments. I had to work out what a curate would be earning and it wasn't much. I got £360 in my first year as a curate and so I wasn't in a position to claim a massive sum.

Ted Dexter had similar difficulties in producing satisfactory calculations despite the additional income which had recently become available to amateurs as well as professionals when MCC lifted regulations on advertising:

Where we were fortunate, I suppose, was that having learnt to play on good wickets at university one trusted the surface in Test matches and continued to play shots. This made some of us reasonably attractive to the advertisers and so provided a useful outside income. So, when it came to calculating broken time, I felt it was necessary to imply that I was the equivalent of an extremely well-paid executive. But it was difficult to take into account irregular outside earnings and it didn't seem to impress those who decide these matters, and I still finished up with substantially less than I might have been earning outside. So in many ways it was a relief when the whole thing was brought together and we all became cricketers.

The problem of amateur expenses had been directly highlighted a few years earlier by one of the game's most eminent professionals, who raised the matter in conversation with the doyen of amateur cricket. In 1958, Jim Laker went to see Gubby Allen:

I told Gubby that I was considering becoming an amateur and I wondered how he would feel about this. He asked me if I'd given it serious consideration and said that, if I had, he thought it was absolutely splendid but wondered why I wanted to do this at that stage of my career. He didn't look best pleased when I told him that I thought I would be better off in financial terms playing as an amateur in the England team in Australia with expenses rather than drawing professional pay. I knew that this was true because Trevor Bailey had told me he would receive £1000 and I was due to get £800.

Jim Laker did, in fact, later become an amateur when playing for a number of seasons for Essex:

Trevor Bailey was the county secretary as well as the captain of Essex, and when we were coming back from playing in a charity match he asked me whether I'd be willing to turn out for the county on the basis of amateur expenses. We were pretty relaxed about the whole thing and, although I didn't make any money, I certainly wasn't out of pocket and I had a good time with my little swansong. Indeed, I got really quite keen and when we came to play Sussex I remember that I did my damnedest when bowling against Ted Dexter. After an over or two he got down to the non-striker's end and said, 'You're trying a bit today, aren't you?' and I said 'Well, Skipper, I thought I might try and impress you sufficiently to ensure that I get chosen to play for the Gentlemen this year!'

When the final decision to abolish amateur status came (and with it the ending of the Gentlemen v. Players matches) it came almost by accident. In 1961, the MCC set up a cricket enquiry committee to look into current problems, particularly in the light of the financial difficulties facing most of the counties. The committee consisted of Sir Hubert Ashton (chairman), Sir William Worsley, Lord Nugent, H. S. Altham, R. Aird, G. O. Allen, B. O. Babb, A. V. Bedser, C. A. F. Hastilow, D. J. Insole, Sir Edward Lewis, J. H. Nash, R. W. V. Robins, A. B. Sellers, The Rev. D. S. Sheppard, J. J. Warr and W. Wooller. The other members of the committee who were unable to attend the meeting at which the proposal for the abolition of the amateur was considered were W. E. Bowes,

D. B. Carr, A. M. Crawley, C. G. Howard and P. B. H. May.
David Sheppard comments:

You can see that there were quite a lot of people who had been on
the 1959 committee, but Cyril Hastilow and I sat tight while
many people came round to the arguments which we had previously put forward. One of the most influential voices was Harry
Altham. He argued that, unless we accepted the change, there
was little likelihood of public-school and university cricketers
continuing to play in the first-class game but that, if we could
make cricket a reasonably attractive career, a number of them
would stay on at least for some years.

Other members of the committee reflected the same sense of
accepting the inevitable. Gubby Allen says, 'I wanted to retain
amateur status but realized the financial problems. I think we might
have kept the distinction going a little while longer but we had to
make the change sooner or later.' For others, like Wilf Wooller, the
change was long overdue: 'I had been up to Lord's just after the war
with J. C. Clay to put forward the proposal which we were now
agreeing and at that time we had been turned down out of hand.'

With the change, however, came a certain sadness and regret on
the part of many amateurs and professionals who had known the
game in the days when – whatever its imperfections – the system
was seen to work in terms of producing enjoyable and well-
supported cricket. But while such sentiments were not universal
and – to a degree – reflected differences in the generation gap, all
those who had been concerned with the matches between the
Gentlemen and the Players are at one in regarding them as a fascinating part of English cricket history.

For the cricket commentator Brian Johnston, the value of the
amateur was 'that he made things happen. When he came in to bat
you were likely to see strokes. If he came on to bowl, you expected
some action even if that sometimes meant that he was going to be
hit all round the field.' Surprisingly, the radical cricket writer
C. L. R. James sees the value of the amateur as 'crucial because he set
standards which the professional sought and achieved both as indi-

viduals as well as cricketers'. Wilf Wooller says, 'However unfash-
ionable it may be to say it, the ending of the amateur has created a
leadership crisis in the game'; while, for Trevor Bailey, 'The modern game is only professional because of sponsorship – remove that
and we should have an all-amateur game.'

In summing up, we cannot do better than turn to the two great
voices of cricket – E. W. Swanton and John Arlott. They are among
those who have selected their best Gentlemen and Players teams in
Appendix II. They were asked to see themselves in the role of
manager of the two teams and to choose the best sides from the ones
they had seen playing since the First World War. Each is well
qualified for the role, and the professionals' attitude towards them
is summed up when Reg Sinfield says, 'It is hard to understand why
they haven't both been knighted for services to the game years ago.'

One of John Arlott's proudest achievements is his presidency of
the Cricketers' Association – the professionals' own trade union.
He was invited to assume this office in recognition of his enthusiastic and longstanding interest in the professional welfare of the
players, from his first timid entrance as a guest in the Hampshire
dressing-room through years of controversy when he did much to
further several professional careers (most notably in his sponsorship of Basil D'Oliveira) and, above all, in his inspired, poetic view
of the true craftsmanlike qualities of the professional cricketer.

Jim Swanton's claims to be the Gentlemen's manager are no less
valid. From his earliest days as a reporter, he took a particular
interest in the public-school and Oxbridge entry into first-class
cricket. More directly, in the sides which he took to the West Indies
and the Far East and in the formation of his own touring team, the
Arabs (which recently celebrated its fiftieth anniversary), he has
given many opportunities for amateurs to enjoy cricket at the
highest levels in many parts of the world.

Jim Swanton has long argued that the value of the amateur
cricketer lay in his independence. Today he says that he is happy
to stand by the remarks he made when news of the amateur abolition reached him in Australia in November 1962. He received
a breakfast-time cable upon which he commented, in part, as
follows:

'Amateurs abolished' it announced laconically, and behind the words one saw finis written to the oldest of all the traditional rivalries of the cricket field. Not only that, of course. The evolution of the game has been stimulated from its beginnings by the fusion of the two strains, each of which has drawn strength and inspiration from the other. English cricket has been at its best when there has been a reasonably even balance between those who have made the game their livelihood and those who have played it, with whatever degree of application and endeavour, basically for relaxation and enjoyment.

John Arlott's view is one which, as ever, is both romantic and pragmatic:

In his period, the amateur played a great part in English cricket. In the Edwardian period certainly. In those days he was both financial patron and someone who could give a certain dash to the game. There was still a case for the amateur between the wars when Tich Freeman chucked 'em up in the air and the amateurs went down the track to hit him and Les Ames could get sixty-odd victims stumped in a season, while many of Tich's other wickets came from catches at long-on and long-off. Yes, that was all splendid. But in the present day, and we had reached it by the sixties, there is no room for the amateur because people simply can't afford to play without pay and shamateurism became increasingly objectionable. Yes, they were right for their time but not today.

Those professionals who played between the wars and in the early post-war years have a different perspective from those who came afterwards. Among the older generation, there is for the most part nothing but regret expressed at the passing of the amateur. Jim Laker, as one who bridged the generation gap, was one of the few to say clearly that the ending of the distinction was one of the best things which happened in his cricketing career. On the other hand, the national cricket coach, Les Lenham, who was just starting to play the game when the amateur was abolished (and whose son is

now making his way in the first-class game), says, 'I never thought
I should hear myself saying this, but we lost a lot when it was no
longer possible for the amateur to play first-class cricket.'

In one narrow sense, Les Lenham is incorrect. A number of
Oxford and Cambridge undergraduates play first-class cricket as
amateurs – the exceptions being those who, by also playing for
counties, have become contracted players. Phil Edmonds recalls
that in 1973:

> I never gave the notion of playing first-class cricket after Cam-
> bridge a lot of thought. It seemed a natural extension of univer-
> sity cricket, but if I was starting all over again I might want to
> give it rather more detailed consideration.

Imran Khan, who left Oxford in the following year (after he had
previously been turned down at Cambridge), adds an overseas
perspective:

> There is no doubt that the system in England still encourages
> university cricketers to stay on in the first-class game. But it is
> still a major decision and some outstanding contemporaries of
> mine at Oxford did not feel able to make that kind of commit-
> ment to cricket compared to other job opportunities. In Australia
> it is still possible to come into a State side and play as an amateur
> before you have to make a decision as to whether or not to
> become a professional.

When Derek Pringle decided to play for England rather than – to
the anguish of many old graduates – captaining Cambridge against
Oxford in 1982, he was recognizing the opportunities open to
university graduates in professional cricket. When asked on that
occasion how many of the Cambridge side had not signed contracts
with counties, he suggested 'about half'.

Tony Brown, who, after his playing days as a fast bowler for
Gloucestershire, had seen a good deal of the game as secretary/
manager first for Gloucestershire and then for Somerset and as
England manager on tour, even sees scope for the cricketing
schoolmaster among the present-day amateur recruits for professional cricket:

I believe that it is as true today as when I came into the first-class game in 1956 that everyone at heart is an amateur. But the great majority of us have to earn a living. Nowadays this means a basic decision at an early age, but you do get the exception like Roger Knight who has been able to combine first-class cricket with work as a schoolmaster in a way that almost resembles the old August amateurs. He played for Surrey, then Gloucestershire, then Sussex, combining his stay with each county with different appointments as a schoolmaster with increasingly senior positions. Finally he went back to Surrey as captain from 1978 to 1983, but he is rather the exception to the general rule, which means you have to commit yourself to the game full-time.

What is certain is that Harry Altham's prediction has proved correct in the sense that a sizeable number of public-school and Oxbridge cricketers who, in the days of the amateur, would have played under that label, now stay on to try their fortunes in a first-class cricket career. It has to be said, however, that they have become indistinguishable in their general approach to the game from all other modern cricketers.

While Jim Laker's main strictures were directed against the last of the 'shamateurs', he accepted that the genuine amateur had played his part. Generally, the independence and colour which such amateurs brought to the game were much missed and, perhaps above all, the discipline which they provided (and which was expected of them) was seen as part of the game's strength in terms of fair and impartial leadership.

The chief criticisms of the amateur came from within their own ranks and ran parallel with the shifts in the pattern of British social history. Thus, the President of the MCC in 1986, Jack Davies (who made his first-class début in 1931), reflected the social stirrings of the Depression years when he described the game in the thirties as 'a bit feudal', and the retiring captain of Middlesex in 1983, Mike Brearley, asked in the terms of one who has grown up with a more self-critical democracy, 'Who bemoans the passing of the amateur? I don't.'

As against these views must be set the many for whom, perhaps, cricket was part of a way of life which did not require deep social evaluation. The admiration of the Gentlemen for their rivals among the Players was generally unforced and unpatronizing. It was born of the hero-worship of youth and the feeling that – as in any other part of life where there are occasional exceptions – taken all in all, one could not find a more admirable person than the dedicated English professional cricketer. In return, these same professional cricketers are quick to enthuse about the virtues that made up the true amateur whose essential gift to the game was leadership. Thus, Sir Leonard Hutton in recent pronouncements still urges the restoration of old-style amateur leadership to offset what he and many others see as the ills of a money-dominated and quarrelling peer group.

Fred Rumsey, who came into the game in 1960 as an established businessman and created the Players' first professional representative body, the Cricketers' Association, in 1968, makes a powerful argument for a reorganization of the first-class game which would include a substantial place for the amateur as in other countries. In particular, he argues in favour of the ending of county teams enjoying limited support for three-day games; he would substitute a system of town teams able to play at weekends with a nucleus of professionals and continuing opportunities for amateurs to test their skills before having to decide whether to become professionals.

There are obvious difficulties in pursuing such proposals and related ones which argue for a sponsored captain or for a move towards the Australian system, whereby first-class cricket is played over successive weekends. In any event, a detailed consideration of such reforms is beyond the scope of this book. But for the many who have expressed concern over perceived changes in the atmosphere and humour of the modern game, perhaps it may be suggested that the cricketers of today – and not just those who recall their predecessors – can glean some insight into the spirit of chivalry and enjoyment which was evident in the hearts and minds of so many of those who have contributed to this book.

Perhaps for all cricketers, the future of the game will be seen at its best if all can meet the Surrey poet Albert Craig's fervent desire that 'All the Gentlemen should be players and all the Players gentlemen.'

APPENDIX I

SCORECARDS FOR GENTLEMEN v. PLAYERS
MATCHES AND OTHER GAMES OF INTEREST
1919–1962

1919	Lord's	Gentlemen of England v. The Australians
1919	Oval	Gentlemen v. Players
1919	Lord's	Gentlemen v. Players
1920	Lord's	Gentlemen v. Players
1921	Oval	Gentlemen v. Players
1921	Eastbourne	An England XI v. The Australians
1921	Scarborough	Gentlemen v. Players
1924	Oval	Gentlemen v. Players
1924	Lord's	Gentlemen v. Players
1925	Lord's	Gentlemen v. Players
1925	Scarborough	Gentlemen v. Players
1927	Scarborough	Gentlemen v. Players
1931	Scarborough	Gentlemen v. Players
1934	Lord's	MCC v. The Australians
1934	Oval	Gentlemen v. Players
1934	Lord's	Gentlemen v. Players
1934	Folkestone	Gentlemen v. Players
1936	Lord's	Gentlemen v. Players
1937	Lord's	Gentlemen v. Players
1938	Lord's	Gentlemen v. Players
1939	Lord's	Gentlemen v. Players
1943	Lord's	England v. The Dominions
1944	Lord's	England v. Australia
1953	Lord's	Gentlemen of England v. The Australians
1946–62	Lord's	Gentlemen v. Players
1947–62	Scarborough	Gentlemen v. Players

LORD'S 1919 – JUNE 23–25
GENTLEMEN OF ENGLAND v. THE AUSTRALIANS

THE GENTLEMEN

Rev. F. H. Gillingham c Gregory b Lampard	83
D. J. Knight lbw b Winning	42
A. J. Evans c Pellew b Stirling	68
P. F. Warner (Capt.) b Gregory	43
Hon. C. N. Bruce b Gregory	11
J. W. H. T. Douglas c Stirling b Collins	56
A. W. Carr st Long b Collins	51
Captain D. C. Robinson c Pellew b Stirling	14
M. Falcon c Lampard b Collins	11
J. C. White st Long b Stirling	5
C. S. Marriott not out	1
Byes 14, leg byes 3	17
Total	402

THE AUSTRALIAN IMPERIAL FORCES

	First Innings		Second Innings	
H. L. Collins (Capt.) c Carr b Douglas	11	— c Evans b Douglas	1
W. L. Trennery lbw b Douglas	1	— c Carr b Evans	40
C. B. Willis c Gillingham b Falcon	6	— b Douglas	6
J. M. Taylor c Carr b Falcon	9	— c Bruce b Falcon	35
A. W. Lampard b Falcon	9	— c Gillingham b Douglas	23
C. E. Pellew c Knight b Douglas	14	— c Douglas b White	15
E. Bull c Gillingham b Falcon	5	— b White	14
J. M. Gregory c Robinson b Falcon	16	— c Robinson b Douglas	12
W. S. Stirling b Falcon	2	— c Gillingham b White	1
S. C. Winning not out	3	— c Evans b White	17
E. J. Long c Carr b Douglas	4	— not out	6
Leg byes	5	Byes 8, leg bye 1, no-balls 5	14
Total	85	Total	184

BOWLING

THE AUSTRALIAN IMPERIAL FORCES

	O.	M.	R.	W.
Gregory	23	2	110	2
Collins	27	7	68	3
Lampard	33	1	121	1
Winning	17	2	48	1
Stirling	14	0	38	3

THE GENTLEMEN

	First Innings					Second Innings			
	O.	M.	R.	W.		O.	M.	R.	W.
Douglas	17.4	3	34	4	Douglas	17	4	40	4
White	3	0	5	0	White	18	7	38	4
Falcon	14	3	41	6	Falcon	11	1	33	1
					Marriott	14	5	30	0
					Evans	9	2	29	1

Umpires: W. A. J. West and W. Smith

Result: The Gentlemen won by an innings and 133 runs.

THE GENTLEMEN

First Innings		*Second Innings*	
Rev. F. H. Gillingham c and b Woolley .	0	— lbw b Woolley	3
Hon. C. N. Bruce c Brown b Woolley .	10	— b Woolley	6
D. C. Robinson b Parkin	15	— b Parkin	2
P. F. Warner (Capt.) c Hendren b Kennedy	57	— b Kennedy	12
J. N. Crawford b Parkin	2	— b Hearne	28
J. W. H. T. Douglas lbw b Woolley	3	— b Kennedy	16
F. T. Mann b Woolley	0	— not out	24
N. E. Haig c Parkin b Woolley	22	— b Woolley	0
M. Falcon not out	10	— not out	4
G. M. Louden c Strudwick b Woolley ..	8		
J. C. White st Strudwick b Parkin	10		
Byes	4	Byes 2, leg byes 3	5
Total	141	Total (7 wkts.)	100

THE PLAYERS

J. B. Hobbs not out	120
J. W. Hearne c Robinson b Louden	23
C. P. Mead not out	64
Byes 7, no-balls 2	9
Total (1 wkt., dec.)	216

E. Hendren, F. E. Woolley, J. T. Tyldesley (Capt.), G. Brown,
A. S. Kennedy, W. Hitch, C. H. Parkin, and H. Strudwick did not
bat.

BOWLING

THE PLAYERS

First Innings	O.	M.	R.	W.	*Second Innings*	O.	M.	R.	W.
Kennedy	18	6	39	1	Kennedy	12	6	24	2
Woolley	30	4	69	6	Woolley	18	6	41	3
Parkin	15.5	2	29	3	Parkin	12	3	21	1
					Hearne	4	2	9	1

THE GENTLEMEN

	O.	M.	R.	W.
White	15	2	50	0
Crawford	9	1	34	0
Louden	15	4	54	1
Falcon	6	0	22	0
Douglas	7	1	31	0
Haig	3	0	16	0

Umpires: H. Butt and F. T. Russell

Result: Drawn.

THE GENTLEMEN

First Innings		*Second Innings*	
Rev. F. H. Gillingham lbw b Parkin	10	— lbw b Parkin	29
D. J. Knight c Kennedy b Parkin	71	— c Hearne b Parkin	124
A. J. Evans c Woolley b Parkin	0	— b Parkin	63
P. F. Warner (Capt.) c Woolley b Parkin	34	— b Woolley	0
Hon. C. N. Bruce b Parkin	9	— hit wkt b Woolley	37
J. W. H. T. Douglas c Gunn b Kennedy	30	— not out	11
M. Falcon lbw b Kennedy	11		
A. W. Carr c Woolley b Kennedy	2	— b Woolley	40
Major D. C. Robinson c Woolley b Kennedy	9	— c Hobbs b Woolley	0
G. T. S. Stevens c Hearne b Parkin	24	— b Bestwick	11
G. M. Louden not out	4		
Byes 4, leg byes 6	10	Bye 1, leg bye 1, no-balls 5	7
Total	214	Total (8 wkts. dec.)	322

THE PLAYERS

J. B. Hobbs c and b Douglas	2	— c Louden b Falcon	113
G. Gunn c Louden b Douglas	1	— b Louden	57
J. W. Hearne b Douglas	5	— not out	32
C. P. Mead c Bruce b Falcon	9	— c Stevens b Falcon	2
E. Hendren c Gillingham b Douglas	42		
F. E. Woolley b Douglas	22		
G. H. Hirst (Capt.) not out	50		
A. S. Kennedy lbw b Stevens	12		
C. H. Parkin b Douglas	9		
A. Dolphin c Louden b Douglas	2		
W. Bestwick b Douglas	0		
Byes 6, leg byes 3, no-balls 2	11	Byes 8, leg byes 3	11
Total	165	Total (3 wkts.)	215

BOWLING

THE PLAYERS

First Innings	O.	M.	R.	W.	*Second Innings*	O.	M.	R.	W.
Kennedy	19	5	36	4	Kennedy	13	2	38	0
Bestwick	3	0	7	0	Bestwick	13.3	2	55	1
Parkin	39.5	9	85	6	Parkin	24	2	109	3
Woolley	31	12	45	0	Woolley	25	7	71	4
Hirst	7	1	18	0	Hirst	5	0	22	0
Hearne	4	0	13	0	Hearne	6	0	20	0

THE GENTLEMEN

	O.	M.	R.	W.		O.	M.	R.	W.
Falcon	12	2	44	1	Falcon	12.1	2	55	2
Douglas	20.5	3	49	8	Douglas	16	0	59	0
Stevens	6	2	28	1	Stevens	14	3	34	0
Louden	9	1	33	0	Louden	15	3	45	1
					Evans	4	0	11	0

Umpires: A. J. Atfield and J. Moss

Result: Drawn.

THE GENTLEMEN

	First Innings		*Second Innings*	
D. J. Knight b Parkin	31	—	b Howell	10
V. W. C. Jupp b Howell	9	—	c Hendren b Rhodes	37
H. Ashton b Parkin	3	—	c Woolley b Howell	9
Hon. L. H. Tennyson b Howell	0	—	c and b Woolley	22
J. W. H. T. Douglas (Capt.) c and b Woolley	7	—	lbw b Rhodes	7
A. P. F. Chapman b Parkin	16	—	not out	27
P. G. H. Fender c Hendren b Woolley	50	—	b Woolley	1
G. T. S. Stevens c Strudwick b Howell	47	—	st Strudwick b Woolley	1
R. H. Bettington b Parkin	0	—	c and b Woolley	2
G. E. C. Wood not out	43	—	c Howell b Woolley	3
G. M. Louden b Howell	13	—	b Hearne	3
Byes 6, leg byes 5	11		Byes	2
Total	230		Total	124

THE PLAYERS

J. B. Hobbs lbw b Bettington	33	—	c Stevens b Bettington	33
C. A. G. Russell b Douglas	93	—	c Douglas b Louden	12
C. P. Mead b Louden	10	—	b Louden	24
J. W. Hearne b Jupp	8	—	not out	37
E. Hendren c Stevens b Jupp	1	—	not out	24
G. Brown b Louden	26			
F. E. Woolley lbw b Douglas	0			
W. Rhodes (Capt.) c Ashton b Douglas	6			
H. Strudwick run out	5			
C. H. Parkin not out	15			
H. Howell c Ashton b Douglas	5			
Byes 14, leg byes 9	23			
Total	225		Total (3 wkts.)	130

BOWLING

THE PLAYERS

	First Innings					*Second Innings*			
	O.	M.	R.	W.		O.	M.	R.	W.
Howell	14.5	1	49	4	Howell	11	2	29	2
Parkin	25	6	92	4	Parkin	12	2	27	0
Woolley	16	5	65	2	Woolley	17	7	20	5
Rhodes	2	0	13	0	Rhodes	14	2	38	2
					Hearne	4.4	1	8	1

THE GENTLEMEN

	O.	M.	R.	W.		O.	M.	R.	W.
Douglas	18.1	4	53	4	Douglas	10	1	44	0
Louden	18	3	46	2	Louden	11	2	41	2
Bettington	14	0	60	1	Bettington	5	0	25	1
Stevens	7	3	19	0					
Jupp	7	1	16	2	Jupp	3	0	11	0
Fender	2	0	8	0	Fender	2.5	2	9	0

Umpires: J. Moss and W. A. J. West

Result: The Players won by seven wickets.

THE GENTLEMEN

First Innings		Second Innings	
A. Jeacocke b Durston 15	—	b Durston	25
J. S. F. Morrison c Brown b Hitch 23	—	b Durston	39
Hon. C. N. Bruce lbw b Parkin 127	—	absent hurt	0
C. H. Titchmarsh b Parkin 56	—	b Parkin	26
J. N. Crawford c Hallows b Hitch 42	—	b Durston	5
Hon. L. H. Tennyson c Hearne b Parkin 49	—	lbw b Hearne	4
E. L. Kidd c Brown b Hitch 19	—	c Ducat b Freeman	59
N. E. Haig c Brown b Parkin 33	—	b Durston	4
P. G. H. Fender c Durston b Parkin 7	—	b Hearne	23
Captain T. O. Jameson st Brown b Freeman 0	—	c Hardinge b Freeman	7
G. E. C. Wood not out 12	—	not out	2
Byes 7, leg byes 13, no-ball 1 21		Byes 4, leg byes 3	7
Total 404		Total 201	

THE PLAYERS

C. Hallows lbw b Haig	42
J. B. Hobbs (Capt.) b Jameson	5
J. W. Hearne lbw b Fender	99
A. Ducat run out	80
H. T. W. Hardinge c Morrison b Haig	127
G. Brown lbw b Fender	77
A. Sandham not out	67
W. Hitch b Crawford	62
C. H. Parkin st Wood b Fender	13
F. J. Durston not out	6
Byes 18, leg byes 11, wide 1	30
Total (8 wkts., dec.)	608

A. P. Freeman did not bat

BOWLING

THE PLAYERS

	First Innings					Second Innings			
	O.	M.	R.	W.		O.	M.	R.	W.
Durston	21	3	75	1	Durston	11	1	32	4
Hitch	23	2	81	3	Hitch	7	1	31	0
Parkin	28.3	4	110	5	Parkin	9	3	28	1
Freeman	22	1	89	1	Freeman	19	3	58	2
Hearne	8	0	28	0	Hearne	9	0	45	2

THE GENTLEMEN

	O.	M.	R.	W.
Haig	55	9	182	2
Crawford	19	0	69	1
James	42	4	129	1
Fender	41	4	150	3
Tennyson	3	0	16	0
Kidd	4	0	32	0

Umpires: A. Millward and T. M. Russell

Result: The Players won by an innings and 3 runs.

AN ENGLAND XI

First Innings		*Second Innings*	
Mr G. N. Foster c Gregory b McDonald	5	— c and b McDonald	11
Mr G. A. Faulkner b Armstrong	3	— c Mailey b Armstrong	153
Mr G. Ashton lbw b Armstrong	6	— lbw b Armstrong	36
Mr H. Ashton b McDonald	0	— lbw b Armstrong	75
Mr A. P. F. Chapman b McDonald	16	— b McDonald	11
Mr C. T. Ashton c Ryder b Armstrong	1	— b McDonald	0
Mr M. Falcon b McDonald	8	— c and b McDonald	17
Mr G. E. C. Wood lbw b Armstrong	1	— b McDonald	2
Mr A. C. MacLaren b McDonald	0	— b McDonald	5
Mr C. H. Gibson not out	1	— not out	0
Mr W. Brearley b Armstrong	1	— run out	0
No-ball 1	1	Byes 10, leg bye 1, no-balls 5	16
Total	43	Total	326

AUSTRALIANS

H. L. Collins b Falcon	19	— c H. Ashton b Gibson	12
W. Bardsley lbw b Faulkner	70	— b Gibson	22
C. G. Macartney b Faulkner	24	— b Falcon	14
T. J. E. Andrews b Faulkner	0	— b Faulkner	31
C. E. Pellew c H. Ashton b Falcon	1	— c H. Ashton b Gibson	16
J. Ryder b Falcon	10	— c G. Ashton b Gibson	28
W. W. Armstrong b Falcon	13	— lbw b Faulkner	11
H. Carter c H. Ashton b Faulkner	10	— c C. T. Ashton b Falcon	16
J. M. Gregory not out	16	— lbw b Gibson	0
E. A. McDonald b Falcon	4	— not out	9
A. A. Mailey b Falcon	4	— b Gibson	0
Bye 1, leg byes 2	3	Leg byes 3, no-balls 5	8
Total	174	Total	167

BOWLING

THE AUSTRALIANS

First Innings	O.	M.	R.	W.	*Second Innings*	O.	M.	R.	W.
Gregory	2	0	6	0	Gregory	9	0	51	0
McDonald	10	2	21	5	McDonald	31	3	98	6
Armstrong	8.1	4	15	5	Armstrong	24.5	6	74	3
					Ryder	5	1	11	0
					Mailey	22	3	76	0

AN ENGLAND XI

	O.	M.	R.	W.		O.	M.	R.	W.
Falcon	18.4	2	67	6	Falcon	18	2	82	2
Gibson	14	2	54	0	Gibson	22.4	6	64	6
Faulkner	16	1	50	4	Faulkner	5	1	13	2

Umpires: H. Butt and J. P. Whiteside

Result: An England XI won by 28 runs.

THE PLAYERS

First Innings			*Second Innings*		
G. Brown b Douglas	6	—	b Jupp	54	
P. Holmes c Stevens b Jupp	31	—	c and b Jupp	50	
J. W. Hearne c Burton b Fender	72				
C. P. Mead c Jupp b Fender	86				
E. Hendren c Burton b Jupp	22	—	c Wood b Fender	23	
F. E. Woolley c Knight b Fender	31	—	c Mann b Jupp	13	
A. Sandham b Fender	7				
W. Rhodes b Haig	6	—	not out	11	
G. H. Hirst (Capt.) c and b Haig	1	—	lbw b Fender	37	
W. Hitch lbw b Haig	15	—	c Fender b Stevens	7	
A. S. Kennedy not out	1				
Byes 16, leg byes 7, no-ball 1	24		Byes 10, leg bye 1, no-ball 1	12	
Total	302		Total (6 wkts., dec.)	207	

THE GENTLEMEN

D. J. Knight c Rhodes b Woolley	7	—	st Brown b Woolley	26	
V. W. C. Jupp lbw b Kennedy	8	—	b Kennedy	0	
N. E. Haig b Rhodes	24	—	b Kennedy	3	
J. W. H. T. Douglas (Capt.) b Rhodes	7	—	c and b Rhodes	11	
F. T. Mann lbw b Kennedy	14	—	b Rhodes	4	
A. P. F. Chapman c Hitch b Hearne	1	—	c Kennedy b Hearne	16	
P. G. H. Fender b Kennedy	23	—	b Hirst	68	
G. T. S. Stevens c Woolley b Hearne	22	—	c Woolley b Rhodes	12	
G. E. V. Crutchley b Kennedy	1	—	c Hendren b Woolley	15	
G. E. C. Wood c Hirst b Woolley	12	—	c Hendren b Hirst	0	
D. C. F. Burton not out	10	—	not out	3	
Byes 11, leg bye 1, wide 1	13		Byes 8, leg byes 2, no-ball 1	11	
Total	142		Total	169	

BOWLING

THE GENTLEMEN

First Innings	O.	M.	R.	W.	*Second Innings*	O.	M.	R.	W.
Haig	19.4	1	62	3	Haig	6	0	28	0
Douglas	19	4	65	1	Douglas	2	0	17	0
Fender	25	5	85	4	Fender	13.3	1	64	2
Jupp	17	5	34	2	Jupp	16	0	60	3
Chapman	4	1	10	0					
Stevens	10	1	22	0	Stevens	6	0	26	1

THE PLAYERS

	O.	M.	R.	W.		O.	M.	R.	W.
Hitch	4	1	10	0	Hitch	5	2	17	0
Kennedy	16	4	26	4	Kennedy	11	5	28	2
Woolley	21	7	45	2	Woolley	14	3	29	2
Rhodes	16	4	28	2	Rhodes	16	7	27	3
Hearne	9	4	20	2	Hearne	12	1	47	1
					Hirst	2.2	0	10	2

Umpires: T. M. Russell and G. P. Harrison

Result: The Players won by 198 runs.

THE PLAYERS

First Innings		*Second Innings*	
J. B. Hobbs c Chapman b Falcon	66	— run out	14
A. Sandham lbw b Fender	124	— lbw b Fender	53
F. E. Woolley c Chapman b Falcon	12	— b Calthorpe	50
J. Seymour c Fender b Falcon	1	— b Fender	12
H. T. W. Hardinge c Wood b Falcon	26		
F. Pearson c Foster b Calthorpe	8	— not out	29
M. W. Tate b Falcon	0	— not out	41
H. A. Peach c Mann b Calthorpe	17		
F. Root c Calthorpe b Falcon	11		
H. Strudwick c Foster b Falcon	0		
H. Howell not out	0		
Byes 13, leg byes 9, no-ball 1	23	Leg byes	11
Total	288	Total (4 wkts.)	210

THE GENTLEMEN

First Innings		*Second Innings*	
H. L. Dales b Howell	0	— b Howell	15
G. E. C. Wood c Root b Pearson	39	— b Root	5
M. K. Foster lbw b Tate	10	— b Tate	23
A. P. F. Chapman c Strudwick b Tate	2	— c Strudwick b Howell	48
P. G. H. Fender c and b Howell	8	— b Howell	38
G. R. Jackson c Peach b Howell	0	— c Woolley b Peach	32
F. T. Mann c Strudwick b Tate	0	— b Tate	42
Hon. F. S. G. Calthorpe b Howell	7	— b Tate	7
N. E. Haig b Howell	2	— c Woolley b Tate	5
A. E. R. Gilligan c Hobbs b Pearson	34	— c Seymour b Woolley	112
M. Falcon not out	2	— not out	34
Bye 1, leg byes 8	9	Byes 12, leg byes 7, no-ball 1	20
Total	113	Total	381

BOWLING

THE GENTLEMEN

First Innings	O.	M.	R.	W.	*Second Innings*	O.	M.	R.	W.
Gilligan	14	2	53	0	Gilligan	4	1	14	0
Falcon	17	1	78	7	Falcon	9	0	49	0
Calthorpe	24.3	4	84	2	Calthorpe	16	1	54	1
Haig	17	5	40	0	Haig	10	2	32	0
Fender	7	3	10	1	Fender	10.5	4	50	2

THE PLAYERS

	O.	M.	R.	W.		O.	M.	R.	W.
Howell	14	1	44	5	Howell	17	0	71	3
Tate	12	2	33	3	Tate	26	4	98	4
Root	4	0	9	0	Root	20	3	64	1
Pearson	3.2	0	18	2	Pearson	8	1	33	0
					Peach	9	4	43	1
					Woolley	9.1	1	52	1

Umpires: T. M. Russell and H. Young

Result: The Players won by six wickets.

LORD'S 1924 – JULY 16–18
GENTLEMEN v. PLAYERS

THE PLAYERS

J. B. Hobbs (Capt.) c Lyon b White	118
H. Sutcliffe c Douglas b Robertson-Glasgow	20
J. W. Hearne c Stevens b Robertson-Glasgow	61
F. E. Woolley c MacBryan b Douglas	38
E. Hendren c Stevens b Douglas	5
E. Tyldesley c sub. b Douglas	46
R. Kilner c Robertson-Glasgow b White	113
M. W. Tate c and b Robertson-Glasgow	50
A. P. Freeman c Bryan b White	19
G. Duckworth c White b Douglas	7
H. Howell not out	0
Byes 28, leg byes 8, no-ball 1	37
Total	514

THE GENTLEMEN

	First Innings		Second Innings	
J. C. W. MacBryan b Howell	18	—	lbw b Freeman	35
J. L. Bryan c Woolley b Howell	5	—	c Hendren b Freeman	35
G. T. S. Stevens lbw b Freeman	21	—	not out	42
A. W. Carr b Freeman	8	—	c Tyldesley b Kilner	7
M. K. Foster c Howell b Freeman	0	—	c Woolley b Kilner	3
J. W. H. T. Douglas not out	17	—	c Hearne b Woolley	24
M. D. Lyon lbw b Freeman	11	—	c Tate b Kilner	0
A. E. R. Gilligan (Capt.) c Tyldesley b Freeman	33	—	c Freeman b Kilner	0
J. C. White c Woolley b Freeman	0	—	c Tate b Kilner	1
P. G. H. Fender run out	5	—	absent, hurt	0
R. C. Robertson-Glasgow b Howell	9	—	c Woolley b Kilner	0
Bye 1, no-balls 2	3		Byes 3, leg byes 3	6
Total	130		Total	153

BOWLING

THE GENTLEMEN

	O.	M.	R.	W.
Douglas	32.2	6	107	4
Robertson-Glasgow	43	6	157	3
Gilligan	12	2	42	0
White	33	8	71	3
Fender	8.3	0	28	0
Stevens	18	2	72	0

THE PLAYERS

	First Innings					Second Innings			
	O.	M.	R.	W.		O.	M.	R.	W.
Howell	14.2	2	48	3	Howell	1	0	2	0
Tate	15	3	27	0	Tate	5	2	12	0
Freeman	19	3	52	6	Freeman	13	1	41	2
					Kilner	20	10	20	6
					Hearne	10	3	34	0
					Woolley	4	0	38	1

Umpires: H. Butt and W. Reeves

Result: The Players won by an innings and 231 runs.

THE GENTLEMEN

First Innings		*Second Innings*	
J. L. Bryan lbw b Macaulay	6	— c Kilner b Tyldesley	22
G. T. S. Stevens run out	75	— c and b Kilner	129
K. S. Duleepsinhji c Tyldesley b Kilner	12	— b Macaulay	0
A. W. Carr (Capt.) c Holmes b Tyldesley	82	— c Hearne b Kilner	13
E. W. Dawson b Kilner	33	— b Tyldesley	9
H. J. Enthoven c and b Hearne	36	— c. Sutcliffe b Woolley	8
Hon. F. S. G. Calthorpe b Tyldesley ...	33	— c Tyldesley b Macaulay	1
G. O. Allen lbw b Macaulay	11	— not out	52
P. G. H. Fender b Macaulay	4	— c Hearne b Kilner	32
R. H. Bettington not out	2	— not out	21
N. B. Sherwell, lbw b Tyldesley	0		
Byes 12, leg byes 2, no-ball 1	15	— Byes 15, leg byes 6, wides 5, no-balls 2	28
Total 309		Total (8 wkts., dec.) ...315	

THE PLAYERS

J. B. Hobbs (Capt.) c Allen b Stevens	140		
H. Sutcliffe run out	50		
P. Holmes c Sherwell b Bettington	92		
F. E. Woolley run out	32		
J. W. Hearne c Carr b Fender	6		
E. Hendren c Calthorpe b Allen	28		
R. Kilner c Sherwell b Allen	59		
M. W. Tate c Fender b Stevens	8	— not out	38
G. G. Macaulay b Stevens	11	— not out	11
R. Tyldesley c Bettington b Stevens	0		
H. Strudwick not out	6	— lbw b Calthorpe	0
Byes 11, leg byes 11, wide 1, no-balls 2	25	Byes 8, leg bye 1	9
Total 457		Total (1 wkt.) 58	

BOWLING

THE PLAYERS

First Innings	O.	M.	R.	W.	*Second Innings*	O.	M.	R.	W.
Tate	18	4	57	0	Tate	27	7	56	0
Macaulay	22	6	67	3	Macaulay	31	4	71	2
Kilner	30	10	80	2	Kilner	16	5	37	3
Tyldesley	17.5	5	36	3	Tyldesley	23	8	58	2
Hearne	18	6	54	1	Hearne	5	2	13	0
					Woolley	16	2	52	1

THE GENTLEMEN

	O.	M.	R.	W.		O.	M.	R.	W.
Allen	25	3	82	2	Allen	2	0	17	0
Calthorpe	20	2	78	0	Calthorpe	4	2	7	1
Bettington	18	1	79	1					
Fender	29	6	90	1	Fender	3	0	10	0
Enthoven	6	0	31	0					
Stevens	17.1	0	72	4	Stevens	3	1	7	0
					Duleepsinhji	3	1	8	0

Umpires: W. Reeves and W. A. J. West

Result: Drawn.

THE GENTLEMEN

First Innings		*Second Innings*	
G. T. S. Stevens b Geary	26	— c. Hammond b Tate	11
V. W. C. Jupp c Geary b Hammond	49	— c Geary b Tate	0
K. S. Duleepsinhji c Hammond b Tate	31	— lbw b Tate	10
A. W. Carr, c Hammond b Kennedy	101	— b Kennedy	21
D. R. Jardine lbw b Kennedy	6	— b Geary	5
Hon. L. H. Tennyson run out	1	— b Geary	79
Hon. F. S. G. Calthorpe b Tate	5	— b Hammond	18
J. W. H. T. Douglas (Capt.) b Geary	15	— lbw b Astill	13
F. W. Gilligan c Geary b Tate	18	— not out	21
A. E. R. Gilligan c Geary b Kennedy	10	— b Geary	6
N. E. Haig not out	0	— c Strudwick b Hendren	21
Byes 7, leg bye 1	8	Byes 18, leg byes 12	30
Total	270	Total	235

THE PLAYERS

J. B. Hobbs (Capt.) not out	266
A. Sandham b Jupp	22
C. Hallows c F. W. Gilligan b Stevens	32
E. Hendren c F. W. Gilligan b Haig	129
W. W. Whysall not out	15
Byes 14, leg byes 2	16
Total (3 wkts., dec.)	480

W. R. Hammond, G. Geary, W. E. Astill, M. W. Tate, A. S. Kennedy, and H. Strudwick did not bat

BOWLING

The Players

First Innings	O.	M.	R.	W.	*Second Innings*	O.	M.	R.	W.
Tate	20	3	59	3	Tate	19	4	62	3
Kennedy	19	0	66	3	Kennedy	12	2	25	1
Geary	14	1	50	2	Geary	17	2	53	3
Astill	19	2	52	0	Astill	13	3	29	1
Hammond	8	0	35	1	Hammond	12	1	32	1
					Hendren	1.1	0	4	1

The Gentlemen

	O.	M.	R.	W.
Haig	33	4	94	1
Calthorpe	24	1	104	0
Douglas	15	1	52	0
Stevens	21	0	110	1
Jupp	17	1	81	1
Duleepsinhji	3	0	23	0

Umpires: G. H. Hirst and D. Denton

Result: Drawn.

THE PLAYERS

J. B. Hobbs st F. W. Gilligan b Jupp 119
H. Sutcliffe lbw b Jupp 13
P. Holmes c and b Clay 127
A. Sandham lbw b Jacques 16
E. Tyldesley c sub b Haig 116
M. W. Tate b Jupp 27
H. A. Peach b Jupp 3
G. Geary b Clay 6
W. Rhodes (Capt.) not out 15
J. Mercer b Jupp 35
G. Duckworth not out 1
Byes 20, leg byes 9, wides 2, no-balls 4 35

Total (9 wkts., dec.) 513

THE GENTLEMEN

	First Innings		Second Innings	
L. G. Crawley run out	45	—	c Tyldesley b Mercer	7
T. Arnott c Duckworth b Geary	17	—	lbw b Tate	4
V. W. C. Jupp b Peach	42	—	not out	101
N. E. Haig c Tate b Peach	5	—	st Duckworth b Holmes	85
J. W. H. T. Douglas (Capt.) b Tate	8			
H. J. Enthoven c Geary b Rhodes	40			
F. W. Gilligan b Tate	1			
P. T. Eckersley st Duckworth b Tate ...	36			
A. E. R. Gilligan c Sutcliffe b Tate	46	—	not out	1
J. C. Clay c Sandham b Geary	16			
T. A. Jacques not out	0			
Byes 8, leg byes 7	15		Byes	6
Total 271			Total (3 wkts.) 204	

BOWLING

THE GENTLEMEN

	O.	M.	R.	W.
Jacques	32	4	84	1
Haig	35	8	111	1
Jupp	36	5	158	5
A. E. R. Gilligan	6	2	14	0
Clay	25	4	77	2
Enthoven	2	0	11	0
Arnott	4	0	23	0

THE PLAYERS

	First Innings					Second Innings			
	O.	M.	R.	W.		O.	M.	R.	W.
Mercer	25	4	88	0	Mercer	12	1	19	1
Tate	36	12	55	4	Tate	10	3	22	1
Geary	25.4	9	44	2	Geary	7	0	40	0
Peach	30	11	50	2	Peach	5	1	27	0
Rhodes	20	9	19	1	Rhodes	3	0	30	0
					Sutcliffe	6	0	32	0
					Holmes	4	1	28	1

Umpires: D. Denton and J. Hardstaff

Result: Drawn.

GENTLEMEN v. PLAYERS

THE PLAYERS

First Innings		*Second Innings*	
J. B. Hobbs (Capt.) b Brown	144		
H. Sutcliffe c Robins b Haig	96		
P. Holmes not out	75		
E. Hendren b Jupp	28		
M. Leyland st Gilligan b Jupp	0	— not out	14
E. Paynter lbw b Jupp	6	— not out	13
H. Larwood c Allen b Jupp	11		
H. Verity not out	13		
Byes 20, leg byes 14, wides 7	41		

Total (6 wkts., dec.) 414   Total (0 wkts.) 27

G. Duckworth, T. B. Mitchell, and W. E. Bowes did not bat

THE GENTLEMEN

G. T. S. Stevens b Verity	10
G. D. Kemp–Welch b Larwood	51
R. E. S. Wyatt (Capt.) lbw b Mitchell	92
G. O. Allen lbw b Mitchell	2
V. W. C. Jupp c Hendren b Mitchell	5
H. J. Enthoven b Verity	36
E. W. Dawson b Verity	1
R. W. V. Robins b Bowes	2
N. E. Haig c sub b Bowes	1
F. R. Brown c Paynter b Verity	5
F. W. Gilligan not out	0
Bye 1, leg byes 4	5

Total 210

BOWLING
The Gentlemen

	First Innings				*Second Innings*			
	O.	M.	R.	W.		O.	M.	R.	W.
Allen	14	3	35	0	Haig	4	0	12	0
Haig	14	0	55	1					
Brown	28	2	98	1					
Robins	26	0	75	0					
Jupp	18	2	74	4					
Wyatt	7	0	28	0	Stevens	1	0	1	0
Stevens	2	0	8	0	Enthoven	5	0	14	0

The Players

	O.	M.	R.	W.
Larwood	13	0	34	1
Bowes	22	8	37	2
Verity	25	7	73	4
Mitchell	23.1	6	61	3

Umpires: G. H. Hirst and D. Denton

Result: Drawn.

MCC

	First Innings		*Second Innings*	
Mr R. E. S. Wyatt b Wall	72	—	not out	102
Rev. E. T. Killick c O'Reilly b Wall	3	—	c Woodfull b Grimmett	5
Mr M. J. Turnbull st Oldfield b Fleetwood-Smith	33	—	c Wall b O'Reilly	1
E. Hendren c O'Reilly b Wall	135	—	b O'Reilly	19
Mr B. H. Valentine c Oldfield b O'Reilly	40	—	lbw b O'Reilly	4
Mr A. P. F. Chapman not out	46	—	b Grimmett	1
Mr F. R. Brown c Oldfield b Wall	2	—	c McCabe b Grimmett	12
Mr J. C. White b Grimmett	2	—	c Fleetwood–Smith b Wall	21
Mr I. A. R. Peebles run out	5	—	b Grimmett	0
Mr P. C. Oldfield b Wall	0	—	not out	2
Mr C. S. Marriott b Wall	0			
Byes 11, leg byes 8, wides 3, no-balls 2	24		Byes 12, leg byes 2, wides 1 .	15
Total	362		Total (8 wkts.)	182

THE AUSTRALIANS

W. M. Woodfull c White b Brown	20
W. H. Ponsford not out	281
D. G. Bradman c and b Brown	5
S. J. McCabe b Peebles	192
L. S. Darling c Hendren b White	11
W. A. Brown c Oldfield b Brown	2
W. A. Oldfield b Brown	7
C. V. Grimmett not out	26
Byes 9, leg byes 6	15
Total (6 wkts., dec.)	559

T. W. Wall, W. J. O'Reilly and L. O'B. Fleetwood-Smith did not bat.

BOWLING

THE AUSTRALIANS

	First Innings					*Second Innings*			
	O.	M.	R.	W.		O.	M.	R.	W.
Wall	32.3	10	74	6	Wall	10	1	27	1
McCabe	14	2	53	0					
O'Reilly	23	8	55	1	O'Reilly	21	12	29	3
Grimmett	35	8	81	1	Grimmett	32	5	90	4
Fleetwood-Smith	15	0	72	1	Fleetwood-Smith	6	2	13	0
Darling	2	1	3	0	Darling	3	1	8	0

MCC

	O.	M.	R.	W.
Wyatt	9	1	38	0
Valentine	6	0	28	0
Peebles	40	5	141	1
Marriott	41	9	126	0
Brown	37	2	134	4
White	28	4	77	1

Umpires: A. Morton and J. Hardstaff

Result: Drawn.

THE OVAL 1934 – JULY 11–13
GENTLEMEN v. PLAYERS

THE PLAYERS

A. Sandham b Holmes		65
J. Arnold c Fender b Baxter		125
R. J. Gregory lbw b Baxter		51
H. S. Squires c Machin b Baxter		119
R. Duckfield c sub b Holmes		106
J. W. Lee c Machin b Baxter		4
A. W. Wellard b Baxter		91
A. S. Kennedy (Capt.) not out		40
E. W. Brooks not out		27
Byes 5, leg byes 15, wides 3		23

Total (7 wkts., dec.) 651

J. Mercer and A. R. Gover did not bat

THE GENTLEMEN

First Innings		Second Innings	
R. H. Moore c and b Wellard	12	— c Brooks b Wellard	3
D. P. B. Morkel c Brooks b Gover	0	— lbw b Wellard	1
A. Fairfax c Duckfield b Gover	15	— b Mercer	23
Lord Tennyson c Kennedy b Wellard	5	— lbw b Mercer	42
E. R. T. Holmes (Capt.) c Kennedy b Gover	4	— c Wellard b Mercer	7
H. M. Garland-Wells c Kennedy b Mercer	93	— c and b Lee	0
P. G. H. Fender c Brooks b Gover	10	— b Wellard	21
C. C. Case c Gregory b Gover	11	— b Lee	5
R. S. Machin c Brooks b Wellard	5	— c sub b Gover	25
A. E. G. Baring not out	22	— b Mercer	14
A. D. Baxter b Wellard	0	— not out	6
Byes 9, leg byes 4, wide 1, no-ball 1	15	Byes 4, leg byes 2, wide 1	7
Total	192	Total	154

BOWLING

THE GENTLEMEN

	O.	M.	R.	W.
Baxter	28	3	128	5
Baring	19	1	113	0
Fairfax	15	2	102	0
Morkel	4	0	23	0
Holmes	16	1	110	2
Fender	14	1	75	0
Garland-Wells	16	0	77	0

THE PLAYERS

First Innings	O.	M.	R.	W.	Second Innings	O.	M.	R.	W.
Gover	16	4	57	5	Gover	10	1	34	1
Wellard	17.3	2	60	4	Wellard	13.5	1	53	3
Mercer	9	2	36	1	Mercer	13	3	32	4
Kennedy	4	1	20	0					
Lee	3	1	4	0	Lee	5	0	28	2

Umpires: E. J. Smith and J. Stone

Result: The Players won by an innings and 305 runs.

THE PLAYERS

First Innings		*Second Innings*	
H. Sutcliffe c Holmes b Brown	15	— c Human b Allen	65
A. Mitchell b Allen	0	— c Turnbull b Human	120
W. R. Hammond b Baxter	5	— st Levett b Human	0
J. O'Connor b Holmes	22	— not out	20
M. Leyland st Levett b Brown	80	— c Valentine b Holmes	16
E. Hendren (Capt.) b Baxter	24		
L. E. G. Ames c Melville b Allen	76		
M. S. Nichols c Levett b Allen	27		
H. Verity c Holmes b Brown	1		
J. Smith c Human b Brown	5	— b Holmes	5
T. B. Mitchell not out	1		
Byes 3, leg byes 2, wide 1, no-ball 1	7	Byes 15, leg bye 1, wides 2, no-ball 1	19
Total	263	Total (5 wkts., dec.)	245

THE GENTLEMEN

R. E. S. Wyatt (Capt) c Ames b T. B. Mitchell	34	— not out	104
C. F. Walters c Hammond b T. B. Mitchell	12	— b Nichols	79
A. Melville c Verity b Nichols	12	— lbw b Nichols	1
M. J. Turnbull b T. B. Mitchell	11		
J. H. Human b Hammond	66		
B. H. Valentine b Nichols	19	— b Verity	19
E. R. T. Holmes b Nichols	0		
G. O. Allen lbw b Verity	63		
F. R. Brown not out	35	— not out	23
W. H. V. Levett b T. B. Mitchell	4		
A. D. Baxter b Verity	0		
Byes 4, leg byes 12, no-balls 5	21	Byes 5, leg bye 1	6
Total	277	Total (3 wkts.)	232

BOWLING

THE GENTLEMEN

First Innings	O.	M.	R.	W.	*Second Innings*	O.	M.	R.	W.
Allen	26	6	62	3	Allen	18	6	44	1
Baxter	20	4	52	2	Baxter	21	4	56	0
Brown	31.5	8	106	4	Brown	16	4	33	0
Holmes	22	8	36	1	Holmes	11.3	1	38	2
					Human	11	1	37	2
					Valentine	2	0	18	0

THE PLAYERS

	O.	M.	R.	W.		O.	M.	R.	W.
Smith	24	8	55	0	Smith	9	1	42	0
Nichols	22	6	40	3	Nichols	14	3	63	2
T. B. Mitchell	30	8	94	4	T. B. Mitchell	3	0	31	0
Verity	17.4	5	41	2	Verity	15	4	61	1
O'Connor	2	0	7	0					
Hammond	11	3	19	1	Hammond	2	0	18	0
					Sutcliffe	2	0	11	0

Umpires: A. Morton and J. Hardstaff

Result: The Gentlemen won by seven wickets.

THE PLAYERS

First Innings		*Second Innings*	
J. B. Hobbs (Capt.) b Allom	24	— c Garland-Wells b Read	18
C. J. Barnett c Powell b Read	3	— c Jahangir Khan b Read	14
F. E. Woolley c Mitchell-Innes b Allom	15	— lbw b Jahangir Khan	18
W. R. Hammond c Mitchell-Innes b Jahangir Khan	13	— b Jahangir Khan	46
L. E. G. Ames c Powell b Read	54	— c Tennyson b Read	4
C. C. Dacre b Allom	0	— absent, ill	0
G. Geary b Read	39	— c Walters b Read	109
G. A. E. Paine lbw b Garland-Wells	3	— c Hamilton b Allom	39
A. W. Wellard b Read	2	— c Hamilton b Allom	0
M. W. Tate not out	18	— not out	20
A. P. Freeman b Read	11	— c and b Jahangir Khan	1
Leg bye 1, wide 1, no-balls 2	4	Byes 5, leg byes 5, no-ball 1	11
Total	186	Total	280

THE GENTLEMEN

C. F. Walters st Ames b Freeman	14	— b Tate	10
R. H. Moore lbw b Freeman	14	— b Wellard	4
C. P. Hamilton lbw b Tate	50	— b Hammond	19
N. S. Mitchell-Innes c Woolley b Freeman	16	— st Ames b Freeman	27
B. H. Valentine c Wellard b Freeman	47	— b Freeman	18
A. G. Powell c Woolley b Paine	62	— b Tate	10
H. M. Garland-Wells c Woolley b Tate	16	— c Wellard b Freeman	52
M. J. C. Allom c Paine b Freeman	20	— not out	7
M. Jahangir Khan c Freeman b Geary	7		
Lord Tennyson (Capt.) not out	3	— not out	50
H. D. Read b Geary	1		
Byes 6, wides 2	8	Byes 9, leg byes 5, wide 1	15
Total	258	Total (7 wkts.)	212

BOWLING

THE GENTLEMEN

First Innings	O.	M.	R.	W.	*Second Innings*	O.	M.	R.	W.
Read	17.5	1	73	5	Read	15	0	98	4
Allom	16	4	45	3	Allom	18	1	63	2
Jahangir Khan	13	2	46	1	Jahangir Khan	19.3	3	91	3
Garland-Wells	5	1	18	1	Hamilton	3	0	17	0

THE PLAYERS

	O.	M.	R.	W.		O.	M.	R.	W.
Wellard	21	5	71	0	Wellard	7	2	21	1
Tate	19	5	37	2	Tate	22	7	54	2
Freeman	24	9	69	5	Freeman	21.5	1	86	3
Geary	16.1	1	48	2	Geary	12	4	13	0
Paine	12	4	25	1	Paine	4	0	13	0
					Hammond	2	1	10	1

Umpires: F. Chester and A. E. Street

Result: The Gentlemen won by 3 wickets.

THE GENTLEMEN

First Innings		Second Innings	
R. E. S. Wyatt b Gover	0	c Hammond b Sinfield	4
N. S. Mitchell-Innes lbw b Gover	3	c Copson b Sinfield	19
A. Melville c Verity b Copson	1	b Verity	13
M. J. Turnbull c Gimblett b Gover	4	lbw b Verity	1
T. N. Pearce b Gover	1	st McCorkell b Verity	85
E. R. T. Holmes b Gover	30	c Fishlock b Hammond	37
G. O. Allen (Capt.) lbw b Copson	3	c Copson b Hammond	13
F. R. Brown c Copson b Gover	55	c Hammond b Sinfield	4
W. H. V. Levett not out	9	not out	15
J. W. A. Stephenson b Copson	9		
K. Farnes b Copson	5		
Byes 4, leg byes 6	10	Leg byes 3, no-ball 1	4
Total	130	Total (8 wkts., dec.)	195

THE PLAYERS

First Innings		Second Innings	
H. Gimblett c and b Stephenson	3	b Farnes	1
C. J. Barnett c Levett b Allen	0	lbw b Stephenson	2
W. R. Hammond (Capt.) b Stephenson	72	b Farnes	7
M. Leyland b Stephenson	0	b Allen	11
J. Hardstaff c Pearce b Stephenson	69	b Farnes	4
L. B. Fishlock not out	21	not out	26
R. A. Sinfield lbw b Stephenson	0	not out	12
M. McCorkell b Stephenson	0		
H. Verity b Stephenson	2		
A. R. Gover c Levett b Stephenson	3		
W. Copson b Stephenson	8		
Byes 14, leg byes 2	16		
Total	194	Total (5 wkts.)	63

BOWLING

THE PLAYERS

First Innings	O.	M.	R.	W.	Second Innings	O.	M.	R.	W.
Gover	15	3	41	6	Gover	12	2	46	0
Copson	17.1	6	29	4	Copson	13	1	25	0
Verity	15	5	35	0	Verity	26.3	13	33	3
Sinfield	6	3	15	0	Sinfield	23	7	39	3
					Hammond	8	2	32	2
					Leyland	4	1	16	0

THE GENTLEMEN

	O.	M.	R.	W.		O.	M.	R.	W.
Allen	14	3	46	1	Allen	2	0	16	1
Farnes	16	3	43	0	Farnes	9	3	22	3
Stephenson	16.5	6	46	9	Stephenson	9	3	20	1
Brown	7	0	37	0	Brown	2	0	5	0
Wyatt	1	0	6	0					

Umpires: J. Hardstaff and J. Newman

Result: Drawn.

THE GENTLEMEN

First Innings		Second Innings	
R. E. S. Wyatt lbw b Wellard	15	— c Ames b Smith	9
N. S. Mitchell-Innes c Ames b Wellard	4	— lbw b Hammond	50
C. S. Dempster c Compton b Smith	25	— c Wellard b Smith	0
N. W. D. Yardley b Hammond	7	— b Wellard	4
R. C. M. Kimpton b Wellard	59	— c Ames b Goddard	3
H. G. Owen-Smith b Smith	7	— c Ames b Hammond	27
F. R. Brown c Ames b Hammond	0	— c Hardstaff b Goddard	47
C. R. Maxwell st Ames b Goddard	35	— b Goddard	8
A. B. Sellers (Capt.) st Ames b Goddard	4	— not out	20
K. Farnes c Ames b Wellard	1	— b Wellard	0
D. H. MacIndoe not out	0	— run out	0
Byes 4, leg byes 4	8	Byes 4, leg byes 12	16
Total	165	Total	184

THE PLAYERS

First Innings		Second Innings	
L. Hutton b Brown	34	— retired, hurt	1
C. J. Barnett c and b Farnes	14	— b Farnes	20
J. Hardstaff c Wyatt b Macindoe	39	— b Brown	27
W. R. Hammond (Capt.) c Maxwell b Farnes	68		
E. Paynter c Owen-Smith b Brown	12	— not out	37
D. C. S. Compton st Maxwell b Brown	0	— not out	34
L. E. G. Ames b Farnes	0		
James Langridge not out	24		
A. W. Wellard c and b Macindoe	7		
J. Smith b Farnes	16		
T. W. Goddard c Maxwell b Farnes	0		
Byes 3, leg byes 11, wide 1	15	Byes	2
Total	229	Total (2 wkts.)	121

BOWLING

THE PLAYERS

First Innings	O.	M.	R.	W.	Second Innings	O.	M.	R.	W.
Smith	12	1	43	2	Smith	11	0	31	2
Wellard	21	5	62	4	Wellard	17.5	2	44	2
Hammond	13	2	34	2	Hammond	12	4	33	2
Langridge	2	0	8	0	Langridge	4	2	2	0
Goddard	5.5	1	10	2	Goddard	17	2	58	3

THE GENTLEMEN

	O.	M.	R.	W.		O.	M.	R.	W.
Farnes	22	2	65	5	Farnes	7	0	28	1
Macindoe	17	4	62	2	Macindoe	6	0	24	0
Wyatt	6	3	3	0	Wyatt	4	1	18	0
Brown	15	1	53	3	Brown	6	2	25	1
Yardley	2	0	9	0					
Owen-Smith	6	1	22	0	Owen-Smith	2	0	9	0
					Mitchell-Innes	3.1	0	15	0

Umpires: F. Chester and J. Hardstaff

Result: The Players won by eight wickets.

THE GENTLEMEN

First Innings		*Second Innings*	
B. O. Allen c Price b Pollard	10	— b Pollard	5
P. A. Gibb lbw b Smith	18	— c and b Smith	24
R. E. S. Wyatt lbw b Smith	4	— c Smith b Smailes	30
W. R. Hammond (Capt.) c Compton b Pollard	46	— c Price b Smith	37
N. W. D. Yardley c Price b Smailes	88	— b Smith	34
H. T. Bartlett not out	175	— c Compton b Smith	1
R. H. Moore b Nichols	24	— b Smith	4
F. R. Brown c and b Smith	23	— b Smailes	6
R. J. O. Meyer lbw b Smith	0	— not out	14
Captain J. W. A. Stephenson c Price b Nichols	6		
K. Farnes c Price b Pollard	10	— not out	16
Byes 2, leg byes 3, no-balls 2	7	Leg bye	1
Total	411	Total (8 wkts., dec.) ...172	

THE PLAYERS

W. J. Edrich c Stephenson b Farnes	0	— c Gibb b Meyer	78
L. Hutton lbw b Farnes	52	— lbw b Brown	6
W. F. Price c Hammond b Farnes	0	— c Gibb b Farnes	5
E. Paynter c Gibb b Stephenson	36	— lbw b Stephenson	12
J. Hardstaff b Farnes	25	— b Brown	0
F. E. Woolley (Capt.) c Gibb b Meyer ..	41	— c Moore b Brown	8
D. C. S. Compton b Farnes	6	— lbw b Farnes	45
M. S. Nichols b Farnes	23	— not out	31
T. F. Smailes b Farnes	19	— b Stephenson	20
T. P. B. Smith not out	9	— c and b Farnes	9
R. Pollard b Farnes	5	— c Farnes b Stephenson	13
Leg byes	2	Byes 4, wide 1	5
Total	218	Total 232	

BOWLING

THE PLAYERS

	First Innings					*Second Innings*			
	O.	M.	R.	W.		O.	M.	R.	W.
Nichols	29	2	117	2	Nichols	7	1	17	0
Pollard	27.5	4	60	3	Pollard	22	4	53	1
Smith	38	6	140	4	Smith	27	6	68	5
Smailes	21	2	87	1	Smailes	11	0	33	2

THE GENTLEMEN

	O.	M.	R.	W.		O.	M.	R.	W.
Farnes	21.3	6	43	8	Farnes	24	6	60	3
Stephenson	21	4	46	1	Stephenson	21.4	6	63	3
Brown	24	3	82	0	Brown	18	3	75	3
Meyer	9	0	34	1	Meyer	16	4	29	1
Wyatt	5	1	11	0					

Umpires: F. Chester and J. Hardstaff

Result: The Gentlemen won by 133 runs.

LORD'S 1939 – JULY 5–7
GENTLEMEN v. PLAYERS

THE PLAYERS

First Innings		Second Innings	
H. Gimblett b Farnes	52	— b Brocklebank	14
L. Hutton lbw b Stephenson	1	— b Stephenson	86
E. Paynter (Capt.) lbw b Stephenson	4	— b Stephenson	18
D. C. S. Compton b Stephenson	58	— c Brocklebank b Stephenson	70
J. Hardstaff b Farnes	23	— not out	3
H. E. Dollery c Chalk b Farnes	70		
G. H. Pope st Griffith b Brocklebank	7		
W. F. Price lbw b Brocklebank	38		
D. V. P. Wright hit wkt b Farnes	0		
W. Copson b Farnes	0		
W. E. Bowes not out	1		
Byes 9, leg byes 5, wides 2	16	Byes 7, leg byes 4	11
Total	270	Total (4 wkts., dec.)	202

THE GENTLEMEN

First Innings		Second Innings	
F. G. H. Chalk c Hutton b Bowes	5	— c Wright b Copson	8
R. E. S. Wyatt c Price b Bowes	35	— retired, hurt	16
G. F. H. Heane b Bowes	24	— b Wright	25
W. R. Hammond (Capt.) b Pope	20	— c Wright b Copson	4
B. H. Valentine c Price b Copson	10	— c Price b Bowes	8
H. T. Bartlett c Hutton b Copson	15	— b Wright	60
F. R. Brown c Dollery b Copson	0	— c Paynter b Wright	22
S. C. Griffith not out	15	— c Bowes b Wright	10
Captain J. W. A. Stephenson not out	16	— absent, hurt	0
K. Farnes did not bat	0	— not out	1
J. M. Brocklebank did not bat	0	— b Pope	0
Byes 11, leg byes 2, no-balls 5	18		
Total (7 wkts., dec.)	158	Total	154

BOWLING

THE GENTLEMEN

First Innings	O.	M.	R.	W.	Second Innings	O.	M.	R.	W.
Farnes	19.6	2	78	5	Farnes	11	2	35	0
Stephenson	22	5	63	3	Stephenson	12.6	0	78	3
Wyatt	4	0	20	0	Wyatt	1	0	1	0
Brown	5	0	29	0	Brown	4	0	32	0
Brocklebank	16	3	64	2	Brocklebank	9	2	45	1

THE PLAYERS

	O.	M.	R.	W.		O.	M.	R.	W.
Bowes	17	0	34	3	Bowes	8	1	25	1
Copson	20	5	49	3	Copson	9	0	35	2
Pope	14	4	23	1	Pope	4.2	0	22	1
Wright	7	0	34	0	Wright	9	0	72	4

Umpires: J. Hardstaff and E. J. Smith

Result: The Players won by 160 runs.

ENGLAND

First Innings		*Second Innings*	
H. Gimblett (*Somerset*) c Sismey b Roper	10	— b Roper	0
Capt J. D. Robertson (*Middlesex*) b Constantine	33	— c Sismey b Roper	1
L Cpl L. H. Compton (*Middlesex*) b Martindale	1	— b Martindale	1
Sgt Instr D. C. S. Compton (*Middlesex*) run out	58	— c Miller b Martindale	17
Sq Ldr L. E. G. Ames (*Kent*) c and b Clarke	133	— c Sismey b Martindale	13
Major E. R. T. Holmes (*Surrey*) c and b Clarke	39	— not out	45
Flt Lt R. W. V. Robins (*Middlesex*) b Martindale	2	— not out	69
2nd Lt T. E. Bailey (*Royal Marines*) not out	30		
L Cpl A. W. H. Mallett (*Royal Marines*) lbw b Clarke	2		
Sgt T. G. Evans (*Kent*) b Clarke	5	— b Roper	0
Byes 5, leg byes 5, no-ball 1	11	Byes 3, leg bye 1	4
Total (9 wks., dec.)	324	Total (6 wkts., dec.)	150

Flt Sgt A. V. Bedser (*Surrey*) did not bat.

THE DOMINIONS

F/O D. K. Carmody (*Australia*) c Evans b Mallett	43	— c Ames b D. Compton	49
Lt C. S. Dempster (*New Zealand*) c Ames b Bedser	18	— b Mallet	113
Sgt K. R. Miller (*Australia*) c L. Compton b D. Compton	32	— c Evans b Bedser	2
Sgt J. A. Workman (*Australia*) c Mallett b Bedser	8	— b D. Compton	16
L. N. Constantine (*West Indies*) c Mallett b D. Compton	2	— c L. Compton b Bedser	21
O/Cdt D. P. Morkel (*S. Africa*) lbw b D. Compton	2	— c and b Bedser	0
E. A. Martindale (*West Indies*) b D. Compton	4	— c D. Compton b Bedser	0
F/O S. G. Sismey (*Australia*) lbw b Bedser	0	— c Bedser b Robertson	70
P/O A. D. McDonald (*Australia*) lbw b D. Compton	0	— not out	9
C. B. Clarke (*West Indies*) c and b D. Compton	0	— b D. Compton	52
F/O A. W. Roper (*Australia*) not out	0	— c Bailey b Robertson	2
Byes 3, leg bye 1, no-balls 2	6	Byes 11, wides 1, no-balls 5	17
Total	115	Total	351

BOWLING

The Dominions

First Innings	O.	M.	R.	W.	*Second Innings*	O.	M.	R.	W.
Roper	9	0	51	1	Roper	7	1	36	3
Martindale	10	0	50	2	Martindale	9	1	28	3
Clarke	19.7	1	89	4	Clarke	3	0	29	0
Constantine	10	0	61	1	Constantine	4	0	32	0
Miller	4	1	25	0	Miller	4	1	21	0
Morkel	1	0	6	0					
McDonald	8	1	31	0					

ENGLAND

	O.	M.	R.	W.		O.	M.	R.	W.
Bedser	10.6	1	33	3	Bedser	25	1	108	4
Bailey	4	0	15	0	Bailey	6	1	31	0
Mallett	8	1	26	1	Mallett	9	4	28	1
Robins	3	0	20	0	Robins	12	0	75	0
D. Compton	8	2	15	6	D. Compton	20	3	60	3
					L. Compton	3	0	12	0
					Holmes	1	0	14	0
					Robertson	1	0	6	2

Result: England won by 8 runs.

LORD'S 1944 – AUGUST 7
ENGLAND v. AUSTRALIA

ENGLAND

Flt Sgt C. Washbrook c Roper b Cristofani	20
F/O R. T. Simpson st Sismey b Ellis	16
Lt J. D. Robertson st Sismey b Cristofani	15
Flt Lt W. R. Hammond c Roper b Ellis	105
Sq Ldr W. J. Edrich c Workman b Cristofani	14
Capt. D. C. H. Townsend b Ellis	6
Sgt L. J. Todd b Roper	1
Lt A. W. H. Mallett b Roper	16
Lt T. E. Bailey lbw b Roper	13
Sgt T. G. Evans not out	10
Lt D. V. P. Wright c Williams b Ellis	4
Byes 4, leg byes 2	6
Total	226

AUSTRALIA

Flt Lt S. G. Sismey b Bailey	10
Flt Sgt J. A. Workman run out	8
P/O K. R. Miller c and b Todd	85
Flt Sgt C. P. Calvert c Hammond b Wright	10
F/O R. M. Stanford b Mallett	36
F/O E. A. Williams c Evans b Wright	2
Flt Lt J. R. Henderson lbw b Wright	31
F/O D. R. Cristofani b Wright	0
Flt Lt A. D. McDonald c Bailey b Wright	0
Flt Lt A. W. Roper b Wright	2
F/O R. S. Ellis not out	5
Byes 2, leg bye 1, no-ball 1	4
Total	193

BOWLING

AUSTRALIA

	O.	M.	R.	W.
Roper	13	3	37	3
Calvert	16	2	38	0
Cristofani	22	4	63	3
Ellis	24.5	3	82	4

ENGLAND

	O.	M.	R.	W.
Bailey	13	3	46	1
Todd	12	2	35	1
Wright	18.2	3	62	6
Edrich	2	0	8	0
Mallett	16	5	38	1

Result: England won by 33 runs.

THE PLAYERS

L. B. Fishlock c Griffith b Knott 83
C. Washbrook b Trapnell 105
J. T. Ikin b Mallett 81
D. C. S. Compton b Davies 87
J. Hardstaff (Capt.) c Griffith b Davies 15
H. E. Dollery not out 4
T. G. Evans not out 0
    Byes 9, leg byes 14, wide 1 24

    Total (5 wkts., dec.) 399

E. P. Robinson, R. Pollard, W. E. Hollies and L. Gray did not bat

THE GENTLEMEN

First Innings		*Second Innings*	
A. P. Singleton run out 15	—	c Evans b Gray	0
J. G. W. Davies c Evans b Pollard 9	—	c Ikin b Pollard	1
N. W. D. Yardley c Evans b Hollies ... 21	—	c Dollery b Pollard	0
W. R. Hammond (Capt.) c Dollery b			
Pollard 70	—	b Robinson	0
M. P. Donnelly b Hollies 9	—	c Ikin b Robinson	29
B. H. Valentine lbw b Pollard 14	—	c Washbrook b Pollard	5
A. W. H. Mallett c Evans b Gray 0	—	c Ikin b Robinson	16
S. C. Griffith c Dollery b Pollard 0	—	c Compton b Robinson	20
B. M. W. Trapnell not out 0	—	c Pollard b Hollies	14
J. N. Bartlett b Pollard 0		not out	17
C. J. Knott b Gray 3	—	c Evans b Pollard	12
Leg byes 3 3		Leg bye 1	1
Total 144		Total 115	

BOWLING

THE GENTLEMEN

	O.	M.	R.	W.
Mallett	28	3	85	1
Trapnell	18	5	58	1
Davies	24	6	80	2
Knott	32	7	72	1
Singleton	4	0	26	0
Bartlett	10	2	42	0
Yardley	3	0	12	0

THE PLAYERS

First Innings	O.	M.	R.	W.	*Second Innings*	O.	M.	R.	W.
Pollard	18	6	32	5	Pollard	7.5	4	21	4
Gray	12.2	3	29	2	Gray	10	4	15	1
Hollies	27	5	53	2	Hollies	9	2	33	1
Robinson	14	7	27	0	Robinson	12	0	45	4

Umpires: F. Chester and G. Beet

Result: The Players won by an innings and 140 runs.

LORD'S 1947 – JULY 16–18
GENTLEMEN v. PLAYERS

THE GENTLEMEN

First Innings			*Second Innings*	
G. L. Willatt b Walsh	23	—	c Fletcher b Gladwin	5
H. A. Pawson c Evans b Butler	4	—	lbw b Gladwin	5
W. J. Edrich lbw b Wright	79	—	c Gladwin b Butler	5
M. P. Donnelly not out	162	—	c Compton b Butler	6
R. T. Simpson c Ames b Walsh	4	—	b Gladwin	0
N. W. D. Yardley (Capt.) b Gladwin	9	—	lbw b Barnett	46
K. Cranston c Evans b Butler	16	—	c Walsh b Butler	47
T. E. Bailey lbw b Walsh	0	—	st Evans b Walsh	1
F. R. Brown b Butler	0	—	b Walsh	35
S. C. Griffith lbw b Butler	2	—	not out	39
A. W. H. Mallett b Wright	0	—	c Wright b Compton	14
Bye 1, leg bye 1, no-ball 1	3		Byes 5, leg bye 1	6
Total	302		Total	209

THE PLAYERS

C. Washbrook b Edrich	101	—	not out	3
J. D. Robertson lbw b Cranston	28	—	not out	0
L. E. G. Ames (Capt.) c Mallett b Cranston	6			
D. C. S. Compton c Griffith b Bailey	11			
C. J. Barnett c Simpson b Mallett	39			
D. G. W. Fletcher c Griffith b Bailey	77			
T. G. Evans lbw b Brown	22			
C. Gladwin not out	31			
J. E. Walsh c Griffith b Bailey	2			
D. V. P. Wright not out	0			
Byes 11, leg byes 6	17			
Total (8 wkts., dec.)	334		Total (0 wkt.)	3

H. J. Butler did not bat

BOWLING

THE PLAYERS

	First Innings					*Second Innings*			
	O.	M.	R.	W.		O.	M.	R.	W.
Butler	24	4	91	4	Butler	21	4	56	3
Gladwin	20	3	66	1	Gladwin	17	7	36	3
Barnett	6	1	20	0	Barnett	3	0	5	1
Wright	14.2	1	40	2	Wright	9	1	33	0
Walsh	18	0	82	3	Walsh	11	0	67	2
					Compton	1.1	0	6	1

THE GENTLEMEN

	O.	M.	R.	W.		O.	M.	R.	W.
Bailey	25	3	83	3					
Edrich	19	4	48	1					
Mallett	23	5	56	1					
Brown	21	2	62	1	Brown	2	0	3	0
Cranston	20	4	61	2					
Donnelly	2	0	7	0					
					Yardley	1.5	1	0	0

Umpires: J. Smart and A. Skelding

Result: Drawn.

THE GENTLEMEN

First Innings		*Second Innings*	
R. E. S. Wyatt lbw b Pollard 1	—	lbw b Howorth 14
D. R. Wilcox c Hutton b Pollard 25	—	c Brookes b Hutton 57
W. J. Edrich lbw b Howorth 31	—	lbw b Hutton 7
M. P. Donnelly c Evans b Howorth 0	—	c Butler b Bedser 1
J. L. Cheetham st Evans b Howorth 3	—	b Howorth 6
N. W. D. Yardley (Capt.) c Washbrook b Bedser 35	—	c and b Hutton 23
K. Cranston b Bedser 10	—	b Howorth 37
G. F. H. Heane b Howorth 0	—	c Bedser b Butler 6
F. R. Brown c Evans b Butler 10	—	c Butler b Bedser 1
W. Wooller not out 3	—	b Howorth 22
A. W. H. Mallett c Pollard b Butler 10	—	not out 36
Leg byes 7		Bye 1, leg byes 4, no-balls 2 . 7
Total 135		Total 217

THE PLAYERS

L. Hutton b Mallett 64
C. Washbrook c Cheetham b Mallett 7
D. G. W. Fletcher c Mallett b Brown 26
D. Brookes lbw b Heane 19
L. B. Fishlock c Mallett b Brown 5
J. Hardstaff (Capt.) lbw b Wooller 32
R. Howorth b Brown 80
T. G. Evans run out 33
A. V. Bedser lbw b Heane 13
R. Pollard not out 37
H. J. Butler b Brown 7
Byes 33, leg byes 6 39

Total 362

BOWLING

THE PLAYERS

First Innings	O.	M.	R.	W.	*Second Innings*	O.	M.	R.	W.
Butler	8.3	3	22	2	Butler	8	1	15	1
Pollard	12	4	20	2	Pollard	8	1	23	0
Bedser	18	6	47	2	Bedser	21	4	47	2
Howorth	17	3	30	4	Howorth	22.5	6	71	4
Hardstaff	3	1	9	0	Hardstaff	2	1	8	0
					Hutton	14	4	46	3

THE GENTLEMEN

	O.	M.	R.	W.
Wooller	19	1	84	1
Mallett	18	5	39	2
Brown	29.3	5	112	4
Heane	27	4	86	2
Cranston	2	1	2	0

Umpires: P. Holmes and F. Root

Result: The Players won by an innings and 10 runs.

THE GENTLEMEN

First Innings		*Second Innings*	
J. G. Dewes b Bedser	45	— not out	74
W. J. Edrich b Pritchard	33	— b Pritchard	41
C. H. Palmer b Pritchard	5	— b Pritchard	0
M. P. Donnelly c Robertson b Wardle	5	— c Hutton b Muncer	19
T. N. Pearce c Wardle b Bedser	51	— not out	17
N. W. D. Yardley (Capt.) b Muncer	61	— c Pritchard b Compton	15
F. G. Mann b Pritchard	41	— st Evans b Muncer	5
K. Cranston c Hutton b Bedser	5		
W. Wooller c Wardle b Bedser	8		
S. C. Griffith not out	2		
P. A. Whitcombe not out	1		
Byes 7, no-balls 2	9	Byes 4, leg byes 5, no-balls 3	12
Total (9 wkts., dec.)	266	Total (5 wkts., dec.)	183

THE PLAYERS

L. Hutton (Capt.) b Cranston	59	— not out	132
C. Washbrook c Wooller b Whitcombe	63	— lbw b Whitcombe	9
J. D. Robertson c Pearce b Yardley	17	— lbw b Edrich	13
D. C. S. Compton b Whitcombe	31	— lbw b Palmer	43
J. F. Crapp b Cranston	1	— not out	24
H. E. Dollery c and b Cranston	18		
T. G. Evans b Cranston	6		
A. V. Bedser c Yardley b Wooller	0		
L. B. Muncer c Whitcombe b Wooller	0		
J. H. Wardle c sub b Wooller	14		
T. L. Pritchard not out	0		
Byes 7, no-ball 1	8	Byes 9, leg byes 3	12
Total	217	Total (3 wkts.)	233

BOWLING

THE PLAYERS

First Innings	O.	M.	R.	W.	*Second Innings*	O.	M.	R.	W.
Bedser	27	5	69	4	Bedser	9	1	20	0
Pritchard	26	5	63	3	Pritchard	11	1	40	2
Wardle	25	8	63	1	Wardle	13	1	47	0
Muncer	22	8	42	1	Muncer	17	6	37	2
Compton	4	1	9	0	Compton	3	0	27	1
Hutton	3	0	11	0					

THE GENTLEMEN

	O.	M.	R.	W.		O.	M.	R.	W.
Whitcombe	29	8	57	2	Whitcombe	13	3	51	1
Wooller	29.1	6	63	3	Wooller	12	0	75	0
Cranston	18	7	33	4	Cranston	7	1	37	0
Edrich	3	0	12	0	Edrich	6	0	21	1
Palmer	14	3	33	0	Palmer	11	1	37	1
Yardley	9	6	11	1					

Umpires: J. Smart and F. Chester

Result: The Players won by seven wickets.

THE GENTLEMEN

First Innings		Second Innings	
J. G. Dewes b Jackson	16	— b Jenkins	33
R. T. Simpson lbw b Jackson	6	— c Langridge b Close	28
W. J. Edrich c Evans b Perks	7	— st Evans b Jenkins	4
G. H. G. Doggart c Evans b Hollies	3	— c Evans b Jenkins	4
N. W. D. Yardley lbw b Hollies	7	— lbw b Jenkins	9
C. B. Van Ryneveld c Evans b Hollies	18	— lbw b Hollies	64
F. G. Mann (Capt.) c Evans b Hollies	17	— c Compton b Jackson	43
A. H. Kardar hit wkt b Close	2	— not out	16
F. R. Brown c Langridge b Close	7	— st Evans b Hollies	2
T. E. Bailey not out	15	— lbw b Hollies	53
S. C. Griffith lbw b Hollies	0	— c Jenkins b Jackson	1
Byes 4, leg byes 3	7	Byes 4, leg byes 6	10
Total	105	Total	267

THE PLAYERS

L. Hutton c Edrich b Brown	25	— c Kardar b Bailey	11
John Langridge lbw b Bailey	31	— c Kardar b Bailey	10
J. D. Robertson b Bailey	1	— c Kardar b Brown	5
D. C. S. Compton (Capt.) lbw b Yardley	33	— c Doggart b Brown	17
T. W. Graveney c Kardar b Brown	2	— b Bailey	5
D. B. Close c Simpson b Brown	65	— c Edrich b Brown	2
R. Jenkins b Bailey	5	— not out	41
T. G. Evans c Griffith b Brown	41	— not out	40
R. T. D. Perks c Dewes b Brown	13		
W. E. Hollies c Bailey b Kardar	5		
L. Jackson not out	8		
Leg byes 2, no-balls 3	5	Byes 5, leg byes 3	8
Total	234	Total (6 wkts.)	139

BOWLING

THE PLAYERS

First Innings	O.	M.	R.	W.	Second Innings	O.	M.	R.	W.
Perks	15	3	22	1	Perks	17	1	60	0
Jackson	13	2	30	2	Jackson	20.2	7	33	2
Hollies	17.3	7	32	5	Hollies	26	10	51	3
Close	7	2	14	2	Close	22	3	52	1
					Jenkins	21	8	48	4
					Compton	6	1	13	0

THE GENTLEMEN

	O.	M.	R.	W.		O.	M.	R.	W.
Bailey	22	4	59	3	Bailey	12	1	35	3
Edrich	9	1	30	0	Edrich	3	0	13	0
Brown	24.4	1	80	5	Brown	15	2	71	3
Yardley	10	3	18	1					
Ryneveld	3	0	17	0					
Kardar	5	1	25	1	Kardar	7	1	12	0

Umpires: T. J. Bartley and H. Elliott

Result: The Players won by four wickets.

LORD'S 1950 – JULY 26–28
GENTLEMEN v. PLAYERS

THE GENTLEMEN

First Innings		*Second Innings*	
R. T. Simpson c and b Bedser	10	— lbw b Hollies	69
J. G. Dewes c Washbrook b Tattersall	94	— b Tattersall	48
G. H. G. Doggart b Wright	75	— lbw b Wright	36
D. B. Carr b Tattersall	0	— c Bedser b Wright	17
D. J. Insole c Evans b Wright	4	— not out	38
N. W. D. Yardley run out	5		
T. E. Bailey c Parkhouse b Bedser	5		
F. R. Brown b Tattersall	122	— not out	22
J. J. Warr b Wright	2		
D. Brennan b Hollies	0		
C. J. Knott not out	1		
Byes 5, leg byes 2	7	Byes 1, leg byes 3, no-ball 1 .	5
Total	325	Total (4 wkts., dec.)	235

THE PLAYERS

H. Gimblett lbw b Brown	23	— c Knott b Bailey	14
C. Washbrook c Insole b Bailey	0	— c and b Brown	43
W. G. A. Parkhouse b Brown	29	— c Brown b Knott	81
D. J. Kenyon lbw b Brown	5	— c Brennan b Bailey	54
H. E. Dollery c Brennan b Doggart	123	— c Yardley b Knott	20
T. G. Evans b Bailey	19	— st Brennan b Knott	9
D. Shackleton c Simpson b Knott	25	— c Insole b Knott	2
A. V. Bedser c Dewes b Knott	59	— b Bailey	10
R. Tattersall lbw b Doggart	12	— st Brennan b Knott	0
D. V. P. Wright not out	6	— not out	2
W. E. Hollies not out	1	— not out	0
Byes 2, leg byes 4	6	Byes 2, leg byes 5	7
Total (9 wkts., dec.)	308	Total (9 wkts.)	242

BOWLING
THE PLAYERS

	First Innings					*Second Innings*			
	O.	M.	R.	W.		O.	M.	R.	W.
Bedser	23	2	77	2	Bedser	12	0	41	0
Shackleton	18	3	51	0	Shackleton	13	0	60	0
Tattersall	16.4	6	38	3	Tattersall	10	0	35	1
Hollies	23	8	49	1	Hollies	12	1	43	1
Wright	25	4	103	3	Wright	9	0	51	2

THE GENTLEMEN

	O.	M.	R.	W.		O.	M.	R.	W.
Bailey	25	6	65	2	Bailey	14	2	59	3
Warr	21	5	66	0	Warr	8	1	38	0
Yardley	10	1	23	0	Yardley	4	0	13	0
Brown	28	3	63	3	Brown	10	0	59	1
Knott	21	2	63	2	Knott	11	0	66	5
Carr	2	0	11	0					
Doggart	4	1	11	2					

Umpires: K. McCanlis and A. Skelding

Result: Drawn.

THE PLAYERS

First Innings		*Second Innings*	
J. T. Ikin b Warr	0	— lbw b Edrich	34
J. D. Robertson lbw b Yardley	80	— run out	20
T. W. Graveney st Brennan b Marlar	37	— c Brennan b Marlar	3
D. C. S. Compton (Capt.) c Yardley b Divecha	150	— not out	74
W. Watson b Edrich	33	— not out	49
L. Hutton b Divecha	19		
T. G. Evans b Divecha	6		
A. V. Bedser c Brennan b Warr	4		
R. Tattersall c Insole b Divecha	17		
J. B. Statham st Brennan b Divecha	6		
M. J. Hilton not out	0		
Byes 2, leg byes 5, no-balls 2	9	Byes 7, leg bye 1	8
Total	361	Total (3 wkts., dec.)	188

1/3 2/101 3/141 4/252 5/301 6/311 7/332
8/336 9/361

1/37 2/57 3/63

THE GENTLEMEN

First Innings		*Second Innings*	
R. T. Simpson b Statham	6	— b Tattersall	16
D. S. Sheppard c Watson b Hilton	31	— lbw b Ikin	39
W. J. Edrich c Robertson b Hilton	36	— b Ikin	36
P. B. H. May not out	119	— b Bedser	24
D. J. Insole c Robertson b Hilton	50	— not out	44
N. W. D. Yardley b Compton	17	— c Graveney b Tattersall	4
N. D. Howard (Capt.) c Robertson b Compton	1	— st Evans b Tattersall	0
R. V. Divecha lbw b Ikin	2	— c Robertson b Bedser	32
D. V. Brennan lbw b Ikin	13	— c Statham b Bedser	3
J. J. Warr st Evans b Ikin	11	— b Bedser	17
R. G. Marlar (did not bat)		— c Compton b Ikin	2
Byes 12, leg byes 3	15	Byes 4, leg byes 6	10
Total (9 wkts., dec.)	301	Total	227

1/11 2/53 3/104 4/198 5/238
6/240 7/245 8/287 9/301

1/23 2/78 3/109 4/122 5/137
6/138 7/183 8/211 9/219

BOWLING

The Gentlemen

	First Innings					*Second Innings*			
	O.	M.	R.	W.		O.	M.	R.	W.
Warr	32	6	100	2	Warr	12	2	34	0
Divecha	21.4	4	81	5	Divecha	10	1	47	0
Yardley	18	4	47	1	Yardley	8	0	30	0
Edrich	20	5	43	1	Edrich	8	2	25	1
Marlar	33	11	81	1	Marlar	18	5	44	1

The Players

	O.	M.	R.	W.		O.	M.	R.	W.
Bedser	18	5	39	0	Bedser	15	1	53	4
Statham	14	5	23	1	Statham	3	0	7	0
Hilton	43	18	90	3	Hilton	18	3	67	0
Tattersall	25	5	62	0	Tattersall	12	0	53	3
Compton	11	0	40	2					
Ikin	14.4	5	32	3	Ikin	8.4	0	37	3

Umpires: H. Elliott and W. F. Price

Result: The Players won by 21 runs.

THE GENTLEMEN

First Innings		Second Innings	
R. T. Simpson c Bedser b Pritchard	12	— b Bedser	7
W. J. Edrich st Dawkes b Bedser	1	— c Wilson b Bedser	17
P. B. H. May c Dawkes b Tattersall	36	— st Dawkes b Walsh	33
G. H. G. Doggart c Preston b Bedser	16	— b Walsh	16
M. C. Cowdrey st Dawkes b Hutton	106	— b Preston	10
D. J. Insole c Dawkes b Walsh	26	— c Dawkes b Bedser	26
W. H. H. Sutcliffe st Dawkes b Hutton	82	— b Bedser	14
N. W. D. Yardley b Hutton	7	— c Wilson b Bedser	1
T. E. Bailey c Wilson b Hutton	7	— not out	32
S. C. Griffith c Preston b Walsh	4	— c Wilson b Pritchard	23
T. A. Hall not out	2	— b Pritchard	1
Byes 13, leg byes 5, wide 1	19	Byes 3, leg-byes 6, no-balls 2	11
Total	318	Total	191

THE PLAYERS

First Innings		Second Innings	
L. Hutton b Hall	78	— c Simpson b Hall	5
J. V. Wilson c Griffith b Bailey	17	— c Griffith b Hall	25
T. W. Graveney b Yardley	71	— lbw b Bailey	23
M. Tompkin c Griffith b Yardley	37	— c Yardley b Edrich	21
W. Watson hit wkt b Doggart	80	— c Doggart b Bailey	4
J. E. Walsh c Simpson b Yardley	9	— lbw b Edrich	0
G. O. Dawkes b Hall	22	— run out	1
A. V. Bedser c Simpson b Yardley	32	— not out	22
R. Tattersall b Yardley	1	— not out	0
T. L. Pritchard b Doggart	6	— b Edrich	12
K. C. Preston not out	6	— b Bailey	5
Byes 3, leg byes 7, wide 1, no-ball 1	12	Byes 6, leg byes 3, no-ball 1	10
Total	371	Total (9 wkts.)	128

BOWLING

THE PLAYERS

First Innings	O.	M.	R.	W.	Second Innings	O.	M.	R.	W.
Bedser	30	9	66	2	Bedser	21	2	57	5
Pritchard	21	4	41	1	Pritchard	8.1	2	25	2
Walsh	21.3	3	91	2	Walsh	23	6	57	2
Preston	12	3	47	0	Preston	13	1	31	1
Tattersall	18	6	34	1	Tattersall	5	1	10	0
Hutton	5	0	20	4					

THE GENTLEMEN

	O.	M.	R.	W.		O.	M.	R.	W.
Hall	22	3	78	2	Hall	9	0	38	2
Edrich	15	2	55	0	Edrich	6	2	9	3
Bailey	27	4	84	1	Bailey	15	0	71	3
Yardley	24	5	93	5					
Insole	4	0	13	0					
Cowdrey	4	0	30	0					
Doggart	1.5	0	6	2					

Umpires: H. G. Baldwin and E. Robinson

Result: Drawn.

THE PLAYERS

First Innings				*Second Innings*	
L. Hutton b Brown	16	—	lbw b Marlar	50
D. G. W. Fletcher b Marlar	59	—	b Bailey	0
J. D. Robertson c Insole b McCarthy	10	—	b Marlar	55
D. C. S. Compton c Bailey b McCarthy	49	—	not out	39
W. Watson b Brown	47			
A. J. Watkins hit wkt b Marlar	24			
T. G. Evans c Brennan b McCarthy	21	—	b Marlar	15
D. Shackleton lbw b Bailey	12			
J. H. Wardle c Brennan b Bailey	11	—	st Brennan b Brown	11
J. C. Laker b Marlar	5			
A. V. Bedser not out	0	—	run out	20
Byes 2, leg byes 7, no-balls 2	11		Byes 8, leg byes 5	13
Total	265		Total (6 wkts., dec.)	203

1/25 2/45 3/117 4/168 5/190 6/221
7/237 8/260 9/265

1/12 2/93 3/120 4/148
5/166 6/203

THE GENTLEMEN

R. T. Simpson c and b Laker	14	—	c Evans b Bedser	19
D. S. Sheppard b Bedser	17	—	lbw b Shackleton	2
G. L. Willatt b Laker	20	—	c Compton b Wardle	26
P. B. H. May b Laker	45	—	c Hutton b Shackleton	19
C. H. Palmer c D. Compton b Laker	0	—	c Hutton b Laker	127
D. J. Insole lbw b Bedser	18	—	c Hutton b Shackleton	46
T. E. Bailey not out	18	—	c Evans b Shackleton	23
F. R. Brown c Evans b Bedser	2	—	c Hutton b Bedser	31
R. G. Marlar b Bedser	4	—	b Laker	7
D. V. Brennan b Laker	0	—	c Hutton b Bedser	5
C. N. McCarthy lbw b Laker	0	—	not out	1
Byes 5, leg byes 3	8		Byes 10, leg byes 4	14
Total	146		Total	320

1/27 2/41 3/76 4/76 5/105 6/131
7/141 8/145 9/146

1/8 2/28 3/54 4/73 5/178
6/235 7/305 8/307 9/317

BOWLING

THE GENTLEMEN

	First Innings					*Second Innings*			
	O.	M.	R.	W.		O.	M.	R.	W.
McCarthy	29	7	63	3	McCarthy	18	2	56	0
Bailey	24.3	6	51	2	Bailey	11	1	53	1
Brown	28	6	50	2	Brown	9.4	2	30	1
Marlar	21	5	77	3	Marlar	11	1	51	3
Palmer	6	3	13	0					

THE PLAYERS

	O.	M.	R.	W.		O.	M.	R.	W.
Bedser	20	6	40	4	Bedser	26	6	93	3
Laker	30	12	48	6	Laker	26.1	5	72	2
Shackleton	10	2	14	0	Shackleton	14	2	39	4
Wardle	20	11	36	0	Wardle	26	7	51	1
					Compton	6	0	38	0
					Watkins	9	4	13	0

Umpires: A. Skelding and A. E. Pothecary

Result: The Players won by 2 runs.

THE PLAYERS

First Innings			*Second Innings*	
D. G. W. Fletcher c Insole b Bailey	....	7	— b Bailey	8
J. V. Wilson c Cowdrey b Palmer		24	— c Insole b McCarthy	16
M. Tompkin b Edrich		98	— c McCarthy b Edrich	64
T. W. Graveney b Palmer		5	— c Brennan b Bailey	43
L. Hutton run out		99	— not out	27
T. G. Evans b McCarthy		10	— c Palmer b Bailey	32
J. H. Wardle c McCarthy b Palmer		31		
R. Smith not out		36		
Leg byes 11		11	Bye 1, leg byes 6, no-balls 5 .	12

Total (7 wkts., dec.) 321
1/16 2/50 3/74 4/230 5/252
6/252 7/321

Total (5 wkts., dec.) ...202
1/26 2/28 3/128 4/164 5/202

J. E. Walsh, A. V. Bedser and D. Shepherd did not bat.

THE GENTLEMEN

First Innings			*Second Innings*	
R. T. Simpson c Hutton b Shepherd	...	33	— c Wardle b Bedser	91
D. J. Insole b Shepherd		21	— c Shepherd b Bedser	0
P. B. H. May b Wardle		4	— b Wardle	31
M. C. Cowdrey b Wardle		6	— lbw b Wardle	13
W. J. Edrich b Walsh		79	— b Shepherd	37
C. H. Palmer c Hutton b Shepherd	....	32	— run out	2
N. W. D. Yardley c Evans b Wardle	...	17	— b Bedser	34
T. E. Bailey c Bedser b Wardle		31	— c Smith b Bedser	24
R. W. V. Robins b Shepherd		25	— not out	14
D. V. Brennan not out		11	— not out	0
C. N. McCarthy st Evans b Wardle	....	8		
Byes 2, leg bye 1		3	Leg byes 6	6

Total 270
1/35 2/47 3/65 4/67 5/151 6/190
7/198 8/251 9/253

Total (8 wkts.) 252
1/1 2/64 3/102 4/174 5/178
6/179 7/232 8/241

BOWLING

THE GENTLEMEN

	First Innings					*Second Innings*			
	O.	M.	R.	W.		O.	M.	R.	W.
McCarthy	17	1	60	1	McCarthy	14	1	28	1
Bailey	24	5	66	1	Bailey	14.5	3	41	3
Palmer	24.4	6	84	3	Palmer	6	1	31	0
Robins	4	0	20	0	Robins	5	0	21	0
Edrich	8	0	38	1	Edrich	9	0	66	1
Yardley	6	0	42	0	Yardley	3	0	3	0

THE PLAYERS

	O.	M.	R.	W.		O.	M.	R.	W.
Bedser	22	6	35	0	Bedser	17	0	59	4
Shepherd	28	5	92	4	Shepherd	12	0	68	1
Wardle	43	23	75	5	Wardle	15	2	61	2
Walsh	13	1	46	1	Walsh	10	0	58	0
Smith	7	0	19	0					

Umpires: A. Skelding and H. G. Baldwin

Result: Drawn.

THE GENTLEMEN

First Innings		*Second Innings*	
R. T. Simpson c Bedser b Tattersall	26	— c Watson b Tattersall	117
D. S. Sheppard c Dooland b Tattersall ..	5	— c Dooland b Bedser	6
W. J. Edrich c Bedser b Tattersall	8	— c Dooland b Tattersall	98
P. B. H. May c Compton b Bedser	32	— c Evans b Dooland	11
C. H. Palmer st Evans b Tattersall	18	— lbw b Bedser	20
D. J. Insole c Watson b Bedser	6	— b Tattersall	4
T. E. Bailey c Evans b Bedser	10	— c Dooland b Bedser	16
F. R. Brown not out	11	— b Tattersall	17
W. Wooller c Graveney b Bedser	0	— b Tattersall	0
D. V. Brennan b Bedser	0	— b Tattersall	0
R. G. Marlar b Tattersall	0	— not out	0
Byes 12, leg bye 1	13	Byes 10, leg byes 12	22
Total	129	Total	311

1/17 2/25 3/52 4/90 5/104 6/118
7/118 8/118 9/120

1/22 2/179 3/207 4/264
5/275 6/276 7/307 8/307 9/307

THE PLAYERS

G. M. Emmett c Bailey b Wooller	4	— c Bailey b Marlar	82
C. Washbrook c Brennan b Wooller	5	— b Marlar	41
T. W. Graveney c Wooller b Bailey	2	— c Wooller b Marlar	2
D. C. S. Compton b Marlar	13	— c Sheppard b Marlar	0
W. Watson b Palmer	29	— c Sheppard b Wooller	9
D. W. Barrick c Sheppard b Marlar	7	— c Brennan b Palmer	17
B. Dooland lbw b Wooller	0	— c Insole b Marlar	31
T. G. Evans b Brown	46	— c and b Marlar	7
R. Tattersall b Bailey	1	— not out	15
A. V. Bedser b Bailey	3	— b Marlar	9
A. E. Moss not out	9	— b Palmer	3
Leg byes 4	4	Byes 5, leg bye 1	6
Total	123	Total	222

1/6 2/9 3/11 4/30 5/46 6/47 7/84
8/111 9/113

1/89 2/112 3/113 4/136
5/140 6/180 7/187 8/196 9/219

BOWLING

THE PLAYERS

	First Innings					*Second Innings*			
	O.	M.	R.	W.		O.	M.	R.	W.
Bedser	21	9	34	5	Bedser	30.3	9	74	3
Moss	6	0	21	0	Moss	14	3	34	0
Tattersall	19.5	4	47	5	Tattersall	21	2	83	6
Dooland	13	6	14	0	Dooland	24	5	80	1
					Compton	8	1	18	0

THE GENTLEMEN

	O.	M.	R.	W.		O.	M.	R.	W.
Bailey	10.4	3	14	3	Bailey	8	1	17	0
Wooller	17	3	30	3	Wooller	15	1	47	1
Marlar	20	9	37	2	Marlar	26	3	79	7
Brown	5	0	21	1	Brown	13	1	55	0
Palmer	4	0	17	1	Palmer	6	0	18	2

Umpires: W. F. Price and J. S. Buller

Result: The Gentlemen won by 95 runs.

LORD'S 1953 – AUGUST 26–28
GENTLEMEN OF ENGLAND v. THE AUSTRALIANS

GENTLEMEN OF ENGLAND

First Innings		*Second Innings*	
R. T. Simpson lbw b Lindwall	5	— c Langley b Miller	5
D. S. Sheppard c Langley b Ring	39	— c sub b Archer	34
W. J. Edrich lbw b Ring	22	— lbw b Lindwall	75
P. B. H. May hit wkt b Johnston	14	— c Harvey b Johnston	50
M. C. Cowdrey c Lindwall b Benaud	50	— c Craig b Johnston	57
C. H. Palmer lbw b Lindwall	3	— b Lindwall	5
T. E. Bailey b Benaud	11	— lbw b Lindwall	4
W. Wooller c McDonald b Benaud	0	— c Langley b Miller	1
D. V. Brennan b Archer	6	— b Lindwall	16
R. G. Marlar b Benaud	0	— b Lindwall	0
G. H. Chesterton not out	0	— not out	0
Byes 5, leg bye 1, no-ball 1	7	Leg-byes 2	2
Total	157	Total	249

1/6 2/51 3/84 4/86 5/95 6/133
7/137 8/157 9/157

1/5 2/77 3/150 4/177 5/199
6/211 7/218 8/249 9/249

THE AUSTRALIANS

A. R. Morris c May b Chesterton	12	— not out	126
C. C. McDonald lbw b Chesterton	15	— b Marlar	25
K. R. Miller lbw b Bailey	14	— c Chesterton b Wooller	67
R. N. Harvey b Bailey	16	— not out	30
I. D. Craig b Marlar	14		
R. Benaud b Marlar	25		
R. G. Archer b Marlar	3		
R. R. Lindwall b Marlar	4		
D. T. Ring b Bailey	5		
G. R. A. Langley b Marlar	15		
W. A. Johnston not out	27		
Byes 4	4	Leg byes 5	5
Total	154	Total (2 wkts.)	253

1/23 2/36 3/52 4/59 5/91
6/95 7/101 8/108 9/108

1/72 2/183

BOWLING

THE AUSTRALIANS

First Innings	O.	M.	R.	W.	*Second Innings*	O.	M.	R.	W.
Lindwall	13	5	33	2	Lindwall	30	8	68	5
Johnston	13	5	21	1	Johnston	20	7	46	2
Archer	19	6	34	1	Archer	12	1	33	1
Ring	24	10	42	2	Ring	1	0	1	0
Benaud	4.4	1	20	4	Benaud	11	0	40	0
					Miller	26	6	59	2

GENTLEMEN OF ENGLAND

	O.	M.	R.	W.		O.	M.	R.	W.
Bailey	14	1	35	3	Bailey	19	1	50	0
Wooller	13	1	35	0	Wooller	10	1	40	1
Chesterton	13	2	31	2	Chesterton	8.2	1	43	0
Palmer	6	2	8	0	Palmer	10	5	29	0
Marlar	14.4	3	41	5	Marlar	29	10	80	1
					Edrich	1	0	6	0

Umpires: G. S. Mobey and D. Davies

Result: The Australians won by eight wickets.

THE PLAYERS

First Innings		*Second Innings*	
L. Hutton c Edrich b Bailey 241	— c Bailey b Marlar 14
F. A. Lowson c Brennan b Surridge 2	— lbw b Marlar 34
M. Tompkin c Marlar b Cowdrey 54	— lbw b Surridge 9
T. W. Graveney c Cowdrey b Marlar .. 11	— b Marlar 14
W. Watson not out 143	— not out 47
R. Smith c Brennan b Surridge 32	
T. G. Evans not out 36	— b Surridge 1
J. H. Wardle (did not bat)	— b Cowdrey 42
Byes 6, leg byes 6, wide 1 13	Leg byes 4 4

Total (5 wkts., dec.) 532   Total (6 wkts., dec.) ...165
1/17 2/181 3/235 4/341 5/434   1/5 2/10 3/88 4/88 5/108 6/165

A. V. Bedser, D. Shepherd and R. Tattersall did not bat.

THE GENTLEMEN

R. T. Simpson c Hutton b Smith 4	— b Shepherd 44
D. J. Insole b Bedser 1	— st Evans b Bedser 9
W. J. Edrich c Watson b Bedser 45	— b Bedser 133
P. B. H. May c Watson b Tattersall 157	— c Evans b Bedser 36
M. C. Cowdrey c Watson b Graveney ..100	— st Evans b Wardle 16
W. H. H. Sutcliffe c Hutton b Graveney 57	— not out 0
N. W. D. Yardley c Hutton b Tattersall 62	— not out 5
T. E. Bailey c Smith b Wardle 1	
D. V. Brennan not out 6	
Byes 6, leg byes 8 14	Byes 4, leg byes 5 9

Total (8 wkts., dec.) 447   Total (5 wkts.) 252
1/17 2/28 3/97 4/302 5/320   1/15 2/97 3/168 4/243 5/243
6/413 7/419 8/447

W. S. Surridge and R. G. Marlar did not bat.

BOWLING

THE GENTLEMEN

First Innings	O.	M.	R.	W.	*Second Innings*	O.	M.	R.	W.
Surridge	21	1	97	2	Surridge	8	1	30	2
Bailey	24	2	96	1	Bailey	10	3	28	0
Yardley	15	0	80	0					
Marlar	28	1	147	1	Marlar	12.4	1	70	3
Cowdrey	5	0	29	1	Cowdrey	5	0	33	1
Edrich	14	3	70	0					

THE PLAYERS

	O.	M.	R.	W.		O.	M.	R.	W.
Bedser	19	6	25	2	Bedser	13	3	38	3
Shepherd	12	0	46	0	Shepherd	8.3	0	56	1
Tattersall	28	7	93	2	Tattersall	9	0	63	0
Smith	15	1	50	1					
Wardle	34	6	106	1	Wardle	17	0	86	1
Hutton	10	2	52	0					
Graveney	9.2	1	47	2					
Evans	3	0	14	0					

Umpires: H. D. Baldwin and A. Skelding

Result: The Gentlemen won by five wickets.

THE PLAYERS

	First Innings			*Second Innings*	
D. Kenyon b Marlar	54	—	lbw b Bailey		0
F. A. Lowson c Sheppard b Warr	7	—	c Barnett b Bailey		12
T. W. Graveney b Bailey	15	—	c Warr b Bailey		18
D. C. S. Compton c Yardley b Marlar	36	—	run out		6
J. M. Parks c Edrich b Marlar	1	—	c Barnett b Marlar		20
T. G. Evans b Bailey	7	—	c Barnett b Warr		38
B. Dooland st Barnett b Marlar	4	—	b Yardley		28
G. A. R. Lock b Marlar	2	—	c Barnett b Warr		34
J. B. Statham c Edrich b Marlar	5	—	not out		17
R. Appleyard run out	6	—	b Marlar		6
P. J. Loader not out	0	—	c May b Warr		2
Byes 4, leg bye 1, no-balls 2	7		Leg byes 5, wide 1, no-balls 4		10
Total	144		Total		191

1/27 2/63 3/96 4/98 5/109 6/114
7/116 8/138 9/139

1/0 2/7 3/28 4/60 5/111
6/115 7/146 8/171 9/182

THE GENTLEMEN

	First Innings				*Second Innings*	
D. S. Sheppard c Lowson b Loader	4	—		b Loader		0
R. T. Simpson lbw b Statham	1	—		c Dooland b Appleyard		17
W. J. Edrich c Lock b Loader	56	—		c Statham b Appleyard		27
P. B. H. May lbw b Loader	6	—		c Evans b Lock		53
M. C. Cowdrey b Loader	0	—		c Compton b Dooland		2
N. W. D. Yardley b Appleyard	18	—		b Statham		9
T. E. Bailey lbw b Dooland	12	—		c Lock b Statham		0
G. Goonesena lbw b Loader	2	—		b Appleyard		23
B. A. Barnett c Evans b Loader	0	—		c Lowson b Lock		6
J. J. Warr not out	7	—		c Statham b Appleyard		13
R. G. Marlar b Loader	7	—		not out		4
Byes 4, leg byes 8, no-ball 1	13			Bye 1, leg byes 3, no-balls 2		6
Total	126			Total		160

1/5 2/5 3/23 4/27 5/76 6/107
7/109 8/109 9/110

1/3 2/90 3/91 4/103 5/103
6/105 7/115 8/139 9/153

BOWLING

THE GENTLEMEN

	First Innings					*Second Innings*			
	O.	M.	R.	W.		O.	M.	R.	W.
Bailey	20.2	6	52	2	Bailey	27	7	62	3
Warr	11	3	23	1	Warr	26.3	9	44	3
Marlar	17	5	47	6	Marlar	9	1	29	2
Goonesena	7	0	15	0	Goonesena	3	0	21	0
					Yardley	10	3	25	1

THE PLAYERS

	O.	M.	R.	W.		O.	M.	R.	W.
Statham	14	5	30	1	Statham	18	7	41	2
Loader	17	4	37	7	Loader	13	3	27	1
Appleyard	11	7	14	1	Appleyard	7.5	1	24	4
Lock	6	4	11	0	Lock	14	7	32	2
Dooland	12	3	21	1	Dooland	14	5	30	1

Umpires: P. Corrall and L. H. Gray

Result: The Players won by 49 runs.

THE PLAYERS

First Innings		*Second Innings*	
A. Hamer lbw b Bailey	5	— c Lewis b Bailey	2
W. Watson c Lewis b Marlar	77	— c Marlar b Bailey	39
J. V. Wilson b Bailey	122	— not out	35
T. W. Graveney lbw b Marlar	11		
J. M. Parks lbw b Surridge	57		
E. A. Bedser run out	2		
T. G. Evans b Bailey	32		
J. H. Wardle st Lewis b Surridge	17		
A. V. Bedser not out	1		
Byes 14, leg byes 8	22	Leg bye 1, wide 1	2

Total (8 wkts., dec.) 346
1/7 2/138 3/192 4/286
5/286 6/297 7/336 8/346

Total (2 wkts., dec.) ... 78
1/9 2/78

R. Appleyard and A. E. Moss did not bat.

THE GENTLEMEN

R. T. Simpson c Wilson b Appleyard	9	— c Watson b Moss	6
W. H. H. Sutcliffe b A. Bedser	9	— c Evans b A. Bedser	14
J. J. Warr b A. Bedser	26	— not out	29
P. B. H. May not out	112	— b Wardle	18
W. J. Edrich c and b E. Bedser	22	— c Hamer b E. Bedser	48
D. J. Insole c Evans b Wardle	0	— b Wardle	12
T. E. Bailey c Evans b E. Bedser	2	— c Appleyard b Wardle	4
N. W. D. Yardley not out	5	— c Wardle b E. Bedser	25
W. S. Surridge (did not bat)		— b E. Bedser	2
E. B. Lewis (did not bat)		— b Wardle	0
R. G. Marlar (did not bat)		— c Moss b Wardle	14
Byes 4, leg byes 3, no-balls 6	13	Leg byes 3, no-ball 1	4

Total (6 wkts., dec.) 198
1/18 2/18 3/89 4/176
5/177 6/192

Total 176
1/9 2/20 3/47 4/82 5/86
6/123 7/129 8/136 9/142

BOWLING

THE GENTLEMEN

First Innings	O.	M.	R.	W.	*Second Innings*	O.	M.	R.	W.
Bailey	26.2	7	92	3	Bailey	11.4	2	22	2
Warr	16	0	84	0	Warr	5	0	24	0
Surridge	16	1	63	2	Surridge	1	0	1	0
Marlar	22	4	63	2	Marlar	5	1	29	0
Yardley	5	0	22	0					

THE PLAYERS

	O.	M.	R.	W.		O.	M.	R.	W.
A. Bedser	15	3	44	2	A. Bedser	5	2	8	1
Moss	9	1	38	0	Moss	5	0	20	1
Appleyard	18	5	31	1	Appleyard	4	1	11	0
Wardle	15	3	42	1	Wardle	18	2	85	5
E. Bedser	7	0	30	2	E. Bedser	11	1	40	3
					Graveney	2	0	8	0

Umpires: A. Skelding and H. G. Baldwin

Result: The Players won by 50 runs.

LORD'S 1955 – JULY 13–15
GENTLEMEN v. PLAYERS

THE PLAYERS

First Innings		*Second Innings*	
D. Kenyon c Barnett b Palmer	32	— c Fellows-Smith b Goonesena	39
W. Watson lbw b Fellows-Smith	2	— c Tordoff b Marlar	29
M. Tompkin c Goonesena b Warr	115	— c Barnett b Goonesena	11
J. M. Parks c Smith b Marlar	35	— c and b Goonesena	8
K. Barrington c Fellows-Smith b Warr	3	— st Barnett b Goonesena	0
H. E. Dollery c Pretlove b Warr	14	— c Goonesena b Marlar	82
F. J. Titmus c Insole b Marlar	40	— lbw b Goonesena	14
L. Harrison c Fellows-Smith b Warr	13	— b Goonesena	20
G. A. R. Lock b Goonesena	28	— not out	9
F. H. Tyson not out	15	— absent hurt	0
A. V. Bedser c Smith b Marlar	2	— lbw b Marlar	0
Byes 6, leg byes 10, wide 1	17	Byes 3, leg byes 2, wides 2, no-ball 1	8
Total	316	Total	220

1/4 2/52 3/175 4/178 5/216 6/216
7/270 8/283 9/308

1/70 2/72 3/82 4/82 5/103
6/138 7/202 8/220 9/220

THE GENTLEMEN

M. J. K. Smith lbw b Titmus	17	— c Harrison b Titmus	28
G. G. Tordoff b Lock	20	— c Barrington b Bedser	44
M. C. Cowdrey retired hurt	0	— c Bedser b Titmus	0
C. H. Palmer c Dollery b Bedser	154	— run out	5
D. J. Insole c Tompkin b Titmus	72	— c Titmus b Lock	1
J. P. Fellows-Smith run out	9	— lbw b Lock	51
J. F. Pretlove c Barrington b Bedser	0	— not out	3
G. Goonesena c Barrington b Titmus	13	— c Lock b Titmus	1
B. A. Barnett not out	22	— b Bedser	2
J. J. Warr c sub b Bedser	11	— run out	21
R. G. Marlar (did not bat)		— c Titmus b Bedser	5
Byes 15, leg byes 3	18	Byes 13, leg byes 6	19
Total (8 wkts., dec.)	336	Total	180

1/51 2/51 3/252 4/290
5/290 6/291 7/313 8/336

1/63 2/65 3/71 4/76 5/112
6/164 7/172 8/172 9/179

BOWLING

THE GENTLEMEN

First Innings	O.	M.	R.	W.	*Second Innings*	O.	M.	R.	W.
Warr	22	5	54	4	Warr	13	3	38	0
Fellows-Smith	24	6	62	1	Fellows-Smith	3	1	11	0
Palmer	13	2	41	1	Palmer	5	1	4	0
Insole	4	0	9	0					
Marlar	21.5	5	61	3	Marlar	24.5	3	76	3
Goonesena	10	0	58	1	Goonesena	26	2	83	6
Pretlove	5	1	14	0					

THE PLAYERS

	O.	M.	R.	W.		O.	M.	R.	W.
Tyson	3	0	7	0					
Bedser	30.4	3	86	3	Bedser	16	4	44	3
Lock	32	10	63	1	Lock	18	2	77	2
Titmus	40	13	139	3	Titmus	10.4	1	40	3
Parks	10	0	23	0					

Umpires: J. S. Buller and K. McCanlis

Result: The Players won by 20 runs.

THE GENTLEMEN

	First Innings		*Second Innings*	
R. T. Simpson c Graveney b A. Bedser	3	—	b Illingworth	33
P. E. Richardson b Munden	46	—	b Shepherd	23
W. J. Edrich c Trueman b A. Bedser	133	—	c Munden b Wardle	18
W. H. H. Sutcliffe b Wardle	55	—	c A. Bedser b Wardle	2
D. J. Insole c Close b Wardle	3	—	run out	48
T. E. Bailey c Trueman b Illingworth	54	—	not out	25
N. W. D. Yardley c Wilson b Trueman	7	—	c Illingworth b E. Bedser	6
G. Goonesena c Wilson b Wardle	13			
J. J. Warr not out	6			
W. S. Surridge lbw b Wardle	1			
E. B. Lewis b Illingworth	3			
Byes 5, leg byes 2	7		Leg byes 3, no-ball 1	4
Total	331		Total (6 wkts., dec.)	159

1/5 2/92 3/198 4/212 5/273 6/287
7/315 8/323 9/324

1/41 2/65 3/75 4/85
5/152 6/159

THE PLAYERS

D. B. Close b Warr	8	—	c Richardson b Bailey	53
T. W. Graveney c Bailey b Goonesena	96	—	c Lewis b Goonesena	27
J. V. Wilson c Goonesena b Bailey	31	—	c Lewis b Bailey	13
R. Illingworth c Yardley b Goonesena	1	—	run out	20
E. A. Bedser c Edrich b Goonesena	2	—	st Lewis b Goonesena	12
V. S. Munden b Bailey	61	—	b Goonesena	3
J. H. Wardle b Goonesena	20	—	lbw b Goonesena	24
G. O. Dawkes lbw b Bailey	1	—	c sub b Goonesena	3
F. S. Trueman c Surridge b Bailey	7	—	not out	29
A. V. Bedser not out	43	—	not out	19
D. J. Shepherd c Simpson b Goonesena	1			
Leg byes 5	5		Leg byes 9, wides 4, no-ball 1	14
Total	276		Total (8 wkts.)	217

1/23 2/85 3/88 4/94 5/177 6/201
7/204 8/216 9/265

1/71 2/95 3/108 4/144 5/150
6/156 7/168 8/168

BOWLING

THE PLAYERS

	First Innings					*Second Innings*			
	O.	M.	R.	W.		O.	M.	R.	W.
Trueman	17	1	60	1	Trueman	4	0	13	0
A. Bedser	16	4	39	2	A. Bedser	6	1	17	0
Shepherd	14	3	34	0	Shepherd	5	1	24	1
Wardle	24	5	81	4	Wardle	13	6	43	2
Close	11	3	48	0					
Munden	12	3	32	1					
Illingworth	10.5	3	30	2	Illingworth	10	1	39	1
					E. Bedser	2.5	0	19	1

THE GENTLEMEN

	O.	M.	R.	W.		O.	M.	R.	W.
Warr	20	1	83	1	Warr	8.5	1	53	0
Surridge	7	0	22	0	Surridge	4	0	28	0
Goonesena	24	3	100	5	Goonesena	15	1	77	5
Bailey	21	5	66	4	Bailey	9	0	45	2

Umpires: H. G. Baldwin and A. Skelding

Result: The Players won by two wickets.

LORD'S 1956 – JULY 18–20
GENTLEMEN v. PLAYERS

THE PLAYERS

A. Wharton c Insole b Bailey 36
A. S. M. Oakman lbw b Marlar 43
T. W. Graveney c Smith b Allan 52
D. C. S. Compton c Warr b Allan 25
C. Washbrook c Melluish b Bailey 21
D. V. Smith c Insole b Warr 5
T. G. Evans b Warr 13
J. C. Laker c Insole b Warr 8
G. A. R. Lock b Bailey 11
F. H. Tyson c Cowdrey b Bailey 3
F. S. Trueman not out 8
     Byes 8, wide 1, no-balls 2 11

    Total 236

1/54 2/107 3/144 4/175 5/186 6/192 7/205 8/215 9/225

THE GENTLEMEN

P. E. Richardson c Lock b Trueman 17
M. C. Cowdrey c Smith b Laker 20
R. T. Simpson st Evans b Laker 18
M. J. K. Smith lbw b Lock 16
D. J. Insole c Evans b Tyson 37
C. H. Palmer c Smith b Lock 32
T. E. Bailey not out 22
J. M. Allan not out 0
     Byes 15, leg bye 1, no-ball 1 17

    Total (6 wkts.) 179
1/43 2/51 3/84 4/84 5/153 6/161

J. J. Warr, M. E. L. Melluish and R. G. Marlar did not bat.

BOWLING

THE GENTLEMEN

	O.	M.	R.	W.
Warr	19	4	48	3
Bailey	23.4	4	66	4
Palmer	7	3	13	0
Marlar	24	4	61	1
Allan	17	3	37	2

THE PLAYERS

	O.	M.	R.	W.
Tyson	13	4	26	1
Trueman	11	2	29	1
Smith	5	1	12	0
Laker	15	7	30	2
Lock	12	1	46	2
Oakman	3	0	19	0

Umpires: T. W. Spencer and W. F. Price

Result: Drawn.

THE GENTLEMEN

First Innings		*Second Innings*	
W. J. Edrich c Hallam b Compton	133	— c Moss b Shepherd	43
W. H. H. Sutcliffe b Tyson	4	— b Wardle	23
C. C. P. Williams c Evans b Tyson	0	— b Shepherd	1
A. C. Walton c and b Wardle	17	— b Compton	18
D. J. Insole b Wardle	37	— st Evans b Wardle	13
T. E. Bailey c Munden b Shepherd	53	— c Compton b Shepherd	0
J. F. Pretlove c Barker b Compton	0	— b Compton	8
S. Singh st Evans b Wardle	55	— c Tyson b Compton	1
G. Goonesena not out	21	— c Compton b Shepherd	23
J. J. Warr c Munden b Shepherd	0	— not out	31
M. E. L. Melluish not out	8	— b Shepherd	6
Byes 4, leg byes 3, no–balls 7	14	Byes 6, leg byes 8, wide 1, no–balls 2	17

Total (9 wkts., dec.) 342

1/10 2/10 3/40 4/126 5/230
6/231 7/285 8/322 9/323

Total 184

1/58 2/86 3/87 4/88 5/88
6/116 7/119 8/126 9/148

THE PLAYERS

M. R. Hallam c Warr b Singh	31	— c Goonesena b Warr	50
G. Barker hit wkt b Goonesena	38	— c sub b Warr	45
T. W. Graveney b Warr	124	— not out	39
W. Watson c and b Goonesena	72	— not out	6
D. C. S. Compton st Melluish b Insole	1	— st Melluish b Warr	29
V. S. Munden b Goonesena	9		
T. G. Evans c Bailey b Goonesena	9		
J. H. Wardle not out	24		
F. H. Tyson b Goonesena	1		
A. E. Moss not out	15		
Byes 8, leg byes 12	20	Byes 7, leg byes 9	16

Total (8 wkts., dec.) 344

1/59 2/95 3/245 4/256 5/277
6/297 7/316 8/319

Total (3 wkts.) 185

1/85 2/117 3/160

D. J. Shepherd did not bat.

BOWLING

THE PLAYERS

First Innings	O.	M.	R.	W.	*Second Innings*	O.	M.	R.	W.
Tyson	11	5	15	2	Tyson	8	5	10	0
Moss	10	2	32	0	Moss	9	2	22	0
Shepherd	22	3	89	2	Shepherd	23	5	61	5
Wardle	30	3	98	3	Wardle	16	3	37	2
Munden	7	1	47	0					
Graveney	7	2	19	0	Graveney	2	0	9	0
Compton	5	0	28	2	Compton	10	3	28	3

THE GENTLEMEN

	O.	M.	R.	W.		O.	M.	R.	W.
Warr	27.3	6	73	1	Warr	19	3	83	3
Bailey	16	3	43	0	Bailey	8	0	30	0
Singh	14	2	45	1					
Goonesena	20	1	113	5	Goonesena	11	2	43	0
Pretlove	6	0	37	0					
Insole	6	1	13	1	Insole	3	0	13	0

Umpires: A. Skelding and H. G. Baldwin

Result: The Players won by seven wickets.

LORD'S 1957 – JULY 17–19
GENTLEMEN v. PLAYERS

THE GENTLEMEN

First Innings		Second Innings	
P. E. Richardson hit wkt b Trueman ...	47	— c Evans b Hollies	13
Rev. D. S. Sheppard c Smith b Trueman	55	— c Compton b Trueman	24
D. J. Insole c Trueman b Tyson	21	— not out	79
P. B. H. May c Graveney b Trueman ..	5	— c Trueman b Laker	8
M. C. Cowdrey b Trueman	6	— lbw b Hollies	8
E. R. Dexter b Laker	13	— st Evans b Smith	13
G. Goonesena b Hollies	6		
C. S. Smith c Compton b Hollies	0		
J. J. Warr st Evans b Laker	0	— st Evans b Laker	13
R. G. Marlar run out	4		
E. B. Lewis not out	9		
Byes 2, leg bye 1	3	Byes 4, leg byes 5	9
Total	169	Total (6 wkts., dec.) ...	167

1/87 2/113 3/131 4/131 5/138
6/152 7/156 8/156 9/156

1/34 2/41 3/79 4/87
5/110 6/167

THE PLAYERS

First Innings		Second Innings	
D. V. Smith c Richardson b Dexter	19	— c May b Goonesena	102
T. H. Clark c Goonesena b Smith	0	— b Smith	10
F. C. Gardner b Smith	0	— c Lewis b Goonesena	48
T. W. Graveney c Goonesena b Warr ...	6	— run out	24
D. C. S. Compton c Cowdrey b Dexter	6	— c Lewis b Dexter	26
D. W. Richardson c Lewis b Dexter	0	— lbw b Dexter	2
T. G. Evans c Smith b Dexter	7	— c May b Dexter	4
F. H. Tyson c Goonesena b Dexter	0	— b Smith	2
J. C. Laker c May b Warr	7	— c Lewis b Warr	5
F. S. Trueman not out	1	— not out	3
W. E. Hollies (did not bat)		— not out	1
		Byes 6, leg byes 7, wide 1, no-ball 1	15
Total (9 wkts., dec.)	46	Total (9 wkts.)	242

1/0 2/0 3/11 4/24 5/30
6/33 7/33 8/38 9/46

1/11 2/156 3/169 4/207 5/217
6/225 7/225 8/230 9/234

BOWLING

The Players

	First Innings					Second Innings			
	O.	M.	R.	W.		O.	M.	R.	W.
Trueman	18	8	38	4	Trueman	10	2	25	1
Tyson	15	4	51	1	Tyson	9	1	37	0
Hollies	18	6	39	2	Hollies	10	1	26	2
Laker	18	6	38	2	Laker	18	5	54	2
					Smith	2.5	0	16	1

The Gentlemen

	O.	M.	R.	W.		O.	M.	R.	W.
Warr	10.2	4	23	2	Warr	20	7	63	1
Smith	5	1	15	2	Smith	16	7	31	2
Dexter	5	2	8	5	Dexter	12	2	47	3
					Marlar	3	0	25	0
					Goonesena	13	2	61	2

Umpires: A. E. Pothecary and W. F. Price

Result: Drawn.

THE GENTLEMEN

First Innings		Second Innings	
P. E. Richardson c Gale b Shepherd	54	— lbw b Trueman	2
W. H. H. Sutcliffe b Tyson	1	— not out	8
M. J. K. Smith b Tyson	1	— c Close b Wardle	50
W. J. Edrich c Reynolds b Shepherd	29	— b Graveney	34
A. C. Walton c Graveney b Wardle	28	— c Shepherd b Graveney	30
E. R. Dexter c Evans b Close	6	— c Taylor b Trueman	88
D. J. Insole b Wardle	35		
T. E. Bailey not out	31		
G. Goonesena not out	22		
Leg byes 3, no-balls 4	7	Byes 4, leg byes 5, no-balls 5	14

Total (7 wkts., dec.) 214   Total (5 wkts., dec.) ...226

1/9 2/20 3/74 4/106   1/2 2/93 3/163 4/209
5/121 6/127 7/173   5/226

J. J. Warr and M. E. L. Melluish did not bat.

THE PLAYERS

D. B. Close b Warr	4	— run out	79
R. A. Gale lbw b Bailey	4	— st Melluish b Goonesena	83
T. W. Graveney b Bailey	13	— b Warr	6
D. W. Richardson b Bailey	0	— not out	54
B. Taylor lbw b Bailey	6	— c Insole b Warr	2
B. Reynolds c Edrich b Insole	75		
T. G. Evans lbw b Dexter	13	— not out	4
F. H. Tyson c Edrich b Insole , , , ,	63		
J. H. Wardle c Bailey b Goonesena	1		
F. S. Trueman run out	7		
D. J. Shepherd not out	10		
Byes 4, wides 5, no-ball 1	10	Byes 4, leg byes 3	7

Total 206   Total (4 wkts.) 235

1/4 2/8 3/8 4/24 5/35 6/59 7/173   1/133 2/200 3/219 4/226
8/174 9/188

BOWLING

THE PLAYERS

	First Innings					Second Innings			
	O.	M.	R.	W.		O.	M.	R.	W.
Trueman	14	1	44	0	Trueman	8	1	23	2
Tyson	13	4	22	2	Tyson	7	1	26	0
Close	11	7	18	1	Close	2	0	21	0
Shepherd	24	7	70	2	Shepherd	12	0	47	0
Wardle	23	5	53	2	Wardle	10	1	60	1
					Graveney	6.2	0	35	2

THE GENTLEMEN

	O.	M.	R.	W.		O.	M.	R.	W.
Warr	17	1	52	1	Warr	12.4	2	72	2
Bailey	20	6	38	4	Bailey	17	2	62	0
Dexter	8	0	32	1	Dexter	4	0	24	0
Goonesena	11	0	58	1	Goonesena	5	0	31	1
Insole	4.1	0	16	2	Insole	4	0	39	0

Umpires: H. G. Baldwin and A. R. Coleman

Result: The Players won by six wickets.

LORD'S 1958 – JULY 16–18
GENTLEMEN v. PLAYERS

THE PLAYERS

First Innings		*Second Innings*	
R. E. Marshall c Ingleby-Mackenzie b			
Wheatley 26	— not out 34		
C. A. Milton c Ingleby-Mackenzie b Warr 101			
T. W. Graveney c and b Marlar 66			
W. Watson c Cowdrey b Marlar 4	— not out 31		
J. M. Parks c Smith b Wheatley 46			
D. V. Smith not out 18			
T. G. Evans not out 41			
Byes 6, leg byes 8 14	Byes 4, wide 1 5		

Total (5 wkts., dec.) 316   Total (0 wkt.) 70

1/133 2/141 3/225 4/227 5/267

G. E. Tribe, J. H. Wardle, F. S. Trueman and J. B. Statham did not bat.

THE GENTLEMEN

P. E. Richardson c Evans b Trueman ... 34	— c Parks b Statham 1
M. J. K. Smith lbw b Statham 0	— c Smith b Wardle 19
R. Subba Row not out 102	— not out 44
R. G. Marlar lbw b Trueman 0	
M. C. Cowdrey b Trueman 1	— not out 14
E. R. Dexter st Evans b Wardle 18	
D. J. Insole b Wardle 11	
A. C. D. Ingleby-Mackenzie c Graveney b	
Trueman 27	— b Wardle 2
G. Goonesena c Evans b Wardle 12	
J. J. Warr not out 4	
Byes 10 10	Leg byes 2 2

Total (8 wkts., dec.) 219   Total (3 wkts.) 82

1/6 2/59 3/63 4/67 5/111   1/1 2/38 3/51
6/131 7/194 8/209

O. S. Wheatley did not bat.

BOWLING

THE GENTLEMEN

	First Innings					*Second Innings*			
	O.	M.	R.	W.		O.	M.	R.	W.
Warr	28	3	81	1	Warr	6	1	22	0
Wheatley	22	5	79	2	Wheatley	5	2	5	0
Dexter	2	0	11	0					
Marlar	27	5	72	2	Marlar	3	0	12	0
Goonesena	11	0	59	0	Goonesena	1	0	8	0
					Subba Row	3	0	18	0

THE PLAYERS

	O.	M.	R.	W.		O.	M.	R.	W.
Trueman	16	4	54	4	Trueman	4	0	15	0
Statham	13	2	49	1	Statham	3	0	10	1
Wardle	25.2	15	55	3	Wardle	9	2	31	2
Tribe	12	3	39	0	Tribe	9	0	24	0
Smith	5	1	12	0					

Umpires: John Langridge and N. Oldfield

Result: Drawn.

THE PLAYERS

First Innings		*Second Innings*	
R. E. Marshall b J. Bailey	25	— c May b Warr	76
R. A. Gale c and b J. Bailey	17	— st Petrie b Goonesena	28
T. W. Graveney lbw b Dexter	40	— c May b J. Bailey	7
D. W. Richardson c Insole b Goonesena	55	— c Petrie b J. Bailey	28
J. V. Wilson c Silk b Dexter	67	— not out	41
B. L. Reynolds lbw b Goonesena	26	— st Petrie b Dexter	58
D. C. Morgan c Dexter b Warr	12	— b Goonesena	1
P. J. Sainsbury c Dexter b Warr	19	— b Dexter	4
T. G. Evans c Richardson b Dexter	14	— st Petrie b Goonesena	7
F. S. Trueman c Goonesena b Dexter	4	— not out	2
J. S. Savage not out	0		
Byes 8, leg byes 3	11	Byes 5, leg byes 3	8
Total	290	Total (8 wkts., dec.)	260

1/40 2/51 3/96 4/151 5/207 6/232
7/268 8/271 9/290

1/105 2/109 3/124 4/184
5/211 6/214 7/227 8/248

THE GENTLEMEN

First Innings		*Second Innings*	
P. E. Richardson c and b Morgan	38	— b Savage	10
D. R. W. Silk lbw b Trueman	69	— c and b Savage	20
M. J. K. Smith c and b Sainsbury	41	— b Sainsbury	20
P. B. H. May c Gale b Sainsbury	15	— c Marshall b Sainsbury	46
E. R. Dexter c Wilson b Sainsbury	35	— c Trueman b Sainsbury	23
D. J. Insole b Savage	2	— b Sainsbury	24
T. E. Bailey b Morgan	42	— c Reynolds b Marshall	9
G. Goonesena c Reynolds b Marshall	26	— c Wilson b Sainsbury	25
E. C. Petrie c Graveney b Trueman	11	— not out	10
J. J. Warr run out	4	— lbw b Sainsbury	7
J. A. Bailey not out	0	— b Savage	2
Byes 2, leg byes 3, no-ball 1	6	Byes 4, leg byes 5, wide 1	10
Total	289	Total	206

1/72 2/131 3/159 4/172 5/188
6/218 7/255 8/284 9/284

1/40 2/48 3/82 4/137 5/141
6/149 7/174 8/195 9/203

BOWLING

THE GENTLEMEN

First Innings	O.	M.	R.	W.	*Second Innings*	O.	M.	R.	W.
T. Bailey	16	3	45	0	T. Bailey	8	0	62	0
Warr	15	1	50	2	Warr	10	1	45	1
J. Bailey	14	2	48	2	J. Bailey	7	0	33	2
Goonesena	21	2	79	2	Goonesena	17	0	87	3
Dexter	11.5	0	57	4	Dexter	7	1	25	2

THE PLAYERS

	O.	M.	R.	W.		O.	M.	R.	W.
Trueman	17	3	53	2	Trueman	4	0	13	0
Morgan	20	5	68	2	Morgan	6	4	10	0
Savage	22	1	78	1	Savage	21.4	3	63	3
Sainsbury	20	5	49	3	Sainsbury	19	2	72	6
Marshall	5	1	24	1	Marshall	4	1	12	1
Gale	4	1	11	0	Gale	2	1	8	0
					Richardson	5	1	18	0

Umpires: A. Skelding and H. G. Baldwin

Result: The Players won by 55 runs.

THE GENTLEMEN

First Innings		Second Innings	
R. Subba Row lbw b Cartwright	18	— lbw b Cartwright	55
R. W. Barber c Murray b Jackson	7	— c Barrington b Trueman	9
M. J. K. Smith c Jackson b Cartwright	79	— c Cartwright b Illingworth	166
P. B. H. May c Close b Trueman	15	— c Barrington b Cartwright	17
E. R. Dexter b Cartwright	3	— c and b Barrington	30
D. B. Carr c Cartwright b Illingworth	5	— not out	4
T. E. Bailey lbw b Illingworth	13	— not out	9
C. B. Howland lbw b Close	36		
D. M. Sayer run out	5		
O. S. Wheatley c Barrington b Close	0		
A. Hurd not out	0		
Byes 4, leg byes 9	13	Byes 21, leg byes 7, no-ball 1	29
Total	194	Total (5 wkts., dec.)	319

1/20 2/42 3/71 4/74 5/83 6/145   1/14 2/187 3/262 4/306 5/306
7/153 8/172 9/179

THE PLAYERS

G. Pullar c Subba Row b Wheatley	25	— not out	22
J. H. Edrich c Carr b Sayer	32	— not out	24
W. G. A. Parkhouse c Dexter b Sayer	28		
D. Brookes b Sayer	10		
K. F. Barrington c Carr b Sayer	4		
D. B. Close b Barber	112		
T. W. Cartwright b Bailey	18		
R. Illingworth c Carr b Barber	100		
J. T. Murray b Sayer	2		
F. S. Trueman not out	13		
H. L. Jackson c Howland b Sayer	2		
Byes 9, leg byes 8, wides 2	19	Leg byes 3	3
Total	365	Total (0 wkt.)	49

1/40 2/89 3/102 4/106 5/115
6/160 7/344 8/347 9/363

BOWLING

THE PLAYERS

First Innings	O.	M.	R.	W.	Second Innings	O.	M.	R.	W.
Trueman	17	2	56	1	Trueman	22	3	55	1
Jackson	14	6	20	1	Jackson	19	6	43	0
Cartwright	21	10	45	3	Cartwright	20	8	41	2
Illingworth	19	7	47	2	Illingworth	26	7	61	1
Close	2.4	0	13	2	Close	12	3	65	0
					Barrington	9	2	25	1

THE GENTLEMEN

	O.	M.	R.	W.		O.	M.	R.	W.
Sayer	28.2	8	69	6	Sayer	5	0	16	0
Bailey	25	7	55	1					
Wheatley	26	4	71	1	Wheatley	4	2	7	0
Hurd	26	5	89	0	Hurd	5	2	17	0
Dexter	12	2	29	0	Dexter	3	2	5	0
Carr	1	0	6	0					
Barber	7	2	27	2	Barber	2	1	1	0

Umpires: N. Oldfield and John Langridge

Result: Drawn.

THE GENTLEMEN

First Innings		Second Innings	
T. E. Bailey c Evans b Trueman	47	— lbw b Rhodes	9
D. Kirby c Barrington b Sainsbury	22	— b Rhodes	6
E. R. Dexter b Illingworth	0	— b Trueman	22
M. J. K. Smith c Rhodes b Illingworth	27	— c Rhodes b Sainsbury	16
D. J. Insole c Trueman b Barrington	30	— c Sainsbury b Trueman	0
A. C. D. Ingleby-Mackenzie st Evans b Sainsbury	104	— b Sainsbury	10
J. R. Burnet b Barrington	8	— c Horton b Sainsbury	0
R. V. C. Robins b Barrington	13	— st Evans b Horton	23
J. Brown not out	15	— c Rhodes b Barrington	9
G. W. Richardson c Padgett b Barrington	0	— c Evans b Horton	10
J. J. Warr b Sainsbury	16	— not out	1
Byes 5, leg byes 5, no-ball 1	11	Byes 6, leg byes 2, no-ball 1 .	9
Total	293	Total	115

1/56 2/57 3/101 4/103 5/193
6/229 7/249 8/267 9/267

1/17 2/30 3/56 4/56 5/68
6/68 7/73 8/99 9/106

THE PLAYERS

P. E. Richardson b Kirby	84	— not out	5
R. E. Marshall c and b Dexter	41	— not out	7
M. J. Horton lbw b Robins	79		
K. F. Barrington b Bailey	32		
D. E. V. Padgett lbw b Bailey	23		
R. Illingworth c Brown b Warr	9		
P. J. Sainsbury c Brown b Dexter	35		
T. G. Evans st Brown b Bailey	65		
F. S. Trueman c Brown b Dexter	4		
A. E. Moss b Dexter	6		
H. J. Rhodes not out	5		
Byes 2, leg byes 5, wides 3, no-balls 3	13	Wides 4	4
Total	396	Total (0 wkt.)	16

1/64 2/194 3/218 4/266 5/269
6/279 7/352 8/362 9/382

BOWLING
THE PLAYERS

	First Innings					Second Innings			
	O.	M.	R.	W.		O.	M.	R.	W.
Trueman	10	1	24	1	Trueman	10	4	30	2
Rhodes	7	3	12	0	Rhodes	4	0	16	2
Moss	8	2	24	0	Moss	3	2	2	0
Illingworth	17	4	51	2	Illingworth	3	1	5	0
Sainsbury	17.3	5	85	3	Sainsbury	11	3	28	3
Barrington	15	2	59	4	Barrington	6	2	10	1
Horton	5	0	27	0	Horton	9.3	4	15	2

THE GENTLEMEN

	O.	M.	R.	W.		O.	M.	R.	W.
Warr	19	2	52	1					
Richardson	15	1	58	0					
Bailey	23	3	91	3					
Dexter	12	0	48	4	Dexter	2	0	7	0
Robins	17	2	86	1	Robins	1	0	5	0
Kirby	12	3	48	1					

Umpires: H. G. Baldwin and D. Davies

Result: The Players won by ten wickets.

LORD'S 1960 – JULY 13–15
GENTLEMEN v. PLAYERS

THE GENTLEMEN

First Innings		*Second Innings*	
R. Subba Row c Horton b Statham	11	— c Horton b Barrington	64
R. M. Prideaux lbw b Allen	22	— b Allen	70
E. R. Dexter c Barrington b Statham ...	0	— run out	7
*M. C. Cowdrey c Barrington b Moss .	24	— c Murray b Jackson	48
M. J. K. Smith c Murray b Moss	17	— not out	28
D. B. Carr not out	25	— not out	2
R. W. Barber lbw b Allen	0		
†A. C. Smith c Jackson b Allen	5		
D. M. Sayer c Statham b Allen	2		
A. J. Corran c Murray b Jackson	0		
A. Hurd b Jackson	0		
Leg byes 2	2	Bye 1, leg byes 7	8

Total 108	Total (4 wkts., dec.) ...227
1/20 2/24 3/49 4/60 5/84	1/134 2/145 3/152 4/218
6/85 7/101 8/108 9/108	

THE PLAYERS

J. H. Edrich b Sayer	69	— st A. Smith b Hurd	21
M. J. Stewart c A. Smith b Hurd	29	— c Corran b Dexter	27
W. E. Russell not out	55	— b Sayer	39
H. Horton not out	4	— b Sayer	0
K. F. Barrington (did not bat)		— b Sayer	32
D. E. V. Padgett (did not bat)		— b Sayer	0
†J. T. Murray (did not bat)		— c Corran b Barber	3
D. A. Allen (did not bat)		— not out	11
*J. B. Statham (did not bat)		— c and b Hurd	6
A. E. Moss (did not bat)		— run out	20
Byes 4, leg byes 6, wide 1	11	Byes 4, leg byes 3, wide 1 ..	8

Total (2 wkts., dec.) 168	Total (9 wkts.) 167
1/40 2/157	1/38 2/40 3/63 4/120 5/120
	6/123 7/129 8/135 9/167

H. L. Jackson did not bat.

BOWLING

THE PLAYERS

First Innings					*Second Innings*			
	O.	M.	R.	W.		O.	M.	R.	W.
Statham	14	5	22	2	Statham	11	2	18	0
Jackson	18.3	6	34	2	Jackson	13	3	46	1
Moss	11	4	21	2	Moss	6	0	23	0
Allen	19	6	29	4	Allen	19	4	51	1
					Barrington	11	0	81	1

THE GENTLEMEN

	O.	M.	R.	W.		O.	M.	R.	W.
Sayer	13	3	45	1	Sayer	11	2	36	4
Corran	12	4	13	0	Corran	4	0	19	0
Dexter	3	0	12	0	Dexter	2	0	7	1
Hurd	11	3	34	1	Hurd	5	0	36	2
Barber	16	2	53	0	Barber	9	1	44	1
					Carr	4	0	17	0

Umpires: W. F. Price and N. Oldfield

Result: Drawn.

THE PLAYERS

First Innings		*Second Innings*	
R. E. Marshall b Richardson	32	— c Insole b Warr	2
W. E. Russell b Warr	27	— b Warr	8
J. H. Edrich c Ingleby-Mackenzie b Hurd	50	— c Brown b Dexter	20
K. F. Barrington b Hurd	71	— st Brown b Hurd	111
★T. W. Graveney run out	50	— c Dexter b Richardson	3
P. J. Sainsbury b Bailey	21	— c Dexter b Richardson	21
†R. Swetman b Bailey	39	— c Hurd b Dexter	14
B. R. Knight c Brown b Bailey	14	— b Hurd	8
D. A. Allen lbw b Bailey	1	— c Ingleby-Mackenzie b Hurd	7
A. E. Moss not out	29	— c Bailey b Hurd	1
H. J. Rhodes not out	7	— not out	17
Bye 1, leg byes 7, no-ball 1	9	Byes 4, leg byes 2, wide 1, no-balls 2	9

Total (9 wkts., dec.) 350
1/49 2/61 3/153 4/191 5/251
6/262 7/288 8/292 9/335

Total 221
1/3 2/23 3/31 4/86 5/92
6/154 7/191 8/196 9/198

THE GENTLEMEN

D. R. W. Silk b Sainsbury	119	— c and b Allen	19
C. T. M. Pugh b Rhodes	15	— b Rhodes	1
E. R. Dexter c Graveney b Sainsbury	22	— b Rhodes	56
M. J. K. Smith c Russell b Sainsbury	63	— c Moss b Sainsbury	74
T. E. Bailey c Graveney b Russell	32	— b Knight	10
★D. J. Insole b Allen	1	— c Rhodes b Sainsbury	30
A. C. D. Ingleby-Mackenzie b Rhodes	8	— run out	17
G. W. Richardson b Moss	4	— c Russell b Allen	22
†J. Brown b Rhodes	1	— b Sainsbury	1
J. J. Warr st Swetman b Allen	16	— b Allen	5
A. Hurd not out	1	— not out	1
Byes 5, leg byes 2, no-balls 5	12	Bye 1, leg byes 3, no-balls 4	8

Total 294
1/19 2/53 3/175 4/229 5/230
6/247 7/258 8/261 9/290

Total 253
1/8 2/49 3/125 4/137 5/202
6/208 7/244 8/245 9/245

BOWLING

THE GENTLEMEN

First Innings	O.	M.	R.	W.	Second Innings	O.	M.	R.	W.
Bailey	24	4	59	4	Bailey	2	0	7	0
Warr	22	4	76	1	Warr	10	1	30	2
Dexter	12	3	17	0	Dexter	14	1	43	2
Richardson	11	0	40	1	Richardson	8	2	19	2
Hurd	24	3	149	2	Hurd	25	4	113	4

THE PLAYERS

	O.	M.	R.	W.		O.	M.	R.	W.
Rhodes	12	3	17	3	Rhodes	7	4	5	2
Moss	17	2	40	1	Moss	3	1	3	0
Knight	8	2	27	0	Knight	5	1	15	1
Sainsbury	24	4	103	3	Sainsbury	22	0	103	3
Allen	21	3	78	2	Allen	16.2	0	82	3
Barrington	2	1	4	0	Barrington	1	0	4	0
Russell	4	1	13	1	Russell	5	0	33	0

Umpires: N. Oldfield and H. G. Baldwin

Result: The Players won by 24 runs.

THE PLAYERS

First Innings		*Second Innings*	
G. Atkinson c Craig b Bailey	4	— lbw b Wheatley	14
W. E. Russell lbw b Dexter	33	— run out	11
*W. Watson b Barber	30	— c Wheatley b Dexter	17
K. F. Barrington b Drybrough	53	— c Brearley b Wheatley	53
W. E. Alley b Piachaud	24	— c May b Dexter	1
D. B. Close c Dexter b Piachaud	14	— not out	94
†J. T. Murray b Drybrough	13	— b Drybrough	52
G. A. R. Lock c Brearley b Drybrough	12	— not out	10
F. S. Trueman b Drybrough	1		
J. Flavell b Piachaud	2		
A. E. Moss not out	0		
Byes 12, leg bye 1, wides 4	17	Byes 9, leg byes 2	11
Total	203	Total (6 wkts., dec.)	263

1/4 2/58 3/87 4/141 5/157
6/175 7/195 8/197 9/203

1/18 2/28 3/46 4/56 5/136
6/218

THE GENTLEMEN

R. W. Barber c Russell b Trueman	11	— b Close	45
E. J. Craig b Trueman	6	— c Alley b Flavell	0
E. R. Dexter lbw b Trueman	0	— c Alley b Flavell	0
*P. B. H. May c Murray b Trueman	79	— b Flavell	7
M. J. K. Smith c Murray b Moss	9	— c Lock b Flavell	5
R. M. Prideaux lbw b Flavell	57	— c Murray b Close	16
T. E. Bailey lbw b Lock	4	— c Trueman b Close	24
†J. M. Brearley c Murray b Trueman	1	— b Lock	6
C. D. Drybrough not out	8	— not out	2
J. D. Piachaud lbw b Flavell	2	— c Barrington b Close	4
O. S. Wheatley b Flavell	0	— b Close	0
		Leg byes 8	8
Total	177	Total	117

1/13 2/13 3/30 4/52 5/142
6/151 7/152 8/171 9/173

1/2 2/2 3/10 4/44 5/64
6/89 7/100 8/111 9/117

BOWLING

THE GENTLEMEN

	First Innings					*Second Innings*			
	O.	M.	R.	W.		O.	M.	R.	W.
Bailey	14	2	33	1	Bailey	26	7	45	0
Wheatley	18	6	32	0	Wheatley	25	5	69	2
Dexter	14	4	33	1	Dexter	17	4	54	2
Barber	10	1	34	1	Barber	2	0	10	0
Piachaud	17.5	11	24	3	Piachaud	11	0	33	0
Drybrough	14	6	30	4	Drybrough	14	4	41	1

THE PLAYERS

	O.	M.	R.	W.		O.	M.	R.	W.
Trueman	18	5	47	5	Trueman	13	3	45	0
Flavell	21.1	4	47	3	Flavell	12	7	15	4
Moss	13	3	37	1	Moss	8	4	7	0
Lock	19	8	46	1	Lock	7	3	14	1
					Close	11	3	23	5
					Barrington	1	0	5	0

Umpires: N. Oldfield and J. F. Crapp

Result: The Players won by 172 runs.

THE PLAYERS

First Innings		Second Innings	
*M. R. Hallam lbw b Wheatley	97	— b Richardson	42
N. Hill c Kirby b Richardson	44	— c A. Smith b Bailey	10
J. H. Edrich c A. Smith b Wheatley	18	— c A. Smith b Bailey	4
G. J. Smith c Brearley b Richardson	23	— c and b Wheatley	23
J. Milner c M. Smith b Richardson	73	— c A. Smith b Richardson	6
†G. Millman c A. Smith b Wheatley	3	— not out	39
B. R. Knight b Wheatley	5	— b Richardson	18
B. Crump c A. Smith b Wheatley	79	— not out	0
M. H. J. Allen c May b Richardson	8		
J. S. Savage c and b Bailey	10		
J. D. F. Larter not out	0		
Leg byes 6, wide 1	7	Wide 1	1
Total	367	Total (6 wkts., dec.)	143

1/77 2/128 3/183 4/185 5/195
6/213 7/303 8/322 9/366

1/21 2/29 3/71 4/79 5/94 6/142

THE GENTLEMEN

D. Kirby b Knight	11	— b Larter	22
R. M. Prideaux run out	21	— b Knight	27
M. J. K. Smith c Allen b Savage	92	— c Smith b Savage	43
*P. B. H. May b Knight	2	— c Crump b Allen	13
A. A. Baig c Millman b Allen	25	— b Savage	0
J. M. Brearley lbw b Savage	5	— c Edrich b Savage	10
T. E. Bailey c Knight b Allen	1	— b Savage	21
D. D. Carr b Knight	56	— st Millman b Allen	6
†A. C. Smith not out	37	— st Millman b Allen	16
G. W. Richardson b Knight	0	— c Edrich b Savage	1
O. S. Wheatley b Larter	2	— not out	34
Byes 8, leg bye 1	9	Leg byes 2	2
Total	261	Total	195

1/18 2/47 3/49 4/153 5/156
6/162 7/170 8/252 9/254

1/49 2/49 3/80 4/89 5/112
6/112 7/131 8/139 9/141

BOWLING

THE GENTLEMEN

First Innings	O.	M.	R.	W.	Second Innings	O.	M.	R.	W.
Bailey	20.2	1	90	1	Bailey	16	4	33	2
Wheatley	26	3	92	5	Wheatley	15	1	38	1
Richardson	21	2	76	4	Richardson	15	3	29	3
Kirby	12	0	43	0	Kirby	3	0	26	0
Carr	15	0	59	0	Carr	4	1	16	0

THE PLAYERS

	O.	M.	R.	W.		O.	M.	R.	W.
Larter	13	2	30	1	Larter	8	2	26	1
Knight	15	4	30	4	Knight	7	1	27	1
Allen	24	9	54	2	Allen	21	3	62	3
Savage	17	5	42	2	Savage	21	3	78	5
Crump	19	4	58	0					
Smith	5	0	38	0					

Umpires: J. S. Buller and D. Davies

Result: The Players won by 54 runs.

GENTLEMEN v. PLAYERS

THE GENTLEMEN

	First Innings		*Second Innings*	
Rev. D. S. Sheppard c and b Titmus	...112	— b Titmus		34
E. J. Craig b Trueman	4	— c Titmus b Trueman		0
*E. R. Dexter c Trueman b Shackleton	55	— run out		1
M. J. K. Smith run out	44	— not out		15
R. M. Prideaux b Trueman	14	— b Shackleton		109
A. R. Lewis lbw b Shackleton	2	— c Andrew b Titmus		10
R. W. Barber run out	0	— not out		3
D. B. Pithey run out	30			
T. E. Bailey c Walker b Shackleton	5			
†A. C. Smith c Sharpe b Shackleton	33			
O. S. Wheatley not out	14			
Byes 4, leg byes 6	10			
Total	323	Total (5 wkts., dec.)		...172

1/12 2/109 3/204 4/221 5/227
6/229 7/239 8/262 9/275

1/0 2/73 3/95 4/115 5/166

THE PLAYERS

M. J. Stewart c A. Smith b Bailey	0	— c A. Smith b Wheatley	3
J. H. Edrich b Bailey	19	— not out	77
P. H. Parfitt c Sheppard d Dexter	9	— c Dexter b Barber	63
T. W. Graveney c Craig b Wheatley	21	— c A. Smith b Bailey	41
P. J. Sharpe c and b Barber	39	— not out	12
P. M. Walker b Bailey	15		
F. J. Titmus c Dexter b Bailey	70		
*F. S. Trueman c Wheatley b Barber	63		
†K. V. Andrew c A. Smith b Bailey	17		
N. Gifford c A. Smith b Bailey	2		
D. Shackleton not out	1		
Byes 4	4	Bye 1, leg byes 10	11
Total	260	Total (3 wkts.)	...207

1/0 2/15 3/41 4/56 5/86
6/104 7/194 8/255 9/257

1/3 2/121 3/177

BOWLING

THE PLAYERS

	First Innings					*Second Innings*			
	O.	M.	R.	W.		O.	M.	R.	W.
Trueman	13	6	59	2	Trueman	10	6	8	1
Shackleton	38	9	101	4	Shackleton	19	8	38	1
Walker	28	4	64	0	Walker	9	2	21	0
Titmus	20	6	46	1	Titmus	24	5	69	2
Gifford	14	4	43	0	Gifford	7	0	36	0

THE GENTLEMEN

	O.	M.	R.	W.		O.	M.	R.	W.
Bailey	30.3	10	58	6	Bailey	13	1	45	1
Wheatley	19	6	37	1	Wheatley	12	1	46	1
Dexter	18	2	49	1	Dexter	7	0	35	0
Barber	21	7	90	2	Barber	7	0	43	1
Pithey	8	2	22	0	Pithey	4	0	27	0

Umpires: H. Yarnold and A. E. Rhodes

Result: Drawn.

THE GENTLEMEN

First Innings		*Second Innings*	
A. R. Lewis c Knight b Lock	35	— c Millman b Trueman	0
R. M. Prideaux b Knight	17	— c Lock b Close	25
*M. J. K. Smith c and b Lock	18	— c Millman b Close	33
R. C. White b Trueman	24	— c Barrington b Trueman	95
D. Kirby c and b Barrington	39	— c Millman b Close	1
†A. C. Smith c Morgan b Lock	34	— c Close b Lock	13
R. A. Hutton b Trueman	7	— c and b Lock	16
C. D. Drybrough c Gale b Lock	12	— c Knight b Lock	16
G. W. Richardson st Millman b Morgan	68	— c Barrington b Trueman	1
R. I. Jefferson c Edrich b Morgan	68	— not out	3
O. S. Wheatley not out	3	— b Trueman	0
Bye 1, wides 2	3	Byes 4, leg byes 9, no-ball 1 .	14
Total	328	Total	217

1/27 2/66 3/72 4/130 5/134
6/148 7/188 8/189 9/319

1/1 2/65 3/80 4/82 5/103
6/139 7/212 8/214 9/215

THE PLAYERS

J. H. Edrich b Richardson	38	— b Hutton	43
N. F. Horner c and b Jefferson	30	— not out	49
R. A. Gale c Richardson b Hutton	31	— c and b Wheatley	88
K. F. Barrington b Drybrough	100	— b Drybrough	25
D. B. Close c Wheatley b Hutton	9		
A. Lightfoot c Wheatley b Jefferson	11		
D. C. Morgan b Richardson	48		
B. R. Knight b Drybrough	14	— not out	5
†G. Millman c Kirby b Jefferson	27		
*F. S. Trueman c White b Jefferson	19		
G. A. R. Lock not out	1		
Bye 1, leg byes 4, wide 1, no-balls 3	9	Leg byes 2	2
Total	337	Total (3 wkts.)	212

1/38 2/89 3/102 4/130 5/163
6/274 7/274 8/296 9/336

1/75 2/147 3/193

BOWLING

THE PLAYERS

	First Innings					*Second Innings*			
	O.	M.	R.	W.		O.	M.	R.	W.
Trueman	12	2	29	2	Trueman	9.5	3	11	4
Knight	8	0	16	1	Knight	5	1	8	0
Lightfoot	15	4	53	0					
Lock	20	3	87	4	Lock	28	3	126	3
Morgan	13.1	1	53	2	Morgan	4	0	14	0
Barrington	17	1	87	1					
					Close	21	8	44	3

THE GENTLEMEN

	O.	M.	R.	W.		O.	M.	R.	W.
Wheatley	7	1	19	0	Wheatley	7	0	56	1
Jefferson	23.5	2	104	4	Jefferson	11	1	53	0
Hutton	16	5	42	2	Hutton	10	2	52	1
Drybrough	23	0	128	2	Drybrough	7	0	38	1
Richardson	11	3	35	2	Richardson	2	0	6	0
					White	1	0	5	0

Umpires: J. S. Buller and W. E. Phillipson

Result: The Players won by seven wickets.

APPENDIX II

RECORDS OF GENTLEMEN v. PLAYERS 1806–1962

Compiled by Philip Defriez, Patrick Allen and Michael Marshall

The statistics in Appendix II follow the format established by Roy Webber in Sir Pelham Warner's book *Gentlemen v. Players 1806–1949*. They have been updated to include the matches played from 1950 to 1962. Following Webber, the matches at Blackpool (1924) and Bournemouth (1925) are excluded from these records while the Canterbury match (1846) has been included.

However, research by members of the Association of Cricket Statisticians as well as errors in Webber's original figures have required substantial corrections and revisions. Some additional material has also been included, most notably in the sequences of results; margins of victory; centuries before lunch; 8 or more wickets in an innings; 12 or more wickets in a match; wicket-keeping statistics (most in an innings and a match); fielding; and most of the material in the miscellany section.

Notes on the averages
1) For ease of comparison, the Webber formula has been followed whenever possible. Thus, the averages have been divided into two sections, the first including cricketers whose last appearance was prior to 1900. The remainder appear in the second section – with one exception: W. G. Grace has been placed in the first section as all but seven of his eighty-five appearances predated 1900.
2) Qualification for inclusion in averages:

   Batting 1806–99 – 15 innings with an average of 10 or more
   　　　　　1900–62 – 8 innings with an average of 10 or more
   Bowling 1806–99[1]　⎫
   　　　　　1900–62　⎬– 10 wickets or more
   Fielding　　　　　– 15 catches or more
   Wicket-keeping　　– 15 dismissals or more

   For added interest, at the end of each section there are included some other notable records by cricketers who do not meet the above qualifications.
3) 'Gentlemen' are shown on the left-hand margin and 'Players' are denoted by inset names. Those who played for both sides are shown as having appeared for the team in which they played the most matches.
4) For the Gentlemen, details of public school, university and county appear as appropriate. For the Players, a number of examples are shown of those who coached at public schools by including such school names in brackets. In cases where a cricketer appeared for two or more counties, only those in which he was playing at the time of his appearance in these matches have been included.

[1] This section includes a Total Wickets (TW) column. This is to indicate those whose total includes wickets for which no detailed bowling analyses were available in the early days of cricket records. Bowling performances in matches against odds are recorded in the 5 wickets in the Innings entries (5I) and in the 10 wickets in the Match (10M) columns but not in the Best Bowling (BB) column.

PART A: STATISTICS

GENTLEMEN v. PLAYERS: 1806–1962

1 RESULTS

Venue	Dates	G.	P.	D.	Tie	Total
Lord's (Dorset Square)	1806	2	0	0	–	2
Lord's	1819–1962	39	68	28	–	135
Oval	1857–1934	16	34	21	1	72
Scarborough	1885–1962	4	15	19	–	38
Folkestone	1925–1936	1	3	4	–	10
Hastings	1889–1903	1	2	4	–	7
Prince's	1873–1877	4	1	0	–	5
Brighton	1845–1881	0	1	2	–	3
Canterbury	1846	0	0	1	–	1
TOTAL	1806–1962	67	126	79	1	273

SEQUENCES

Most consecutive victories	Most consecutive draws
13 – Players – 1854–1861	8 – 1930–1932
6 – Players – 1862–1865	4 – 1911–1913
6 – Gentlemen – 1872–1874	4 – 1926–1927
5 – Players – 1831–1835	
5 – Gentlemen – 1877–1879	
5 – Players – 1900–1901	
4 – Players – 1850–1852	
4 – Gentlemen – 1868–1869	
4 – Players – 1932–1934	
4 – Players – 1954–1955	

The Players won all three games in 1900 and 1921.
The Gentlemen won all three games in 1873.
All three games were drawn in 1922.
All four games were drawn in 1931.

2 TEAM RECORDS

HIGHEST INNINGS TOTALS

Gentlemen	578	Oval	1904
	542	Lord's	1926
	513	Oval	1870
	500–2d	Lord's	1903
Players	651–7d	Oval	1934
	647	Oval	1899
	608–8d	Oval	1921
	579	Lord's	1926
	561–6d	Folkestone	1927
	552–8d	Folkestone	1933
	532–5d	Scarborough	1953
	514	Lord's	1924
	513–6d	Oval	1932
	513–9d	Scarborough	1927
	502–8	Lord's	1900

HIGHEST FOURTH INNINGS TOTALS

Gentlemen	412–8 (and won)	Lord's	1904
Players	502–8 (and won)	Lord's	1900

HIGHEST MATCH AGGREGATES

1396 – 24	Scarborough	1953
1313 – 31	Oval	1925
1293 – 32	Scarborough	1906
1292 – 35	Folkestone	1928
1274 – 38	Lord's	1900
1258 – 30	Oval	1899
1235 – 37	Oval	1906
1218 – 21	Lord's	1926
1218 – 23	Lord's	1903
1213 – 28	Oval	1921

LOWEST INNINGS TOTALS

Gentlemen	31	Lord's	1848
	35	Lord's	1837
	36	Lord's	1831
	37	Lord's	1853
	39	Lord's	1840
	42	Lord's	1833
	42	Lord's	1837
	42	Lord's	1850
	43	Lord's	1855
	48	Lord's	1847
	50	Lord's	1856
Players	24 (1st inns.)	Lord's	1829
	37 (2nd inns.)	Lord's	1829
	42	Lord's	1853
	46	Lord's	1830
	48	Oval	1879

LOWEST MATCH AGGREGATES

188 – 30	Lord's	1837
236 – 41	Lord's	1833
248 – 30	Lord's	1850
268 – 30	Lord's	1832
270 – 40	Lord's	1837
282 – 40	Lord's	1853
282 – 32	Lord's	1867

LARGEST MARGINS OF VICTORY

345 runs	Players	Lord's	1823
285 runs	Players	Lord's	1858
Innings & 181 runs	Players	Lord's	1860
262 runs	Gentlemen	Lord's	1875
Innings & 126 runs	Gentlemen	Oval	1879
Innings & 123 runs	Players	Lord's	1887
Innings & 128 runs	Players	Hastings	1891
Innings & 110 runs	Players	Scarborough	1919
Innings & 231 runs	Players	Lord's	1924
Innings & 305 runs	Players	Oval	1934
Innings & 140 runs	Players	Lord's	1946

SMALLEST MARGINS OF VICTORY

1 wicket	Gentlemen	Lord's	1846
4 runs	Gentlemen	Lord's	1870
1 wicket	Gentlemen	Lord's	1877
1 run	Players	Brighton	1881
5 runs	Gentlemen	Lord's	1888
1 wicket	Gentlemen	Hastings	1889
8 runs	Players	Oval	1893
1 wicket	Gentlemen	Oval	1896
6 runs	Gentlemen	Scarborough	1913
2 runs	Players	Lord's	1952

TIED MATCH

Players	203 & 181	Oval	1883
Gentlemen	235 & 149		

Note. In the match at Brighton in 1881, which the Players won by 1 run, it is stated that an error was found in the score after the match, giving the Gentlemen an extra run and therefore making the result, in effect, a tie.

3 BATTING

	Gentlemen			Players	
Lord's					
102★	W. Ward	1825	113★	T. Beagley	1821
134★	W. G. Grace	1868	100	J. Saunders	1827
109	W. G. Grace	1870	132	T. Hayward	1860
112	W. G. Grace	1872	112★	T. Hayward	1863
163	W. G. Grace	1873	122★	T. Hearne	1866
152	W. G. Grace	1875	102	R. Daft	1872
169	W. G. Grace	1876	111	A. Shrewsbury	1887
103	A. W. Ridley	1876	130★	W. Barnes	1889
107	A. P. Lucas	1882	103	W. Gunn	1892
100	C. T. Studd	1882	116★	T. W. Hayward	1896
107	E. F. S. Tylecote	1883	125	A. Shrewsbury	1897
118	W. G. Grace	1895	139	W. Gunn	1898
104	C. B. Fry	1899	163	J. T. Brown	1900
102★ 136	R. E. Foster	1900	111	T. W. Hayward	1900
			140	J. T. Tyldesley	1901
126	C. B. Fry	1901	141	L. C. Braund	1902
232★	C. B. Fry	1903	100	W. H. Lockwood	1902
168★	A. C. MacLaren	1903	139	A. E. Knight	1903
121	K. S. Ranjitsinhji	1904	104 109★	J. H. King	1904
114	R. H. Spooner	1906			
124	D. J. Knight	1919	123★	T. W. Hayward	1905
101	P. G. H. Fender	1921	146★	T. W. Hayward	1907
160	A. P. F. Chapman	1922	154★	J. B. Hobbs	1911
122	G. T. S. Stevens	1923	113	J. B. Hobbs	1919
120	M. D. Lyon	1923	108	C. P. Mead	1921
129	G. T. S. Stevens	1925	140	J. B. Hobbs	1922
108	A. P. F. Chapman	1926	162	C. A. G. Russell	1922
123	D. R. Jardine	1927	118	J. B. Hobbs	1924
125 103★	K. S. Duleepsinhji	1930	113	R. Kilner	1924
			140	J. B. Hobbs	1925
165	Nawab of Pataudi, Snr.	1932	163	J. B. Hobbs	1926
132	K. S. Duleepsinhji	1932	131	G. E. Tyldesley	1926
104★	R. E. S. Wyatt	1934	107	H. Sutcliffe	1926
175★	H. T. Bartlett	1938	161★	J. B. Hobbs	1932
162★	M. P. Donnelly	1947	110	W. R. Hammond	1932
122	F. R. Brown	1950	120	A. Mitchell	1934
119★	P. B. H. May	1951	105	C. Washbrook	1946
127	C. H. Palmer	1952	101	C. Washbrook	1947
117	R. T. Simpson	1953	132★	L. Hutton	1948
154	C. H. Palmer	1955	123	H. E. Dollery	1950
102★	R. Subba Row	1958	150	D. C. S. Compton	1951
166	M. J. K. Smith	1959	115	M. Tompkin	1955
112	D. S. Sheppard	1962	102	D. V. Smith	1957
109	R. M. Prideaux	1962	101	C. A. Milton	1958
			112	D. B. Close	1959
			100	R. Illingworth	1959
Princes					
104	A. N. Hornby	1873	118	G. Ulyett	1877
110	W. G. Grace	1874			
134	G. F. Grace	1877			
Hastings					
131	W. G. Grace	1894	169	W. Gunn	1891
105	A. O. Jones	1901	117	R. Abel	1892
			108	A. Ward	1897
			124★	G. H. Hirst	1903

Brighton

217	W. G. Grace	1871

Oval

107★	A. Lubbock	1867	119	R. P. Carpenter	1860
165	I. D. Walker	1868	106	R. P. Carpenter	1861
215	W. G. Grace	1870	117	H. H. Stephenson	1864
109★	W. B. Money	1870	134	G. Ulyett	1884
117	W. G. Grace	1872	127	A. Shrewsbury	1886
158	W. G. Grace	1873	151★	A. Shrewsbury	1892
144	A. N. Hornby	1877	168★	R. Abel	1894
100	W. G. Grace	1881	100	F. W. Marlow	1895
159	W. W. Read	1885	195	R. Abel	1899
112★	C. L. Townsend	1899	134★	T. W. Hayward	1899
123	C. J. Burnup	1900	153★	R. Abel	1900
145	B. J. T. Bosanquet	1904	247	R. Abel	1901
140	W. L. Murdoch	1904	177	T. W. Hayward	1902
128	J. H. S. Hunt	1904	203	T. W. Hayward	1904
190	R. H. Spooner	1911	104	J. Hardstaff, Snr.	1906
101	C. B. Fry	1912	158	S. Kinneir	1911
107	G. L. Jessop	1913	123★	J. W. Hearne	1912
127	C. N. Bruce	1921	126	J. W. Hearne	1913
112	A. E. R. Gilligan	1924	156	J. B. Hobbs	1914
130	G. O. B. Allen	1925	120★	J. B. Hobbs	1919
193	D. R. Jardine	1928	127	H. T. W. Hardinge	1921
115	R. E. S. Wyatt	1929	126	T. F. Shepherd	1923
123★	D. R. Jardine	1932	124	A. Sandham	1924
112	L. H. Tennyson	1932	103	J. W. Hearne	1925
			125	A. Sandham	1926
			150	E. H. Hendren	1927
			110	J. B. Hobbs	1931
			120	H. Sutcliffe	1931
			194★	E. H. Hendren	1932
			125	J. Arnold	1934
			119	H. S. Squires	1934
			106	R. G. Duckfield	1934

Scarborough

174	W. G. Grace	1885	125	G. J. Thompson	1900
134	F. S. Jackson	1900	157★	D. Denton	1906
102	T. L. Taylor	1902	122★	E. G. Hayes	1906
102	C. J. Burnup	1902	105	J. T. Tyldesley	1910
137	E. G. Wynyard	1906	223	C. P. Mead	1911
120	K. L. Hutchings	1908	116	J. B. Hobbs	1919
103	B. J. T. Bosanquet	1911	146	J. W. Hearne	1919
119	G. L. Jessop	1913	138	J. B. Hobbs	1920
101	G. A. Faulkner	1913	105	J. B. Hobbs	1923
101	A. P. F. Chapman	1920	100★	E. H. Hendren	1923
100	F. T. Mann	1922	266★	J. B. Hobbs	1925
101	A. W. Carr	1925	129	E. H. Hendren	1925
101★	V. W. C. Jupp	1927	119	J. B. Hobbs	1927
106	M. C. Cowdrey	1951	127	P. Holmes	1927
157	P. B. H. May	1953	116	G. E. Tyldesley	1927
100	M. C. Cowdrey	1953	144	J. B. Hobbs	1931
133	W. J. Edrich	1953	100	J. Hardstaff, Jnr.	1938
112★	P. B. H. May	1954	241	L. Hutton	1953
133	W. J. Edrich	1955	143★	W. Watson	1953
133	W. J. Edrich	1956	122	J. V. Wilson	1954
104	A. C. D. Ingleby-Mackenzie	1959	124	T. W. Graveney	1956
119	D. R. W. Silk	1960	111	K. F. Barrington	1960
			100	K. F. Barrington	1962

Gentlemen				Players	

Folkestone

101	F. S. G. Calthorpe	1927	138	W. R. Hammond	1927
136	B. W. Hone	1932	103	E. H. Hendren	1927
128	C. P. Johnstone	1933	141★	F. E. Woolley	1928
115	R. C. M. Kimpton	1936	118	A. Sandham	1931
			129	T. S. Worthington	1932
			201	L. E. G. Ames	1933
			117	W. H. Ashdown	1933
			109	G. Geary	1934
			106	W. R. Hammond	1935

THREE CENTURIES IN AN INNINGS

Gentlemen	(578)	B. J. T. Bosanquet	145		
		W. L. Murdoch	140		
		J. H. S. Hunt	128	Oval	1904
Players	(579)	J. B. Hobbs	163		
		H. Sutcliffe	107		
		G. E. Tyldesley	131	Lord's	1926
Players	(513–9d)	J. B. Hobbs	119		
		P. Holmes	127		
		G. E. Tyldesley	116	Scarborough	1927
Players	(651–7d)	J. Arnold	125		
		H. S. Squires	119		
		R. G. Duckfield	106	Oval	1934

DOUBLE CENTURIES

Gentlemen	232★	C. B. Fry	Lord's	1903
	217	W. G. Grace	Brighton	1871
	215	W. G. Grace	Oval	1870
Players	266★	J. B. Hobbs	Scarborough	1925
	247	R. Abel	Oval	1901
	241	L. Hutton	Scarborough	1953
	223	C. P. Mead	Scarborough	1911
	203	T. W. Hayward	Oval	1904
	201	L. E. G. Ames	Folkestone	1933

215 centuries were made in the series altogether:
100 for the Gentlemen and 115 for the Players.

CENTURY ON DEBUT IN THE SERIES

Gentlemen	123	C. J. Burnup	Oval	1900
	102★ & 136	R. E. Foster	Lord's	1900
	128	J. H. S. Hunt	Oval	1904
	124	D. J. Knight	Lord's	1919
	120	M. D. Lyon	Lord's	1923
	128	C. P. Johnstone†	Folkestone	1933
	115	R. C. M. Kimpton	Folkestone	1936
	119★	P. B. H. May	Lord's	1951
	106	M. C. Cowdrey	Scarborough	1951
	102★	R. Subba Row	Lord's	1958

†Sole appearance in the series.

Players	100	F. W. Marlow	Oval	1895
	125	G. J. Thompson	Scarborough	1900
	139	A. E. Knight	Lord's	1903
	104 & 109★	J. H. King	Lord's	1904
	104	J. Hardstaff, Snr.	Oval	1906
	223	C. P. Mead	Scarborough	1911
	123★	J. W. Hearne	Oval	1912
	117	W. H. Ashidown†	Folkestone	1933
	106	R. G. Duckfield†	Oval	1934
	119	H. S. Squires†	Oval	1934
	120	A. Mitchell	Lord's	1934
	105	C. Washbrook	Lord's	1946
	101	C. A. Milton†	Lord's	1958

CENTURY IN EACH INNINGS OF A MATCH

Gentlemen	102★ & 136	R. E. Foster	Lord's	1900
	125 & 103★	K. S. Duleepsinhji	Lord's	1930
Players	104 & 109★	J. H. King	Lord's	1904

CARRYING BAT THROUGH COMPLETED INNINGS

Gentlemen	47★	(149)	A. P. Lucas	Oval	1883
	62★	(170)	J. J. Ferris	Scarborough	1892
Players	67★	(115)	E. Lockwood	Oval	1874
	81★	(167)	A. Shrewsbury	Lord's	1891
	151★	(325)	A. Shrewsbury	Oval	1892
	168★	(363)	R. Abel	Oval	1894
	153★	(302)	R. Abel	Oval	1900
	146★	(278)	T. W. Hayward	Lord's	1907
	154★	(292)	J. B. Hobbs	Lord's	1911
	161★	(320)	J. B. Hobbs	Lord's	1932

CENTURY BEFORE LUNCH

Gentlemen	126	C. B. Fry	(Day 2)	Lord's	1901
	112	A. E. R. Gilligan	(Day 3)	Oval	1924
	112	W. G. Grace	(Day 3)	Lord's	1872
	158	W. G. Grace	(Day 1)	Oval	1873
	169	W. G. Grace	(Day 1)	Lord's	1876
	144	A. N. Hornby	(Day 3)	Oval	1877
	109	R. M. Prideaux	(Day 3)	Lord's	1962
	137	E. G. Wynyard	(Day 2)	Scarborough	1906
Players	111	K. F. Barrington	(Day 3)	Scarborough	1960
	122★	E. G. Hayes	(Day 3)	Scarborough	1906
	241	L. Hutton	(Day 1)	Scarborough	1953

†Sole appearance in the series.

RECORD PARTNERSHIPS

Gentlemen

1. 203	W. G. Grace & A. J. Webbe	Lord's	1875
2. 241	W. G. Grace & G. F. Grace	Brighton	1871
3. 309★	C. B. Fry & A. C. MacLaren	Lord's	1903
4. 205	P. B. H. May & M. C. Cowdrey	Scarborough	1953
5. 137	A. P. F. Chapman & D. R. Jardine	Lord's	1926
6. 164	K. L. Hutchings & F. L. Fane	Scarborough	1908
7. 249	W. L. Murdoch & J. H. S. Hunt	Oval	1904
8. 129	T. L. Taylor & E. Smith	Scarborough	1902
9. 193	G. O. B. Allen & N. E. Haig	Oval	1925
10. 134	A. E. R. Gilligan & M. Falcon	Oval	1924

Players

1. 263	J. B. Hobbs & H. Sutcliffe	Lord's	1926
2. 181	J. B. Hobbs & P. Holmes	Scarborough	1927
3. 298	J. B. Hobbs & E. H. Hendren	Scarborough	1925
4. 226	E. H. Hendren & W. R. Hammond	Folkestone	1927
5. 160	J. W. Hearne & F. A. Tarrant	Oval	1912
6. 204	L. E. G. Ames & W. H. Ashdown	Folkestone	1933
7. 184	D. B. Close & R. Illingworth	Lord's	1959
8. 118	A. E. Knight & S. F. Barnes	Lord's	1903
9. 156	T. W. Hayward & J. T. Hearne	Lord's	1896
10. 140★	G. S. Boyes & A. E. Thomas	Folkestone	1930

4 BOWLING

BEST BOWLING FIGURES IN AN INNINGS

Gentlemen	9–46	J. W. A. Stephenson	Lord's	1936
	9–82	D. Buchanan	Oval	1868
	9–105	J. W. H. T. Douglas	Lord's	1914
	8–?	F. W. Lillywhite★	Lord's	1829
	8–?	A. Mynn	Lord's	1848
	8–25	W. G. Grace	Lord's	1867
	8–43	K. Farnes	Lord's	1938
	8–46	S. M. J. Woods	Hastings	1892
	8–49	J. W. H. T. Douglas	Lord's	1919
	8–94	F. G. Bull	Oval	1896

★Given man

Players	10–37	A. S. Kennedy	Oval	1927
	10–90	A. Fielder	Lord's	1906
	9–?	F. W. Lillywhite	Lord's	1837
	9–85	C. H. Parkin	Oval	1920
	8–29	James Lillywhite	Lord's	1862
	8–35	G. H. Hirst	Scarborough	1900
	8–41	A. P. Freeman	Lord's	1929
	8–72	W. H. Lockwood	Scarborough	1892
	8–94	E. F. Field	Scarborough	1911

BEST BOWLING FIGURES IN A MATCH

Gentlemen	14–?	F. W. Lillywhite★	Lord's	1829
	13–172	J. W. H. T. Douglas	Lord's	1914
	12–?	J. Cobbett★	Lord's	1838
	12–77	F. S. Jackson	Lord's	1894
	12–91	P. H. Morton	Oval	1880
	12–125	W. G. Grace	Lord's	1875

| | 12–165 | D. Buchanan | Lord's | 1872 |
| | 12–183 | N. A. Knox | Lord's | 1906 |

*Given men

Players	14–221	A. Fielder	Lord's	1906
	13–?	F. W. Lillywhite	Lord's	1835
	13–?	F. W. Lillywhite	Lord's	1837
	13–141	T. Richardson	Hastings	1897
	13–144	A. P. Freeman	Lord's	1929
	12–?	F. W. Lillywhite	Lord's	1840
	12–?	F. W. Lillywhite	Lord's	1841
	12–?	W. Clarke	Lord's	1850
	12–58	A. S. Kennedy	Oval	1927
	12–77	J. Southerton	Prince's	1875
	12–96	F. W. Lillywhite	Lord's	1845
	12–103	C. Blythe	Oval	1909
	12–159	W. Rhodes	Hastings	1901

N.B. All the above bowling figures include performances
in eleven-a-side matches only.

HAT-TRICKS

Gentlemen	E. R. Wilson	Scarborough	1919
	H. J. Enthoven	Lord's	1926
	H. G. Owen-Smith	Folkestone	1935
	C. J. Knott	Lord's	1950
Players	T. Hayward	Lord's	1870
	A. Hill	Lord's	1874
	R. G. Barlow	Oval	1884

BOWLERS UNCHANGED THROUGHOUT BOTH COMPLETED INNINGS

Gentlemen

F. W. Lillywhite* (14) & J. Broadbridge* (5)	Lord's	1829
P. H. H. Bathurst (11–50) & S. M. E. Kempson (9–54)	Lord's	1853
A. G. Steel (9–43) & A. H. Evans (10–74)	Oval	1879
S. M. J. Woods (6–124) & F. S. Jackson (12–77)	Lord's	1894

*Given men

Players

F. W. Lillywhite & J. Broadbridge	Lord's	1832
F. W. Lillywhite (13) & S. Redgate (5)	Lord's	1837
J. Wisden (8) & W. Clarke (12)	Lord's	1850
J. Jackson (11–99) & E. Willsher (6–70)	Lord's	1861
E. Willsher (9–55) & G. F. Tarrant (11–49)	Lord's	1864

5 ALL-ROUND CRICKET

100 RUNS AND 10 WICKETS IN A MATCH

Gentlemen

134*		6–50	&	4–31	W. G. Grace	Lord's	1868
23	110	3–61	&	7–58	W. G. Grace	Prince's	1874
7	152	7–64	&	5–61	W. G. Grace	Lord's	1875

6 FIELDING AND WICKET-KEEPING

MOST DISMISSALS IN AN INNINGS

Gentlemen	5 (3–2)	J. Round	Oval	1867
	(5–0)	A. Lyttelton	Oval	1877
Players	5 (3–2)	T. Box	Lord's	1837
	(2–3)	M. Sherwin	Lord's	1888
	(5–0)	J. H. Board	Oval	1896
	(3–2)	L. E. G. Ames	Lord's	1937
	(2–3)	G. O. Dawkes	Scarborough	1951

MOST DISMISSALS IN A MATCH

Gentlemen	8 (6–2)	A. Lyttelton	Oval	1877
	7 (5–2)	E. F. S. Tylecote	Oval	1876
	6 (0–6)	E. H. Budd	Lord's	1819
	(2–4)	T. Vigne	Lord's	1822
	(6–0)	A. C. Smith	Scarborough	1961
Players	8 (7–1)	A. F. A. Lilley	Lord's	1904
	(6–2)	L. E. G. Ames	Lord's	1937
	7 (6–1)	G. Duckworth	Lord's	1928
	(5–2)	T. G. Evans	Lord's	1949
	(3–4)	G. O. Dawkes	Scarborough	1951
	6 (3–3)	M. Sherwin	Lord's	1888

Note. The figures in brackets above represent catches and stumpings respectively.

MOST CATCHES IN AN INNINGS

Gentlemen	6	A. J. Webbe	Lord's	1877
	5	A. P. Upton	Lord's	1806
		F. Burbidge	Oval	1858
Players	5	L. Hutton	Lord's	1952

MOST CATCHES IN A MATCH

Gentlemen	6	A. P. Upton	Lord's	1806
		A. J. Webbe	Lord's	1877

Note. The names of the Gentlemen are ranged left; the names of the Players are indented.

FIELDERS	Schools		County	Career	Matches	Caught
W. G. Grace			Gloucs	1865–1906	85	97
F. E. Woolley	(King's, Canterbury)		Kent	1909–1938	31	46
G. Ulyett			Yorks	1875–1892	37	35
V. E. Walker	Harrow		Middx	1856–1869	26	27
W. R. Hammond			Gloucs	1923–1946	22	26
E. H. Hendren	(Harrow)		Middx	1919–1934	31	26
G. L. Jessop	Cheltenham GS	CU	Gloucs	1897–1914	26	25
A. E. Trott			Middx	1899–1908	13	25
T. W. Hayward			Surrey	1895–1911	33	24
G. H. Hirst	(Eton)		Yorks	1897–1921	26	24
P. G. H. Fender	St Paul's	Sussex	Surrey	1913–1934	27	23
W. Rhodes	(Harrow)		Yorks	1898–1927	39	23
R. Abel	(Dulwich)		Surrey	1886–1902	34	22
G. A. Lohmann			Surrey	1886–1896	20	22
A. Shaw	(Westminster)		Notts	1865–1881	28	22
J. W. Hearne			Middx	1912–1932	32	20
J. B. Hobbs			Surrey	1907–1934	49	20
A. N. Hornby	Harrow		Lancs	1869–1886	31	20
I. D. Walker	Harrow		Middx	1865–1877	22	20
E. M. Grace			Gloucs	1862–1886	13	19
G. F. Grace			Gloucs	1870–1878	24	19
A. O. Jones	Bedford Modern	CU	Notts	1896–1907	14	18 (+1 stumped)
R. G. Barlow			Lancs	1876–1886	19	17
W. Caffyn	(Eton)		Surrey	1850–1863	18	17
R. P. Carpenter			Cambs	1859–1873	18	17
A. G. Steel	Marlborough	CJ	Lancs	1878–1891	18	17
G. Strachan	Cheltenham Gloucs Middx		Surrey	1871–1880	11	16
W. Barnes			Notts	1879–1892	30	16
L. Hutton			Yorks	1937–1953	12	16
C. G. Lyttelton	Eton	CU	Worcs	1861–1866	12	16 (+3 stumped)
A. Shrewsbury			Notts	1876–1898	30	15
D. C. S. Compton			Middx	1937–1957	14	15
J. W. H. T. Douglas	Felsted		Essex	1906–1927	30	15
F. S. Jackson	Harrow	CU	Yorks	1891–1906	20	15
A. E. Stoddart	St John's Coll.		Middx	1887–1898	21	15

WICKET-KEEPERS			Career	Matches	Dismissals	Ct.	St
T. G. Evans		Kent	1946–1959	20	55	35	20
H. Strudwick		Surrey	1903–1926	23	52	41	11
M. Sherwin		Notts	1883–1893	18	51	41	10
E. F. S. Tylecote	Clifton OU	Kent	1871–1886	17	46	25	21
E. Pooley		Surrey	1866–1879	25	40	29	11
A. F. A. Lilley		Warks	1895–1909	14	38	28	10
G. MacGregor	Uppingham CU	Middx	1890–1907	14	38	31	7
T. Lockyer		Surrey	1854–1866	19	36	27	9
T. Box		Sussex	1834–1853	20	30	13	17
G. Duckworth		Lancs	1924–1935	10	25	17	8
A. Lyttelton	Eton CU	Middx	1876–1881	10	25	18	7
L. E. G. Ames		Kent	1928–1947	12	24	14	10
D. Hunter		Yorks	1891–1909	9	24	16	8
E. G. Wemnan		Kent	1829–1846	17	23	12	11
R. Pilling		Lancs	1879–1884	8	22	17	5
W. Nicholson	Harrow	Middx	1846–1858	14	18	7	11
W. Storer		Derby	1893–1901	13	18	15	3
W. S. Bird	Malvern OU	Middx	1905–1913	7	17	14	3
D. Brennan	Downside	Yorks	1950–1953	6	16	11	5
W. H. V. Levett	Brighton	Kent	1931–1936	8	16	9	7
J. H. Board		Gloucs	1896–1910	5	8	7	1
W. B. Franklin	Repton CU	Bucks	1926–1930	6	10	6	4
S. C. Griffith	Dulwich CU	Sussex	1938–1951	7	10	9	1
F. H. Huish		Kent	1902	1	2	1	1
J. Hunter		Yorks	1885	1	1	1	–
H. Martyn	Exeter GS OU	Somerset	1899–1906	5	6	6	–
J. T. Murray		Middx	1959–1961	3	8	8	–
J. M. Parks		Sussex	1954–1958	4	1	1	–
H. Philipson	Eton OU	Middx	1887–1892	6	6	4	2
J. Round	Eton	Essex	1864–1868	4	8	5	3
A. C. Smith	KES, B'ham OU	Warks	1960–1962	4	13	12	1
E. J. Smith		Warks	1911–1928	6	13	8	5

PART B: AVERAGES

7 BATTING AVERAGES (1806–1899)

Note. The names of the Gentlemen are ranged left; the names of the Players are indented.

			Career	M.	I.	N.O.	Runs	H.S.	100s	Avge
W. G. Grace		Gloucs	1865–1906	85	151	10	6008	217	15	42.61
T. Hayward		Cambs	1860–1871	12	19	3	614	132	2	38.38
A. Shrewsbury		Notts	1876–1898	30	53	7	1729	151*	4	37.59
W. Yardley	Rugby CU	Kent	1869–1874	9	15	3	435	83	–	36.25
T. Hearne		Middx	1863–1869	9	16	2	474	122*	1	33.86
W. Gunn		Notts	1881–1898	31	54	3	1666	169	3	32.67
G. F. Grace		Gloucs	1870–1878	24	40	8	1008	134	1	31.50
A. Lubbock	Eton	Kent	1866–1871	8	15	2	396	107*	1	30.46
W. W. Read		Surrey	1877–1896	24	41	2	1128	159	1	28.92
T. Beagley		Hants	1819–1836	16	27	7	569	113*	1	28.45
G. Ulyett		Yorks	1875–1892	37	65	0	1791	134	2	27.55
W. Barnes		Notts	1879–1892	30	51	5	1263	130*	1	27.46
W. Searle		Surrey	1822–1832	10	17	3	381	60	–	27.21
W. Bates		Yorks	1880–1887	16	29	3	698	87	–	26.85
R. P. Carpenter		Cambs	1859–1873	18	28	1	725	119	2	26.85
T. C. O'Brien	St Charles' Coll. OU	Middx	1884–1896	12	18	2	420	90	–	26.25
J. Saunders		Surrey	1822–1831	9	15	1	364	100	1	26.00
A. G. Steel	Marlborough CU	Lancs	1878–1891	18	29	5	610	76	1	25.42
R. Daft		Notts	1858–1879	24	43	4	985	102	1	25.26
W. Mortlock		Surrey	1854–1868	10	18	2	403	78	–	25.19
A. P. Lucas	Uppingham CU Surrey Middx	Essex	1876–1889	19	35	3	786	107	1	24.56
A. W. Ridley	Eton OU Hants	Middx	1873–1883	14	22	2	491	103	1	24.55
A. N. Hornby	Harrow	Lancs	1869–1886	31	51	1	1220	144	2	24.40
R. D. Walker	Harrow OU	Middx	1863–1868	10	18	1	412	92	1	24.24
John Lillywhite		Sussex	1851–1860	11	17	3	335	66	–	23.93

	School	County	Career	M.	I.	N.O.	Runs	H.S.	100s	Avge
J. Broadbridge		Sussex	1822–1835	12	20	3	391	49	—	23.00
J. Selby		Notts	1875–1882	11	22	0	502	88	—	22.82
J. M. Read		Surrey	1882–1895	18	26	2	546	71	—	22.75
G. Parr		Notts	1846–1865	22	32	2	676	77	—	22.53
E. Lockwood		Yorks	1869–1883	28	55	1	1179	97	—	21.83
E. Willsher		Kent	1856–1873	21	34	11	497	77	—	21.61
I. D. Walker	Harrow	Middx	1865–1877	22	38	6	680	165	1	21.25
A. E. Stoddart	St John's Coll.	Middx	1887–1898	21	37	0	785	85	—	21.22
H. Jupp		Surrey	1865–1880	33	64	0	1344	72	—	21.00
J. Walker	CU	Middx	1852–1863	9	18	4	290	98	—	20.71
J. Wisden		Sussex	1848–1859	15	24	3	423	58	—	20.14
R. Peel		Yorks	1887–1897	20	28	4	476	71*	—	19.83
J. Guy		Notts	1838–1852	17	29	3	515	65	—	19.81
H. H. Stephenson	(Uppingham)	Surrey	1857–1869	14	24	3	424	117	1	19.27
W. Ward	Winchester	Hants	1819–1838	18	33	3	570	102*	1	19.00
C. G. Lyttelton	Eton CU	Worcs	1861–1866	12	23	0	428	81	—	18.61
J. Briggs		Lancs	1884–1896	17	25	2	420	85	—	18.26
J. A. Dixon		Notts	1888–1898	11	20	1	347	53	—	18.26
T. Humphrey		Surrey	1865–1870	10	19	0	346	64	—	18.21
T. Lockyer		Surrey	1854–1866	19	27	3	422	76*	—	17.58
G. A. Lohmann		Surrey	1886–1896	20	28	2	457	58	—	17.58
E. F. S. Tylecote	Clifton OU	Kent	1871–1886	17	29	4	438	107	1	17.52
F. P. Miller		Surrey	1855–1863	12	24	2	385	55	—	17.50
R. G. Barlow		Lancs	1876–1886	19	37	2	611	65	—	17.46
E. G. Wenman		Kent	1829–1846	17	25	2	401	73*	—	17.43
E. M. Grace		Gloucs	1862–1886	13	25	1	417	71	—	17.38
J. Grundy		Notts	1851–1868	19	30	2	467	69*	—	16.68
G. R. C. Harris	Eton OU	Kent	1875–1884	13	22	1	347	85	—	16.52
A. Mynn		Kent	1832–1852	21	38	0	605	66	—	15.92
E. Pooley		Surrey	1866–1879	25	48	3	708	85	—	15.73
T. Emmett	(Rugby)	Yorks	1869–1885	25	50	7	675	57	—	15.70
W. Oscroft		Notts	1871–1880	15	29	0	451	73	—	15.55
C. G. Taylor	Eton CU	Sussex	1836–1846	12	21	2	290	89	—	15.26
V. E. Walker	Harrow	Middx	1856–1869	26	46	14	482	51	—	15.06
H. R. J. Charlwood		Sussex	1868–1881	10	20	1	285	85	—	15.00
F. Pilch		Kent	1827–1849	24	36	3	492	60	—	14.91
J. Jackson		Notts	1857–1864	13	19	4	219	41	—	14.60

Name	School(s)	County	Years	M	I	NO	Runs	HS	100	Avge
M. McIntyre		Notts	1871–1875	9	17	1	232	56	—	14.50
G. Griffith		Surrey	1860–1870	11	18	2	230	35	—	14.38
A. W. T. Daniel	Harrow CU	Middx	1862–1876	8	16	1	214	51	—	14.27
A. Greenwood		Yorks	1873–1876	8	16	0	228	51	—	14.25
W. Flowers		Notts	1882–1894	18	30	2	397	50	—	14.18
James Lillywhite, Jnr		Sussex	1862–1877	15	29	5	329	39	—	13.71
A. Shaw		Notts	1865–1881	28	53	7	602	70	—	13.09
E. T. Drake	Westminster CU	Bucks	1854–1864	14	16	2	183	58	—	13.07
W. Nicholson	Harrow	Middx	1846–1858	14	27	2	322	31	—	12.88
N. Felix	Kent	Surrey	1831–1852	20	35	2	402	88	—	12.18
J. Shuter	Winchester	Surrey	1879–1890	9	15	0	182	41	—	12.13
T. Box		Sussex	1834–1853	20	31	3	331	39	—	11.82
G. Wootton		Notts	1862–1870	12	21	7	164	27	—	11.71
W. Attewell		Notts	1885–1898	18	28	5	267	51*	—	11.61
C. G. Lane	Westminster OU	Surrey	1857–1861	9	18	0	207	47	—	11.50
H. R. Kingscote	Harrow		1825–1834	8	15	0	172	38	—	11.47
G. Strachan	Cheltenham Gloucs Middx	Surrey	1871–1880	11	17	3	160	34	—	11.43
W. Caffyn	(Eton)	Surrey	1850–1863	18	27	1	288	48	—	11.08
C. F. Buller	Harrow	Middx	1865–1874	10	18	1	181	41	—	10.65
A. Haygarth	Harrow Sussex	Sussex	1846–1859	16	30	1	299	53*	—	10.31
J. Southerton	Surrey Sussex	Hants	1870–1877	9	15	6	91	39*	—	10.11
F. Beauclerk	Hants	Kent	1806–1824	7	12	1	207	58	—	18.82
W. Beldham	Hambledon	Surrey	1806–1821	5	7	1	73	23*	—	12.17
I. F. W. Bligh	Eton CU	Hants	1879–1880	3	5	2	55	14	—	18.33
E. H. Budd		Hants	1806–1830	9	13	1	315	69	—	26.25
J. Caesar		Surrey	1856–1863	10	14	1	235	51	—	18.08
J. H. Dark			1835	1	1	0	0	0	—	0.00
W. G. Grace, Jnr	Clifton CU	Gloucs	1894–1897	2	4	0	35	16	—	8.75
L. H. Gwynn	Dublin U	Ireland	1895–1896	2	4	0	105	80	—	26.25
H. Jenner(-Fust)	Eton CU	Kent	1827–1836	9	16	0	132	32	—	8.25
F. E. Lacey	Sherborne CU	Hants	1892	1	1	0	22	22	—	22.00
W. Lambert		Surrey	1806	2	3	0	102	57	—	34.00
A. Lyttelton	Eton CU	Middx	1876–1881	10	14	0	269	66	—	19.21
W. E. Midwinter		Gloucs	1878–1882	6	12	1	181	35	—	16.45
R. A. H. Mitchell	Eton OU	Warks	1862–1871	8	13	1	322	76	—	26.83
J. Nyren	Hambledon	Hants	1806	2	3	1	6	4	—	3.00
L. C. H. Palairet	Repton OU	Somerset	1892–1898	6	12	0	235	54	—	19.58
R. M. Poore		Hants	1899	2	3	0	52	27	—	17.33
C. T. Studd	Eton CU	Middx	1881–1883	6	12	3	313	100	1	34.78

		Career	M.	I.	N.O.	Runs	H.S.	100s	Avge
C. I. Thornton	Eton CU Kent Middx	1869–1875	3	6	0	59	34	–	9.83
A. J. Webbe	Harrow OU Middx	1875–1877	7	11	1	116	65	–	11.60

8 BOWLING AVERAGES (1806–1899)

		Career	M.	Runs	Wkts	Avge	TW	5I	10M	BB
W. Ashby	Kent	1821–1830	9	–	–	–	53	4	1	4-?
S. Redgate	Notts	1835–1843	10	–	–	–	47	3	1	5-?
J. Cobbett	Surrey	1832–1841	11	–	–	–	41	5	1	6-?
T. C. Howard	Hants	1806–1829	7	–	–	–	33	–	–	4-?
J. Broadbridge	Sussex	1822–1835	12	–	–	–	23	2	–	3-?
W. Mathews	Surrey	1824–1830	5	–	–	–	19	2	–	7-?
F. Beauclerk	Kent	1806–1824	7	–	–	–	14	1	–	3-?
A. J. Lowth	Winchester OU Hants	1836–1841	2	–	–	–	14	1	–	5-?
G. Brown	Hants	1820–1830	6	–	–	–	13	–	–	4-?
F. W. Lillywhite	Sussex	1829–1849	21	330	41	8.05	175	22	8	9-?
F. H. Farrands	Notts	1870	1	88	10	8.80	–	1	1	6-23
W. Martingell	Surrey Kent	1844–1858	13	236	26	9.08	–	1	–	7-19
A. H. Evans	Hants	1878–1885	7	366	39	9.38	–	4	1	7-31
G. F. Tarrant	Cambs	1862–1864	4	290	30	9.67	–	4	–	7-17
G. Parr	Notts	1846–1865	22	159	16	9.94	71	1	–	6-42
W. R. Hillyer	Kent	1838–1851	15	282	27	10.44	–	7	3	6-40
P. H. Morton	Rossall CU Surrey	1880–1882	2	185	17	10.88	18	2	–	6-41
G. E. Yonge	Eton OU	1847–1852	5	124	11	11.27	50	1	1	5-32
W. Clarke	Notts	1846–1853	10	272	24	11.33	73	5	1	7-?
F. H. H. Bathurst	Winchester Hants	1831–1854	21	403	35	11.51	–	7	1	7-?
Alfred Payne	OU	1854–1864	6	219	19	11.53	–	2	1	6-26
J. Jackson	Notts	1857–1864	13	825	69	11.96	45	6	1	6-31
A. P. Lucas	Uppingham CU Surrey Middx	1876–1889	19	256	21	12.19	–	–	–	4-12
J. Wisden	Sussex	1848–1859	15	394	32	12.31	21	3	–	6-23
H. Arkwright	Harrow CU	1862–1864	2	142	11	12.91	–	–	1	7-83
H. W. Fellows	Eton	1847–1851	6	40	3	13.33	–	2	–	7-?
W. Barnes	Notts	1879–1892	30	961	72	13.35	–	5	2	7-58
H. Pigg	Abingdon House CU N'hants	1889–1891	2	164	12	13.67	–	1	1	7-55
J. Grundy	Notts	1851–1868	19	368	26	14.15	36	–	–	5-42

Name		County	Years		Runs	Wkts	Avge				Best
A. Mynn		Kent	1832–1852	21	443	31	14.29	107	9	3	8-?
J. Dean	(Winchester)	Sussex	1843–1857	18	218	15	14.53	19	–	–	4-30
D. Buchanan	Rugby CU	Warks	1868–1874	10	1295	87	14.89	–	9	5	9-82
A. G. Steel	Marlborough CU	Lancs	1878–1891	18	1520	99	15.35	–	6	–	7-27
E. Willsher		Kent	1856–1873	21	1151	75	15.35	–	5	2	6-29
A. Shaw		Notts	1865–1881	28	2101	134	15.68	–	10	1	7-17
E. M. Grace		Gloucs	1862–1886	13	675	43	15.70	–	5	–	6-25
W. S. Patterson	Uppingham CU	Lancs	1876–1877	3	350	22	15.91	–	1	–	7-58
F. W. Milligan	Eton	Yorks	1897–1898	4	257	16	16.06	–	2	–	7-61
R. Peel		Yorks	1887–1897	20	771	48	16.06	–	2	–	6-34
G. F. Grace		Gloucs	1870–1878	24	945	58	16.29	–	3	–	6-56
C. K. Francis	Rugby OU	Middx	1870–1875	6	361	22	16.41	–	–	–	4-45
G. Griffith		Surrey	1860–1870	11	417	25	16.68	–	2	–	6-51
C. A. Smith	Charterhouse CU	Sussex	1888–1891	3	185	11	16.82	–	–	–	3-23
W. Attewell		Notts	1885–1898	18	964	57	16.91	–	4	1	6-24
V. E. Walker	Harrow	Middx	1856–1869	26	1075	62	17.34	–	4	–	6-57
A. Appleby		Lancs	1867–1887	12	1025	59	17.37	–	4	–	6-33
W. Flowers		Notts	1882–1894	18	756	43	17.58	–	2	–	6-40
J. Briggs		Lancs	1884–1896	17	986	56	17.61	–	5	–	6-104
S. Christopherson	Uppingham	Kent	1884–1885	4	427	24	17.79	–	2	–	7-24
C. G. Taylor	Eton CU	Sussex	1836–1846	12	232	13	17.85	29	1	2	5-46
C. D. B. Marsham	OU		1854–1862	10	862	48	17.96	–	3	–	6-40
H. H. Stephenson	(Uppingham)	Surrey	1857–1869	14	306	17	18.00	–	–	–	4-11
R. G. Barlow		Lancs	1876–1886	19	762	42	18.14	–	–	–	4-23
E. Wainwright	(Winchester S'bury)	Yorks	1892–1897	7	327	18	18.17	–	2	–	5-37
J. J. Ferris		Gloucs	1891–1894	8	600	33	18.18	–	4	–	7-28
G. A. Lohmann		Surrey	1886–1896	20	1619	89	18.19	–	2	–	6-57
W. Caffyn	(Eton)	Surrey	1850–1863	18	462	25	18.48	–	1	–	7-52
W. G. Grace		Gloucs	1865–1906	85	5073	271	18.72	10	21	6	8-25
T. Nixon		Notts	1851–1853	4	38	2	19.00	–	1	–	5-?
F. Silcock		Essex	1866–1874	7	475	25	19.00	–	2	–	7-132
C. A. Absolom	KCS, London CU	Kent	1868–1874	7	429	22	19.50	–	1	–	5-56
G. Strachan	Cheltenham Gloucs Middx	Surrey	1871–1880	11	279	14	19.93	–	1	–	6-31
James Lillywhite, Jnr		Sussex	1862–1877	15	706	35	20.17	–	1	–	8-29
F. Morley		Notts	1874–1881	15	1155	57	20.26	–	5	1	6-36
G. Wootton		Notts	1862–1870	12	801	39	20.54	–	2	–	6-24
H. Rotherham	Uppingham	Warks	1880–1884	5	458	22	20.82	–	2	–	6-41
T. Hayward		Cambs	1860–1871	12	459	22	20.86	–	1	–	5-86
W. R. Gilbert	Middx	Gloucs	1874–1877	4	316	15	21.07	–	1	–	5-93

		Career	M.	I.	N.O.	Runs	H.S.	100s	Avge
W. Bates	Yorks	1880–1887	16	718	34	21.12	–	2	–	6-50
A. Hill	Yorks	1874–1882	11	852	40	21.30	–	3	–	6-77
C. T. Studd	Eton CU — Middx	1881–1883	6	540	25	21.60	–	2	–	5-45
G. Bennett	Kent	1865–1866	4	390	18	21.67	–	1	–	5-73
C. G. Lyttelton	(Brighton) — Worcs	1861–1866	12	286	13	22.00	–	–	–	4-67
A. W. Mold	Eton CU — Lancs	1893–1895	4	446	20	22.30	–	2	–	7-85
F. Martin	Kent	1891–1897	5	287	12	23.92	–	1	–	6-83
J. C. Shaw	Notts	1871–1874	10	1157	46	25.15	–	3	–	7-72
E. Peate	Yorks	1881–1886	11	996	39	25.54	–	3	–	5-51
J. Southerton	Hants	1870–1877	9	810	31	26.13	–	2	1	6-38
H. V. Page	Surrey Sussex Cheltenham OU — Gloucs	1884–1894	8	263	10	26.30	–	–	–	3-41
F. G. Bull	Essex	1896–1897	3	565	21	26.90	–	1	1	8-94
A. W. Ridley	Audley House Eton OU Hants — Middx	1873–1883	14	525	19	27.63	–	–	–	4-41
W. F. Maitland	Harrow OU — Essex	1864–1869	9	362	13	27.85	–	1	–	5-104
R. D. Walker	Harrow OU — Middx	1863–1868	10	428	15	28.53	–	–	–	4-55
A. E. Stoddart	St John's Coll. — Middx	1887–1898	21	557	19	29.32	–	1	–	5-34
T. Emmett	(Rugby) — Yorks	1869–1885	25	1130	38	29.74	–	–	–	4-76
G. Ulyett	Yorks	1875–1892	37	927	30	30.90	–	–	–	4-39
F. P. Miller	Surrey	1855–1863	12	608	20	30.40	–	–	–	4-101
E. A. Nepean	Sherborne OU — Middx	1887–1892	6	440	11	40.00	–	1	–	4-125
M. McIntyre	Notts	1871–1875	9	702	17	41.29	–	–	–	5-47
H. Jenner(-Fust)	Eton CU — Kent	1827–1836	9	–	–	–	8	–	3-?
W. Lambert	Surrey	1806	2	–	–	–	4	–	4-?
F. R. Spofforth	Derby	1890–1897	3	311	9	34.56	–	–	–	4-71
J. Willes	Kent	1806	2	–	–	–	3	–	1-?

9 BATTING AVERAGES (1900–1962)

Name	School	County	Career	M.	I.	N.O.	Runs	H.S.	100s	Avge
J. H. King		Leics	1904–1909	5	9	3	468	109*	2	78.00
D. R. Jardine	Winchester OU	Surrey	1924–1933	12	18	2	1029	193	3	64.31
A. Sandham		Surrey	1921–1934	16	19	2	962	125	3	56.59
L. Hutton		Yorks	1937–1953	12	22	3	1070	241	2	56.32
J. W. Hearne	(Westminster)	Middx	1912–1932	32	47	12	1923	146	4	54.94
J. B. Hobbs		Surrey	1907–1934	49	79	5	4052	266*	16	54.76
W. Watson	Yorks	Leics	1951–1961	10	19	5	748	143*	1	53.43
G. E. Tyldesley		Lancs	1922–1928	8	12	2	516	131	2	51.60
M. Tompkin		Leics	1951–1955	4	8	0	409	115	1	51.13
K. S. Duleepsinhji	Cheltenham CJ	Sussex	1925–1932	7	12	1	547	132	3	49.73
P. Holmes		Yorks	1919–1931	13	20	3	833	127	1	49.00
D. B. Close		Yorks	1949–1962	6	10	1	440	112	1	48.89
J. V. Wilson		Yorks	1951–1958	5	10	2	391	122	1	48.88
H. Sutcliffe		Yorks	1923–1938	18	29	5	1113	120	2	46.38
T. W. Hayward		Surrey	1895–1911	33	61	6	2535	203	7	46.09
E. H. Hendren	(Harrow)	Middx	1919–1934	31	39	6	1516	194*	5	45.94
A. C. MacLaren	Harrow	Lancs	1893–1909	12	18	2	728	168*	1	45.50
E. G. Wynyard	Charterhouse	Hants	1897–1906	5	10	2	357	137	1	44.63
C. B. Fry	Repton OU Sussex	Hants	1893–1914	20	39	1	1681	232*	4	44.24
K. F. Barrington		Surrey	1955–1962	7	11	0	484	111	2	44.00
W. J. Edrich	(Westminster)	Middx	1938–1957	15	30	0	1318	133	3	43.93
C. A. G. Russell		Essex	1920–1922	6	9	0	383	162	1	42.56
C. J. Burnup	Malvern CU	Kent	1900–1903	6	11	0	465	123	2	42.27
W. W. Whysall		Notts	1923–1929	5	8	1	294	88	–	42.00
J. H. Edrich		Surrey	1959–1962	6	12	1	415	77*	1	41.50
G. H. Hirst	(Eton)	Yorks	1897–1921	26	41	10	1280	124*	1	41.29
R. Abel	(Dulwich)	Surrey	1886–1902	34	55	5	2055	247	5	41.10
G. W. Beldam		Middx	1902–1907	7	11	1	410	80	–	41.00
R. E. Marshall	(King's, Taunton)	Hants	1958–1960	4	8	2	243	76	1	40.50
D. C. S. Compton		Middx	1937–1957	14	25	3	889	150	1	40.41
C. P. Mead		Hants	1911–1928	16	23	2	844	223	2	40.19
M. J. K. Smith	Stamford OU Leics	Warks	1955–1962	13	25	2	921	166	1	40.04
C. Washbrook		Lancs	1946–1956	7	11	1	398	105	2	39.80
L. E. G. Ames		Kent	1928–1947	12	16	0	629	201	2	39.31
P. B. H. May	Charterhouse CU	Surrey	1951–1961	13	26	2	943	157	3	39.29

Player	School / University & clubs	County	Career	M.	I.	N.O.	Runs	H.S.	100s	Avge
Nawab of Pataudi, Snr	OU	Worcs	1931–1933	5	8	1	274	165	1	39.14
W. R. Hammond	Malvern OU	Gloucs	1923–1946	22	32	2	1173	138	3	39.10
D. J. Knight		Surrey	1919–1921	4	8	0	306	124	1	38.25
J. T. Brown		Yorks	1896–1921	10	18	1	645	163	1	37.94
R. M. Prideaux	Tonbridge CU Kent	N'hants	1960–1962	5	10	0	378	109	1	37.80
A. P. F. Chapman	Uppingham CU	Kent	1920–1936	21	33	2	1162	160	3	37.48
J. T. Tyldesley		Lancs	1898–1919	22	36	2	1265	140	2	37.21
M. S. Nichols		Essex	1930–1936	7	9	3	222	47	—	37.00
R. Kilner		Yorks	1919–1926	7	8	0	295	113	1	36.88
H. T. W. Hardinge		Kent	1911–1924	6	10	0	257	127	1	36.71
A. W. Carr	Sherborne	Notts	1919–1929	11	19	0	692	101	1	36.42
J. W. Hitch		Surrey	1912–1923	10	13	3	363	68*	—	36.30
J. Hardstaff, Jnr		Notts	1935–1947	9	14	2	434	100	1	36.17
C. H. Palmer	Halesowen GS Worcs	Leics	1948–1956	6	11	0	395	154	2	35.91
G. O. B. Allen	Eton CU	Middx	1923–1938	11	16	2	497	130	1	35.50
J. H. Parsons		Warks	1914–1931	7	12	2	355	72	—	35.50
D. Denton		Yorks	1901–1919	18	28	3	879	157*	1	35.16
E. G. Hayes	(Winchester)	Surrey	1903–1914	12	22	1	708	122*	1	33.71
F. E. Woolley	(King's, Canterbury)	Kent	1909–1938	31	47	2	1510	141*	1	33.56
G. Brown		Hants	1919–1930	9	10	1	301	80*	—	33.44
M. P. Donnelly	OU Middx	Warks	1946–1948	4	8	1	231	162*	1	33.00
W. L. Murdoch		Sussex	1891–1904	8	13	2	362	140	1	32.91
B. J. T. Bosanquet	Eton OU	Middx	1899–1911	10	18	0	592	145	2	32.89
M. W. Tate	(Tonbridge)	Sussex	1923–1934	16	22	8	455	64	—	32.50
H. M. Garland-Wells	St Paul's OU	Surrey	1928–1938	5	10	2	258	93	—	32.25
R. E. S. Wyatt	Warks	Worcs	1926–1947	23	42	2	1290	115	2	32.25
R. H. Spooner	Marlborough	Lancs	1903–1919	17	33	0	1055	190	2	31.97
	Harrow CU	Yorks	1891–1906	20	36	3	1052	134	1	31.88
P. E. Richardson	Worcs	Kent	1955–1959	13	13	1	374	84	—	31.17
G. T. S. Stevens	U.C.S. OU	Middx	1919–1931	17	28	3	772	129	2	30.88
G. J. Thompson	(Rugby Clifton Stowe)	N'hants	1900–1911	9	13	2	337	125	1	30.64
T. W. Graveney	Gloucs	Worcs	1949–1962	17	31	1	877	124	1	29.23
C. L. Townsend	Clifton	Gloucs	1896–1900	17	17	1	465	112*	1	29.06
K. S. Ranjitsinhji	CU	Sussex	1893–1912	14	25	2	668	121	—	29.04
L. C. Braund	(Repton)	Somerset	1901–1907	7	12	1	316	141	1	28.73
A. O. Jones	Bedford Modern CU	Notts	1896–1907	14	26	4	628	105	1	28.55
F. T. Mann	Malvern CU	Middx	1914–1930	14	22	1	598	100	1	28.48

Player	School (Univ)	County	Years	M	I	NO	Runs	HS	100	Avge
F. H. Gillingham	Dulwich, OU	Essex	1908–1925	4	8	1	198	75	—	28.29
F. L. Fane	Charterhouse, OU	Essex	1906–1913	6	11	1	282	61	—	28.20
D. L. A. Jephson	Clapham, CU	Surrey	1894–1902	11	20	8	336	59	1	28.00
A. E. R. Gilligan	Dulwich, CU	Sussex	1922–1927	9	13	1	335	112	1	27.92
P. F. Warner	Rugby, OU	Middx	1897–1919	24	46	1	1248	97	1	27.73
W. Storer		Derby	1893–1901	13	24	2	608	93	1	27.64
L. H. Tennyson	Eton	Hants	1920–1935	21	36	3	910	112	1	27.58
D. S. Sheppard	Sherborne, CU	Sussex	1951–1962	6	12	0	329	112	—	27.42
C. J. B. Wood	Wellingborough	Leics	1900–1906	4	8	0	219	68	—	27.38
J. R. Gunn	(Harrow)	Notts	1900–1913	15	24	3	571	75	1	27.19
W. Rhodes	(Harrow)	Yorks	1898–1927	39	60	12	1296	82	1	27.00
W. H. H. Sutcliffe	Rydal	Yorks	1951–1957	6	12	2	269	82	—	26.90
M. Leyland		Yorks	1928–1938	11	17	2	402	80	1	26.80
T. L. Taylor	Uppingham, CU	Yorks	1900–1902	4	8	0	213	102	—	26.63
G. Gunn	(Harrow)	Notts	1908–1928	7	14	0	372	83	1	26.57
M. C. Bird	Harrow	Surrey	1909–1913	5	9	1	211	56	—	26.38
A. P. Day	Malvern	Kent	1911–1914	6	12	1	288	73	1	26.18
C. N. Bruce	Winchester, OU	Middx	1919–1928	8	12	0	313	127	1	26.08
K. L. Hutchings	Tonbridge	Kent	1906–1911	7	13	0	339	120	—	26.08
H. J. Enthoven	Harrow, CU	Middx	1925–1934	6	8	0	207	40	—	25.88
A. W. Wellard		Somerset	1931–1938	5	10	1	231	91	1	25.67
J. D. B. Robertson		Middx	1947–1952	5	10	1	229	80	—	25.44
E. W. Dawson	Eton, CU	Leics	1925–1931	10	8	0	203	95	—	25.38
J. Tunnicliffe	(Clifton)	Yorks	1897–1906	18	17	0	431	55	—	25.35
D. J. Insole	Monoux, CU	Essex	1951–1960		33	3	758	79*	—	25.27
William Quaife		Warks	1897–1913	12	20	0	501	79	2	25.05
M. C. Cowdrey	Tonbridge, OU	Kent	1951–1960	9	17	2	374	106	—	24.93
S. G. Smith		N'hants	1909–1914	5	10	0	249	65	—	24.90
M. W. Payne	Wellington, CU	Middx	1904–1907	5	9	1	198	69	—	24.75
S. F. Barnes	Lancs	Staffs	1902–1914	8	11	3	197	56	—	24.63
E. Paynter		Lancs	1931–1939	5	10	2	196	45	—	24.50
A. F. A. Lilley		Warks	1895–1909	14	23	3	484	74	—	24.20
W. Brockwell		Surrey	1894–1902	10	15	0	361	81	—	24.07
C. P. McGahey		Essex	1897–1905	8	16	1	360	68	—	24.00
H. K. Foster	Malvern, OU	Worcs	1896–1910	8	16	0	383	72	—	23.94
T. G. Evans		Kent	1946–1959	20	30	5	598	65	—	23.92
N. W. D. Yardley	St Peter's, York, CU	Yorks	1937–1955	16	31	2	693	88	—	23.90
V. W. C. Jupp	Burgess Hill, Sussex	N'hants	1920–1931	10	17	1	382	101*	1	23.88
R. T. Simpson	Nottingham HS	Notts	1947–1956	13	25	0	593	117	1	23.72

	School/Univ	Team	Career	M.	I.	N.O.	Runs	H.S.	100s	Avge
G. Geary	(Charterhouse)	Leics	1925–1934	9	11	1	237	109	1	23.70
F. A. Tarrant		Middx	1903–1914	17	31	2	684	79	–	23.59
H. G. Owen-Smith	OU	Middx	1931–1937	5	9	0	212	67	–	23.56
G. L. Jessop	Cheltenham GS CU	Gloucs	1897–1914	26	49	2	1107	119	2	23.55
M. D. Lyon	Rugby CU	Somerset	1923–1930	6	10	0	235	120	1	23.50
F. R. Brown	Leys CU Surrey	N'hants	1931–1953	16	29	5	562	122	1	23.42
J. R. Mason	Winchester	Kent	1894–1913	11	20	1	441	72	–	23.21
F. S. Trueman		Yorks	1955–1962	4	13	6	161	63	–	23.00
D. B. Carr	Repton OU	Derby	1950–1961	17	8	3	115	56	–	23.00
W. H. Lockwood		Surrey	1892–1902	13	27	3	547	100	1	22.79
A. Ward		Lancs	1889–1900	21	24	7	540	108	1	22.50
T. E. Bailey	Dulwich CU	Essex	1947–1962	16	37	7	665	54	–	22.17
A. S. Kennedy	(Cheltenham)	Hants	1914–1934	4	16	4	266	59*	–	22.17
C. F. Walters	Neath GS	Worcs	1932–1934	27	8	0	176	79	–	22.00
P. G. H. Fender	St Paul's Sussex	Surrey	1913–1934	6	46	1	988	101	1	21.96
A. Jeacocke		Surrey	1921–1933	9	9	1	175	44	–	21.88
C. J. Barnett		Gloucs	1933–1947	24	16	1	328	52	–	21.87
N. E. Haig	Eton	Middx	1919–1932	15	39	4	764	98	–	21.83
E. Smith	Clifton OU	Yorks	1891–1906	9	26	4	480	76	–	21.82
J. H. Wardle		Yorks	1948–1958	12	10	5	195	42	–	21.67
A. V. Bedser		Surrey	1947–1955	5	16	5	237	59	–	21.55
G. A. R. Lock		Surrey	1954–1962	4	8	3	107	34	–	21.40
L. G. Wright		Derby	1893–1905	7	8	0	168	51	–	21.00
A. E. Moss		Middx	1953–1961	8	8	4	83	29*	–	20.75
R. W. V. Robins	Highgate CU	Middx	1928–1952	10	13	2	227	48	–	20.64
E. R. Dexter	Radley CU	Sussex	1957–1962	8	19	0	392	88	–	20.63
F. R. Foster	Solihull	Warks	1910–1914	9	15	1	288	69	–	20.57
E. R. T. Holmes	Malvern OU	Surrey	1927–1936	9	15	0	304	84	–	20.27
J. N. Crawford	Repton	Surrey	1906–1921	5	17	2	303	71*	–	20.20
H. Ashton	Winchester CU	Essex	1920–1927	6	9	1	179	31	–	19.89
P. R. Le Couteur	OU		1910–1911	10	9	2	138	70	–	19.71
S. Haigh	(Winchester)	Yorks	1898–1910	4	13	3	195	51	–	19.50
N. S. Mitchell-Innes	Sedbergh OU	Somerset	1934–1937	11	12	2	156	50	–	19.50
C. H. Parkin		Lancs	1919–1923	8	13	2	194	45	–	19.40
J. Iremonger	(Dulwich Harrow)	Notts	1902–1911	8	13	0	248	43	–	19.08
G. E. C. Wood	Cheltenham CU	Kent	1920–1932	8	12	3	171	43*	–	19.00
G. Goonesena	CU	Notts	1954–1958	8	12	2	187	26	–	18.70

Name	School	Univ.	County	Years	M	I	NO	Runs	HS	100	Avge
M. Falcon	Harrow	CU	Norfolk	1911–1927	14	26	11	277	75	–	18.47
E. G. Arnold			Worcs	1899–1908	7	11	0	203	89*	–	18.45
S. C. Griffith	Dulwich	CU	Sussex	1938–1951	7	13	4	166	39*	–	18.44
F. L. Bowley	(Repton Haileybury)	CU	Worcs	1904–1914	4	8	1	128	47	–	18.29
J. L. Bryan	Rugby	CU	Kent	1923–1928	5	8	0	142	35	–	17.75
H. A. Carpenter			Essex	1896–1902	10	17	1	282	58	–	17.63
G. R. Jackson	Harrow		Derby	1924–1927	4	8	0	135	42	–	16.88
F. S. G. Calthorpe	Repton	CU	Warks	1920–1933	12	22	0	371	101	1	16.86
J. T. Hearne			Middx	1893–1904	14	26	7	319	71	–	16.79
R. H. B. Bettington	(Harrow)	OU	Middx	1920–1928	5	9	2	116	39	–	16.57
M. J. C. Allom	Wellington	CU	Surrey	1930–1934	8	9	4	81	22	–	16.20
J. H. Board			Gloucs	1896–1910	5	8	1	113	50	–	16.14
N. A. Knox	Dulwich		Surrey	1906–1910	5	8	3	80	35	–	16.00
J. J. Warr	Ealing CGS	CU	Middx	1950–1960	14	21	6	240	31*	–	16.00
J. C. White	Taunton		Somerset	1914–1930	12	18	10	127	23	–	15.88
M. B. Hawke	Eton	CU	Yorks	1887–1908	10	15	0	236	38	–	15.73
A. E. Trott			Middx	1899–1908	13	21	3	281	49*	–	15.61
J. W. H. T. Douglas	Felsted		Essex	1906–1927	30	56	7	757	72	–	15.45
D. C. Robinson	Marlborough		Gloucs	1912–1919	6	12	0	183	58	–	15.25
W. H. B. Evans	Malvern	OU	Hants	1903–1909	5	9	0	137	39	–	15.22
K. Farnes	Romford	CU	Essex	1933–1939	7	11	5	90	22*	–	15.00
H. L. Simms	Malvern		Sussex	1912–1913	5	8	0	117	41	–	14.63
B. H. Valentine	Repton	CU	Kent	1932–1946	7	14	1	190	47	–	14.62
J. Sharp			Lancs	1907–1911	6	11	1	146	48	–	14.60
T. Richardson			Surrey	1895–1903	8	14	2	174	43	–	14.50
A. E. Relf			Sussex	1903–1913	9	12	0	173	65	–	14.42
R. H. Moore	(Wellington)		Hants	1934–1938	4	8	0	114	45	–	14.25
A. Melville		OU	Sussex	1934–1936	4	8	0	109	40	–	13.63
W. B. Franklin			Bucks	1926–1930	6	9	2	93	30	–	13.29
G. W. Richardson	Repton	CU	Derby	1959–1962	4	8	0	106	68	–	13.25
H. D. G. Leveson-Gower	Winchester	OU	Surrey	1895–1920	11	17	6	140	35	–	12.73
G. Duckworth			Lancs	1924–1935	10	9	2	88	32	–	12.57
I. A. R. Peebles	Glasgow A.	OU	Middx	1927–1935	9	12	3	110	27	–	12.22
A. P. Freeman			Kent	1921–1936	13	12	2	119	32*	–	11.90
H. Strudwick			Surrey	1903–1926	23	28	12	187	48*	–	11.69
G. M. Louden			Essex	1919–1925	8	9	5	46	13	–	11.50
S. M. J. Woods	Brighton	CU	Somerset	1888–1902	16	25	3	250	52	–	11.36
H. Verity			Yorks	1931–1936	7	8	3	56	13*	–	11.20
W. H. V. Levett	Brighton		Kent	1931–1936	8	12	4	86	15*	–	10.75

			Career	M.	I.	N.O.	Runs	H.S.	100s	Avge
H. Martyn	Exeter GS OU	Somerset	1899–1906	5	9	1	85	26	—	10.63
O. S. Wheatley	KES, B'ham CU Warks	Glam	1958–1962	6	8	3	53	34*	—	10.60
C. P. Buckenham	(Repton)	Essex	1907–1913	6	10	1	92	40	—	10.22
W. E. Astill	(Tonbridge)	Leics	1923–1928	5	4	0	60	37	—	15.00
R. W. Barber	Ruthin CU	Lancs	1959–1962	4	7	1	75	45	—	12.50
J. M. Brearley	City of London CU	Middx	1961	2	4	0	22	10	—	5.50
R. E. Foster	Malvern OU	Worcs	1900–1907	4	7	1	352	136	2	58.67
R. Illingworth		Yorks	1955–1959	3	4	0	130	100	1	32.50
James Langridge		Sussex	1930–1937	5	6	2	204	87	—	51.00
John G. Langridge		Sussex	1933–1949	2	3	0	49	31	—	16.33
A. R. Lewis	Neath GS CU	Glam	1962	2	4	0	47	35	—	11.75
P. A. Perrin	Margate	Essex	1896–1906	2	4	0	59	32	—	14.75
R. Subba Row	Whitgift CU	N'hants	1958–1960	3	6	2	294	102*	1	73.50
F. J. Titmus		Middx	1955–1962	2	3	0	124	70	—	41.33
M. J. L. Turnbull	Downside CU	Glam	1933–1936	4	7	0	102	72	—	14.57

10 BOWLING AVERAGES (1900–1962)

			Career	M.	Runs	Wkts	Avge	5I	10M	BB
R. Pollard		Lancs	1938–1947	3	209	15	13.93	1	—	5-32
C. Blythe		Kent	1909–1913	3	287	20	14.35	2	1	7-55
D. M. Sayer	Maidstone GS OU	Kent	1959–1960	2	166	11	15.09	1	—	6-69
S. F. Barnes		Staffs	1902–1914	8	686	45	15.24	3	1	7-38
A. R. Gover		Surrey	1934–1936	3	201	13	15.46	1	—	6-41
W. H. Lockwood		Surrey	1892–1902	17	1216	77	15.79	6	1	8-72
W. E. Bowes		Yorks	1931–1939	6	370	23	16.09	—	—	3-29
A. Fielder	(Rugby)	Kent	1906–1910	4	435	27	16.11	2	1	10-90
H. L. Simms	Malvern	Sussex	1912–1913	5	504	30	16.80	2	—	6-49
W. C. Smith		Surrey	1910–1911	4	304	18	16.89	2	—	7-61
C. S. Marriott	St Columba's CU Lancs	Kent	1921–1933	4	240	14	17.14	—	—	4-55
J. C. Laker	(Cranleigh)	Surrey	1952–1957	3	242	14	17.29	1	—	6-48
C. W. L. Parker		Gloucs	1925–1926	3	191	11	17.36	1	—	5-42
J. W. A. Stephenson	Clayesmore	Essex	1936–1939	4	445	25	17.80	1	1	9-46

Name	School/Univ.	County	Years	M	Runs	Wkts	Avge	5wi	10wm	Best
H. J. Butler		Notts	1947	2	184	10	18.40	—	—	4-91
K. Farnes	Romford CU	Essex	1933–1939	7	693	37	18.73	3	—	8-43
H. I. Young		Essex	1899–1900	2	188	10	18.80	1	—	5-56
H. D. Read	Winchester	Essex	1934–1935	2	246	13	18.92	1	—	5-73
H. Verity		Yorks	1931–1936	7	515	27	19.07	2	—	6-57
F. J. Durston		Middx	1921–1932	7	632	33	19.15	—	1	4-32
W. E. Hollies		Warks	1946–1957	4	326	17	19.18	1	—	5-32
A. S. Kennedy	(Cheltenham)	Hants	1914–1934	16	1169	60	19.48	3	1	10-37
S. M. J. Woods	Brighton CU	Somerset	1888–1902	16	1493	75	19.91	6	2	8-46
T. B. Mitchell		Derby	1931–1934	4	280	14	20.00	—	1	4-27
W. Rhodes	(Harrow)	Yorks	1898–1927	39	2086	103	20.25	4	—	6-27
M. Leyland		Yorks	1928–1938	11	244	12	20.33	1	—	7-94
A. V. Bedser		Surrey	1947–1955	12	1152	56	20.57	2	—	5-34
T. Richardson		Surrey	1895–1903	8	1306	63	20.73	5	3	7-43
E. R. Dexter	Radley CU	Sussex	1957–1962	10	543	26	20.88	1	—	5-8
P. J. Sainsbury		Hants	1958–1960	3	440	21	20.95	—	—	6-72
A. P. Freeman		Kent	1921–1936	13	1720	82	20.98	11	3	8-41
D. B. Close		Yorks	1949–1962	6	298	14	21.29	1	—	5-23
T. W. J. Goddard		Gloucs	1929–1938	4	279	13	21.46	—	—	4-58
F. S. Trueman		Yorks	1955–1962	11	731	34	21.50	1	—	5-47
G. W. Richardson	Winchester	Derby	1959–1962	4	263	12	21.92	—	—	4-76
W. W. Odell		Leics	1903–1907	5	440	20	22.00	1	—	6-54
W. R. Hammond	(Rugby, Clifton, Stowe)	Gloucs	1923–1946	22	756	34	22.24	—	—	4-53
G. J. Thompson		N'hants	1900–1911	9	670	30	22.33	1	—	6-59
D. W. Carr	Sutton Valence	Kent	1909–1913	5	537	24	22.38	2	—	6-71
C. M. Wells	Dulwich CU Surrey	Middx	1892–1901	4	247	11	22.45	—	—	4-80
W. Brearley		Lancs	1903–1911	7	1092	48	22.75	3	—	7-103
N. A. Knox	Dulwich	Surrey	1906–1910	5	661	29	22.79	4	1	7-52
E. G. Arnold	(King's, Canterbury)	Worcs	1899–1908	7	675	29	23.28	2	1	5-63
F. E. Woolley		Kent	1909–1938	31	1417	60	23.62	2	—	6-69
A. E. Relf	(Wellington)	Sussex	1903–1913	9	568	24	23.67	—	—	4-33
J. S. Savage		Leics	1958–1961	2	261	11	23.73	—	—	5-78
G. H. Hirst		Yorks	1897–1921	26	1284	54	23.78	1	—	8-35
D. A. Allen	(Eton)	Gloucs	1960	9	240	10	24.00	—	—	4-29
G. Geary		Leics	1925–1934	9	720	30	24.00	1	—	5-52
L. C. Braund	(Charterhouse)	Somerset	1901–1907	7	552	23	24.00	2	—	6-50
W. S. Lees		Surrey	1904–1906	4	389	16	24.31	2	—	6-92
W. Brockwell	(Repton)	Surrey	1894–1902	10	439	18	24.39	1	—	5-82
C. I. J. Smith		Middx	1934–1937	4	244	10	24.40	—	—	3-31

Name		County	Career	M.	Runs	Wkts	Avge	5I	10M	BB
A. E. Thomas		N'hants	1928–1930	3	269	11	24.45	1	–	5-58
E. R. Wilson	Rugby CU	Yorks	1902–1922	4	416	17	24.47	–	–	4-102
F. A. Tarrant		Middx	1903–1914	17	956	39	24.51	3	–	5-36
C. H. Parkin		Lancs	1919–1923	11	1155	47	24.57	3	1	9-85
J. W. H. T. Douglas	Felsted	Essex	1906–1927	30	2216	90	24.62	5	1	9-105
S. G. Smith		N'hants	1909–1914	5	271	11	24.64	1	–	5-40
R. Tattersall		Lancs	1950–1953	5	518	21	24.67	2	1	6-83
A. W. Wellard		Somerset	1931–1938	6	525	21	25.00	1	–	5-45
H. Howell		Warks	1920–1925	8	758	30	25.27	2	–	6-40
F. R. Foster	Solihull	Warks	1910–1914	8	835	33	25.30	1	–	5-83
J. R. Mason	Winchester	Kent	1894–1913	11	759	30	25.30	2	–	6-90
J. T. Hearne	(Harrow)	Middx	1893–1904	14	1248	49	25.47	4	1	6-57
J. W. Hitch		Surrey	1912–1923	10	920	36	25.56	2	–	7-59
M. S. Nichols		Essex	1930–1938	7	642	25	25.68	–	–	3-17
C. P. Buckenham	(Repton)	Essex	1907–1913	6	593	23	25.78	1	–	5-96
S. Hargreave		Warks	1902–1904	3	364	14	26.00	1	–	6-53
W. M. Bradley	Alleyn's	Kent	1897–1903	2	783	30	26.10	2	–	6-82
R. G. Marlar	Harrow CU	Sussex	1951–1958	10	1061	40	26.53	2	–	7-79
W. T. Greswell	Repton	Somerset	1909–1928	4	294	11	26.73	–	–	4-60
R. Kilner		Yorks	1919–1926	7	496	18	27.56	1	–	6-20
G. G. Macaulay		Yorks	1922–1925	3	305	11	27.73	–	–	3-63
T. E. Bailey	Dulwich CU	Essex	1947–1962	21	2023	72	28.10	1	–	6-58
A. D. Baxter	Loretto	Lancs	1934	3	339	12	28.25	1	–	5-128
G. G. Napier	Marlborough CU	Middx	1904–1913	7	735	26	28.27	1	–	6-39
V. W. C. Jupp	Burgess Hill Sussex	N'hants	1920–1931	10	738	26	28.38	1	–	5-158
P. R. Le Couteur	OU		1910–1911	6	658	23	28.61	–	–	5-98
S. Haigh	(Winchester)	Yorks	1898–1910	10	631	22	28.68	1	–	5-55
G. Goonesena	CU	Notts	1954–1958	8	893	31	28.81	4	1	6-83
C. J. Cortright		Essex	1893–1900	4	490	17	28.82	1	–	7-73
H. A. Gilbert	Tonbridge OU	Worcs	1908–1910	4	405	14	28.93	1	–	6-112
G. M. Louden	Charterhouse	Essex	1919–1925	8	666	23	28.96	2	–	5-49
E. Smith	Clifton OU	Yorks	1891–1906	15	1043	36	28.97	3	–	6-86
G. O. B. Allen	Eton OU	Middx	1923–1938	11	882	30	29.40	2	1	5-40
J. R. Gunn	(Harrow)	Notts	1900–1913	15	947	32	29.59	2	1	6-64
M. W. Tate	(Tonbridge)	Sussex	1923–1934	16	1553	52	29.87	2	–	7-148
F. S. Jackson	Harrow CU	Yorks	1891–1906	20	1507	50	30.14	3	1	7-41
D. V. P. Wright	(C'house Tonbridge)	Kent	1939–1950	3	333	11	30.27	–	–	4-72

Player	Schools / Univ.	County	Years	M	R	W	Avge	5wi	10wm	Best
J. H. Wardle		Yorks	1948–1958	9	1110	36	30.83	2	–	5-75
G. A. R. Lock		Surrey	1954–1962	5	502	16	31.38	–	–	4-87
H. G. Owen-Smith	OU	Middx	1931–1937	5	314	10	31.40	–	–	4-26
M. Falcon	Harrow, CU	Norfolk	1911–1927	14	1304	41	31.80	3	1	7-78
T. W. Hayward		Surrey	1895–1911	33	318	10	31.80	–	–	4-43
A. E. Trott		Middx	1899–1908	13	1376	43	32.00	2	–	6-142
G. L. Jessop	Cheltenham GS, CU	Gloucs	1897–1914	26	1029	32	32.16	–	–	3-23
M. J. C. Allom	Wellington, CU	Surrey	1930–1934	8	749	23	32.57	–	–	4-55
C. B. Fry	Repton, OU, Sus-ex	Hants	1893–1914	20	400	12	33.33	1	–	5-90
J. N. Crawford	Repton	Surrey	1906–1921	9	601	18	33.39	1	–	6-54
T. G. Wass		Notts	1904–1908	3	340	10	34.00	1	–	5-95
D. L. A. Jephson	Clapham, CU	Surrey	1894–1902	11	626	18	34.77	1	–	6-21
J. W. Hearne	(Westminster)	Middx	1912–1932	32	1708	49	34.86	1	–	5-53
H. A. Peach		Surrey	1923–1928	6	431	12	35.92	–	–	3-42
R. C. Robertson-Glasgow	Charterhouse, OU	Somerset	1924–1935	5	580	16	36.25	1	–	5-85
A. O. Jones	Bedford Modern, CU	Notts	1896–1907	14	544	15	36.27	1	–	5-67
J. A. Newman		Hants	1922–1928	6	364	10	36.40	–	–	3-44
D. J. Shepherd		Glam	1952–1957	5	587	16	36.69	1	–	5-61
F. R. Brown	Leys, CU	N'hants	1931–1953	16	1486	39	38.10	1	–	5-80
H. V. Hesketh-Prichard	Fettes	Hants	1903–1905	3	384	10	38.40	1	–	5-80
G. T. S. Stevens	U.C.S., OU	Middx	1919–1931	17	976	25	39.04	1	–	5-62
O. S. Wheatley	KES, B'ham, CU, Warks	Glam	1958–1962	6	551	14	39.36	1	–	5-92
J. E. Walsh		Leics	1947–1952	3	401	10	40.10	–	–	3-82
R. E. S. Wyatt	Warks	Worcs	1926–1947	23	689	17	40.53	–	–	3-46
J. C. White	Taunton	Somerset	1914–1930	12	875	21	41.67	–	–	3-71
N. W. D. Yardley	St Peter's, York, CU	Yorks	1937–1955	16	512	12	42.67	1	–	5-93
I. A. R. Peebles	Glasgow A., OU	Middx	1927–1935	9	834	19	43.89	1	–	6-105
J. J. Warr	Ealing CGS, CU	Middx	1950–1960	14	1411	32	44.09	–	–	4-54
B. J. T. Bosanquet	Eton, OU	Middx	1899–1911	10	709	16	44.31	1	–	6-60
F. S. G. Calthorpe	Repton, OU	Warks	1920–1933	12	1158	25	46.32	1	–	6-88
C. L. Townsend	Clifton	Gloucs	1896–1900	9	749	16	46.81	–	–	4-58
R. W. V. Robins	Highgate, CU	Middx	1928–1952	8	661	14	47.21	1	–	5-26
P. G. H. Fender	St Paul's, Sussex	Surrey	1913–1934	27	2184	46	47.48	–	–	4-85
E. R. T. Holmes	Malvern, OU	Surrey	1927–1936	11	553	11	50.27	–	–	2-18
N. E. Haig	Eton	Middx	1919–1932	24	1816	36	50.44	–	–	3-23
A. E. R. Gilligan	Dulwich, CU	Sussex	1922–1927	9	642	12	53.50	–	–	3-63
R. H. B. Bettington	OU	Middx	1920–1928	5	562	10	56.20	–	–	4-136
W. E. Astill	(Tonbridge)	Leics	1923–1928	5	281	8	35.13	–	–	3-39
T. W. Cartwright		Warks	1959	1	86	5	17.20	–	–	3-45

			Career	M.	Runs	Wkts	Avge	5I	10M	BB
J. C. Clay	Winchester	Glam	1923–1935	3	229	5	45.80	—	—	2-63
N. Gifford		Warks	1962	1	79	0	—	—	—	0-36
R. Illingworth		Yorks	1955–1959	3	233	8	29.13	—	—	2-30
James Langridge		Sussex	1930–1937	5	123	5	24.60	—	—	3-36
H. Larwood		Notts	1927–1932	5	299	7	42.71	—	—	4-54
H. J. Rhodes		Derby	1959–1960	2	50	7	7.14	—	—	3-17
D. Shackleton		Hants	1950–1962	3	303	9	33.67	—	—	4-39
G. H. T. Simpson-Hayward	Malvern	Worcs	1903–1908	2	84	5	16.80	1	—	5-17
J. B. Statham		Lancs	1951–1960	4	200	8	25.00	—	—	2-22
F. J. Titmus		Middx	1955–1962	2	294	9	32.67	—	—	3-40
F. H. Tyson		N'hants	1955–1957	5	194	6	32.33	—	—	2-15
W. Voce		Notts	1932	1	84	1	41.67	—	—	1-84

PART C: MISCELLANY

11 UNUSUAL EVENTS AND OTHER RECORDS

UNUSUAL EVENTS

1832   In an attempt to restore balance in a series which had become one-sided in favour of the Players, the Gentlemen defended wickets five inches lower in height and two inches less in width than the normal stumps used by the Players. In a parallel experiment in 1837, the Players defended four stumps with a height of thirty-six inches and a width of twelve inches. Despite these attempts to shorten the odds, the Players won both games by an innings.

1836   N. Darnell, A. J. Lowth and W. L. Pakenham, all of Winchester College, appeared for the Gentlemen while still at school.

1845   The match at Brighton was staged for the benefit of G. Brown. The only other Gentlemen and Players matches at Brighton in 1871 and 1881 were also arranged as benefit matches for John Lillywhite and James Lillywhite, Jnr, respectively.

1846   A. Haygarth (Gentlemen) took four hours to score 26 runs at Lord's.

1870   F. H. Farrands (Players) took 10–88 (4–63 and 6–25) at Lord's in his only game in the series.

1872   R. Daft (Players) scored 9 runs from a shot off I. D. Walker at the Oval.

1876   A. Shaw (Players) had, at one stage in the Gentlemen's first innings, bowling figures of 48–40–12–3 at Prince's. W. G. Grace (Gentlemen) had match figures of 156–86–184–8 at the Oval. The 156 overs of four balls represented 624 deliveries – the highest number ever by a bowler on either side in the series.

1880   A. Shaw (Players) bowled 14 consecutive maiden 4-ball overs at Lord's.

1882   A. P. Lucas (Gentlemen) went one hour without adding to his score during an innings of 20 at the Oval.

1891–1901   The Gentlemen's limited bowling resources were evident when 9 bowlers were used in a single innings in the matches at Hastings in 1891 and 1897, the Oval in 1899 and 1901. In all the Gentlemen used 10 bowlers in the match at Hastings in 1897.

1896   K. S. Ranjitsinhji (Gentlemen) hit 11 fours in his innings of 47 at Lord's.

1911–26   Nine bowlers were used in a match by the Players at Scarborough in 1911 and by the Gentlemen at Lord's in 1926.

1919   G. T. S. Stevens (University College School) appeared for the Gentlemen while still at school.

1919   J. B. Hobbs made a century for the Players in all three matches, scoring 120* at the Oval, 113 at Lord's and 116 at Scarborough.

1922   A. W. Carr (Gentlemen) hit three consecutive sixes off F. E. Woolley at Scarborough.

1927   I. A. R. Peebles made his début in first-class cricket when appearing for the Gentlemen at the Oval.

1934   The Players scored 608–7 on the first day at the Oval.

1937–38   W. R. Hammond led each side to victory in successive years at Lord's – the Players in 1937 and the Gentlemen in 1938.

1938   H. T. Bartlett (Gentlemen) hit

28 runs off 1 over (664444) from T. P. B. Smith at Lord's.

1949   T. G. Evans (Players) scored 6 all run (with no overthrows) off T. E. Bailey at Lord's.

1950   F. R. Brown (Gentlemen) scored 122 out of 131 runs added during his innings at Lord's.

1953–56   W. J. Edrich (Gentlemen) made three centuries in four matches at Scarborough in 1953, 1955 and 1956 and, on each occasion, his score was 133.

OTHER RECORDS

PLAYED FOR BOTH SIDES

R. Daft	Gentlemen – 1858	Players – 1860–1879
E. J. Diver	Gentlemen – 1884	Players – 1886–1899
W. C. Dyer	Gentlemen – 1825	Players – 1821
W. J. Edrich	Gentlemen – 1947–1957	Players – 1938
W. R. Hammond	Gentlemen – 1938–1946	Players – 1923–1937
J. H. Parsons	Gentlemen – 1929–1931	Players – 1914–1927
P. E. Richardson	Gentlemen – 1955–1958	Players – 1959
Lord Strathavon	Gentlemen – 1827	Players – 1819

GIVEN MEN

The following Players appeared as given men for the Gentlemen:

W. Beldham	(1)	1806		Lord's		
J. Broadbridge	(1)	1829		Lord's		
J. Cobbett	(2)	1835,	1838	Lord's		
T. C. Howard	(1)	1820		Lord's		
W. Lambert	(2)	1806		Lord's		
F. W. Lillywhite	(3)	1829,	1830	Lord's	1846	Canterbury
W. Martingell	(1)				1846	Canterbury
W. Mathews	(1)	1825		Lord's		
F. Pilch	(2)	1830,	1838	Lord's		
S. Redgate	(1)	1835		Lord's		
E. G. Wenman	(1)	1838		Lord's		

The Gentlemen played 18 men in 1836, 17 in 1827 (both matches), 16 in 1825, 1833 and 1837, 14 in 1824, 12 in 1829 and 1830, all matches at Lord's.

The Players played only 9 men in 1831 at Lord's.

MOST APPEARANCES

85	W. G. Grace	Gentlemen	1865–1906
49	J. B. Hobbs	Players	1907–1934
39	W. Rhodes	Players	1898–1927
37	G. Ulyett	Players	1875–1892
34	R. Abel	Players	1886–1902
33	T. W. Hayward	Players	1895–1911
33	H. Jupp	Players	1865–1880
32	J. W. Hearne	Players	1912–1932
31	W. Gunn	Players	1881–1898
31	E. H. Hendren	Players	1919–1934
31	A. N. Hornby	Gentlemen	1869–1886
31	F. E. Woolley	Players	1909–1938
30	W. Barnes	Players	1879–1892
30	J. W. H. T. Douglas	Gentlemen	1906–1927
30	A. Shrewsbury	Players	1876–1898

FAMILY TIES

FATHER & SON

Beauclerk	F.	& C.W.	Gentlemen
Buller	A.W.	& C.F.	Gentlemen
Carpenter	R.P.	& H.A.	Players
Doggart	A.G.	& G.H.G.	Gentlemen
Dowson	E.	& E.M.	Gentlemen
Evans	A.H.	& A.J.	Gentlemen
Freemantle	A.	& G.	Players
Grace	W.G.	& W.G., Jnr.	Gentlemen
Halliwell	R.B.	& E.A.	Gentlemen
Hammond	J.	& C.J.	Players
Hardstaff	J.	& J., Jnr.	Players
Hayward	D.	& T.	Players
Hornby	A.N.	& A.H.	Gentlemen
Johnson	G.R.	& P.R.	Gentlemen
Lillywhite	F.W.	& John	Players
Mann	F.T.	& F.G.	Gentlemen
Parks	J.H.	& J.M.	Players
Robins	R.W.V.	& R.V.C.	Gentlemen
Sewell	T.	& T., Jnr.	Players
Tate	F.W.	& M.W.	Players
Townsend	F.	& C.L.	Gentlemen

Daft	R.	Gentlemen & Players	H.B.	Gentlemen
Hutton	L.	Players	R.A.	Gentlemen
Sutcliffe	H.	Players	W.H.H.	Gentlemen

BROTHERS (3 OR MORE)

Foster	5	G.N., H.K., M.K., R.E. & W.L.	Gentlemen
Gilligan	3	A.E.R., A.H.H. & F.W.	Gentlemen
Grace	3	E.M., G.F. & W.G.	Gentlemen
Grimston	3	E.H., J.W. & R	Gentlemen
Lyttelton	3	A., C.G. & E.	Gentlemen
Marsham	3	C.D.B., C.J.B. & R.H.B.	Gentlemen
Walker	6	A.H., F., I.D., J., R.D. & V.E.	Gentlemen

SOME OVERSEAS CRICKETERS WHO PLAYED
FOR THE GENTLEMEN

Australia	*South Africa*	*West Indies*
B. A. Barnett	G. A. Faulkner	J. H. Cameron
R. H. B. Bettington	J. P. Fellows-Smith	G. Challenor
E. H. Butler	C. N. McCarthy	I. H. Ross
A. G. Fairfax	A. Melville	S. G. Smith
J. J. Ferris	D. P. B. Morkel	
B. W. Hone	H. G. Owen-Smith	
R. C. M. Kimpton	D. B. Pithey	
P. R. Le Couteur	R. M. Poore	
L. O. S. Poidevin	C. O. H. Sewell	
F. R. Spofforth	J. H. Sinclair	
S. M. J. Woods	H. W. Taylor	
	C. B. Van Ryneveld	
	R. C. White	*Pakistan*
		A. H. Kardar

348

New Zealand	Ceylon	India
C. S. Dempster	G. Goonesena	A. H. Baig
M. P. Donnelly	J. D. Piachaud	R. V. Divecha
T. C. Lowry		K. S. Duleepsinhji
E. C. Petrie		M. Jahangir Khan
		Nawab of Pataudi, Snr
		K. S. Ranjitsinhji
		S. Singh

12 BEST TEAMS 1919–1962

Sir Pelham Warner in his book *Gentlemen versus Players* selected the best teams he had seen in the period 1919–49 as follows:

The Gentlemen: 1926, 1930 and 1932.
The Players: 1923, 1926, 1928, 1929, 1932, 1938 and 1939.

These were teams which actually appeared, but in the period with which this book is principally concerned, 1919–62, the opportunity has been taken to indulge in that sport beloved of so many cricket followers – that of choosing sides to comprise the best cricketers available throughout the entire period.

As indicated in Chapter 12, the case for inviting Jim Swanton to select and manage the Gentlemen's XI and for John Arlott to do the same for the Players' XI was powerful and appealing. It was agreed that the sides should be listed in batting order and that W. R. Hammond and W. J. Edrich should not be considered (because of their appearances for both sides); otherwise a free choice was available to both selectors from the twenties to the sixties. Their selections follow, together with their additional comments:

E. W. SWANTON'S GENTLEMEN'S XI

'Here is my Gentlemen's XI drawn from those XIs seen over the period 1928–1962 in G. v. P. matches, with a few comments:

M. C. Cowdrey	G. O. Allen (captain)
G. T. S. Stevens	T. E. Bailey
K. S. Duleepsinhji	J. C. White
P. B. H. May	S. C. Griffith
D. R. Jardine	K. Farnes
E. R. Dexter	

'Of this side eight made Test hundreds – as have at least four others for whom room regrettably could not be found: Wyatt, Chapman, Robins, and Sheppard. Farnes and Allen take the new ball, followed perhaps by Bailey. Stevens and White provide the spin. Dexter can be called upon at a pinch. The fielding should be brilliant near the wicket, perhaps not so brilliant at long range. 7 Cantabs, 3 Oxonians! Although, in my view, all "chose themselves" except Stevens, Bailey and White, a next best side does not fall far behind except as regards fast bowling. Here is the 2nd XI:

Rev. D. S. Sheppard		R. W. V. Robins (or P. G. H. Fender)
C. F. Walters		M. D. Lyon
M. P. Donnelly	(or Nawab of Pataudi)	Capt. J. W. A. Stephenson
R. E. S. Wyatt	(or M. J. K. Smith)	J. C. Clay
A. P. F. Chapman	(captain)	I. A. R. Peebles
F. R. Brown	(or N. W. D. Yardley)	(or C. S. Marriott)

'Brown or Wyatt would have to share the new ball with Stephenson, with Peebles, Clay and Robins to provide the spin: six bowlers in all. In the 27 names above there are, incidentally, 15 captains of England.'

John Arlott was happy to leave the side below as one which 'picked itself':

J. B. Hobbs	L. C. Braund
L. Hutton (captain)	M. W. Tate
D. C. S. Compton	H. Larwood
C. P. Mead	J. C. Laker
W. Rhodes	F. H. Tyson
L. E. G. Ames	

However, in a letter to the author dated 22 January 1987, he added the following comments on his choice of captain:

My choice of Hutton is based on a number of arguments: the first pro for many years to captain England in face of some really niggling prejudice; a superb tactician; a man who made good a horrible psychological disadvantage; and, above all – and superbly – a winner, *and* a winner in Australia.

Turning to some of the greatest performers in the two sides, it seemed appropriate to give the captains of the last Gentlemen and Players match at Lord's, and the authors of this book's Foreword, the opportunity to have their say. However, interestingly, each expressed a fascination in selecting the other side, *i.e.* F. S. Trueman opted to select the Gentlemen's XI, mainly consisting of the best of those against whom he played, while E. R. Dexter decided to do the same for the Players. In Fred Trueman's case this arose because of his fascination with the concept which the author put to him of the 'professional amateur' – one who played more like a professional than an amateur. His selection shows his regard for some doughty opponents (including some who pre-date his own playing career), although he emphasizes that the team selected is one which best fits the 'professional amateur' category rather than one ideally suited for its playing balance.

F. S. TRUEMAN'S 'PROFESSIONAL AMATEURS' GENTLEMEN'S XI

R. E. S. Wyatt	T. E. Bailey
D. R. Jardine	W. Wooller
P. B. H. May	A. B. Sellers (captain)
A. W. Carr	D. V. Brennan
D. B. Carr	W. S. Surridge
	J. C. Laker (Essex amateur vintage)

For Ted Dexter, the choice of an 'amateur professional' side – those who during his playing years played the game with the gusto and relish traditionally associated with the old-style amateur – still allowed the selection of a well-balanced side.

E. R. DEXTER'S 'AMATEUR PROFESSIONAL' PLAYERS' XI

C. Milburn	T. G. Evans
R. E. Marshall	D. W. White
T. W. Graveney	F. E. Rumsey
D. C. S. Compton (captain)	B. D. Wells
G. Cox	W. E. Hollies
B. R. Knight	

Finally, the author could not resist adding his own selection of two sides from all those who took part in the Gentlemen v. Players from 1919 to 1962. Unlike the earlier selections, this choice is made on the basis of performances in the series as reflected in the averages. While averages based on limited appearances in annual encounters may seem arbitrary, it is of interest to identify those who had achieved outstanding success against their traditional opponents. Apart from excluding Hammond and Edrich from consideration, the only self-imposed rules required the teams to have five batsmen, an all-rounder, one wicket-keeper, two fast bowlers and two spin bowlers, and for all candidates to have played in at least three matches. The following sides emerged:

TOP OF THE AVERAGES GENTLEMEN'S XI

D. R. Jardine (captain)	S. C. Griffith
Nawab of Pataudi, senior	E. R. Wilson
K. S. Duleepsinhji	J. W. A. Stephenson
P. B. H. May	C. S. Marriott
E. R. Dexter (or G. O. Allen)	K. Farnes
M. J. K. Smith	

TOP OF THE AVERAGES PLAYERS' XI

J. B. Hobbs	D. B. Close
L. Hutton (captain)	J. C. Laker
A. Sandham	C. W. L. Parker
J. W. Hearne	A. R. Gover
W. Watson	R. Pollard
L. E. G. Ames	

The only arbitrary or postponed decisions related to the choice of the captain and the all-rounders on each side. For the Gentlemen, strangely, E. R. Dexter was ahead of G. O. Allen in the bowling averages while the situation was reversed in the batting averages – hence their joint inclusion as alternative all-rounders. For the Players, D. B. Close's high ranking in both batting and bowling averages puts him out on his own. There was no meaningful statistical evidence for the selection of the two captains but a Jardine/Hutton encounter would have a fascination all its own.

SELECT
BIBLIOGRAPHY

The basic reference books consulted were the *Wisden Cricketers' Almanacks*; E. W. Swanton, *Barclay's World of Cricket* (Collins Willow, 1980 and 1986); Philip Bailey, Philip Thorn and Peter Wynne-Thomas, *Who's Who of Cricketers* (Newnes Books, with the Association of Cricket Statisticians, 1984); Robert Brooke, *The Collins Who's Who of English First-class Cricket 1945–1984* (Collins Willow, 1985); Christopher Martin-Jenkins, *The Complete Who's Who of Test Cricketers* (Orbis, 1980); Peter Wynne-Thomas, *England on Tour* (Hamlyn, 1982); and Sir Pelham Warner, *Gentlemen v. Players 1806–1949* (Harrap, 1950). Finally, notwithstanding the immense value of the various works of my friend Bill Frindall, it was a particular pleasure to discover that Test records were covered by the work of another old colleague from BBC cricket commentating days, the late-lamented Arthur Wrigley, whose *Book of Test Cricket 1876–1964* (Epworth, 1965) precisely met my needs.

Other published sources to which reference is made or which are quoted in the text are listed below. The two monthly magazines, *The Cricketer* and *Wisden Cricket Monthly*, have both provided invaluable information.

Andrews, W. H. R., *The Hand that Bowled Bradman: Memories of a Professional Cricketer* (Macdonald, 1973)

Arlott, J., *Fred: Portrait of a Fast Bowler* (Eyre & Spottiswoode, 1972)

Bedser, A. V. and E. A., *Twin Ambitions* (Stanley Paul, 1986)

Birley, D., *The Willow Wand* (Macdonald & Jane's, 1979)

Bowen, R., *Cricket: A History* (Eyre & Spottiswoode, 1970)

Callaghan, J., *Yorkshire's Pride* (Pelham, 1984)

Cardus, N., *English Cricket* (Collins, 1945)

Carr, A. W., *Cricket with the Lid Off* (Hutchinson, 1935)

Coldham, J. D., *Northamptonshire Cricket: A History* (Heinemann, 1959)

Cowdrey, M. C., *MCC: The Autobiography of a Cricketer* (Hodder & Stoughton, 1976)

Douglas, C., *Douglas Jardine: Spartan*

Cricketer (George Allen & Unwin, 1984)

Down, M., *Is It Cricket?* (Queen Anne Press, 1985)

Foot, D., *Cricket's Unholy Trinity* (Stanley Paul, 1985)

Frith, D., *The Slow Men* (Corgi Books, 1985)

Gibson, A., *The Captains of England* (Cassell, 1979)

Graveney, T. W., *The Heart of Cricket* (Arthur Barker, 1983)

Green, B., *The Wisden Book of Obituaries* (Queen Anne Press, 1986)

Gregory, K., *In Celebration of Cricket* (Granada, 1978)

Harris, Lord, *A Few Short Runs* (Murray, 1921)

Hawke, Lord, *Recollections and Reminiscences* (Williams & Norgate, 1924)

Hutton, Sir Leonard, *Fifty Years in Cricket* (Star Books, 1984)

Ibbotson, Doug, and Dellor, Ralph, *A Hundred Years of the Ashes* (Rothmans, 1982)

Insole, D. J., *Cricket from the Middle* (Heinemann, 1960)

James, C. L. R., *Beyond a Boundary* (Hutchinson, 1963)

Lee, F. S., *Cricket, Lovely Cricket* (Stanley Paul, 1960)

Lemmon, D., *Percy Chapman: a Biography* (Queen Anne Press, 1984)
Johnny Won't Hit Today (George Allen & Unwin, 1983)

Leveson Gower, Sir Henry, *Off and On the Field* (Stanley Paul, 1953)

May, P. B. H., *A Game Enjoyed* (Stanley Paul, 1986)

Moorhouse, G., *Lord's* (Hodder & Stoughton, 1983)

Murphy, P., *Tiger Smith of Warwickshire and England* (Lutterworth Press, 1981)

Parker, Grahame, *Gloucestershire Road: A History of Gloucestershire County Cricket Club* (Pelham, 1983)

Parkin, C. H., *Cricket Reminiscences, Humorous and Otherwise* (Hodder & Stoughton, 1923)
Cricket Triumphs and Troubles (Nicholls, 1936)

Peebles, I. A. R., *Spinner's Yarn* (Collins, 1973)

Pollard, J., *Australian Cricket: The Game and the Players* (Hodder & Stoughton, 1983)

Rait Kerr, D., and Peebles, I., *Lord's 1946–70* (Harrap, 1971)

Root, F., *A Cricket Pro's Lot* (Edward Arnold, 1937)

Sheppard, Rev. D. S., *Parson's Pitch* (Hodder & Stoughton, 1964)

Snow, E. E., *Leicestershire Cricket 1949–1977* (Stanley Paul, 1977)

Sutcliffe, Herbert, *For Yorkshire and England* (Edward Arnold, 1935)

Swanton, E. W., *As I Said at the Time* (Collins Willow, 1983)

Tate, M. W., *My Cricketing Reminiscences* (Stanley Paul, 1934)

Tennyson, Lord, *From Verse to Worse* (Cassell, 1933)

Various, *County Champions* (Heinemann, 1982)

Warner, Sir Pelham, *Lord's 1787–1945* (Harrap, 1946)

Williams, M., *Double Century* (Collins Willow, 1985)

Woolley, F. E., *The King of Games* (Stanley Paul, 1936)

Wyatt, R. E. S., *Three Straight Sticks* (Stanley Paul, 1951)

Wynne-Thomas, P., and Arnold, P., *Cricket in Conflict* (Newnes, 1984)

PICTURE CREDITS

Yorkshire in 1946 *Yorkshire Post*
Glamorgan in 1948 *G. A. Copinger*
Len Hutton at Lord's, 1951 *Sport and General*
Peter May, 1953 *Sport and General*
Gentlemen's XI at Scarborough, 1952 *Scarborough C.C.*
Colin Cowdrey, 1951 *G. A. Copinger*
Cyril Washbrook, 1956 *Sport and General*
Gentlemen's XI at Scarborough, 1955 *Scarborough C.C.*
Surrey Championship County, 1952 *Surrey C.C.C.*

Surrey 2nd XI, 1954 *Surrey C.C.C.*
E. R. Dexter, 1957 *Scarborough C.C.*
MCC in Australia, 1954–55 *G. A. Copinger*
Gentlemen's XI at Lord's, 1961 *Michael Marshall*
J. R. Burnet *G. A. Copinger*
W. S. Surridge *G. A. Copinger*
Players' XI at Scarborough, 1960 *Scarborough C.C.*
E. R. Dexter, 1962 *Sport and General*
F. S. Trueman, 1962 *Michael Marshall*

INDEX